ST. PAUL'S EPHESUS

Figure 1   The Roman Province of Asia at the time of Saint Paul

ST. PAUL'S EPHESUS

Texts and Archaeology

JEROME MURPHY-O'CONNOR, O.P.

A Michael Glazier Book

LITURGICAL PRESS
Collegeville, Minnesota

www.litpress.org

A Michael Glazier Book published by Liturgical Press

1   2   3   4   5   6   7   8

Library of Congress Cataloging-in-Publication Data

Murphy-O'Connor, J. (Jerome), 1935–
    St. Paul's Ephesus : texts and archaeology / Jerome Murphy-O'Connor.
      p.   cm.
    "A Michael Glazier book."
    Includes bibliographical references and index.
    ISBN 978-0-8146-5259-6
     1. Ephesus (Extinct city)—Church history.   2. Ephesus (Extinct city)—Antiquities.   3. Artemis (Greek deity)—Cult—Turkey—Ephesus (Extinct city) 4. Ephesus (Extinct city)—Religion.   5. Bible. N.T. Epistles of Paul—History. I. Title.   II. Title: Saint Paul's Ephesus.

BR185.M87 2008
225.9′3—dc22

                                2007044977

To my colleagues and students
at the École Biblique de Jérusalem
where I have now taught for forty years.

CONTENTS

PART 1: THE ANCIENT TEXTS

HISTORIANS

Poets and Novelists

PART 2

FOREWORD

The fourth-century B.C.E. poet Duris of Elaea called Ephesus "the most besung of all the Ionian cities."[1] In fact, it is mentioned over five hundred times in Greek literature alone.[2] It was the western terminus of the road from India and the capital of perhaps the richest province in the Roman empire. It enshrined the Temple of Artemis, one of the seven wonders of the world. The city was also Paul's base for just over two years, and because of the letters he wrote from Ephesus it is the best documented period of his career. Toward the end of the first century C.E. the city became the home of the evangelist who produced the final version of the Fourth Gospel. Ephesus, in consequence, has a claim on the attention of anyone interested in the origins of Christianity or in the life of one of the most extraordinary cities of antiquity.

Our knowledge of its rich history derives from scattered allusions in a variety of Greek and Latin authors. The references have been combined in any number of scientific works, where they are synthesized and summarized. Such concentration on the essentials inevitably robs the texts of their immediacy, vigor, and charm. It is a way of learning the basic facts about the city, but it leaves the city's personality in the shadows. For grasping the ethos of Ephesus there is no alternative to the first-hand accounts of visitors. These reflect the moods the city inspired in the writers and the small things that caught their fancy.

Thus I quote from a wide variety of authors and as extensively as possible. The unfortunate consequence is a certain amount of repetition. The data on a given point sometimes appear in a number of different places. These disadvantages, however, are easily transformed into benefits. The personal assemblage of data permits a critical assessment, and repetitiousness raises the important questions of sources and traditional themes.

In the sister volume, *St. Paul's Corinth: Texts and Archaeology* (2002), I presented the authors in roughly chronological order insofar as this could be established. On reflection I find this to be rather meaningless, since each one covers material from different ages. The latest author in date may deal with the earliest historical period.

Thus in this volume I divide the authors into two groups within which I follow a simple alphabetical order. The first, "Historians," is self-explanatory, and many of the names found in my Corinth book also appear here. The second category, "Poets and Novelists," is at first sight surprising. Corinth did attract the attention of a number of poets, but no novelist ever set a story there. Ephesus, on the contrary, figures prominently in a series of novelistic works. For their appeal these needed to paint a realistic background, but their real importance lies in what they reveal of the perception of Ephesus in the popular mind. Only in these texts does it become clear to what extent Ephesians looked back to a glorious Greek past without any Romans.

I make Strabo the opening chapter, both because he was just a generation before Paul and because his lengthy account touches on all the significant aspects of the history of Ephesus. It is the best introduction to the different facets of the city's life.

The framework of the section devoted to each author is substantially the same. It opens with a brief presentation of the writer's life in which particular attention is paid to the nature of the work from which the citation is taken and to the question of whether he actually visited Ephesus. The text is then quoted at length and is followed by a commentary. The function of the latter is to heighten the intelligibility of the text and also, when necessary, to raise critical questions concerning the reliability or completeness of the information.

The other principal source of our knowledge of Ephesus is archaeological excavation. In 1995 the Austrian Archaeological Institute, Vienna, celebrated one hundred years of research at Ephesus. During that century the number of volumes published on various aspects of the vast site might give the impression that all had been smooth sailing. In fact there had been serious storms, of which the most dangerous was the First World War (1914–1918). Work resumed at Ephesus only in 1926, and then solely because of the efforts of Gustaf Adolf Deissmann, professor of New Testament in the University of Berlin (1908–1935).

Best known for his foundational methodology of giving primacy to papyri and inscriptions in the study of New Testament Greek,[3] Deissmann was the first New Testament scholar to realize the importance of the archaeological exploration of Ephesus.[4] While other scholars concentrated their researches on the geography and monuments of the Holy Land,[5] he believed strongly that the historical background of early Christianity must be sought throughout the Greco-Roman world. Ephesus, he believed, was the ideal site to test this hypothesis. It had been Paul's base for a considerable time and had become an influential Christian center by the end of the first century.

Deissmann visited Ephesus in 1906 and again in 1909. Thus he was able to appreciate fully the report on the sorry condition of the site sent to him in 1925 by Joseph Keil (1878–1963), who had been working with the Austrians at Ephesus since 1904. Tons of mud were deposited on excavated areas when the ruins were flooded periodically. The roots of the abundant vegetation were fragmenting fragile decorative masonry. Earthquakes in 1919 and 1924 had caused structural damage.

The Austrian Archaeological Institute alone was licensed by Turkey to excavate at Ephesus, but it had no money. Deissmann used his immense prestige to raise funds from various organs of the German government, and from the Rockefeller family in New York, in order to put Keil and an Austrian team back in the field. Such altruism at a time when archaeology was highly nationalistic only serves to underline Deissmann's generosity of spirit.[6] The Austrians proved themselves fully worthy of Deissmann's trust. Their subsequent record of excavation, restoration, and publication is unlikely ever to be surpassed.

In addition to their impeccable scientific publications, German-speaking archaeologists working on major sites in western Turkey share another unusual trait. They write guidebooks to their excavations. Walter Radt's guide to Pergamum comes immediately to mind, as does Joseph Keil's guide to Ephesus. It was not surprising, therefore, that the field archaeologists who have dedicated their lives to Ephesus should have made a guidebook their contribution to the celebration of the centenary of their work there.

Under the editorship of Peter Scherrer, fifteen Austrians and twelve Turks combined to produce the authoritative *Ephesus: The New Guide*, which is written with the zest of first-hand knowledge and incorporates the most recent research. Different opinions among members of the team are reported as alternative hypotheses and, where appropriate, older interpretations are modified or discarded. It is a model of its genre.

Finally, I must express my gratitude to those who contributed in various ways to the production of this book. My nephew James Murphy-O'Connor and Norman Sheppard graciously procured the reconstruction drawing of the Artemision, which does so much to justify the reputation of this extraordinary building. I am also indebted to my colleagues Jean-Michel de Tarragon and Jean-Baptiste Humbert for improving the drawing electronically. Alain Chambon generously contributed three maps. I am deeply obliged to Keiran O'Mahoney for sending me books I could not find here.

Jerome Murphy-O'Connor, o.p.
Jerusalem
31 May 2007

ACKNOWLEDGMENTS

Parts of the following translations are reprinted by kind permission of the publishers, Harvard University Press, Cambridge Massachusetts, and the Trustees of the Loeb Classical Library (LCL). Copyright © by the President and Fellows of Harvard College. The Loeb Classical Library ® is a registered trademark of the President and Fellows of Harvard College. Each item in the list contains these elements: (1) author, (2) work, (3) volume(s) = LCL number(s), (4) translator(s), and (5) copyright year(s).

Achilles Tacitus. *Leucippe and Clitophon*. L045 (Stephen Gaselee), 1917.

Aelian. *Historical Miscellany*. L486 (Nigel Guy Wilson), 1997.

Appian. *Roman History* II = L003, IV = L005 (Horace White), 1912.

Athenaeus. *The Deipnosophists* I = L204, II = L208, III = L224, VI = L327, VII = L345 (Charles Burton Gulick), 1951 (I), 1928 (II), 1929 (III), 1930 (IV), 1940 (VI), 1941 (VII).

Caesar. *Civil Wars* II = L039 (Arthur George Peskett), 1914.

Callimachus. *Hymns and Epigrams*. L129 (Alexander W. Mair), 1955.

Cicero. *Letters to Atticus* XXII = L007N, XXIII = L008N, XXIV = L097N (David R. Shackleton Bailey), 1999.

Cicero. *Letters to His Friends* XXV = L205N, XXVI = L216N, XXVII = L230N (David R. Shackleton Bailey), 2001.

Cicero. *Letters to Quintus* XXVIII = L462/L462N (David R. Shackleton Bailey), 2002.

Cicero. *The Verrine Orations. I Against Verres* VII = L221 (Leonard H. G. Greenwood), 1928.

Cicero. *On the Orator* III = L348 (Edward W. Sutton and Harris Rackham), 1942.

Cicero. *On Divination* XX = L154 (William A. Falconer), 1923.

Dio Cassius. *Roman History* IV = L066, V = L082, VI = L083, VII = L175, VIII = L176 (Earnest Cary), 1916 (IV), 1917 (V-VI), 1924 (VII), 1925 (VIII).

Dio Chrysostom. *Discourses* III = L358 (Henry Lamar Crosby), 1940.

Diogenes Laertius. *Lives of Eminent Philosophers* II = L185 (Robert D. Hicks), 1931.

Frontinus. *Stratagems, Aqueducts*. L174 (Charles E. Bennett), 1925.

Greek Anthology III = L084 (William R. Paton), 1948.

Herodotus. *History* I = L002, III = L119 (Alfred D. Godley), 1931 (119), 1922 (III).

Ignatius of Antioch. *Letter to the Ephesians* in *Apostolic Fathers* I = L024 (Bart D. Ehrman), 2003.

Josephus. *Antiquities of the Jews* X = L489, XI = L410 (Ralph Marcus), 1943 (X), 1963 (XI).

Josephus. *Jewish War* IV = L210 (Henry St. John Thackeray), 1928.

Livy. *History of Rome* I = L114, IX = L295, X = L301, XI = L313 (B. O. Foster) [I], (Evan T. Sage) [IX-XI], 1919 (I), 1936 (IX), 1958 (X), 1936 (XI).

Martial. *Epigrams* I = L094 (David R. Shackleton Bailey), 1993.

Pausanias. *Description of Greece* I = L093, II = L188, III = L272, IV = L297 (William H. S. Jones) [I, III-IV], (Henry A. Ormerod) [II], 1918 (I), 1926 (II), 1933 (III), 1935 (IV).

Philostratus. *Life of Apollonius of Tyana* I = L016, II = L017 (Frederick C. Conybeare), 1912.

Philostratus. *Lives of the Sophists*. L134 (Wilmer C. Wright), 1952.

Pliny. *Natural History* II = L352, IV = L370, IX = L394, X = L419 (Harris Rackham) [II, IV, IX], (D. E. Eichholz) [X], 1942 (II), 1945 (IV), 1952 (IX), 1962 (X).

Pliny the Younger. *Letters and Panegyrics* I = L055, II = L059 (Betty Radice), 1969.

Plutarch. *Moralia* III = L245 (Frank C. Babbit), 1931.

Plutarch. *Moralia* IV = L305 (Frank C. Babbit), 1936.

Plutarch. *Moralia* IX = L245 (Edwin L. Minar), 1961.

Plutarch. *Moralia* X = L321 (Harold N. Fowler), 1927.

Plutarch. *Parallel Lives* II = L047 (Bernadotte Perrin), 1914.

Plutarch. *Parallel Lives* IV = L080 (Bernadotte Perrin), 1916.

Plutarch. *Parallel Lives* VI = L099 (Bernadotte Perrin), 1918.

Plutarch. *Parallel Lives* IX = L101 (Bernadotte Perrin), 1920.

Seneca. *Epistulae Morales* VI = L077 (Richard M. Gummere), 1925.

Strabo. *Geography* II = L050, V = L211, VI = L241 (Horace L. Jones), 1949 (II), 1954 (V, VI).

Tacitus. *Annals* III = L249, IV = L312 (John Jackson), 1937.

Valerius Maximus. *Memorable Sayings and Doings* II = L493 (David R. Shackleton Bailey), 2000.

Vitruvius. *On Architecture* I = L251, II = L280 (Frank Granger), 1931 (I), 1934 (II).

Xenophon of Athens. *Hellenica* I = L088 (Carleton L. Brownson), 1918.

* * * * * * * * *

Parts of Graham Anderson's translation of Xenophon of Athens, *An Ephesian Tale*, in *Collected Ancient Greek Novels*, edited by B. P. Reardon (1989) are published with the permission of the University of California Press.

Parts of the translations of *The Acts of John* and *The Acts of Paul* in Edgar Hennecke and Wilhelm Schneemelcher, *New Testament Apocrypha II*, are published with the permission of Westminster John Knox Press.

Parts of *New Documents Illustrating Early Christianity IV*, edited by Greg Horsley in 1987, are published with the permission of the Ancient History Documentary Research Centre, Macquarie University, Australia.

LIST OF ILLUSTRATIONS

Fig. 1. The Roman Province of Asia at the time of Saint Paul.
Adapted from the *Tübinger Atlas des Vorderen Orients*, BV7 (1983).

Fig. 2. The moving shoreline of Ephesus.
A. At the time of the Ionian settlement.
B. In the Roman period.
Based on Friedmund Hueber, *Ephesos. Gebaute Geschichte*. Mainz: von Zabern, 1997, figs. 2, 39.

Fig. 3. Arthur Henderson's reconstruction of the Hellenistic Temple of Artemis at Ephesus.
Arthur Henderson, "The Hellenistic Temple of Artemis at Ephesus," *Journal of the Royal Institute of British Architects* 22 (1915): 133.

Fig. 4. Arthur Henderson's plan of the Hellenistic Temple of Artemis at Ephesus.
Arthur Henderson, "The Hellenistic Temple of Artemis at Ephesus" *Journal of the Royal Institute of British Architects* 22 (1915): 131.

Fig. 5. Roman Ephesus.
Based on Friedmund Hueber, *Ephesos. Gebaute Geschichte*. Mainz: von Zabern, 1997, fig. 48.

Fig. 6. Central Ephesus ca. 50 C.E.
Adapted from Wilhelm Alzinger, "Ephesos vom Beginn der römischen Herrschaft in Kleinasien bis zum Ende der Principatzeit: Archäologischer Teil," in *Aufstieg und Niedergang der Römischen Welt* II.7.2 (1980): 760.

Fig. 7. Terrace Houses at Ephesus.
Adapted from Selahattin Erdemgil, et al., *The Terrace Houses in Ephesus*. Istanbul: Hitit Color, n.d., 16–18, 36–37.

Part 1

THE ANCIENT TEXTS

HISTORIANS

STRABO INTRODUCES EPHESUS

What is known about Strabo must be gleaned from his great surviving work *Geography*. He was born into a rich family of Amasia in Pontus in 64 or 63 B.C.E. Wealth gave him an extensive Greek education and the lifelong leisure to travel while devoting himself to intellectual pursuits. At the age of twenty he made the first of several visits to Rome, where Tyrannion may have stimulated his interest in geography. He certainly visited Asia, and draws attention to what he was "shown" in Ephesus. In philosophy he was a Stoic and fervently admired the administration that had given his world the *pax Romana*. It has been argued that Strabo wrote his *Geography* in Rome about 19 C.E., but this seems unlikely because he would then have been too old a man to undertake what he knew to be a colossal task (1.1.23). Thus it seems more probable that he wrote in his hometown about 7 B.C.E., and produced an updated edition in 18 C.E. He must have died not long afterward.

Strabo begins his *Geography* with a description of the Iberian peninsula, whose Sacred Cape (modern Cape Saint Vincent in Portugal) "is the most westerly point, not only of Europe, but of the whole inhabited world" (3.1.4). Then, following Eratosthenes, he moves systematically eastward to "the most remote peaks of the mountain chain that form the northern boundary of India" (2.1.1). Thus his first reference to Ephesus occurs in the context of his treatment of Transalpine Gaul (4.1.1).

MARSEILLES, DAUGHTER OF EPHESUS

Massilia was founded by the Phocaeans. . . . It is on the headland, however, that the Ephesium and also the temple of the Delphinian Apollo are situated. The latter is shared in common by all Ionians, whereas the Ephesium is a temple dedicated solely to the Ephesian Artemis.

When the Phocaeans were setting sail from their homeland an oracle was delivered to them, it is said, to use for their voyage a guide received from the Ephesian Artemis. Accordingly, some of them put in at Ephesus and inquired in what way they might procure from the goddess what had been enjoined upon them. Now the goddess in a dream, it is said, had stood beside Aristarcha, one of the women held in very high honour, and commanded her to sail away with the Phocaeans taking with her a certain reproduction [of Artemis] which was among the sacred images.

> This done, and the colony finally settled, they not only established the temple but also did Aristarcha the exceptional honour of appointing her priestess. Further, in the colonial cities [of Marseilles] the people everywhere do this goddess honours of the first rank, and they preserve the artistic design of the "xoanon" the same, and all the other usages precisely the same as is customary in the mother-city. . . . In the cities they founded in Iberia as strongholds against the Iberians they also taught the Iberians the sacred rites of the Ephesian Artemis, as practiced in the fatherland, so that they sacrifice by the Greek rites. (*Geography* 4.1.4-5)

Massilia is Marseilles, on the south coast of France. Its foundation by settlers from Phocaea, the most northerly of the Ionian cities in Asia Minor (modern Eski Foç),[1] is confirmed by Herodotus (*Histories* 1.163) and Thucydides (*History* 1.13). Somewhat surprisingly, the austere Aristotle (384–322 B.C.E.), as quoted by Athenaeus (*Deipnosophists* 576a-b), makes their arrival a true romance. The daughter of the local king, who had to select a husband that day, fell in love with the handsome Greek leader; her father immediately offered him land to found a city. The foundation date of around 600 B.C.E. given by the Sicilian historian Timaeus of Tauromenium is confirmed by archaeology. The oldest imported Greek pottery is dated to the transition period between the seventh and sixth centuries.[2]

The poverty of their land made the Phocaeans renowned seafarers, and no one questions their importance in the colonization of the French and Spanish coasts. This makes it all the more surprising that the two oldest sanctuaries should evoke other Ionian cities. Apollo Delphinius, a sea-god not to be confused with the Delphic Apollo, was indeed common to all Ionians, but he seems to have been particularly associated with Miletus, also a great colonizing city.[3] Strabo leaves no doubt about the association of Artemis with Ephesus, which he will develop in great detail below (p. 15), and even manages to give the impression that the Phocaeans were somehow guided to Marseilles by Ephesus. It seems logical to infer "that the foundation of Marseilles was initiated by several Ionian cities—thereafter the Phocaeans took over from the Ephesians and the Milesians."[4]

The religious influence of Ephesus remained strong in the western Mediterranean. Strabo mentions temples of Ephesian Artemis in the towns founded by Marseilles on the eastern coast of Spain at Hemeroscopeium (3.4.6), Rhodus and Emporium (3.4.8),[5] and on an island in the delta of the river Rhone (4.1.8).

A statue of Artemis is mentioned in the foundation story of Marseilles. It was brought from Ephesus and reproduced for the temples in its daughter cities. Veneration of such cult statues was well established by the seventh century B.C.E.,[6] and there are many references to the primordial statue at Ephesus itself. Strabo also reports that the statue brought by the colonists to Marseilles was copied by the Romans and placed on the Aventine Hill in Rome (4.1.5). Since that statue had only two breasts it must be assumed that the Ephesian original was the same.[7]

Figures of Artemis with multiple round protuberances between neck and waist first appear on coins of the second century B.C.E.[8] The oft-reproduced statues with the same motif preserved in the Ephesus museum at Selçuk date to the second century C.E.[9] Apparently the iden-tification of the protuberances as breasts was first advanced by the early-third-century Christian writer Minucius Felix: "Diana is sometimes short-kilted for the hunt, while at Ephesus she is figured with many breasts and paps" (*Octavius* 23.5). He saw them as a symbol of the deca-dence of pagan religion. Some modern scholars think them to be the testicles of sacrificed bulls. The debate seems not to have come to any satisfactory conclusion.[10] It has, of course, been suggested that the original bulls' testicles were misinterpreted as breasts in the later imperial period.[11]

EPHESUS FOUNDED BY AMAZONS

A peculiar thing has happened in the case of the account we have of the Amazons; for our accounts of other peoples keep a distinction between the mythical and the historical elements, for the things that are ancient and false and monstrous, but history wishes for the truth, whether ancient or recent, and contains no monstrous element, or else only rarely.

But as regards the Amazons, the same stories are told now as in early times, though they are marvellous and beyond belief. For instance, who could believe that an army of women, or a city, or a tribe, could ever be organized without men, and not only be organized, but even make inroads upon the territory of other people, and not only overpower the peoples near them to the extent of advancing as far as what is now Ionia, but even send an expedition across the sea as far as Attica. For this is the same as saying that the men of those times were women and that the women were men. Nevertheless, even at the present time these very stories are told about the Amazons, and they intensify the peculiarity above mentioned and our belief in the ancient accounts rather than those of the present time.

At any rate the founding of cities and the giving of names to them are ascribed to the Amazons, as, for instance, Ephesus and Smyrna and Cyme and Myrine. (*Geography* 11.5.3-4; cf. 12.3.21)

Strabo is still a long way from Ephesus, but his eastward journey has brought him to the mountains above Albania, where some claimed the Amazons live. Others placed them in the northern foothills of the

Caucasus Mountains. In any case Strabo here offers the classical picture of an exclusively female society, whose right breasts were seared off in childhood and who mated periodically with the Gargarians in order to beget children, the Gargarians taking the males and the Amazons the females (11.5.1-2). According to Diodorus Siculus, on the contrary, it was a society governed by women who went to war and allocated only domestic tasks to men (2.45.1-5; 3.53.1-3).[12]

Strabo's report that Ephesus was founded by Amazons is supported by Pliny alone (5.31.115; p. 104). Callimachus (*Hymns* 3, line 237; p. 166), Pomponius Mela (*De Chorographia* 1.78), and somewhat ambiguously Pausanias (compare 4.31.8 and 7.2.7; see p. 97) claim only that the Amazons founded the sanctuary of Artemis. It may be thought, however, that this was equivalent to founding the city because of the attraction the temple had for the outsiders it drew to settle there. While Diodorus Siculus lists Myrinia, Cyme, Mytilene, Pitane, and Priene as Amazon foundations, he says nothing about Ephesus or Smyrna (3.55.6-7).

Strabo's complete skepticism regarding the Amazons (cf. 12.3.22) is shared by his slightly older contemporary Diodorus Siculus: "when any writers recount their prowess, men consider the ancient stories about the Amazons to be fictitious tales" (2.46.6). Even though Strabo's critique may be tinged with patriarchalism, its common sense is undeniable. This makes it all the more remarkable that a male-dominated world should have ascribed the founding of seven important cities to women who were not goddesses. The situation is made even more complex by the fact that no cities in Greece are credited to the Amazons, even though it hosted a number of cult sites dedicated to them.[13]

The only common denominator I can find for the seven cities is that they are all sited on the sea and constitute a cluster in the middle of the west coast of Asia Minor. Only Priene is south of Ephesus. Moving north from Ephesus, the figure between the names in the following list is the distance in kilometers as the crow flies: Ephesus, 60 Smyrna, 40 Cyme, 10 Myrina, 15 Pitane, 45 Mytilene.[14]

It is difficult to work out what these cities might have gained by thinking of their origins in terms of Amazons. They were undoubtedly exotic, which was a strong point in their favor. Yet the Amazons had another, much less attractive side. Most fundamentally they were women. Many would have agreed with Heracles who "felt that it would ill accord with his resolve to be the benefactor of the whole race of mankind if he should suffer any nations to be under the rule of women" (Diodorus Siculus, 3.54.3). Moreover, they were losers. Whatever conquests they made were always short-lived. In the *Iliad* they are regularly vanquished (2.814; 3.189; 6.186). They were defeated by Dionysus near Ephesus (Pausanias, 7.2.4-7), by Heracles in his ninth labor (Diodorus Siculus,

2.46.3), and by Theseus when they invaded Attica (Plutarch, *Theseus* 26). A city might claim a consistent winner with pride—many put themselves under the patronage of Heracles[15]—but why honor those who cannot guarantee protection?

Nonetheless, statues of Amazons stood in the sanctuary of Artemis from the classical age to the Roman period (Pliny, 34.19.53; p. 113).

ATHENS COLONIZES IONIA

> Pherecydes says concerning this seaboard that Miletus and Myus and the parts around Myucale and Ephesus were in earlier times occupied by Carians. . . . He also says that Androclus, legitimate son of Codrus the king of Athens, was the leader of the Ionian colonisation, which was later than the Aeolian, and that he became the founder of Ephesus, and for this reason, it is said, the royal seat of the Ionians was established there. And till now the descendants of his family are called kings; and they have certain honours, I mean the privilege of front seats at the games and of wearing purple robes as insignia of royal descent. (*Geography* 14.1.3)

Strabo's source is Pherecydes of Athens, who is dated in the middle of the fifth century B.C.E.[16] Codrus was king of Athens in the eleventh century B.C.E., and Androclus was one of his sons who led the colonization of Ionia (see Pausanias, 7.2.8-9; p. 97). The early date is, of course, suspect, and is likely to be a retrojection in time of the situation in the fifth century B.C.E. when Athens exercised real power after the Ionian revolt. The legendary colonization is "essentially an Athenian imperial fiction of the 5th cent BC."[17]

If Strabo's "till now" (*eti nun*) is taken literally, it would mean that the family of Androclus had survived into the first century B.C.E. While not absolutely impossible, this does seem rather incredible. The story is taken up by Pausanias (7.2.9; p. 97).

Eleven other cities in addition to Ephesus were founded in the first wave of colonization, namely Miletus, Myus, Lebedus, Colophon, Priene, Teos, Erythrae, Phocaea, Clazomenae, Chios, and Samos.

THE SITE OF THE FIRST SETTLEMENT

> These are the the twelve Ionian cities, but at a later time Smyrna was added, being induced by the Ephesians to join the Ionian League, for the Ephesians were fellow-inhabitants of the Smyrnaeans in ancient times, when Ephesus was also called Smyrna. And Callinus somewhere so names it, when he calls the Ephesians Smyrnaeans in the prayer to Zeus, "and pity the Smyrnaeans"; and again, "remember, if ever the Smyrnaeans burnt up beautiful thighs of oxen in sacrifice to thee."

> Smyrna was an Amazon who took possession of Ephesus, and hence the name both of the inhabitants and of the city, just as certain of the Ephesians were called Sisyrbitae after Sisyrbe. Also a certain place belonging to Ephesus was called Smyrna, as Hipponax plainly indicates, "He lived behind the city in Smyrna between Tracheia and Lepra Acte," for the name Lepra Acte was given to Mount Pion, which lies above the present city and has on it part of the city's wall.
>
> At any rate the possessions behind Pion are still now referred to as in the "opistholeprian" territory, and the country alongside the mountain round Coressus was called "Tracheia." The city was in ancient times around the Athenaeum, which is now outside the city near the Hypelaeus, as it is called. So that Smyrna was near the present gymnasium, behind the old city, but between Tracheia and Lepra Acte. On departing from the Ephesians, the Smyrnaeans marched to the place where Smyrna now is, which was in the possession of the Leleges, and, having driven them out, they founded the ancient Smyrna, which is about 20 stadia distant from the present Smyrna. (*Geography* 14.1.4)

According to the Austrian archaeologists the original Ionian settlement was on the thirty-four-meter-high hill on which the so-called Macellum is now located,[18] which for convenience and neutrality I shall call Hill 34 rather than prejudge the issue by adopting their name, "The Ionian Acropolis." This area does show traces of occupation in the eighth century B.C.E., and before the bay silted up it would have been surrounded by water on two sides (see fig. 2). Certainly the Ionians who founded Miletus at about the same time chose an almost identical site.[19] How does Hill 34 square with what the literary sources tell us?

The most detailed form of the founding legend is furnished by Athenaeus (361d-e; p. 47). Among other things it tells us that a temple of Athena marked the spot where the boar died on a mountain that is called Tracheia ("Rough"). Strabo also says that "the city in ancient times was around the Athenaeum," but he adds the crucial supplementary information that this site "is now outside the city," by which he can only mean that it was outside the Hellenistic wall (see 14.1.21 below). Hill 34 is in fact outside a city wall dated with some hesitation to 191 B.C.E.[20]

Strabo, however, also twice tells us that Smyrna lay "behind the old city but between Tracheia and Lepre Acte," and he says that the latter was a name given to Mount Pion. In fact it was a nickname meaning "the leprous escarpment" and is perfectly appropriate to the modern Panayir Dagh, whose crumbling surface still suggests rotting skin. Pausanias thought it "strange" (7.5.10). Panayir Dagh, "mountain of the pilgrimage," takes its name from a chapel to which the Armenians of Izmir come every year in May to celebrate the feast of St. John the Theologian. It has two small peaks; the northern is 131 meters high and the southern 155 meters. It does dominate the Hellenistic city in the valley

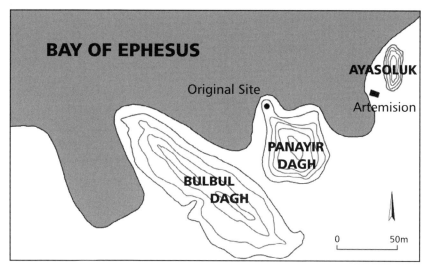

At the time of the Ionian settlement

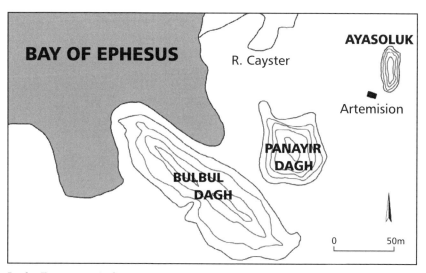

In the Roman period

Figure 2   The Moving Shoreline of Ephesus

between it and the Bulbul Dagh, and on it a section of the Hellenistic wall is still visible.

Before we continue, it is appropriate here to say a word about the Bulbul Dagh, "mountain of the nightingales." Its highest point (358 meters) lies southwest of the southern peak of Panayir Dagh. From there it slopes gradually to the WNW for some four kilometers. An inscription on the south side of the square tower popularly known as the "Prison of St. Paul" tells us (a) that the forty-five-meter-high knob with which Bulbul Dagh terminates on the WSW was called Hermaion, from a no-longer-extant sanctuary of Hermes; (b) that the ninety-six-meter-high hill closer to the city was called the Hill of Astuagus; and (c) that in 287 B.C.E. the sea washed the foot of that part of Bulbul Dagh.[21]

To return to Strabo, his placing of Smyrna in the valley *between* Tracheia and Panayir Dagh means that the latter cannot be Tracheia, an identification the archaeologists claim as further justification for their interpretation of Hill 34.[22] Strabo is entirely logical in placing Smyrna "behind the city," because one would naturally think of the "front" of a settlement on Hill 32 as being the seaward side.

Strabo further identifies Tracheia as "the country alongside the mountain round Coressus." In order to clarify what this means we have to draw in three other texts. Herodotus tells us that in 489 B.C.E. the Ionians "left their ships at Coressus in Ephesian territory" (5.100; p. 72), which implies that Coressus was a coastal village with a harbor. In 409 B.C.E. Thrasyllus disembarked half his troops "near Coressus" and "all the rest near the marsh on the opposite side of the city" (Xenophon of Athens, *Hellenica* 1.2.7). The latter can only be the marshy area around the mouth of the Marnas river between the city and the Artemision. Coressus once again appears as a coastal village. Finally, a first-century C.E. papyrus is absolutely explicit in speaking of "the harbor called Coressus (*ton limena ton Korēsson kaloumenon*)."[23]

Such consistency is interrupted by Athenaeus' statement that the Ionians "settled Tracheia and the areas on the slopes of Coressus (*ktizousi Trēcheian kai ta epi Korēsson*)" (361e; p. 47). The natural reading is that "Tracheia" and "the slopes of Coressus" are two different places. But if Tracheia is Hill 34, where then is Coressus? It has been suggested that it is Panayir Dagh,[24] but that would mean that the same small hill had three different names—Mount Pion, Lepre Akte, and Coressus—which seems excessive, to say the least, particularly since no justification is forthcoming.

An alternative reading of the text of Athenaeus is to take *kai*, "and," in the well-attested explanatory sense,[25] and thus translate "Tracheia, that is to say, the areas on the slopes of Coressus." In other words, the proper name of the hill Coressus came from the coastal village at the foot of the hill, and the nickname "Rough" described what sort of terrain it was. The situation is exactly parallel to that of Mount Pion, which had the nickname Lepre Akte.

The conclusion of this rather protracted analysis is that Hill 34 satisfies the exigencies of all the literary evidence as to the location of Coressus. Inevitably confusion has been generated by the fact that the same little coastal village gave its name both to a harbor in front and to the mountain behind. It is not an objection to say that the "mountain" is only thirty-four meters high, because the Ionian "city" of Ephesus would probably rank as a mere hamlet in the modern sense. The temptation to move the name Coressus to the much higher Bulbul Dagh should be resisted, *pace* the Schindler map of the environs of Ephesus.

In this hypothesis the harbor of Coressus could be either northeast or southwest of Hill 34. Over the centuries the name might even have moved from the former to the latter when the first silted up. There is little doubt that in the Hellenistic period the harbor lay southwest of Hill 34, as we shall see below in *Geography* 14.1.24.

It would appear that when the Ionians arrived they found two villages in the area they planned to settle, Coressus and Smyrna. The Greeks took the high ground of Hill 34, whose roughness had inhibited the two villages from doing anything with it. The Ionians needed the harbor of Coressus, and the village seems to have been happy to be absorbed into a new dynamic urban entity. Pausanias laughs at the idea of making a real distinction between Ephesus and Coressus (5.24.8). The people of Smyrna thought otherwise and, according to Strabo, preferred to move elsewhere.

Deep probes beneath the western edge of the *Tetragonos Agora*, the "Square Marketplace" (see p. 197), brought to light evidence of a very early settlement that the archaeologists identify as the Smyrna mentioned here.[26] Increasing prosperity was evident in the changing building styles from the eighth to the sixth centuries b.c.e. Thereafter the site seems to have been abandoned. The identification with Smyrna seems rather arbitrary. It could equally well be Coressus.

Strabo, of course, knew of a city called Smyrna (modern Izmir) located 320 stadia as the crow flies from Ephesus (14.1.2), and his enthusiastic description (14.1.37) clearly indicates that he visited it. He claims that it was not on the original site, and he implies that Antigonus and Lysimachus were responsible for the move. The latter had enforced a somewhat similar move in Ephesus (14.1.21 below; p. 17). It must have been an irresistible temptation for Strabo to attribute the first settlement to those who had left Ephesus. A sudden cultural shift is in fact attested for the seventh century b.c.e.[27] His explanation of the similarity of names is ingenious, but it is perfectly possible to think that the village of Smyrna was progressively incorporated into an expanding Ephesus, and that the name of the town up the coast was a pure coincidence.

THE NAME OF ARTEMIS

> Artemis has her name from the fact that she makes people *artimeas*. (*Geography* 14.1.6)

The justification for this parenthetical aside is simply an associative train of thought. In writing of Miletus, Strabo naturally mentions the great temple of Apollo at Didyma and notes that the Milesians pray to Apollo as *Oulios*, that is the god of "health and healing." This immediately evoked his sister, Artemis, whose name had a similar etymology. *Artemēs*, "secure and healthy," is the adjective derived from *artemeō*, "to be safe and sound."[28] Here, therefore, Artemis is defined in terms of the benefits she confers on others, which goes a long way toward explaining her great popularity at Ephesus.

For Plato (*Cratylus* 406B), however, her name came from *artemes*, "strong-limbed," which defined the goddess in herself.[29] The same approach is taken by Liddell, Scott, and Jones's *Lexicon*, but they suggest that her name is derived from *artamos*, "butcher," the substantive from *artameō*, "to cut into pieces."[30] Justification for this hypothesis is not difficult to find. For example, when Artemis feared that Actaeon would boast of having seen her naked she changed him into a stag, and with his own pack of fifty hounds tore him to pieces.[31]

WINE GOOD AND BAD

> The island of Samos does not produce good wine, although good wine is produced by the islands all round (although most of the whole of the adjacent mainland produces the best of wines), for example Chios and Lesbos and Cos. And indeed the Ephesian and Metropolitan wines are good; and Mount Mesogis and Mount Tmolus and the Catacecaumene country and Cnidos and Smyrna, and other less significant places, produce exceptionally good wine, whether for enjoyment or medicinal purposes. (*Geography* 14.1.15)

Metropolis is just north of Ephesus on the road to Smyrna. The two mountain ranges are the southern and northern limits respectively of the Cayster valley, at whose mouth Ephesus is located. The Catacecaumene country is inland from Smyrna, and Cnidos is a peninsula far to the south.

Pliny the Elder is of a very different opinion. The island wines, he believes, are by far the best, and he is rather critical of the two mountain wines:

that of Mount Tmolus is not esteemed as a wine to drink neat, but because being a sweet wine an admixture of it gives a sweetness to the dry quality of the remaining vintages, at the same time giving them age, as it at once makes them seem more mature. . . . As for the vintage of (Mount) Mesogis, it has been found to cause headache, and that of Ephesus has also proved to be unwholesome, because sea-water and boiled must are employed to season it. (NH 14.9.74-75)

The use of must, i.e., the expressed juice of the grape before fermentation, is understandable, but the use of seawater seems rather curious. However, there is no mistake, because just before this paragraph Pliny compliments the wine of Clazomenae (between Ephesus and Smyrna) on its improvement "now that they have begun to flavour it more sparingly with sea-water" (73), and he goes on to speak of "sea-flavoured" and "sea-treated" wine (78). Later in his work Pliny draws on classical handbooks of oenology to explain how the Greeks prepare wine: "In Greece, on the other hand, they enliven the smoothness of their wines with potter's earth or marble dust or salt or sea-water, while in some parts of Italy they use resinous pitch for this purpose" (NH 14.24.120). It would seem that the purpose of this was to increase the acidity of the wine.

EPHESUS, BIRTHPLACE OF ARTEMIS AND APOLLO

After the Samian strait, near Mount Mycale, as one sails [north] to Ephesus, one comes on the right to the seaboard of the Ephesians, and a part of this seaboard is held by the Samnians. First is the Panionium . . . then comes Neapolis . . . then Marathesium . . . then Pygela. . . . Then comes the harbour called Panormus, with a temple of the Ephesian Artemis, and then the city Ephesus.

On the same coast, slightly above the sea, is also Ortygia, which is a magnificent grove of all kinds of trees, of the cypress most of all. It is traversed by the Cenchrius River, where Leto is said to have bathed herself after her travail [in giving birth to Artemis and Apollo]. For here is the mythical scene of the birth, and of the nurse Ortygia, and of the holy place where the birth took place, and of the olive tree nearby, where the goddess is said first to have taken a rest after she was relieved from her travail.

Above the grove lies Mount Solmissus, where, it is said, the Curetes stationed themselves, and with the din of their arms frightened Hera out of her wits when she was jealously spying on Leto, and when they helped Leto to conceal from Hera the birth of her children. There are several temples in the place, some ancient and others built in later times. And in the most ancient temples are many ancient wooden images, but in those of later times there are works of Scopas, for example, Leto holding a sceptre and Ortygia standing beside her with a child in each arm.

A general festival is held there annually. And by a certain custom the youths vie for honour, particularly in the splendour of their banquets there.

> At that time also a special college of the Curetes holds symposiums and performs certain mystic sacrifices. (*Geography* 14.1.20)

Leto had been made pregnant by Zeus, who was married to Hera. The latter naturally resented his infidelities, and persecuted his paramours. Thus she would have killed Leto and her children. This is perhaps the fullest version of the tradition attaching the birth of the twins Artemis and Apollo to the vicinity of Ephesus. A competing story, found in the Delian section of the archaic *Homeric Hymn to Apollo*, gives the honor to Delos,[32] which the Ephesians fiercely denied (Tacitus, *Annals* 3.61; p. 135). The qualification of Ortygia as a nurse, however, must derive from the Delian legend, according to which Artemis was born first and immediately helped her mother in the birth of Apollo.[33]

The basis of the claim of Delos is the appearance of the word "Ortygia" in the tradition. It means "Quail (*ortyx*) island," and was the name of a small island very close to Delos. Other places, however, are also called Ortygia,[34] because the quail is a migratory bird. Moreover, Delos is far too small to have a river. According to Pausanias the river Cenchrius is in the land of the Ephesians (7.5.10). But where precisely? In 1904 it was thought that the river flowed due north to join the Cayster.[35] The *Barrington Atlas* (map 61, E2), on the contrary, shows the river flowing southwest to the sea. In the first opinion Orthygia is four kilometers southwest of the city, whereas in the second it is twelve kilometers due south. The name of the place no doubt derives from the association with Artemis, whose sacred bird was the lascivious quail.[36]

The Curetes were young divine warriors from Crete and were the male equivalent of Nymphs. Their role here parallels what they did at the birth of Zeus, when they made a great deal of noise to frighten off his father Cronus, who was accustomed to swallowing his children immediately after their birth (Strabo, 10.3.11). Without the willingness of the Curetes to take up arms Artemis would not have been born near Ephesus. Thus they could claim that without them the city would not exist. Understandably, therefore, they played a major role in the celebration of the birthday of Artemis in the persons of the members of the college that perpetuated their memory.[37]

The myth of the birth of Artemis was not just a curious story that attracted antiquarians. There is evidence to confirm Strabo's assertion that the festival was celebrated annually with great pomp well into the third century C.E., even though it is impossible to reconstruct either the exact history or the precise details.[38] Artemis permeated the consciousness of the Ephesians to the point that it was a rock-bottom element in their collective and individual identities.[39]

Scopas (active 370–20 B.C.E.) was reckoned among the three principal Greek sculptors of gods and worked almost exclusively in marble.[40] There is some doubt whether the temples were in Ortygia, on Mount Solmissus, or in Ephesus itself. The last would seem to be the most probable, in which case the statue in question would have been carved around 350 B.C.E. when the temple of Artemis was rebuilt.[41]

The Ephesian legend should have guaranteed Apollo equal importance in Ionia. It did in fact contain a number of temples dedicated to him, notably at Didyma, but the feeling that Ionia, and particularly Ephesus, were the domain of Artemis is perfectly articulated by Himerios: "When the leader of the Muses divided all the earth beneath the sun with his sister, although he himself dwells among the Greeks, he appointed that the inheritance of Artemis would be Ephesus."[42]

A MOVING HISTORY

The city of Ephesus was inhabited both by Carians and by Leleges, but Androclus drove them out and settled the most of those who had come with him around the Athenaeum and the Hypelaeus, though he also included a part of the country situated on the mountain around Coressus. Now Ephesus was thus inhabited until the time of Croesus, but later the people came down from the mountainside and abode around the present temple until the time of Alexander.

Lysimachus built a wall round the present city, but the people were not agreeably disposed to change their abodes to it. Therefore he waited for a downpour of rain and himself took advantage of it and blocked the sewers so as to inundate the city. The inhabitants were then glad to make the change. He named the city after his first wife Arsinoë. The old name, however, prevailed. There was a senate (*gerousia*), which was conscripted. With these were associated the *Epicleti*, as they were called, who administered all the affairs of the city. (*Geography* 14.1.21)

Strabo has already dealt with the colonization of Ionia (see above). Once again he locates the earliest settlement by reference to the temple of Athena and the spring Hypelaeus, which was obviously unique because of the "oily" (*hypelaios*) taste of its water. We saw above that the temple should be located on the northwestern spur of the Panayir Dagh. Croesus, the last king of Lydia (560–546 B.C.E.), subjugated the Greek cities on the west coast of Asia Minor but did not expel the inhabitants. He beseiged but did not capture Ephesus because of a strategem of the inhabitants, which is explained by Herodotus (1.26; p. 68) and Aelian (3:26). On the defeat of Croesus by Cyrus the Great in 546 B.C.E. Ephesus became part of the Persian empire, and there remained with minor interruptions until Alexander the Great defeated the Persians in 334 B.C.E. at the battle of the river Granicus (modern Kocabas) in northwestern Asia Minor.

Alexander the Great (356–323 B.C.E.) visited Ephesus at least once (see below). Under his will Lysimachus (355–281 B.C.E.), one of the "Successors" (*diadochi*), received Thrace as his portion of the known world, but invaded Asia in 302 B.C.E. and participated in the decisive battle of Ipsus against Antigonus in 301 B.C.E. For his share in this victory he was rewarded with the lands of Asia Minor north of the Taurus range.

According to Strabo, in the period between Croesus and Lysimachus Ephesus moved twice. The site of the original settlement, as we have seen, was on a promontory of Panayir Dagh. The *terminus ad quem* of the first move was the area around "the present temple." It is immediately tempting to think that Strabo had in mind a new temple of Athena. His next subject, however, is the temple of Artemis (next section), and there can be little doubt that once the Artemision began to grow in importance it became "*the* temple" in Ephesus. Its popularity attracted immense crowds of visitors and it was natural for the inhabitants to move to where the business was. The same thing has occurred elsewhere. In the Holy Land, for example, the original villages of Bethany and Hebron moved to cluster around the revenue-producing Tomb of Lazarus and Tomb of the Patriarchs respectively.

The Artemision was located much closer to modern Selçuk than to ancient Ephesus. It lies in the valley on the north side of both the Marnas and the Selinus rivers, and that was where the Ephesians settled. Only this makes the rather drastic action taken by Lysimachus intelligible. It was clear to any prescient observer that as the river Cayster brought down more and more mud (see Pliny, 5.31.115; p. 104) the risk of both the Marnas and Selinus rivers backing up increased exponentially. Not only was occasional flooding inevitable, but a silted-up river delta very quickly becomes a malarial swamp.[43] At the time of Augustus the maintenance of drainage ditches in the Marnas valley was a serious drain on the finances of the Artemision.[44] Even today the plain west of Selçuk can turn into a lagoon after heavy rain.[45]

The first move down the hill to the valley cannot have taken place before 409 B.C.E., which is the date of the attack on Ephesus by the Athenian Thrasyllus, which is thus described by Xenophon of Athens:

> Having disembarked the hoplites near Coressus (*pros Korēsson*), and the cavalry, peltasts, marines and all the rest near the marsh on the opposite side of the city (*pros ton elos epi ta hetera tēs poleōs*), he led forward the two divisions at daybreak. (*Hellenica* 1.2.7)

The marshy area is the valley of the Marnas around the Artimision, and Coressus can only be a coastal village at the foot of the northwest ridge of the Panayir Dagh and distinct from Ephesus itself. The fact that the Ephesians did not begin to drift down to surround the Artemision for at least fifty years after the completion of the temple (see next section) suggests that, despite the latter's magnificence, it took some time to establish its reputation and to attract visitors in significant numbers.

The second move occurred around 294 B.C.E.,[46] when Lysimachus "at Ephesus founded the modern city which reaches to the sea" (Pausanias, 1.9.7). As we saw above, he was awarded western Asia, but to make his possession a reality he then had to take the individual cities, and he used a clever trick to capture Ephesus.

> When Lysimachus, king of the Macedonians, was besieging the Ephesians, these were assisted by the pirate chief Mandro, who was in the habit of bringing into Ephesus galleys laden with booty. Accordingly, Lysimachus bribed Mandro to turn traitor, and attached to him a band of dauntless Macedonians to be taken into the city as captives, with hands pinioned behind their backs. These men subsequently snatched weapons from the citadel and delivered the town into the hands of Lysimachus. (Frontinus, *Strategems* 3.3.7)

Lysimachus used an equally clever stratagem to compel the inhabitants to move to the present location of the city between Bulbul Dagh and Panayir Dagh. Not unnaturally, the inhabitants did not want to move away from their livelihoods, which depended on the Artimision. The tactic adopted by Lysimachus to force them was simple. He took out of commission whatever system of drainage the town enjoyed. The rainwater, in consequence, had nowhere to go, and the inhabitants experienced at first hand what flooding was like. This made them finally see reason and they were happy to move to a site that was not only safer but much better protected. To increase the population, Lysimachus also brought in new settlers (Pausanias, 1.9.7; p. 100).

Lysimachus' defensive wall was ten meters high and 9.65 kilometers long. Parts of it are still visible on the summit of Bulbul Dagh and on the northeast side of Mount Pion (Panayir Dagh). It was 2.4 to three meters thick, increasing to more than four meters as it descended into the valley between the two mountains. Square towers reinforced the wall, particularly at strategic points and where it changed direction.[47]

Lysimachus also changed the way the city was governed. He replaced the old Greek democracy with an oligarchical government dominated by the *gerousia* and the *epikletoi*. These latter are literally "men specially summoned," and presumably served as a sort of executive committee.

After the death of Lysimachus, Seleucids and Ptolemies fought over Ephesus. It eventually became subject to the Attalids of Pergamum when Antiochus III the Great (223–187 B.C.E.) was defeated at the battle of Magnesia near Sipylum (modern Manisa) in 190 B.C.E. He had wintered in Ephesus in 196 B.C.E., and of him Plutarch tells the following story:

"Seeing the priestess of Artemis surpassingly beautiful in her appearance, he straightway marched forth from Ephesus, for fear that even against his determination he might be constrained to commit an unholy act" (183F). This renunciation of the *droit du seigneur* is certainly rare, if not unique. If true, it highlights the awe in which the temple of Artemis was held. The last of the Attalids, Attalus III (170–133 B.C.E.), willed his kingdom to the Romans (see 14.1.38 below).

THE TEMPLE OF ARTEMIS

As for the temple of Artemis, its first architect was Chersiphron; and then someone else made it larger. But when it was set on fire by a certain Herostratus, the citizens erected another and better one, having collected the ornaments of the women and their own individual belongings, and having sold also the pillars of the former temple.

Testimony is borne to these facts by the decrees that were made at that time. Artemidorus says: Timaeus of Tauromenium, being ignorant of the decrees and being anyway an envious and slanderous fellow (for which reason he was also called *Epitimaeus* [Calumniator]), says that they exacted means for the restoration of the temple from the treasures deposited in their care by the Persians; but there were no treasures on deposit in their care at that time, and, even if there had been, they would have been burned along with the temple; and after the fire, when the roof was destroyed, who could have wished to keep deposits of treasure lying in a sacred enclosure open to the sky?

Now Alexander, Artemidorus adds, promised the Ephesians to pay all expenses, both past and future, on condition that he should have the credit therefore on the inscription, but they were unwilling, just as they would have been far more unwilling to acquire glory by sacrilege and a spoliation of the temple. And Artemidorus praises the Ephesian who said to the king [Alexander] that it was inappropriate for a god to dedicate offerings to gods.

After the completion of the temple, which, he says, was the work of Cheirocrates (the same man who built Alexandreia and the same man who proposed to Alexander to fashion Mount Athos into his likeness, representing him as pouring a libation from a kind of ewer into a broad bowl, and to make two cities, one on the right of the mountain and the other on the left, and a river flowing from one to the other)—after the completion of the temple, he says, the great number of dedications in general were secured by means of the high honour they paid their artists, but the whole of the altar was filled, one might say, with the works of Praxiteles. They showed me also some of the works of Thrason, who made the chapel of Hecatē, the waxen image of Penelopē, and the old woman Eurycleia.

They had eunuchs as priests, whom they called Megabyzi. And they were always in quest of persons from other places who were worthy of this preferment, and they held them in great honour. And it was obligatory for maidens to serve as colleagues with them in their priestly office. But though at the present time some of their usages are being preserved, yet others are not. (*Geography* 14.1.22-23)

The extent of the influence of the temple of Artemis is best articulated by Apollonius of Tyana in a letter to the Ephesians: "Your temple is thrown open to all who would sacrifice, or offer prayers, or sing hymns, to suppliants, to Hellenes, barbarians, free men, to slaves" (*Letter* 67). Nonetheless, Richard Oster is entirely correct in writing, "the quintessence of Artemis was forever related to the well being of Ephesus."[48] He further qualifies the relationship between the goddess and the city as a "covenant bond," which is illustrated in various ways, two of which are particularly striking.[49] Coins show Artemis wearing a mural crown to symbolize her protection of the city's defenses and thereby its general welfare. The city is given the title *neokōros tēs Artemidos* at least from the time of Nero.[50] The title *neokōros* is normally used of the official in charge of the proper administration of a temple. To find it predicated of a city is most unusual and affirms the conviction of Ephesus that it was the divinely appointed keeper and protector of the cult of Artemis. The city is also represented on coins as a woman holding in her hand the temple or the statue of the goddess.

It should not be assumed that the official line on the relationship of the temple to the city always reflected reality. The temple was administered by frail human beings who sometimes did not maintain the standards demanded by their offices. In 22 C.E. the right of asylum was so abused that the emperor Tiberius had to step in (Tacitus, *Annals* 3.60-63; p. 135). At the time of Paul's presence in Ephesus the emperor Claudius had to instruct the proconsul of Asia, Paullus Fabius Persicus, to deal with a whole series of corrupt practices that had practically beggared the temple of Artemis.[51]

Although the temple of Artemis is mentioned frequently in the literary sources, it was considered to be so well known that the precise location is never given. Its discovery was due to the tenacity of an Englishman, John Turtle Wood, who searched for seven years before finding it buried under eight meters of alluvial deposit on New Year's Day 1870. The crucial clue was furnished by an inscription found in the theatre. It mentioned a procession from the Magnesian Gate to the temple. This gate could only have been at one point in the encircling wall. When Wood excavated there he found an inscription that made the identity of the gate certain. Just outside was a covered portico that Wood immediately realized must be the one mentioned by Philostratus as linking the Magnesian Gate with the temple of Artemis (*Lives of the Sophists* 2.23; p. 173). His excavation (1870–1874) brought to light two huge temples, one built on top of the other. Subsequent excavations revealed that they had been erected on the ruins of much older sanctuaries probably dedicated to Cybele and Demeter.

According to Vitruvius "the temple of Diana at Ephesus was planned in the Ionic style by Chersiphron of Cnossus [on Crete] and his son Metagenes" (7 pref. 16; also Pliny, 7.38.125). He is very precise in saying "planned" because Pliny twice noted that the temple took 120 years to complete, even though "the whole of Asia" was working on it (16.79.213; 36.21.95). Vitruvius waxes lyrical on the ingenuity Chersiphron used to move marble from the quarry to the site (10.2.11-15; p. 143). Herodotus (*History* 1.92) notes that the columns were paid for in great part by Croesus (560–546 B.C.E.), which implies that the temple was started sometime in the middle of the sixth century B.C.E. In writing "someone else made it larger" Strabo seems to imply that the design was altered in the course of the work. Vitruvius merely says, "Afterwards Demetrius, a temple-warden of Diana and Paeonius of Ephesus are said to have completed it" (7 pref. 16). Paeonius seems to have been an architect, because he also worked on the temple of Apollo at Miletus (ibid.).

This temple measured 142 x 73 meters (Pliny, 36.21.95-97; p. 118), and was the largest building of its time in Rome, Greece, or Asia. The famous Parthenon at Athens, for example, measured only 69.5 x 30.88 meters.[52] Today huge buildings are to accommodate large numbers. In antiquity, on the contrary, temples were simply a setting for the statue of the god or goddess. The most striking example is perhaps the temple of Zeus at Olympia, where the statue dominated the interior space (see p. 161). Here there is not the slightest hint that the cult statue of Artemis was unusually large. All the religious ceremonies took place outside the building in the open. The great altar of the Artemision is twenty-nine meters from the steps leading up to the main entrance of the temple on the west.

It has been suggested that the Cretan architects were familiar with the great buildings of the Egyptians and that this influenced their ambitious design.[53] However, one should not forget the mobility of craftsmen in the ancient world, which meant that knowledge and skills had wide distribution. Greek sculptors, for example, worked on the great palace at Persepolis in Persia, which was built between 500 and 460 B.C.E.[54]

The date of the destruction of this first temple was widely remembered because it coincided with the birth of Alexander the Great in 356 B.C.E. Plutarch records a striking comment: "Hegesias the Magnesian made an utterance frigid enough to have extinguished that great conflagration. He said, namely, it was no wonder that the temple of Artemis was burned down, since the goddess was busy bringing Alexander into the world" (*Alexander* 3.6; p. 123). Had Artemis been at home in Ephesus, the disaster would not have happened.

Strabo is unusual in mentioning the name of the arsonist. Aulus Gellius recorded that "the common council of Asia decreed that no one should ever mention the name of the man who had burned the temple of Diana [= Artemis] at Ephesus" (*Attic Nights* 2.6.18). This is the background to the fuller note by Valerius Maximus: "Here is appetite for glory involving sacrilege. A man was found to plan the burning of the temple of Ephesian Diana so that through the destruction of this most beautiful building his name might be spread through the whole world. This madness he unveiled when put upon the rack. The Ephesians had wisely abolished the memory of the villain by decree" (8. 14, ext. 5).[55]

It is noteworthy that in this context both Cicero and Plutarch record that the magi who saw the destruction of the temple of Artemis interpreted it as the portent of further disaster. For Cicero they wailed, "Asia's deadly curse was born last night." For Plutarch they cried aloud that "woe and great calamity for Asia had that day been born." With the benefit of hindsight we may understand that the allusion can only be to the fact that Alexander made Asia the battleground on which his war with Persia was fought, even though it lasted less than a year.

Strabo attributes the design of the new temple, the one that became truly famous, to Cheirocrates. This appears to be an error. According to a note on the Loeb translation it should be Deinocrates of Macedonia.[56] It is rather extraordinary that he was as much a foreigner as the architect of the original temple. For a description of his achievement see Pliny (36.21.95-97; p. 116). Strabo had visited it personally ("they showed me").

The restoration must have begun immediately. This can be deduced from the charge of Timaeus of Tauromenium (ca. 350–260 B.C.E.) that money for the rebuilding of the temple was taken from deposits put there for security by various Persians who were expelled by Alexander in 334 B.C.E. Clearly Artemidorus, who wrote between 104 and 101 B.C.E., took this as a slander on his native city. His refutation, however, contains an uncomfortable element of bluster that brings its credibility into question. In any case it is compromised by its implausibility. Temples always served as depositories for valuables. Gold is not destroyed by fire; it may melt but will again solidify. A roof will not guarantee the security of gold, and guards can be employed in a roofless temple.

According to Aelius Aristides the rebuilt temple of Artemis was "the general bank of Asia" (*Orations* 23.24). This is confirmed by Julius Caesar for the first century B.C.E. (*Civil Wars* 3.33, 105; p. 32) and for the early second century C.E. by Dio Chrysostom (*Orations* 31.54-55; p. 64).

It is clear from Strabo that work on the new temple was still in progress when Alexander the Great came to Ephesus in 334 B.C.E. The city offered him no resistance. It was typical of him to want to reciprocate with a generous gesture, in this case by covering all past construction expenses and guaranteeing future ones. His desire for sole credit on the founding inscription, however, suggests that his lust for glory was another, and perhaps more powerful, motive. Given the ecumenical character of the temple of Artemis, the reaction of the Ephesians is rather surprising. Their refusal can hardly have been for religious reasons. It was probably much more personal. The financial sacrifices they had already made showed how much of themselves they had invested in the restoration of the temple. Perhaps they felt that by letting such a powerful figure pay for everything they would be surrendering control. This was selfish, perhaps, but it took courage to refuse any request of Alexander.

The interpretation of what is said in Strabo's last paragraph regarding the cult personnel is complicated by the final sentence, which appears to suggest that the author was aware that what he was describing was no longer current practice. In this perspective the imperfect tense should be interpreted strictly: "They used to have eunuchs, whom they would call *megabyzoi*. . . . It was customary for virgins to serve as priestesses." To support this view Christine Thomas draws attention to an inscription from the mid-fourth century B.C.E. that reads, "[Megabyzos,] son of Megabyzos, temple warden of the temple of Artemis in Ephesus."[57] Clearly Megabyzos *père*, at least, was not a eunuch!

If *megabyzos*, a Persian word meaning "set free by god,"[58] had become merely a generic proper name, its use in both the singular and the plural is no longer a problem. Pausanias declared, "I know that the 'entertainers' of the Ephesian Artemis live in a similar fashion [in sexual and ritual purity], but for a year only, the Ephesians calling them Essenes" (8.13.1). Inscriptions show that these were priests who sacrificed to Artemis in addition to other functions.[59] Perhaps their temporary chastity led to the erroneous conclusion that the priests of Artemis were eunuchs. The meaning of "Essene" (*essēn*) has not been clarified.[60] Some twenty-three sacerdotal positions, honorary titles, and clerical functionaries associated with the temple of Artemis are mentioned in inscriptions.[61]

The "maidens," of course, were virgins. They did not, however, serve for life. They could marry after a period of service, and inscriptions reflect their pride in their daughters who served Artemis in their turn.[62] According to Plutarch, "At Ephesus they call each one of the servants of Artemis, first a novice (*Mellieren*), then a priestess (*Hieren*), and thirdly an ex-priestess (*Parieren*)" (*Moralia* 795D). Another office open to women was that of *kosmēteira tēs Artyemidos*, which is interpreted as meaning a female magistrate.[63]

THE RIGHT OF ASYLUM

But the temple remains a place of refuge, the same as in earlier times, although the limits of the refuge have often been changed. For example, when Alexander extended them for a stadium, and when Mithridates shot an arrow from the corner of the room and thought it went a little further than a stadium, and when Anthony doubled this distance and included within the refuge a part of the city. But this extension of the refuge proved harmful, and put the city in the power of criminals. Therefore, it was nullified by Augustus Caesar. (*Geography* 14.1.23)

Asylum is simply the modified transcription of the Greek *asylos*, "inviolable," which was predicated of territory immune from the power of the state. The only modern parallel is an embassy, a space in which the host nation has no sovereignty. Cardinal Stefan Wyszynski saved himself from the communist regime in Poland by finding asylum in the American embassy in Warsaw.

In antiquity Greek temples were considered automatically inviolable because of their sanctity. In them individuals could take refuge. This situation was formalized in the mid-third century B.C.E. when grants of immunity were made by the civil power. None is recorded after the Roman review of that status in 22–23 C.E. Between those two dates some ninety grants are known.[64] The right to asylum was not absolute. It could not be proper for a criminal to escape justice by taking up residence in a temple (e.g., Josephus, *Antiquities* 16.168; p. 81). Thus the temple authorities had to determine whether a claim for asylum was justified.[65] See Plutarch, *Parallel Lives: Antony* 5.1.4 (p. 125).

The ideal asylum seeker would have been someone like Ptolemy XII Auletes, the legitimate king of Egypt, who in 58 B.C.E. was dethroned by the Alexandrians. Fearing for his life, he sought refuge in the temple of Artemis in Ephesus (Dio Cassius, 39.16.3), where he remained until he was convinced that the danger no longer existed.

It is easy to think of ways in which the safeguard of assessment of individual cases could be nullified. That this in fact happened at the temple of Artemis is clear from Apollonius of Tyana: "But I do condemn the people who by night and by day share the home of the goddess. Otherwise I should not see issuing thence thieves and robbers and kidnappers and every sort of wretch or sacrilegious rascal. For your temple is just a den of robbers" (*Letter* 65). The final phrase evokes Jeremiah 7:11, which was used by Jesus apropos of the Temple in Jerusalem (Mark 11:17 and parallels).

In Strabo's text what Augustus nullified was not the right of asylum as such, but the extension that Mark Antony had irresponsibly granted. In order to define precisely the limits of the territory sacred to the goddess, in 6 or 5 B.C.E. Augustus erected a surround wall with an inscription: "the *temenos* of Artemis is inviolate, the whole area inside the perimeter. Whoever transgresses (this provision) will have himself to blame."[66] Within the wall was included an Augusteum in which the emperor was worshiped.[67] This was a development without parallel in the long history of the Artemision, and effectively made Augustus the "partner" of the goddess.

The presentation of the Artemision's historical claim to inviolability to the senatorial review board set up by Tiberius in 22 C.E. is reported in considerable detail by Tacitus (*Annals* 3.60-63; p. 135). Understandably, no mention is made of the disgraceful Ephesian Vespers in 88 B.C.E., in which, on the orders of Mithridates, the Ephesians violated the sanctuary of Artemis to murder the innocent Romans who had sought asylum there (Appian, *Mithridatic Wars* 12.4.23; p. 41). Rome reacted by removing its privilege of inviolability, which was only restored by Julius Caesar some forty years later.[68]

In novels dated to the second century C.E. Ephesus has the widespread reputation of being "the last hope of desperate individuals, a haven of possible security for those battered by fate."[69] See, for example, Achilles Tatius, *Leucippe and Clitophon* (p. 150).

THE HARBORS OF EPHESUS

> The city has both an arsenal and a harbour. The mouth of the harbour was made narrower by the engineers, but they, along with the king who ordered it, were deceived as to the result, I mean Attalus Philadelphus. For he thought that the entrance would be deep enough for large merchant vessels—as also the harbour itself, which formerly had shallow places because of the silt deposited by the Cayster River—if a mole were thrown up at the mouth, which was very wide, and therefore ordered that the mole should be built. But the result was the opposite, for the silt, thus hemmed in, made the whole of the harbour as far as the mouth more shallow. Before this time, the ebb and flow of the tides would carry away the silt and draw it to the sea outside. Such then is the harbour. And the city, because of its advantageous situation in other respects, grows daily more prosperous, and is the largest emporium in Asia this side of the Taurus. (*Geography* 14.1.24)

Today Ephesus is some seven kilometers from the sea. The silt carried down by the river Cayster has pushed out the coastline. Pliny notes that at the time of the Ionian colonization the sea "used to wash up to the temple of Diana [= Artemis]," whereas in his time the island of Syrie had become "part of the mainland" (2.87.201, 204). For a map of the coastline in the early historic period see figure 2, page 11.

The original harbor was close to the Artemision. Hence its name, "the Sacred Harbor" (Athenaeus, 361d-e; p. 47). How long it lasted before silting up remains a mystery, but when the temple of Artemis was rebuilt after the fire of 356 B.C.E. its floor had to be raised 2.6 meters in order to keep it above the rising water table.[70] When Lysimachus relocated the city (see above), he developed a new harbor farther to the west. In fact, this may have been his primary motive. He would have realized that a deep harbor was indispensable to the future prosperity of Ephesus. There is no doubt about the location of this harbor. The almost circular shape clearly visible in aerial photographs has been confirmed archaeologically. The great paved road (five hundred meters long and eleven meters wide) laid out in the first century B.C.E., running out from the theatre, terminates at the Middle Harbor Gate. The Northern and Southern Harbor Gates on either side have also been identified. All that we are told about this harbor is that in 190 B.C.E. "its mouth was like a river, long, narrow, and full of shoals," and that it could contain eighty-nine warships (Livy, 37.14.7; p. 88). Clearly the sea must have been pushed back considerably since the harbor first came into use.

This is the harbor Strabo describes. Originally it was four to six meters deep.[71] The problem of its silting up forced Attalus II of Pergamum (220–138 B.C.E.) to take action, but the "solution" only made the problem worse. The mole has not been discovered. Nonetheless, this harbor appears to have remained in use into the late Roman period. The Southern Harbor gate is dated to around 200 C.E., the Middle Harbor Gate to the time of Hadrian (117–138 C.E.), and the Northern Harbor Gate to the mid-third century C.E.[72] The harbor obviously remained a focal point of the city, but it would seem that only small, lightly laden boats could enter it.

Since Strabo mentions it (14.1.20), the third harbor, Panormus, must have been in existence when he wrote. Therefore it must have been developed by the Romans, probably in the first half of the first century B.C.E. It would have been used by larger seagoing vessels. It is usually located farther to the west in the little bay at the northwest tip of the Bulbul Dagh. It lies at the outlet of a mountainous valley whose periodic floodwaters could have served to flush the harbor free of silt.

If Ephesus was to continue to be "the largest emporium in Asia this side of the Taurus" a functioning harbor was essential, and a series of inscriptions attests to efforts to keep the harbor dredged.[73] In describing the career of Marcius Barea Soranus, who was proconsul of Asia in 61 C.E., Tacitus gave him credit for having "industriously cleared the harbor of Ephesus" (*Annals* 16.23). Hadrian adopted a more radical solution to the silting up of the ports. An inscription dated to 129 C.E. gives him credit for diverting the river Cayster farther to the north.[74]

FISHY BUSINESS IN EPHESUS

If merchant ships took pride of place in the harbor of Ephesus, fishing boats also had their importance. In antiquity both rich and poor lived essentially on bread, fish, olive oil, and wine. Fish, be it fresh, dried, or in the form of *garum*, was the principal, if not the only, source of protein. A fascinating insight to this industry at Ephesus at the time of Paul is provided by an inscription on a large *stele* found *in situ* in the southeast corner of the harbor at Ephesus and dated to 54–59 c.e.[75] It records the contributions of the members of an association of fishermen and fish-mongers toward the construction of a customs house (*telōnion*) at the harbor for the collection of the fishery tax. The mention of "columns" and "paving of the open area" as items specifically paid for in addition to "tiles" suggests that the edifice was built at the same time as a portico that served either as the city's wholesale or retail fish market. Fresh fish got premium prices because it was much tastier than salted or dried fish. On seafood from Ephesus see Athenaeus, 87c (p. 49). Another inscription suggests that people tended to work timber and stone on the wharf; such activities had to be forbidden by the proconsul because they damaged the quay area.[76]

At first it might seem a little odd for tradespeople to erect a building to take their own taxes, but reflection shows it to be a smart move. The state or city collected the fishery tax in the usual way, by farming it out to tax-collectors. It was to the advantage of everyone in the fishery business to have the process of payment take place in their own building. It permitted them to control its fairness, and if necessary to correct an injustice by the presence of menacing numbers. At the same time, of course, they protected their monopoly.

The original list contained perhaps a hundred names, of which eighty-nine remain clear enough to be studied. The breakdown reveals a wide range of social and legal status.[77] There were forty-three or forty-four Roman citizens, which can be further subdivided into those of Roman/Italian descent (eighteen or nineteen), Greeks who were granted citizenship (nine), and those bearing slave names, who won their citizenship through military service or manumission (sixteen). In addition there were between thirty-six and forty-one Greeks, presumably citizens of Ephesus, and between two and ten slaves. Nothing can be said about the remaining names. In other words, the membership of the fishery association reflected the diversity of the city's inhabitants.

This is perhaps a convenient place to list other professional guilds in Ephesus attested by inscriptions: silversmiths (Acts 19:25), *to synedrion tōn argyrokopōn*,[78] doctors (p. 84), bakers (cf. p. 1), wine dealers, wool dealers and garment sellers (cf. p. 211), towel weavers, hemp dealers, cobblers, temple builders and carpenters, sawyers, knob-turners, surveyors, workers in the private baths. Some or all of these may have housed their officers in a "portico of the corporations."[79]

WORTHIES OF EPHESUS

Notable men have been born in this city. In ancient times, Heraclitus the Obscure, as he is called; and Hermodorus concerning whom Heraclitus himself says, "It were right for the Ephesians from youth upwards to be hanged, who banished their most useful man saying, 'Let no man of us be most useful; otherwise, let him be elsewhere and with other people.'" Hermodorus is reputed to have written certain laws for the Romans. And Hipponax the poet was from Ephesus; and so were Parrhasius the painter and Apelles, and more recently Alexander the orator, surnamed Lychnus [Lamp], who was a statesman, and wrote history, and left behind him poems in which he describes the position of the heavenly bodies, and gives a geographic description of the continents, each forming the subject of a poem. (*Geography* 14.1.25)

This is an extraordinary little digression because in the next section (below) Strabo returns to practical matters such as fishing rights and taxes. He did, however, single out some of the major cultural figures in the history of Ephesus.

Heraclitus was one of the fathers of philosophy but earned his nickname by his tendency to argue by means of indirect references. According to Dio Chrysostom he was self-taught (*Oration* 55.1). He is also coupled with Hermodorus by Diogenes Laertius, who shows that Strabo caught his spirit correctly:

Heraclitus, son of Bloson or, according to some, of Heracon, was a native of Ephesus. He flourished in the 69th Olympiad [504–500 B.C.E.]. He was lofty-minded above all other men, and over-weening, as is clear from his book in which he says, "Much learning does not teach understanding; else would it have taught Hesiod and Pythagoras, or again, Xenophanes and Hecataeus." For "this one thing is wisdom, to understand thought, as that which guides all the world everywhere." And he used to say that "Homer deserved to be chased out of the lites and beaten with rods, and Archilochus likewise."

Again he would say, "There is more need to extinguish insolence than an outbreak of fire," and "The people must fight for the law as for city-walls." He attacks the Ephesians, too, for banishing his friend Hermodorus. He says, "The Ephesians would do well to end their lives, every grown man of them, and leave the city to beardless boys, for that they have driven out Hermodorus, the worthiest man among them, saying 'We will have none who is worthiest among us; or if there be any such, let him go elsewhere and consort with others."

And when he was requested by them to make laws, he scorned the request because the state was already in the grip of a bad constitution. He would retire to the temple of Artemis and play at knuckle-bones with the boys. And when the Ephesians stood around him and looked on, he said,

"Why, you rascals, are you astonished? Is it not better to do this than to take part in your civil life?" (*Lives of Eminent Philosophers* 9.1-3)

Hipponax is dated to the late sixth century B.C.E., but remained a popular figure right up to the time of Strabo, who quotes him in 14.1.4 (above). He did not take himself very seriously and used colorful, vulgar language both to entertain his readers and to excoriate his enemies.

Pliny would certainly have approved of Strabo's choice of artists, for he says of Parrhasius:

> Parrhasius also, a native of Ephesus, contributed much to painting. He was the first to give proportions to painting and the first to give vivacity to the expression of the countenance, elegance of the hair and beauty of the mouth. Indeed it is admitted by artists that he won the palm in the drawing of outlines. . . . There are many other pen-sketches still extant among his panels and parchment, from which it is said that artists derive profit. . . . Parrhasius was a prolific artist, but one who enjoyed the glory of his art with unparalleled arrogance, for he actually adopted certain surnames, calling himself the "Bon Viveur" and in some other verses "Prince of Painters," who had brought the art to perfection. (NH 35.36. 67-72)

Athenaeus confirms what Pliny says of the arrogance of Parrhasius:

> To such an extent were the delights of luxury and sumptuous expense cultivated among the ancients that even the Ephesian painter Parrhasius dressed himself in purple and wore a gold crown on his head, as Clearchus records in his *Lives*. For he indulged in luxury in a way offensive to good taste and beyond his station as a painter, and yet in talk claimed the possession of virtue, inscribing on the works of art wrought by him the following verse: "A man who lives in dainty style and at the same time honours virtue, has written these words." (543 c-d)

The real star on Strabo's list is undoubtedly Apelles who, according to Pliny, "surpassed all the painters that preceded and all who were to come after him; he dates in the 112th Olympiad [332–329 B.C.E.]" (35.79). He then goes on to give a detailed account of his career (35.79-97; p. 108), in the course of which he tells the famous horse story, which is also mentioned by other writers, e.g., Aelian:

> Alexander looked at Apelles' portrait of him in Ephesus and did not give it the praise which its artistry deserved. When his horse was brought along it whinnied at the horse in the picture as if it too were real, and Apelles said, "Your majesty, the horse certainly seems to have much better taste in art than you do." (*Historical Miscellany* 2.3)

Nonetheless, Pliny records that "This ruler [Alexander] also issued a proclamation that only Apelles should paint his picture, only Pyrgoteles sculpture his statue and only Lysippus cast him in bronze" (7.38.125).

The untouchable prestige of Alexander attracted stories of cheeky remarks from his inferiors, e.g., "When Diogenes was sunning himself in Craneum, Alexander came and stood over him and said, 'Ask of me anything you desire.' To which he replied, 'Stand out of my light!'"[80]

Strabo gives more space to Alexander the Lamp than to any of the others, presumably because he felt that they were in the same line of business. He was a polymath and ethnographer of the first century B.C.E. who perhaps belonged to Miletus rather than to Ephesus. Strabo would no doubt disagree with the assessment of the *Oxford Classical Dictionary*, "His encyclopaedic industry is evident; nothing suggests any concern for originality" (60b).

There is one extraordinary omission from Strabo's list of the worthies of Ephesus, namely, the great geographer Artemidorus of Ephesus, who flourished around 104–101 B.C.E., who is praised for his accuracy by Diodorus Siculus (3.11.2) and is quoted by Strabo on numerous occasions throughout his work. The omission is all the more surprising in that Artemidorus has just been cited approvingly (14.1.22) and will appear again in the very next section.

One might have thought that Zenodorus of Ephesus would also have merited inclusion. Born about 325 B.C.E., he became the founding head of the great library of Alexandria around 284 B.C.E. and was the first to attempt to produce a critical edition of Homer's *Illiad* and *Odyssey*.[81] Strabo, however, twice disagrees with his emendations (9.2.35; 12.3.8), which perhaps explains why he was not a contender for praise here.

NORTH OF EPHESUS

After the outlet of the Cayster River comes a lake that runs inland from the sea, called Selinusia; and next comes another lake that is confluent with it, both affording great revenues. Of these revenues, though sacred, the kings deprived the goddess, but the Romans gave them back. And again the tax-gatherers forcibly converted the tolls to their own use, but when Artemidorus was sent on an embassy, as he says, he got the lakes back for the goddess, and he also won the decision over Heracleotis, which was in revolt, his case being decided at Rome. In return for this the city erected in the temple a golden image of him. In the innermost recess of the lake there is a temple of a king, which is said to have been built by Agamemnon.

Then one comes to the mountain Gallesius, and to Colophon, an Ionian city, and to the sacred precinct of Apollo Clarius, where there was once an ancient oracle. (*Geography* 14.1.26-27)

The two lakes are located in the northwest corner of the Cayster valley.[82] In estimating the value of the fisheries on the sacred lakes one must keep in mind that fish was by far the most important source of

protein in the ancient world, and that in antiquity rivers and lakes provided the bulk of the fish caught. One would not be surprised were these
lakes protected by a warning similar to the one found on an inscription
at Smyrna dated to 1 B.C.E.:

> Do not harm the sacred fish, nor damage any of the goddess' utensils, nor
> carry anything out of the sanctuary to steal it. May the one who does any
> of these things be destroyed wretchedly by a terrible destruction, being
> eaten by fish. But if any of the fish dies, let it be offered on the same day
> on the altar. And may those who join in watching over and who increase
> the valuables of the goddess and her fish-pond have from the goddess
> enjoyment of life and successful labour.[83]

The revenues, which belonged to the temple of Artemis, were appropriated by the Attalids of Pergamum and were restored to the Artemision
only when the Romans inherited their kingdom in 133 B.C.E. Ten years
later, however, C. Sempronius Gracchus "changed history by providing
that the tithe of Asia was to be sold in Rome by the censors every five
years."[84] Each time the bidding went higher, new sources of income in
Asia had to be found by the tax-gatherers, who tended to infringe the
law by taxing temple land their contracts declared exempt. Ephesus
resisted renewed infringment of the rights of the Artemision in 104 B.C.E.
by sending an embassy to the Senate headed by Artemidorus, the eminent geographer. His successful argument would have been based on
documentation similar to a letter from the consuls in Rome to the city of
Oropos in central Greece dated 73 B.C.E.: "Concerning the land of Oropos
about which there was a dispute with the publicans, according to the
(state) contract this land is exempted, so that the publicans may not collect its taxes; we have made our decision in accordance with the decree
of the senate."[85] Eternal vigilance on behalf of the temple was necessary
for its prosperity.

The lakes no doubt were a gift to the temple. It was also endowed
with land, as were monasteries in later centuries. Such estates made a
significant contribution to the upkeep of the temple and its cult. The
properties belonging to Artemis in the Cayster valley are known in broad
outline through the discovery of a series of boundary markers ranging
in date from Augustus to Trajan. A typical one reads: "In accordance
with the ordinance of the emperor Nerva Trajan Caesar Augustus Germanicus Dacius (this) sacred boundary mark of Artemis (*horos hieros
Artimidos*) was placed (here) in the proconsulship of Fabius Postumius,
in line with the edict of Tullius."[86] The involvement of the emperor and
of the most senior Roman official in the province underlines the importance Rome attached to the security of the temple estates. Two sections
of the river Cayster passed through these estates, and tax was paid to
the temple on any fish caught there.[87]

It is very odd that Strabo should speak of the oracle at Claros as if it were a curiosity of the past. It had been the most celebrated oracular site in Asia Minor for three hundred years and would become even more celebrated in the next three hundred years because of its accurate prediction of the death of Germanicus, the son of the emperor Tiberius, in 18 C.E. (see Tacitus, *Annals* 2.54; p. 134). Due to its having been built across a narrow but deep natural fissure around 400 B.C.E. a prostyle temple (22 x 15 meters) in Ephesus is also identified as an oracular temple dedicated to Apollo.[88] Perhaps this was the temple of Didymaean Apollo at Ephesus that Gaius planned to finish.[89]

EPHESUS PASSES INTO THE HANDS OF ROME

After Smyrna one comes to Leucae, a small town, which after the death of Attalus Philomotor was caused to revolt by Aristonicus, who was reputed to belong to the royal family and intended to usurp the kingdom. Now he was banished from Smyrna after having been defeated in a naval battle near the Cymaean territory by the Ephesians, but he went up into the interior and quickly assembled a large number of resourceless people, and also of slaves, invited with a promise of freedom whom he called Heliopolitae. Now he first fell upon Thyateira unexpectedly, and then got possession of Apollonis, and then set his efforts against other fortresses.

But he did not last long. The cities immediately sent a large number of troops against him, and they were assisted by Nicomedes the Bithynian and by the kings of the Cappadocians. Then came five Roman ambassadors, and after that an army under Publius Crassus the consul, and after that Marcus Perperna, who brought the war to an end, having captured Aristonicus alive and sent him to Rome. Now Aristonicus ended his life in prison; Perpernas died of disease; and Crassus, attacked by certain people in the neighborhood of Leucae, fell in battle. And Manius Aquillius came over as consul with ten lieutenants and organised the province into the form of government that still now endures. (*Geography* 14.1.38)

Earlier Strabo had noted laconically, "Attalus, surnamed Philometer, reigned five years [138–133 B.C.E.], died of disease, and left the Romans his heirs. The Romans proclaimed the country a province, calling it Asia, by the same name as the continent" (13.3.2). Here he fills out the picture considerably. Attalus III was nicknamed "the mother lover," which perhaps explains why he died childless and diseased. His surrender of his kingdom to foreigners was of course resented, but the only one to take action was Aristonicus, who is thought to have been an illegitimate son of Eumenes II of Pergamum (197–158 B.C.E.).

The other cities led by Ephesus would have none of it and had checked the revolt by the time Rome intervened in 131 B.C.E. to claim its inheritance of an immensely valuable territory. A diplomatic effort was followed by a military offensive. Aristonicus succeeded in killing the first Roman commander, the consul Publius Licinius Crassus, but was sent to Rome as a prisoner by his successor, Marcus Perperna, who died in Pergamum in 129 B.C.E.[90]

Manius Aquillius arrived in 129 B.C.E. with a senatorial commission to determine the boundaries of the province and to set up a constitutional administration. Its structure can be worked out from numerous inscriptions. The citizens were divided into five "tribes," each headed by a *phylarchos*. These were thought to go back to the Ionian colonization, namely the Ephesians, the Karenaeans, the Teians, the Euonumoi, and the Bembinaeans. A sixth "tribe," Sebaste, was added probably during the reign of Augustus.[91] If the city's origins were Greek, its rebirth was Roman, and the dominance of the latter is underlined by the fact that the Sebaste ranked second in the order of precedence by the middle of the first century C.E.[92]

Each "tribe" contained six "thousands." From these citizens were drawn the members of the two-house system that in theory governed the city: (1) a "council" (*boulē*), whose membership was fixed at 450,[93] headed by a "secretary (*grammateus*) of the council," and (2) an "assembly of the people" (*ekklēsia tou dēmou*), also headed by a *grammateus tou dēmou*. "Secretary" in these contexts carries the connotation of the modern Secretary of State; this person was a senior official with real administrative power. In a number of cases the *grammateus tou dēmou* also enjoyed the title of "Asiarch," which connoted an administrative, not a religious function.[94] The two titles appear in Acts 19:31-35.

Official Roman documents copied by Josephus are addressed "to the magistrates, council, and people of Ephesus (*Ephesiōn archousi boulē dēmō*)."[95] The members of the *ekklēsia* were so numerous that it had to meet in the great theater.[96] There was also a *gerousia* ("senior citizens") headed by its own secretary, which had great influence but was not a political instrument.

To a great extent this was window-dressing, because Rome deliberately and systematically subverted the Greek ideal of the *boulē* as the executive committee of an *ekklēsia* whose membership changed regularly and often. Such potential instability was deemed intolerable. Rome was too clever to modify the traditional institutions of the Greek cities, because that would have been deeply resented. Instead it preserved the form while radically changing the content. It introduced a property qualification for membership in the *ekklēsia* and tended to grant its members life tenure. Thus Rome ensured that whatever power the city retained was wielded by those with an aversion to change and a strong personal interest in preserving the *status quo*.[97]

Such were the natural allies of Rome. Not only did they not rock the boat, but their behavior tended to loosen their grip on what little power remained to them. The Greek proclivity to emulation (*philotimia*) now had only one outlet, internal competition. Plutarch was fully alert to the unfortunate consequences.

> Those who invite the governor's decision on every decree, meeting of a council, granting of a privilege, or administrative measure, force their governor to be their master more than he desires. And the cause of this is chiefly the greed and contentiousness of the leading citizens. For either, in cases in which they are injuring their inferiors, they force them into exile from the state, or, in matters concerning which they differ among themselves, since they are unwilling to occupy an inferior position among their fellow-citizens, they call in higher powers. As a result, council (*boulē*), popular assembly (*dēmos*), courts (*dikastēria*), and the entire local government lose their authority. (*Moralia* 814F-815A)

Aquillius also gave Asia its first Roman roads. These are known from seven milestones inscribed with his name. They show that he had made Ephesus the capital of the new province in place of Pergamum (modern Bergama), the capital of the Attalid kingdom, because the bilingual (Latin and Greek) milestone found near Pergamum marks the 131st mile, which means that Ephesus was the *caput viae*.[98] The other great road he paved was the "common highway" to the east, of which Strabo will speak below (p. 36).

SOUTH OF EPHESUS

> In the interior above the Ionian seaboard there remain to be described the places in the neighbourhood of the road that leads from Ephesus to Antiochia and the Maeander River. These places are occupied by Lydians and Carians mixed with Greeks.
>
> The first city that one comes to after Ephesus is Magnesia, which is an Aeolian city, and is called "Magnesia on the Maeander," for it is situated near that river. But it is much nearer the Lethaeus River, which empties into the Maeander and has its beginning in Mount Pactyes, the mountain in the territory of the Ephesians. . . .
>
> In the present city [of Magnesia] is the shrine of Artemis Leucophryenē, which in the size of its shrine and in the number of its votive offerings is inferior to the temple in Ephesus, but in the harmony and skill shown in the structure of the sacred enclosure is far superior to it. And in size it surpasses all the sacred enclosures in Asia except two, those at Ephesus and at Didyma. (*Geography* 14.1.38-40)

The southeastern gate of Ephesus is the Magnesian Gate. From there it is roughly twenty kilometers to Magnesia on the Maeander river (modern Menderes). The qualification is made necessary by the fact that there were a number of other Magnesias, notably Magnesia near Sipylum (modern Manisa), north of Ephesus. Strabo is rather pedantic in pointing out (correctly) that Magnesia is not actually on the Maeander. The usage, however, is understandable because this river stretches far into the interior, and was much better known than its tiny tributary the Lethaeus. Even in his time it had become proverbial for its twists and turns. Strabo wrote, "its course is so exceedingly winding that everything winding is called 'meandering'" (12.8.15). Like the Cayster, the Maeander carried down so much silt (Strabo, 15.1.16) that Miletus, the rival of Ephesus, became almost unusable as a port in the Roman period, and is now far from the sea.[99]

The temple of "white-robed" Artemis at Magnesia was designed by Hermogenes of Alabanda in Caria (Vitruvius, 3.2.6) who appears to have been active either in the late second or early first century B.C.E.[100] Clearly Strabo thought it superior in design to the much more famous temple of Artemis in Ephesus, which might explain why he does not classify the latter as one of the wonders of the world (see Antipater of Sidon, *Greek Anthology* 9.58; p. 160).

Didyma is sixteen kilometers south of Miletus, and the temple was an oracular shrine of Apollo, which after being refounded by Alexander the Great about 331 B.C.E. became extremely important and influential.[101] The Antioch in question can only be Antiochia ad Maeandrum, which is much further up the valley of the Maeander.[102]

THE ROAD SYSTEM AROUND EPHESUS

Artemidorus says that as one goes from Physcus, in the Peraea of the Rhodians, to Ephesus, the distance to Lagina is 850 stadia. And then to Alabanda 250 stadia more. And to Tralles, 160 stadia. But one comes to the road that leads into Tralles after crossing the Maeander River, at about the middle of the journey, where are the boundaries of Caria. The distance all told from Physcus to the Maeander along the road to Ephesus amounts to 1180 stadia.

Again, from the Maeander, traversing next in order the length of Ionia along the same road. The distance from the river to Tralles is 80 stadia. Then to Magnesia, 140 stadia. To Ephesus, 120 stadia. To Smyrna, 320 stadia. And to Phocaea and the boundaries of Ionia, less than 200. So that the length of Ionia in a straight line would be, according to Artemidorus, slightly more than 800 stadia.

Since there is a kind of common highway constantly used by all who travel from Ephesus towards the east, Artemidorus traverses this too. From Ephesus to Carura, a boundary of Caria towards Phrygia, through Magnesia, Tralles, Nyssa, and Antioch on the Maeander is a journey of 740 stadia. (*Geography* 14.2.29)

Strabo here describes two of the major roads of antiquity. The first is the great north-south route in western Asia Minor. The second is the "common highway" running from Ephesus to India. His source, Artemidorus of Ephesus, as we have seen, was a great geographer, who attempted to calculate the length and breadth of the inhabited world (Pliny, 2.242-43).

Strabo starts from the southern end at Physcus (modern Marmaris) on the southern coast of Caria. The first part of the route, as far as Idyma, follows a valley cutting across the base of the peninsula of Cnidus. A mountain section brings it into the headwaters of the Marsyas, which it follows closely from Alabanda to the Maeander river. From Tralles (modern Aydin) it runs due west to Magnesia on the Maeander, where it angles northwest to Ephesus.[103] From Ephesus the route went up the Cayster valley to Anokome and then passed through a series of interconnecting river valleys to Smyrna (modern Izmir). Thereafter it followed the coastline.[104] It was first paved by the Roman consul Manius Aquillius between 129 and 126 B.C.E. (see above, p. 35). The great valley of the Maeander is the logical border between Caria on the south and Ionia on the north.

The distances given by Strabo are not in fact accurate. Curiously, they are too high for Caria and too low for Ionia. In Caria he gives the distance from Physcus to the Maeander river as 1180 stadia, which is equivalent to 215 kilometers (134 miles), whereas it is in fact about 150 kilometers (93 miles). His stage figures for Ionia add up to 860 stadia, which works out at 156 kilometers (97 miles), but the real distance is close to 200 kilometers (124 miles). According to Pliny (5.114), Magnesia on the Maeander was fifteen Roman miles from Ephesus and eighteen miles from Tralles.

The route to the north, of course, did not end at Phocas. In fact, it cut across the base of the peninsula on which that city is situated and angled into the valley of the river Caicus to reach Pergamum (modern Bergama) before continuing into the Troad.[105]

The "common highway" from Ephesus to India should perhaps be called the Great Trunk Road in order to bring out its military and commercial importance. From Tralles it runs along the north side of the Maeander river, crossing to the south bank at Antioch on the Maeander. At Carura it turns southeast into the Lycus valley, in which are the Pauline churches of Colossae, Laodicea, and Hierapolis.[106] Strabo's 740 stadia equals 134 kilometers (84 miles), whereas the real distance is 150 kilometers (93 miles). It was paved by Manius Aquillius between 129 and 126 B.C.E. at least as far as Apamea (modern Dinar).[107] Paul would have traveled this road on his way to Ephesus from Galatia in the late summer of 52 C.E.

Strabo's text continues to enumerate the cities and stages across Anatolia to the river Euphrates: Laodicea on the Lycus–Apamea–Metropolis–Philomelion–Tyraion–Laodicea–Katacecaumene–Koropassus–Garsaura–Mazaka/Caesarea–Tomisa.[108] The last section coincides with "the royal road" described by Herodotus (*History* 5.53-54; p. 71).

APPIAN

Appian was born toward the end of the first century C.E. and died about 165. He concludes the preface to his history of Rome with the words, "I am Appian of Alexandria, a man who reached the highest place in my native country, and have been, in Rome, a pleader of causes before the emperors, until they deemed me worthy of being their procurator." He must, in consequence, have acquired Roman citizenship. His use of a wide range of Greek and Latin sources shows high personal intelligence in the way he selected, condensed, and organized his material.[109]

HANNIBAL IN EPHESUS

> A rumour having spread that Ptolemy Philopator was dead, Antiochus hastened to Egypt in order to seize the country while bereft of a ruler. While on this journey Hannibal the Carthaginian met him at Ephesus . . . where he was received in a magnificent manner because of his great military reputation. (*Syrian Wars* 11.1.4)

While there can be little doubt about the ambition of Antiochus III the Great (223–187 B.C.E.) to add Egypt to his kingdom in Syria, the encounter with Hannibal that Appian uses to date his journey is impossible. Ptolemy IV Philopator ruled from 221–204 and was immediately succeeded by Ptolemy V Epiphanes. Hannibal could have encountered Antiochus only much later. Hannibal left Italy in 203 after fifteen fruitless years of trying to conquer Rome, and was finally defeated at Zama in north Africa in 202. Thereafter he confined himself to domestic affairs. His enemies, however, accused him of conspiring with Antiochus III. Before the Roman commission of enquiry reached Carthage, Hannibal fled east, and ultimately encountered Antiochus III, whom he endeavored to persuade to go to war with Rome. This encounter is dated to 195 B.C.E.[110]

A WITTICISM OF HANNIBAL

> In the meantime Roman ambassadors, and among them Scipio, who had humbled the Carthaginian power, were sent, like those of Antiochus, to ascertain his designs and to form an estimate of his strength. Learning that the king had gone to Pisidia, they waited for him at Ephesus. There they

entered into frequent conversations with Hannibal. . . . It is said that at one of their meetings in the gymnasium Scipio and Hannibal had a conversation on the subject of generalship, in the presence of a number of bystanders, and that Scipio asked Hannibal whom he considered the greatest general, to which the latter replied, "Alexander of Macedon." On this Scipio made no comment, yielding, as it seemed, the first place to Alexander, but proceeded to ask Hannibal whom he placed next. Hannibal replied, "Pyrrhus of Epirus" because he considered boldness the first qualification of a general; for it is not possible to find two kings more enterprising than these. Scipio was rather nettled by this, but nevertheless he asked Hannibal to whom he would give the third place, expecting that at least the third would be assigned to him. But Hannibal replied, "To myself; for when I was a young man I conquered Spain and crossed the Alps with an army. . . . I invaded Italy. . . ." As Scipio saw that he was likely to prolong his self-laudation he said, laughing, "Where would you have placed yourself, Hannibal, if you had not been defeated by me?" Hannibal, now perceiving his jealousy, replied, "I should have put myself before Alexander." Thus Hannibal persisted in his self-laudation, but flattered Scipio in a delicate manner by suggesting that he had conquered one who was the superior of Alexander. (*Syrian Wars* 11.2.9-10)

Alexander the Great would have been first on anyone's list of great generals. No doubt Pyrrhus of Epirus (319–272 B.C.E.) was included among Hannibal's choices because he, too, had invaded Italy with elephants among his forces.[111] He defeated the Romans at Heraclea (280 B.C.E.) and at Ausculum the following year. After losing to them at Malventum in 275 he returned to his homeland just as Hannibal had done. The Scipio in question is P. Cornelius Scipio Africanus, who defeated Hannibal at the battle of Zama in 202 B.C.E.

Although this story is also reported by Plutarch, *Lives: Titius Flaminius*, 21.3, and by Livy, *Roman History* 35.14, one can only comment "if it is not true, then it should be," or as the Italians say, *si non e vero e ben trovato*. In fact, most scholars consider it to be fictitious. Cicero admiringly records another retort by Hannibal in Ephesus in *On the Orator* 2.18.75 (p. 59).

EPHESIANS ACT AGAINST ROME

Then [When Mithridates took Ephesus], the Ephesians even overthrew the Roman statues which had been erected in their cities—for which they paid the penalty not long afterward. (*Mithridatic Wars* 12.3.21)

Mithridates VI Eupator Dionysius (120–63 B.C.E.), king of Pontus, was Rome's most dangerous enemy in the first century B.C.E. His control of almost the complete circuit of the Black Sea gave him enormous resources in men and materials.[112] When his armies swept into Asia at the beginning of the First Mithradaic War (89–85), he was warmly supported by Ephesus, which with other cities deeply resented having been handed over to Rome by the will of Attalus III in 133 B.C.E., because this made its inhabitants liable to the intolerable exactions of Roman tax-collectors. The system of taxation imposed on Asia was probably unique in the Roman empire.[113]

In 123 B.C.E. the tribune C. Sempronius Gracchus introduced a law whereby the taxes of Asia were to be auctioned in Rome by the censors every five years.[114] "What Gracchus certainly did was entirely to reorganize the system of taxation. He substituted for the Attalid taxes, which were probably many and various, two uniform taxes for the whole province, a tithe on arable land and pasture dues on grazing land. The new system was modelled on that of Sicily with the important exception that the taxes were farmed not locally but by the censors in Rome. The contracts thus fell to Roman companies instead of to local men, a circumstance that was to prove disastrous to the province."[115]

The last point has been well developed by Stephen Mitchell:

> The right to collect the various Asian taxes was certainly exploited to the full by profiteers. Should the Asian communities be unable to produce the sums demanded of them, they might be compelled to borrow, often at punitive rates of interest, from Roman bankers and moneylenders. Their chief security was certainly land, with the result that individual Romans from the start began to acquire property in Asia, either in default of debt payments, or by direct purchase from landowners unable to raise the capital to pay Roman levies by other means. The need to pay taxes also forced the cities of Asia to sell other assets, primarily to Roman buyers, notably works of art, manufactured goods in increasing quantities, and slaves.[116]

From the perspective of citizens of Ephesus more and more of their land and cultural heritage was being ripped away by Roman fingers. It was easy for Mithridates to win support.

But there were also those who resisted, refusing to believe that Mithridates could hold out against the might of Rome. Two inscriptions contain letters sent by the king to a satrap in Caria, in which he says of his enemy Chairemon that "having heard of my coming (*parousia*) he has escaped to the temple of Ephesian Artemis," where the king thought Chairemon abused the right of asylum, "from there he sends out letters to our common enemies, the Romans; and his immunity from punishment for the crimes that have been committed is an incitement to activities against us."[117] The right of asylum would carry no weight against the wishes of a powerful monarch; see what is said below regarding Mark Antony.

Resistance in Ephesus was minimal, and its choice was disastrous. It was to be repeated many times in the future. Not only did Ephesus pick the wrong side in the war between Mithridates and Rome, but it opted for Pompey against Caesar, for the assassins of Caesar against Mark Antony, and for the latter against Octavian.[118]

EPHESIANS KILL ITALIANS

Mithridates wrote secretly to all his satraps and city governors (*poleōn archousi*) that on the 30th day thereafter they should set upon all Romans and Italians in their towns, and upon their wives and children and their freedmen of Italian birth, kill them and throw their bodies out unburied, and share their goods with King Mithridates.

The Ephesians tore away the fugitives, who had taken refuge in the temple of Artemis, and were clasping the images of the goddess, and slew them. [Other cities also slaughtered those who had sought refuge in temples.] Such was the awful fate that befell the Romans and Italians in Asia, men, women, and children, their freedmen and slaves, all who were of Italian blood. By which it was made very plain that it was as much hatred of the Romans that impelled the Asians to commit these atrocities. (*Mithridatic Wars* 12.4.22-23)

This barbarous order led to the deaths of a great number of Italians. Valerius Maximus (9.2.4 ext. 3) estimates the figure at eighty thousand, whereas Plutarch (*Parallel Lives: Sulla* 24.4) nearly doubles that figure to one hundred fifty thousand. Mithridates' motive was no doubt twofold. On the one hand he provided welcome release for the hatred the Greek cities in Asia bore toward their blood-sucking occupiers, while on the other hand he got the Asians to commit themselves so openly and decisively that there could be no going back. This tactic did not work. Appian comments: "They paid a double penalty for their crime—one at the hands of Mithridates himself, who ill-treated them perfidiously not long afterward, and the other at the hands of Cornelius Sulla" (12.4.23), the Roman general who eventually defeated Mithridates.

EPHESIANS MURDER ZENOBIUS

When Zenobius approached Ephesus with his army, the citizens ordered him to leave his arms at the gates, and come in with only a few attendants. He obeyed the order and paid a visit to Philopoemen (the father of Monima, the favourite wife of Midthridates), whom the latter had appointed overseer of Ephesus (*episkopon Ephesiōn*), and summoned the Ephesians to the assembly. They expected nothing good from him, and adjourned the meeting until the next day. During the night they met and encouraged one another, after which they cast Zenobius into prison and put him to death. Then they manned the walls, organized the population, brought in supplies from the country, and put the city in a state of complete defence.

When the people of Tralles, Hypaepa, Mesopolis, and several other towns heard of this, fearing lest they should meet the fate of Chios, they followed the example of Ephesus.

Mithridates sent an army against the revolters and inflicted terrible punishments on those whom he captured, but as he feared other defections, gave freedom to the Greek cities, proclaimed the cancelling of debts, gave the right of citizenship to all sojourners therein, and freed the slaves. He did this hoping (as indeed it turned out) that the debtors, sojourners, and slaves would consider their new privileges secure only under the rule of Mithridates, and would therefore be well disposed toward him. (*Mithridatic Wars* 12.7.48)

The citzens of Ephesus had taken fright at the punishment that Mithridates had inflicted on the inhabitants of Chios on the mere suspicion that they were leaning toward Rome. Zenobius was the general in charge of that brutal operation (Appian, 12.7.46-47). It was probably sheer arrogance, and a conviction of the terror inspired by Mithridates, that allowed him to enter Ephesus without a military escort. The violence of the reaction of the Ephesian authorities betrays their panic. Understandably they did not think of protesting their innocence of any conspiracy with Rome or envisage negotiating with Mithridates. The experience of Chios had excluded both these options. They might, however, have considered using Zenobius as a bargaining counter.

EPHESUS PUNISHED BY SULLA

Having settled the affairs of Asia, Sulla bestowed freedom on the inhabitants of Illium, Chios, Lycia, Rhodes, Magnesia, and some others, either as a reward for their cooperation, or a recompense for what they had suffered from their loyalty to him [Sulla], and inscribed them as friends of the Roman people.

Then he distributed his army among the remaining towns and issued a proclamation that the slaves who had been freed by Mithridates should at once return to their masters. As many disobeyed and some of the cities revolted, numerous massacres ensued, of both free men and slaves on various pretexts. The walls of many towns were demolished. The Cappadocian faction, both men and cities, were severely punished, and especially the Ephesians, who, with servile adulation of the king [Mithridates] had treated the Roman offerings in their temples with indignity. (*Mithridatic Wars* 12.9.61)

The "Cappadocian faction," to which Ephesus belonged, were the most dedicated of Mithridates' supporters, and they suffered in the winter of 85–84 B.C.E. To have soldiers billeted on a city meant continual uncontrolled harassment of the population and a heavy financial burden for individuals; see Plutarch, *Sulla* 25.2 (p. 125).

In addition Sulla imposed a fine on Asia equivalent to five years' annual taxes to be paid at once. This caused great distress: "The cities oppressed by poverty borrowed it at high rates of interest and mortgaged their theatres, their gymnasiums, their walls, their harbours, and every other scrap of public property, being urged on by the soldiers with contumely" (Appian, 12.9.63). This was the end of the First Mithridatic War (85 B.C.E.).

POMPEY DEPARTS FROM EPHESUS

> At the end of the winter Pompey distributed rewards to the army. . . . Then he marched to Ephesus, embarked for Italy, and hastened to Rome, having dismissed his soldiers at Brundisium to their homes, a democratic action which greatly surprised the Romans. (*Mithridatic Wars* 12.17.116)

This dry little summary hides three years of incredible achievements in the East. After crushing the pirates in the eastern Mediterranean, Pompey (106–48 B.C.E.) was given charge of the provinces of Cilicia, Bithynia, and Pontus in 66 B.C.E. Quickly defeating Mithridates, he continued to push east, annexing Syria and Judea and extending Roman rule to the Euphrates. In 62 B.C.E. he brought his army west into Asia, where he distributed the spoils of his campaigns to his troops, who would not have to fight again. That he chose to leave from Ephesus underlines its importance as a port. A great number of ships were needed to transport his soldiers across the Aegean and Adriatic seas to Brundisium (modern Brindisi) on the east coast of Italy.

MARK ANTONY AT EPHESUS

> Octavian then proceeded towards the Adriatic, but when Antony arrived at Ephesus he offered a splendid sacrifice to the city's goddess, and pardoned all those who, after the disaster to Brutus and Cassius, had fled to the temple as suppliants, except Petronius, who had been privy to the murder of Caesar, and Quintus, who had betrayed Dolabella to Cassius at Laodicea.
>
> Having assembled the Greeks and other peoples who inhabited the Asiatic country around Pergamum, and who were present on a peace embassy, and others who had been summoned thither, Antony addressed them as follows:
>
> "Your king Attalus, O Greeks, left you to us in his will and straightway we proved better to you than Attalus had been, for we released you from the taxes that you had been paying to him, until the action of popular agitators also among us made these taxes necessary. But when they became necessary we did not impose them upon you according to a fixed evaluation so that we could collect an absolutely certain sum, but we required

you to contribute a portion of your yearly harvest in order that we might share with you the vicissitudes of the seasons. When the publicans, who farmed these collections by the authority of the Senate, wronged you by demanding more than was due, Gaius (Julius) Caesar remitted to you one-third of what you had paid to them and put an end to their outrages; for he turned over to you the collection of the taxes from the cultivators of the soil. And this was the kind of man that our honourable citizens called a tyrant and you contributed vast sums of money to the murderers of your benefactor and against us, who were seeking to avenge him." (*Civil Wars* 5.1.4)

After the defeat of Brutus and Cassius (the assassins of Julius Caesar) at Philippi in 42 B.C.E. Octavian returned to Italy, while Mark Antony the following year crossed the Aegean to Asia. Ephesus was the obvious port of arrival. It had the facilities to handle an army of six legions and ten thousand horse (5.1.3).[119]

The goddess, of course, is Artemis, and the temple is hers. No doubt Antony was surprised to find that some of his old enemies had sought refuge there. Although Brutus and Cassius had held the east, there is nothing to indicate that Ephesus was wholeheartedly on their side. Refugees would have been interested only in the temple of Artemis there, which was internationally recognized as *the* place of refuge. Asylum, however, was not absolute. While some were worthy of the protection of the goddess, others were not. Antony's discriminatory judgment was perfectly in keeping with the best traditional practice (see Strabo, 14.1.23; p. 24). Later he was not so scrupulous (see below).

Mark Antony's speech is a perfect illustration of how ancient historians worked. Appian certainly puts the words into Antony's mouth; there would have been no stenographic record. The essential fact, however, that Julius Caesar changed the Roman tax system in Asia in 48 B.C.E. is confirmed by Dio Cassius: "He did away with the publicans, who had been abusing the people most cruelly, and he converted the amount accruing from the taxes into a joint payment of tribute" (*Roman History* 42.6.3).

The savage ruthlessness of the tax collectors has been highlighted above, apropos of *Mithridatic Wars* 12.3.21. The significance of the change introduced by Caesar is well brought out by David Magie:

> The most notable of Caesar's measures, however, deal with the taxation of the province of Asia. Perceiving, apparently, that the amounts previously paid to Rome were excessive, especially in the present depleted state of the province, he remitted one third of the amount which Asia had hitherto paid. Then, taking a step of much greater consequence, he abolished the old method of collecting the taxes through contracts with the tax-farming corporations. This was now replaced by a new system, by which amounts were raised by the communities themselves and paid directly to the

quaestor of the province. This change, to be sure, affected the direct taxes only; the indirect levies, such as the customs-duties, were still collected, like the income from the state-owned properties and utilities, by the agents of the old corporations.[120]

Augustus put the tax system for Asia inaugurated by Caesar on a more stable foundation by instituting a periodic census, which provided an objective basis for determining what communities should pay.[121]

As Antony says, the province of Asia had been well plundered by Brutus and Cassius, the assassins of Julius Caesar. They had been empowered by the Senate to collect the normal taxes and to take as "loans" whatever else was required. They allowed only two years for the collection of the tribute of ten years to be paid. "Total collections must have been more than 25,000 talents (150,000,000 denarii)."[122] It is relatively easy to translate this figure into modern terms. At that time a day's wage for an unskilled laborer was half a denarius. In Jerusalem today the same workman would earn five dollars per hour, hence forty dollars for an eight-hour day. In consequence, a denarius is worth eighty dollars in today's terms, which is what one of Paul's skilled secretaries would have earned. Thus 150,000,000 denarii is equivalent to $1,200,000,000. Broughton offers a rough estimate of the population of the province of Asia at the time as 4,600,000.[123] Thus Brutus and Cassius took a minimum of $260 from every man, woman, and child—in cash up front. Antony himself was only slightly less demanding.[124]

THE EXCESSES OF MARK ANTONY

Straightway Antony's former interest in public affairs began to dwindle. Whatever Cleopatra ordered was done, regardless of laws, human or divine. While her sister Arsinoë was a suppliant in the temple of Artemis Leucophryne at Miletus, Antony sent assassins thither and put her to death. . . . Antony ordered the priest of Artemis at Ephesus, whom they called the Megabyzus, and who had once received Arsinoë as queen, to be brought before him, but in response to the supplications of the Ephesians, addressed to Cleopatra herself, released him. So swiftly was Antony transformed, and this passion was the beginning and end of evils that afterwards befell him. (*Civil Wars* 5.1.9)

This text is confused. If Arsinoë had sought refuge in Miletus, why should Antony want to kill the chief priest of the temple of Artemis in Ephesus? Josephus in this instance is probably more accurate in writing "Cleopatra got her sister Arsinoë to be slain, by the means of Antony, when she was a suppliant at Diana's temple at Ephesus."[125] The poor woman had sought asylum in the temple. In this case Antony would have wanted to distract public attention from his guilt by righteously punishing the dereliction of duty by the authorities of the temple of Artemis, who should have protected their suppliant.

Beneath the Octogonal Monument on Curetes' Street, whose decoration places it firmly in the period 50–20 B.C.E., was found a marble sarcophagus containing the body of a girl of fifteen or sixteen. She is identified as Arsinoë.[126]

ATHENAEUS

Of Athenaeus we know only that he was a native of Naucratis in Egypt and that he was active in Rome about 200 C.E. The one work that has come down to us is *Deipnosophistai*, which is usually translated as "The Learned Banquet." Those with a more developed sense of humor might call it "The Gastronomers" or "The Supping Sophists." It is really an encyclopedia. Athenaeus used the device of friends chatting around a table and capping each others quotations to collect and arrange a vast body of material. "He cites some 1,250 authors, gives the titles of more than 1000 plays, and quotes more than 10,000 lines of verse."[127] Many of the works he cites no longer exist, and without the industry of Athenaeus our knowledge of ancient literature would be immeasurably poorer. The *Deipnosophistai* contains twenty-five references to Ephesus covering a surprising number of subjects ranging from the sublime to the ridiculous.

THE FOUNDATION OF EPHESUS

Creophylus, in *Chronicles of the Ephesians*, says that the founders of Ephesus, after suffering many hardships because of the difficulties of the [first] site [they had selected], finally sent to the oracle of the god and asked where they should build their city. And he declared to them that they should build a city "wheresoever a fish shall show them and a wild boar shall lead the way."

It is said, accordingly, that some fishermen were eating their noonday meal in the place where are the spring today called Hypelaeus and the Sacred Harbour. One of the fish popped out with a live coal and fell into some straw, and a thicket in which a wild boar happened to be was set on fire by the fish. The boar, frightened by the fire, ran up a great distance on a mountain which is called Tracheia (Rough), and when brought down by a javelin, fell where today stands the temple of Athena.

So the Ephesians crossed over from the island after living there 20 years, and [this time] settled Tracheia and the areas on the slopes of Coressus (*ktizousi Trēcheian kai ta epi Korēsson*). They also built a temple of Artemis overlooking the market-place, and a temple of the Pythian Apollo at the harbour. (361d-e)

This translation reflects the necessary corrections made to the Greek text by P. Fournier.[128] Nothing is known about Creophylus, but his narrative has an internal logic that gives it plausibility. Its discretion regarding the identity of the original Ephesians is also a recommendation. Other sources identify the settlers as Ionians led by Androclus, the son of Codrus who was the king of Athens in the eleventh century B.C.E.,[129] which is sometimes dismissed as "essentially an Athenian imperial fiction of the fifth cent. B.C.E."[130]

It is certainly Athenian propaganda to suggest that its citizens were the first to erect the world-renowned temple to Artemis (= Diana) at Ephesus. Antipater of Sidon calls Ephesus "the city of Androclus" and Artemis "the queen of the Ionians" (*Greek Anthology* 9.790). That this false claim continued to circulate is explicitly confirmed by Dionysius of Halicarnassus in the first century C.E. (*Roman Antiquities* 4.25.4), and is implied by its explicit repudiation by Pausanias a century later: "the cult of the Ephesian Artemis is far more ancient still than the coming of the Ionians" (7.2.6; p. 97).

The original settlers were probably a reconaissance party sent to evaluate the prospects of the area (farming, fishing, trade, commerce) with a view to colonization. Their first base was on an island, which offered evident advantages in terms of security. This can only be Syrie (modern Kourou-Tepe), which by the time of Paul had become part of the coast due to the accumulation of mud brought down by the river Cayster (Pliny, 5.31.115; p. 104). After twenty years of observation they decided that the area was worth massive investment. This made it all the more important to have the approval of the god by his designation of a site for the future city.

The fact that two of the three temples mentioned were dedicated to Athena and Pythian Apollo unambiguously indicates that the settlers were Athenians who had appealed to the oracle at Delphi for guidance. The siting of the temple of Apollo at the harbor was no doubt a gesture to the fishermen who had unconsciously revealed the meaning of the oracular directive.

The spring called Hypelaeus must have been a well-known landmark because of the "oily" (*hypelaios*) taste of its water. Unfortunately it can no longer be located. Since the temple of Artemis once had sea frontage before the Cayster valley silted up (Pliny, 2.201) the "sacred harbor" must have been immediately to its south, and may have coincided with the mouth of the river Marnas. On the precise location of the first settlement see the commentary on Strabo, 14.1.4 (p. 11).

The site chosen by the original settlers facilitated access to the rich farmlands of the Marnas valley, but its rough mountainous character became a definite disadvantage as the city grew, and subsequently it moved twice (see Strabo, 14.1.21; p. 17).

TEMPLE MUSEUM

> Alexander of Cythera, as Juba says, perfected the "psaltery" (*psaltērion*) with a large number of strings, and since in his old age he lived in the city of Ephesus, he dedicated this invention, as the most ingenious product of his skill, in the temple of Artemis. (183c)

This report comes from Juba II, king of Mauretania, who lived in the second half of the first century B.C.E. and who among other learned works wrote a treatise on Greek and Roman antiquities. Cythera is the island off Cape Malea, the southern tip of the Peloponnese. It had a musical history (598e), but nothing is known of the Alexander mentioned here. It is entirely natural that a musician should move from a poor island to a major city where he could earn a much better livelihood. Perhaps he traveled to Ephesus in search of new experiences after having played in Corinth and/or Athens, both much closer to home. Votive offerings might have great intrinsic value, but what really mattered was their importance to the giver. The gift had to be a sacrifice, and Alexander's choice probably symbolized the end of his musical career. Craftsmen often dedicated their tools to a god or goddess on retirement. On other votive offerings to Artemis at Ephesus see Pausanias, 4.31.8 (p. 101). The unforeseen, and perhaps unintended, result was that the temple of Artemis also functioned as a museum for objects of cultural significance.

SEAFOOD FROM EPHESUS

> As for mussels, those from Ephesus and similar kinds are better in flavour than scallops, but are inferior to cockles; they tend to cause urination rather than loosening of the bowels. (87c)

> Mussels are moderately nourishing; they promote digestion and are diuretic. The best are the Ephesian, especially when taken in the autumn. (90d)

> In Ephesus also are smooth cockles, not to be despised. (92d)

> Ask for a parrot-fish from Ephesus, but in winter eat mullets which have been caught in sandy Teichioessa, a village of Miletus. (320a)

> Omit not the fat gilt-head from Ephesus, which people there call *ioniscus*. Buy it, that nursling of the holy Selinus. Wash it with care, then bake and serve it whole even though it measure ten cubits. (328b)

The last three citations are culled from Archestratus of Gela on the south coast of Sicily. He was a poet of the mid-fourth century who wrote up his culinary tour of the Mediterranean in a work that survives only in the citations of Athenaeus.[131] The latter also preserves the judgment of Daphnus of Ephesus, "Archestratus made a voyage around the world to satisfy his stomach and appetites even lower" (116f.). The river Selinus runs beside the temple of Diana in Ephesus; see Strabo, 8.7.5. On the organization of the fishing industry at Ephesus see Strabo (p. 27).

LUXURY GOODS

With reference to the Ephesians themselves Democritus of Ephesus, in the first of his two books *On the Temple of Ephesus*, tells the story of their luxury and of the dyed garments which they wore, writing as follows, "The garments of the Ionians are violet-dyed, and crimson, and yellow, woven in a lozenge pattern. But the top borders are marked at equal intervals with animal patterns. Then there are robes called *sarapeis* died with quince-yellow, crimson, and white, others again with sea-purple. And long robes (*kalasireis*) of Corinthian manufacture. Some of these are crimson, others violet, others dark red. One might also buy these robes in flame-color or sea-green. There are also Persian *kalasireis*, which are the finest of all. One might also see, Democritus goes on, the so-called *aktaiai*, and this in fact is the most costly among the Persian wraps. It is compactly woven to give solidity and lightness, and is strewn all over with gold beads. All the beads are fastened to the inner side of the robe by a purple cord attached at the centre." All these, he says, are used by the Ephesians in their devotion to luxury. (525c)

To such an extent were the delights of luxury and sumptuous expense cultivated among the ancients that even the Ephesian painter Parrhasius dressed himself in purple and wore a gold crown on his head, as Clearchus records in his *Lives*. For he indulged in luxury in a way offensive to good taste and beyond his station as a painter, and yet in talk claimed the possession of virtue, inscribing on the works of art wrought by him the following verse: "A man who lives in dainty style and at the same time honors virtue, has written these words." (543cd)

Ephesus in earlier times excelled in perfumes, particularly of the kind called *megalleion*, but does so no longer. (689a)

Nothing is known about Democritus of Ephesus, but if the social mores he criticizes were those that influenced Parrhasius we can say that he was speaking of the fifth or early fourth century B.C.E. Pliny, who offers a much more positive appreciation of Parrhasius (35.67-72; cf. p. 30), dates him to 397 B.C.E., which might be rather too late.[132] Ephesus must have been exceptionally prosperous for it to have become a symbol of luxury, but the last citation suggests that this reputation had not endured indefinitely. The context of the note on perfume makes it clear that the failure was due to a drop in standards because "the excellence of the perfume is due in each case to those who furnish the materials, the material itself, and the manufacturers, rather than to the localities" (688f).

MAGIC SPELLS

> Hence one might appropriately quote for this wise philosopher [Anax-
> archus of Abdera] the verses from *The Harp-maker* of Anaxilas: "Oiling his
> skin with yellow unguents, flaunting soft cloaks, shuffling fine slippers,
> munching bulbs, bolting pieces of cheese, pecking at eggs, eating peri-
> winkles, drinking Chian [wine], and what is more, carrying about, on little
> bits of stitched leather, lovely Ephesian letters (*Ephesēia grammata kala*).
> (548c)

Since Anaxilas is to be dated to the mid-fourth century B.C.E.,[133] this
is the earliest allusion to "the Ephesian letters." The phrase remained
current into the first century C.E. Plutarch insists that someone with bad
taste can be led to appreciate good art "just as sorcerers advise those
possessed by demons to recite and name over to themselves the Ephesian
letters" (*Moralia* 706E). Clearly it is question of a magical formula to ward
off evil spirits. Its six-word content is given by Clement of Alexandria
(ca. 150–ca. 211): *askion, kataskion, lix, tetrax, damnameneus, aisia* (*Stromateis*
5.242). Even in antiquity the meaning of the words was unclear, which
fostered fantastic speculation. This eventually bred a tendency to call all
unintelligible spells "Ephesian Letters," but this was not the case in
antiquity.[134] The formulation of Anaxilas would appear to suggest that
the individual words were inscribed on different pieces of leather, which
could then be shuffled to produce different arrangements. If one was felt
not to be working, another combination could be tried.

CAESAR

Julius Caesar (100–44 B.C.E.) had a long and turbulent career in Roman politics before his conquest of Gaul gave him a taste for absolute power. His enemies were wary of his influence, and to escape impeachment, once he had disbanded the legions he had trained to storm the heavens, he invaded Italy in 49 B.C.E., thus beginning a civil war. He wrote seven books on the Gallic war and three on the civil war in order to ensure that his point of view would have a place in history. He was assassinated in the Curia on 15 March 44 B.C.E. Such was his impact that his personal name was used as the title of emperors and kings from the time of Augustus (63 B.C.E.–14 C.E.)

ROBBING THE BANK

> At Ephesus Scipio gave orders that sums of money deposited there in former times should be removed from the temple of Diana. And a certain date having been appointed for this transaction, when they had come to the shrine and with them a number of men of the senatorial order whom Scipio had invited, a dispatch is handed to him from Pompey stating that Caesar had crossed the sea with his legions, that Scipio was to make haste to come to him with his army, and to put everything else aside. On receipt of this dispatch, he dismisses those whom he had invited, and himself begins to prepare for his journey into Macedonia, and a few days later he set out. This circumstance secured the safety of the money at Ephesus. (*Civil Wars* 3.33)

> On Caesar's arrival in Asia he found that T. Amplius had attempted to remove sums of money from the temple of Diana, and that with this object he had summoned all the senators from the province, that he might employ them as witnesses in reference to the amount of the sum, but he had fled when interrupted by Caesar's arrival. So on two occasions Caesar saved the Ephesian funds. (*Civil Wars* 3.105)

The sanctity of the temple of Artemis (= Diana) assured safety to all who sought refuge within its walls. It was also thought that the power of the goddess protected money deposited there. Thus the temple became "the general bank of Asia" (Aelius Aristides, *Orations* 23.24). The most detailed discussion of this aspect of the temple of Artemis in Ephesus is given by Dio Chrysostom (*Orations* 31.54-55; p. 64). Not surprisingly, it attracted the attention of those desperate for money but deprived of religious scruples.

Of such, Caecilius Metellus Pius Scipio was a prime example. According to Caesar, "any mode of exaction, provided a name could be found for it, was deemed a sufficient excuse for compelling contributions" (*Civil Wars* 3.32). Pompey was married to Scipio's daughter and had saved him from prosecution. They stood together against Caesar when he invaded Italy in 49 B.C.E. Caesar beseiged Pompey at Dyrrhachium in western Greece, but though the siege failed, Pompey retreated inland to Thessaly, whence he sent word to his ally Scipio in Asia. Rather than take ship across the Aegean, Scipio preferred the much longer northern route through Macedonia. Did he plan to arrive too late to face the redoubtable Caesar? In any case, he commanded the center at Pharsalus, where he and Pompey were decisively defeated by Caesar in 48 B.C.E.

Caesar followed Pompey to Egypt, and after his death delayed there in dalliance with Cleopatra VII. In the spring of 47 B.C.E. he moved north into Syria and swung west through Asia to take ship from Ephesus to Italy. T. Amplius was a supporter of Pompey and feared being subject to Caesar's wrath.

Whatever their personal motives, it is clear that Scipio and Amplius wanted to make their theft look as official as possible by surrounding themselves with provincial senators. The fact that they achieved nothing (how long does it take to fill bags with gold coins?) suggests that they encountered determined opposition from the temple authorities.

CICERO

Marcus Tullius Cicero was born in 106 B.C.E. and was executed in 43 B.C.E. Into those sixty-three years he crammed an incredible amount of activity both intellectual and practical. He came to prominence in public life at a time when the political institutions of Rome were quaking under the opressive weight of an expanding empire. How he survived the pressures generated by stronger personalities and conflicting political theories is not our concern here. It is more important to know that he wrote voluminously, speeches for both the prosecution and the defense (for he was the most eminent lawyer in Rome), philosophical works, and above all personal letters.

These letters were not intended for publication, and apparently it was only in the year before his death that he entertained the idea that a collection might be useful to posterity (*Atticus letter* 410; 16.5.5). His best friend Titus Pomponius Atticus preserved the 426 letters written to him, whereas Cicero's long-time secretary, Marcus Tullius Tiro, after his master's death published 435 letters to other friends, of which he must have kept copies. Tiro may also have been responsible for the collections of the twenty-seven letters to Cicero's brother Quintus and the twenty-four letters to a friend, M. Junius Brutus. A new numbering system for the letters has been introduced by D. R. Shackleton-Bailey in his recent translation, but I give the old numbers after the semicolon.

EPHESUS, THE GATEWAY TO ASIA

26 July 51
We arrived at Ephesus on 22 July, 559 days after the battle of Bovillae. Our voyage was free from danger and seasickness, but rather slow because of the unstalwart quality of the Rhodian open craft. As to the concourse of deputations and individuals and the huge crowds which welcomed me even at Samos and in quite astounding numbers at Ephesus, I expect you have already heard, or if not, why should you worry. However the tithe farmers were as eagerly to the fore as though I had come to them with full powers and the Greeks as though I had been governor of Asia (*Ephesio praetori*). (*Atticus letter* 106; 5.13)

27 July 51
Until I get settled somewhere you must not expect my letters to be long or always in my own hand. At present we are en route, and it is a hot and

dusty road. I sent off a letter from Ephesus yesterday and I am sending this from Tralles. (*Atticus letter* 107; 5.14)

27 or 28 July 51
I arrived at Tralles on 27 July. . . . I expect to reach Laodicea on 31 July. I shall stay only a very few days, to collect the sum due on my Treasury draft. Then I shall proceed to join the army, so that I should expect to be in the neighbourhood of Iconium about the Ides of August [13 August]. . . . You say you asked Scaevola to take charge of the province in your absence pending my arrival. I saw him in Ephesus and he was on a familiar footing with me during the three days I spent in the city, but I heard nothing from him about any instructions from you. (*Friends letter* 68; 3.5.4-5)

19 December 51
You know about my arrival in Ephesus, indeed you have congratulated me on the assemblage that day, one of the most flattering experiences of my life. From there, getting wonderful welcomes in such towns as there were, I reached Laodicea on 31 July. There I spent two days with great acclaim, and by dint of courteous speeches effaced all earlier grievances. I did the same at Apamea, where I spent five days, and at Synnada (three days), at Philomelium (five days), at Iconium (ten days). My administration of justice in these places lacked neither impartiality nor mildness nor responsibility. . . . After encamping for five days at Cyubistra in Cappadocia . . . I marched forthwith into Cilicia through the Gates of Taurus. I reached Tarsus on 5 October. (*Atticus letter* 113; 5.20; cf. *Friends letter* 110; 15.4.2)

1 October 50
I had no sooner set about writing to you and picked up my pen than Batnius arrived at my house in Ephesus straight from shipboard and gave me your letter on 29 September. . . . Etesians (winds) of unusual strength have held me up. An open boat too cost us twenty days at Rhodes. I am giving this letter to L. Tarquinius on the Kalends of October (1 October) as I take ship from Ephesus. He is leaving port along with ourselves, but has less to cumber his voyage. We shall be waiting for calm spells to suit the Rhodian craft and the other long ships. (*Atticus letter* 122; 6.8)

46–44
C. Curtius Mithres is, as you know, the freedman of my very good friend Postumus, but he pays as much respect and attention to me as to his own ex-master. At Ephesus, whenever I was there, I stayed in his house as though it was my home, and many incidents arose to give me proof of his good will and loyalty to me. (*Friends letter* 297; 13.69.1)

5 January 49
You should also bear in mind that I deposited the whole of the sum which had legally accrued to me with the tax farmers at Ephesus, that it amounted

to HS 2,200,000, and that Pompey has taken the lot. (*Friends letter* 128; 5.20.9)

Early April 50
Important private business obliged Pomptinus [Cicero's *legatus*] to leave me, greatly to my regret. He was at Ephesus, just taking ship, when he heard that your interests were at stake, and at once returned to Laodicea. (*Friends letter* 73; 3.10.3)

3 September (or shortly after) 51
I expect that Proconsul M. Bibulus, who left by sea from Ephesus for Syria about the Ides of August [13 August], has already arrived in his province, since he had favourable winds. I presume that everything will be more reliably reported to the Senate in a dispatch from him. (*Friends letter* 103; 15.3.2)

The purpose of these citations is to underline the extent to which Ephesus was the gateway not only to Asia but to all points farther east. Cicero's experience was typical not only for Roman officials, but for all who had business in Asia or any of the eastern provinces.

On his way to take charge in Bithynia on the north coast of modern Turkey, Pliny the Younger landed in Ephesus and then worked his way north, partly by land and partly by sea (*Letters* 10.15; 10.17A; p. 120). Cicero reports that M. Bibulus sailed from Ephesus to Syria, presumably to Antioch-on-the-Orontes, and made such a quick passage that in just a little over two weeks (13 August–1 September) he had not only reached his destination but had familiarized himself with the situation there. Over a century later Paul followed the same route when he sailed to Jerusalem for the last time (Acts 20:17–21:3).

Cicero himself reached Ephesus on 22 July 51 and remained there for several days before setting out for the province of Cilicia, where he had been appointed governor. He was received by the Propraetor of Asia, M. Minucius Thermus, to whom he subsequently wrote several letters looking for favors (*Friends* 13.55, 56, 57). He certainly enjoyed the enthusiastic reception he received because he tells Atticus about it twice. The Ephesians had clearly learned that Rome was to be placated and that it was wise to curry favor with senior officials who might be friends at court should it become necessary at some time in the future.

Leaving Ephesus on 27 July, Cicero reached Tralles the following day, and arrived in Laodicea, the westernmost city in his province, on 31 July. Laodicea is the town in the Lycus valley to which Paul wrote a letter now lost. In the vicinity were Colossae and Hierapolis (Col 4:13-16). If Cicero took four days to cover the 120 kilometers (72 miles) from Ephesus to Laodicea, he averaged only thirty kilometers (18 miles) per day. No doubt this was due to the welcome he received in the towns along the way. Each time he would have had to make a gracious speech.

A private citizen on urgent business, such as Epaphras bringing the news of the Colossian heresy to Paul in Ephesus, could have done the journey easily in three days. The Lycus valley was comfortably within the missionary outreach of Ephesus (cf. p. 210). Cicero's figures provide an invaluable baseline for the speed of Paul's movements on the same road.

From Ephesus, Cicero had followed what Strabo calls "the common highway" to the east because it was used by everyone (*Geography* 14.2.29; p. 36). He stayed on that great road through Apamea, Synnada, Philomelus, Iconium, and Cybistra, where he swung east and south into the Cilician Gates, the main pass through the Taurus mountains that brought him to Tarsus.[135]

This, of course, was the route Paul took first with Barnabas to evangelize Iconium, Lystra, Derbe, and Antioch in Pisidia (Acts 13–14), and twice subsequently, on his second journey (Acts 16–18) and later when Ephesus was his goal (Acts 19:1). Cicero followed the same route when he had finished his term of office and was returning to Rome.

It was no doubt on this occasion that he deposited 2,200,000 sesterces in Ephesus. The fact that he handed over this rather large sum to the Roman tax-collectors, who were effectively bankers to the state,[136] suggests that these were not his personal funds, but the profits of his government of Cilicia. Cicero leaves a misleading impression of Pompey's action because a year later the money was still in Ephesus, and it was Cicero who withdrew half of it to give to Pompey. (*Atticus letter* 211; 11.1.2)

RUNAWAY SLAVES

Between 25 October and 10 December 59
A slave called Licinus (you know him) belonging to our friend Aesopus has run away. He was in Athens with Patro the Epicurean passing as a free man, and passed from there to Asia. Later, one Plato of Sardia, an Epicurean, who is a good deal in Athens and was there when Licinus arrived, having later learned from a letter of Aesopus' that he is a runaway, arrested him and gave him into custody in Ephesus; but from his letter we are not sure whether the fellow was put into gaol or into the mill.

However that may be, he is in Ephesus, so will you please search for him and take good care either to send him to Rome or to bring him with you? Don't consider what he's worth. Such a good-for-nothing can't be worth much. But Aesopus is so distressed by the slave's criminal audacity that you can do him no greater favour than by getting him back his property. (*Quintus letter* 2; 1.2.14)

In 70 B.C.E.
Not long ago Marcus Aurelius Scaurus asserted that, while serving as quaestor at Ephesus, he was forcibly prevented from removing from the temple of Diana his own slave, who had there taken sanctuary. And on his

application an Ephesian of the highest rank named Pericles was summoned
for trial to Rome, on the grounds that he had been responsible for this act
of injustice. (*Against Verres* 2.1.85)

Neither of these stories provides a precise parallel to the case of
Onesimus, a slave of Philemon, one of Paul's converts, who ran from his
home in Colossae to Ephesus. Onesimus was seeking a friend of his
master's to intercede with Philemon on his behalf.[137] He intended to
return home. These two individuals, on the contrary, wanted to be rid
of their masters permanently, but took different options. The first simply
acted as if he were a freeman. The risk was not great. There was no police
force that on request would hunt down runaway slaves. If the owner
wanted to recover his property he had to use whatever resources he or
his friends possessed. One tactic was to put up posters offering a reward
for recovery, such as the following one dated 13 August 156 B.C.E.:

> On 16 Epeiph (year) 25, a slave of Aristogenes, son of Chrysippos from
> Alabanda, envoy, fled "in Alexandria" by the name of Hermon, also called
> Neilos, Syrian by birth from Bambyke, about 18 years of age, medium
> height, beardless, with strong calfs, dimple in chin, mole on nose on the
> left, scar above corner of mouth on the left, tattooed on right wrist with
> two foreign letters, having of coined gold 3 minae, 10 pearls, an iron ring
> on which an oil-bottle and strigils (are represented), having about his body
> a cloak and loin-cloth.
>
> Whoever brings this (slave) back will receive (2) 3 bronze talents, show-
> ing (him) at the temple (1) 2 talent, with a man of substance and legally
> actionable (3) 5 talents. He who wishes should disclose information to the
> agents of the *strategos*.[138]

The physical description of the runaway slave is supplemented by
other information, e.g., that he was wearing an iron ring around his arm
or neck. The motifs would suggest that he was the owner's personal
bath attendant. The figures in brackets reflect a first edition of the poster;
the amount of the reward was subsequently increased. There are three
levels of reward: (a) for bringing the slave back in person; (b) for specify-
ing in which temple he had taken refuge; and (c) for naming the person
who had taken him into his employ. The greatest reward goes to (c)
because in addition to getting his slave back the original owner could
sue the new one.

Given the extremely low level of literacy, the probable impact of such
posters would have been on other owners and their educated servants.
These, of course, had a vested interest in maintaining the system, and
presumably would have kept their eyes peeled for the fugitive in a casual
and non-systematic way.

The tactic adopted by Aesopus, a tragic actor who gave Cicero elocu-
tion lessons, was to write to his friends in the hope that they might have

remembered the appearance of the fugitive. In this instance it worked. Licinius was apprehended and handed over to the authorities in Ephesus to be held until Aesopus devised some way to get him back to Rome. This is where Cicero came in. As a favor to his old teacher he commissioned his brother Quintus to do the needful.

The slave of Marcus Aurelius Scaurus actualized the possibility mentioned in the wanted poster (above). He ran only as far as the temple of Diana (= Artemis), which enjoyed the privilege of immunity. Whether he believed that this would be sufficient to win him freedom is anyone's guess, but his master knew perfectly well that it did not. It would have been most detrimental to public order were criminals or slaves to put themselves out of the reach of the law simply by sauntering into a temple. "Commonly, one who took refuge in a temple was required by the temple to undergo a kind of trial to determine whether his flight was 'just.' The god was not obliged to accept and protect every suppliant, only those who had a just claim."[139] In the case of a slave the crucial question to which the priests had to find an answer concerned the slave's treatment by his master. Was he handled cruelly or unjustly? If so, the priest had to strive to secure an improvement in the slave's condition, e.g., by arranging his or her sale to a new master. Asylum amounted to no more than a cooling-down period or breathing space.[140]

One will not be far wrong in assuming that the young Roman *quaestor* asserted his right in such a high-handed and arrogant fashion that the temple authorities simply refused out of sheer contrariness. Scaurus must have appealed to the emperor for an Ephesian city father to be brought to trial in Rome, where he would have been treated with little sympathy.

ANOTHER HANNIBAL STORY

Nor do I need any Greek professor to chant at me a series of hackneyed axioms, when he himself never had a glimpse of a law-court or judicial proceeding, as the tale goes of Phormio the well-known Peripatetic. When Hannibal, banished from Carthage, had come in exile to Antiochus at Ephesus and, inasmuch as his name was highly honoured all the world over, had been invited by his hosts to hear the philosopher in question, if he so pleased, and he had intimated his willingness to do so, that worthy individual is said to have held forth for several hours upon the functions of a commander-in-chief and military matters in general.

Then, when the other listeners, vastly delighted, asked Hannibal for his opinion of the eminent teacher, the Carthaginian is reported to have thereupon replied, in no very good Greek but at any rate candidly, that time and again he had seen many old madmen, but never one madder than Phormio.

And upon my word he was right, for what better example of prating insolence could there be than for a Greek, who had never seen a foeman or a camp, or even had the slightest connection with any public employment, to lecture on military matters to Hannibal, who all these years had been disputing empire with the Roman people, the conquerors of the world? (*On the Orator* 2.18,75)

Once again (cf. Appian, *Syrian Wars* 11.2.9-10; p. 39) this story of Hannibal carries no guarantee of historicity. It is precisely the sort of example a clever orator would think up. Had it actually happened, Hannibal's response would certainly have been articulated with the expressive invective of an old soldier.

DIO CASSIUS

Born in Nicea in Asia Minor around 160 C.E., Cassius Dio held a number of high offices in Rome culminating in a shared consulship with the emperor Alexander Severus in 229. He is remembered, however, for his eighty-volume history of Rome from its legendary beginnings until his retirement in 229. He made excellent use of the annalistic tradition represented by Polybius, Livy, and Tacitus. Only books 36–54, which cover the period 68–10 B.C.E., have survived intact. Books 1–21 have been preserved in a paraphrase made by Zonaras in the twelfth century C.E., while books 51–80 exist only in an abridgment made by Xiphilinus, an eleventh-century monk of Constantinople.

MARK ANTONY VIOLATES THE TEMPLE OF ARTEMIS

During this same period, following the battle at Philippi, Mark Antony came to the mainland of Asia, where he levied contributions upon the cities and sold the positions of authority. Some of the districts he visited in person and to others he sent agents. Meanwhile he fell in love with Cleopatra, whom he had seen in Cilicia, and thereafter gave not a thought to honour but became the Egyptian woman's slave and devoted his time to his passion for her. This caused him to do many outrageous things, and in particular to drag her brothers from the temple of Artemis at Ephesus and put them to death. (*Roman History* 48.24.1-2)

There is common agreement that Mark Antony at the behest of Cleopatra violated the temple of Artemis (= Diana) by killing one or more of her relatives who had taken refuge there. According to Dio Cassius here it was her two brothers, but elsewhere he implies that only one brother was alive at this time (*Roman History* 42.43.4). For Josephus, however, it was her sister Arsinoë whom Cleopatra had killed (*Ant.* 15.86). See Appian, *Civil Wars*, 5.1.9 (p. 45).

EPHESUS HONORED

Caesar, meanwhile, besides attending to the general business, gave permission for the dedication of sacred precincts in Ephesus and in Nicaea to Rome and to Caesar his father, whom he named the hero Julius. These cities had at that time attained chief place in Asia and in Bithynia respectively. He commanded that the Romans resident in these cities should pay honour to these two divinities. But he permitted the aliens, whom he styled Hellenes, to consecrate precincts to himself, the Asians to have theirs in Pergamum, and the Bithynians theirs in Nicomedia. (*Roman History* 51.20.6)

The Caesar in question had begun life in 63 B.C.E. as C. Octavius. His mother was a niece of Julius Caesar, who adopted her son in 45 B.C.E. and made him his heir. He achieved mastery of the Roman world by defeating Mark Antony in 31 B.C.E. and capturing Alexandria the following year. In the glow of definitive victory he thought it appropriate to honor two provinces that were a rich source of revenue while at the same time glorifying the patron who had given him his chance. This event is dated to 29 B.C.E., two years before the senate voted Octavian the title Augustus.

Ephesus and Pergamum (modern Bergamum) were perennial rivals in Asia, as were Nicea (modern Iznic) and Nicomedia (modern Izmit) in Bithynia. Pergamum had been the capital of the Attalid kingdom, but lost its primacy when Rome took over in 133 B.C.E. Its place was taken by Ephesus, which as time went on showed that it fully merited the title of the "chief city" of Asia. One would expect a sanctuary dedicated to Rome and Caesar to be a double-cella podium temple. With some hesitation this temple is identified with the small prostyle peripteros temple in the center of the State Agora.[141]

If the emperor had decided to reward the achievement of Ephesus, he also felt it appropriate to remind the city of its past[142] by awarding an even greater honor to Pergamum. It was given the right to have a temple to a reigning emperor. Ephesus was again passed over in 26 C.E. when Tiberius decided it had sufficient glory in the temple of Artemis (= Diana).[143]

CHEAP GLORY

Gaius ordered that a sacred precinct should be set apart for his worship at Miletus in the province of Asia. The reason he gave for choosing this city was that Diana had preempted Ephesus, Augustus Pergamum, and Tiberius Smyrna. But the truth of the matter was he desired to appropriate to his own use the large and exceedingly beautiful temple which the Milesians were building to Apollo. (*Roman History* 59.28.1)

Nicknamed *Caligula*, "little boots," by his father's soldiers on the Rhine when he was a little boy, Gaius succeeded Tiberius as emperor in 37 C.E. He was not averse to accepting homage amounting to deification. This episode is dated to 40 C.E., but the procedure that makes him look mean and grasping is far from typical. He relished building, and his investments in this line were economically advantageous to the state.[144]

For Augustus and Pergamum see 51.20.6 (above). For Tiberius and Smyrna see Tacitus, *Annals* 4.55-56 (p. 137). Miletus (modern Milet) is some eighty kilometers from Ephesus, whose elders Paul summoned to meet him there (Acts 20:17-38). During the winter of 64–65 C.E. it was the scene of Paul's last days in Asia (2 Tim 4:20).[145]

ASTROLOGER HONORED

> Vespasian banished the astrologers from Rome, even though he was in the habit of consulting all the best of them himself, and, by way of showing a favour to Barbillus, a man of that profession, had even permitted the Ephesians to celebrate some sacred games, a privilege he granted to no other city. (*Roman History* 65.9.2)

The "science" of converting astronomical data into predictions regarding human affairs originated in Babylon. By the first century B.C.E. it commanded respect and credence throughout the Roman empire. Men such as T. Claudius Thrasyllus and his son T. Claudius Balbillus (whom Dio incorrectly calls Barbillus) were the confidants of emperors from Tiberius to Vespasian. Since astrologers could be seen as a potential threat to public order, Vespasian's expulsion order of 70 C.E. merely repeated the ineffective edicts of previous emperors.[146] That Vespasian would make himself an exception fits with his personal predilection for signs and portents, which is well documented by Suetonius (*Vespasian* 4-5). Moreover, Balbillus was exceptionally gifted as both a scholar and an administrator, having served as Prefect of Egypt from 55 to 59 C.E.[147] In Ephesus, his native city, he founded a festival, the *Balbilleia*, which quickly established itself as one of the major sacred games.[148] It included competitions for children.[149]

DIO CHRYSOSTOM

Dio Cocceianus was born about 40 C.E. in Prusa in Bithynia of a wealthy family who gave him an excellent rhetorical education in Rome. He won his title of "Chrysostomos" (the golden-mouthed) through a series of seventy-eight orations that manifested his great gifts as an orator. Many were display-speeches glorifying cities (e.g., Tarsus) or events (e.g., the Olympic Games). They were pronounced between 97 and 112 C.E., when he would have been in his fifties. His stock themes of nature, virtue, and philanthropy were those of a Stoic teacher, but he was a close observer of the world around him and "he gives a vivid and detailed picture of the life of his times."[150]

THE BANK OF ASIA

> You know about the Ephesians, of course, and that large sums of money are in their hands, some of them belonging to private citizens and deposited in the temple of Artemis, not alone money of the Ephesians, but also of aliens and of persons from all parts of the world, and in some cases of commonwealths and kings, money which all deposit there in order that it may be safe, since no one has ever yet dared to violate that place, although countless wars have occurred in the past and the city has often been captured.
>
> Well, that the money is deposited on state property is indeed evident, but it is also evident, as the lists show, that it is the custom of the Ephesians to have these deposits officially recorded. Well then, do they go on and take any of these monies when any need arises, or do they "borrow" them at any rate—an act which, perhaps, will not appear at all shocking? No, on the contrary, they would sooner, I imagine strip off the adornment of the goddess than touch this money. Yet you would not say that the Ephesians are wealthier than yourselves [the Rhodians]. The very opposite is the case. For not only were you the richest of the Greeks in former times, but now you are still richer. Whereas the Ephesians, one can see, are less prosperous than many. (*Oration* 31.54-55)

Temples of all sorts attracted wealth. Not only were votive offerings often of great intrinsic value, but the inviolability of a sanctuary appeared to guarantee the security of the cash and valuables deposited there. We are told of the Jewish temple in Jerusalem, for example, that "in the treasuries of Jerusalem are stored many thousands of private deposits not belonging to the temple account" (4 Macc 4:3). The more powerful the divinity, the greater the wealth of the temple. Thus with pardonable hyperbole Josephus claims that "the entire riches of the Jews were heaped up" in the Jerusalem temple.[151]

The immense prestige of the temple of Artemis at Ephesus made it a magnet for deposits, and Dio Chrysostom is certainly correct in saying that kings and commoners from all over the world entrusted it with funds. With good reason, therefore, Aelius Aristides in the second century c.e. called it "the general treasury of Asia (*tamieion te koinon tēs Asias)" (Oration* 23.24); this echoes "the house of gold" (*Nephelai*, 599-600), which was the assessment of Aristophanes some seven hundred years earlier.

In terms of what Dio Chrysostom says, it would be better to call the temple of Artemis a "depository" rather than a "bank."[152] A bank in the modern sense receives money on deposit and it is then free to use that money for its own purposes, e.g., to make loans on which it gains interest. The wealth deposited in the Artemision was there to be stored for security. The temple had no authority to do anything more unless it was explicitly authorized by the depositor, who then retained full responsibility.

If a temple made loans, and there is evidence that the Artemision did,[153] such funds came from its own resources. In addition to state contributions and tithes it received donations, gifts, and bequests like all religious institutions. Lucian mentions the offering of "ingots of gold" (*Sky-man* 24). Its great landholdings and fishing rights produced immense revenues. It is improbable that all this income was required for the upkeep and functioning of the temple. The surplus could and should have been employed for the public good: e.g., after a bad harvest a farmer might need to borrow in order to buy seed for the next sowing.

T. Robert S. Broughton highlights two factors that affected the development of temple banks in the Hellenistic and Roman periods.[154] First, as the need for sophisticated banking services grew, temple banks tended to come under civic control. In Ephesus the *gerousia* appears to have functioned as a regulatory agency that supervised the use of temple funds and could also be used by the temple authorities to put pressure on the municipality. Second, the temple bank was gradually restricted to deposits and reserves by the invention of the public bank and the spread of private banking. Broughton does not believe that temple banks had ever committed serious funds to commercial loans or other hazardous kinds of credit. Mortgages and blue-chip investments were their traditional market. The money of the goddess was not to be gambled with.

At the end of the first Mithridatic War the financial situation in Asia was so desperate that the council of Ephesus, in order to maintain its population, was forced to pass a decree canceling debts to the city and to the temple of Artemis. It offers an intriguing picture of financial life in 85 B.C.E.

> All registered (as debtors) in any way by the sacred or public accountants shall be restored to full rights, and registrations and debts against them shall be null and void; any listed for judgments sacred or public, or fines, sacred or public, or other debts in any way shall all be released, and actions based on these shall be invalid, but actions based on previously existent arrangements shall stand according to the laws for all who are named in the sacred leases (of land of Artemis) and the public tax contracts.
>
> With respect to loans of sacred funds all debtors and agents are released from their obligations except in the case of funds lent upon mortgages by boards (of magistrates or priests) or by money-lenders designated by them, and upon these the interest shall be remitted from the coming year until the people meet with better times; all persons upon the citizen roll up to the present time shall have full rights and share in these privileges. Cases at law, sacred and public, shall be voided except those dealing with mis-bounding of property and disputes about inheritance. . . .[155]

Obviously, then as now, many lived on credit.

Dio Chrysostom is certainly wrong in saying that no one had ever tried to violate the temple of Artemis. Mark Antony stole from it, and Augustus had to make restitution.[156] An inscription mentions "the abundance of revenues which were restored to the goddess by the deified Augustus."[157] On two occasions only the fortuitous arrival of Julius Caesar prevented theft from the temple (p. 32). It would be extraordinary if these were the only attempts to misappropriate funds from the Artemision. The temple in Jerusalem was looted regularly.[158]

It is rather surprising that Dio Chrysostom should conclude with a reference to the relative lack of prosperity of Ephesus. This is probably just a rhetorical flourish designed to win the approval of his audience, the people of the island of Rhodes, because, according to modern authorities, "the building programs of the Flavian and Antonine periods seem to reflect marked growth commencing with the reign of Domitian [81–96 C.E.]."[159]

HERODOTUS

Herodotus was a native of Halicarnassus (modern Bodrum), which is 110 kilometers (66 miles) due south of Ephesus as the crow flies. He is thought to have been born around 484 B.C.E. Certainly he was alive during the first (461–446 B.C.E.) and second (431–404 B.C.E.) Peloponnesian Wars, which began and ended the preeminence of Athens in Greece. As a young man he spent some time on Samos and also lived for a while in Athens. Inherited wealth gave him the opportunity to travel, and he used it to the full. He shows personal knowledge of the whole coastline of Asia Minor. He visited Syria and perhaps got as far as Mesopotamia. He traveled up the Nile as far as Aswan, and west along the coast of Egypt into Cyrenaica. His value as a historian has been vigorously debated. He has been dismissed as at best a storyteller and at worst a liar. Both are exaggerations, and he certainly cannot be accused of being credulous. He does report the views of those who should know, but affirmations of his acceptance of what he has been told are much rarer than explicit expressions of disbelief. In the last analysis each report has to be judged on its own merits, and the inaccuracy of one cannot be permitted to generate false assumptions regarding the veracity of others.

ARTEMIS PROTECTS EPHESUS

After the death of Alyattes his son Croesus came to the throne [ca. 560 B.C.E.], being then 35 years of age. The first Greeks whom he attacked were the Ephesians. These being besieged by him, dedicated their city to Artemis. This they did by attaching a rush-rope (*schoinion*) to the city wall from the temple of the goddess, standing seven stadia away from the ancient city, which was then being besieged. These were the first whom Croesus attacked. Afterwards he made war on the Ionian and Aeolian cities in turn. (*History* 1.26)

Another version of this story is provided by Aelian:

Pindar, son of Melas and grandson of the Lydian Alyattes on his mother's side, became tyrant of Ephesus by succession. In his punishments he was stern and unyielding, but in other respects he seemed to be reasonable and patriotic, and he was thought to take many precautions to prevent his country being enslaved by the barbarians. The following appears to show that this was true.

> When his maternal uncle Croesus was conquering Ionia and sent envoys to Pindar to demand that Ephesus submit to him, the request was refused and Croesus began a siege of the city. When one of the fortification towers was destroyed—it was later known as the Tower of Treason—and he could see disaster looming, Pindar advised the Ephesians to attach cords from the city gates and towers to the columns of the temple of Artemis as if they were consecrating the city to Artemis. He hoped by this means to ensure that Ephesus would not be captured. He advised them to go to plead with the Lydian. When the Ephesians displayed their credentials as suppliants, Croesus is said to have laughed and accepted the stratagem in good part, allowing the Ephesians unmolested freedom, while he ordered Pindar to leave the city. (*Historical Miscellany* 3.26)

The intention of the Ephesians is unambiguous. When the city was menaced by Croesus of Lydia they wanted to secure for their city the inviolability of the sanctuary of Artemis, even though the temple was not within the city. A space had to be bridged by the rush-rope. The technical details are another matter altogether. Herodotus' account is far from satisfactory.

He distinguishes between "the city" and "the ancient city." Prior to the time of Croesus the settlement was on a spur on the northwest of the Panayir Dagh. This was Tracheia, to which the Ionian colonists had moved when they finally determined to settle permanently in the Cayster valley (Athenaeus, 361d-e; p. 47). It is in fact seven stadia (roughly a mile) from the Artemision. And here we encounter the first problem. It is difficult to imagine a rope being carried this distance through a besieging army!

Herodotus shows himself to be so familiar with the island of Samos (e.g., 3.60) that he is thought to have lived there for some time. In this case it would be surprising if he had not made a visit to Ephesus. The fame of the Artemision was by then widespread. Thus we can assume that he had a general idea of the topography. At the time of his visit, however, the Ephesians had moved from Tracheia to surround the Artemision (see Strabo, 14.1.21; p. 17). The majority no doubt took up residence on the low ridge of Ayasoluk (sometimes Ajasoluk), which was safe from the flooding that endangered the plain.[160] It would be natural, therefore, for Herodotus to think of Tracheia as "the ancient city" and to treat Ayasoluk simply as "the city." The *temenos* wall of the Artemision would have run very close to Ayasoluk, and to throw a rope from one to the other would have been perfectly feasible. This hypothesis, however, does not account for the "seven stadia." It may have been a misplaced recollection of whatever source Herodotus was using. The distance is mentioned again by Xenophon of Ephesus (p. 177).

It is entirely possible that Aelian knew Herodotus, but the plethora of extra details means that he certainly had another source for the story of the miraculous escape of Ephesus. In it the credit for the strategem is given to a certain Pindar. Despite his eminent family connections nothing is known about this individual, other than the fact that a family member had preceded him as "tyrant" of Ephesus. "Tyrant" originally had none of the negative overtones it later acquired. It was simply a title given to those in Greek states in the seventh and sixth centuries B.C.E. who took power by force in the conviction that expanding cities needed to be governed by a single mind. Pindar's resistance to his uncle, Croesus, was no doubt motivated by self-interest.

It was natural for Aelian, or his source, to assume that the temple of Artemis was in the center of the city because that is where the most important temples of Rome and Athens were located. It was never the case with Ephesus at any time in its long history. If the story of the reaction of Croesus to the childish ploy is not historical, it nonetheless carries a degree of truth because, as the next section shows, he treated Ephesus very well.

RICH AS CROESUS

Now there are many offerings of Croesus in Hellas, and not only those whereof I have spoken. There is a golden tripod at Thebes in Boeotia, which he dedicated to Apollos of Ismenus; at Ephesus there are the oxen of gold and the greater part of the pillars; and in the temple of Proneïa at Delphi, a golden shield. All these yet remained till my lifetime, but some other of the offerings have perished. And the offerings of Croesus at Branchidae of the Milesians, as I have heard, are equal in weight and like to those at Delphi. (*History* 1.92)

The simile "rich as Croesus" is justified by reports such as this regarding his great wealth and generosity. His gifts to Thebes and Delphi betray the close ties that linked western Asia Minor to Greece. He was equally munificent to the two great shrines in his own domain. The Branchidae were the priestly clan who administered the great oracular temple of Apollo in Didyma, some sixteen kilometers (10 miles) south of Miletus. Nothing else is known of the golden oxen of Ephesus. Were they simply symbolic sacrificial animals? The "pillars" can only be those of the Artemision, and this text is the reason why the foundation of the archaic temple is dated in the mid-sixth century B.C.E.

GREEK DIALECTS

Now these Ionians, who possessed the Panionion, had set their cities in places more favoured by skies and seasons than any country known to us. For neither to the north of them nor to the south nor to the east nor to the west does the land accomplish the same effect as Ionia, being affected here by cold and wet, there by heat and drought. Not all use the same speech, but four different dialects.

Miletus lies furthest south among them, and next to it come Myus and Priene. These are settlements in Caria, and they use a common language.

Ephesus, Colophon, Lebedos, Teos, Cloazomenae, Phocaea, all of them being in Lydia, have a language in common which is wholly different from the speech of the three cities aforementioned.

There are yet three Ionian cities, two of them situated on the islands of Samos and Chios, and one, Erythrae, on the mainland. The Chions and Erythraeans speak alike, but the Samians have a language which is their own and none others'. (*History* 1.142)

Herodotus later tells us that "The Panionion is a sacred ground in Mycale . . . a western promontory of the mainland opposite Samos" (1.148). It was the central sanctuary of the twelve-city Ionian League, where its members met to celebrate an annual festival and whenever necessary to formulate common policy in time of need. Diodorus Siculus, writing in the first century B.C.E., brings the history up to date:

In Ionia nine cities were in the habit of holding a common assemblage of all the Ionians and of offerings sacrifices of great antiquity on a large scale to Poseidon in a lonely region near the place called Mycale. Later, however, as a result of the outbreak of wars in this neighbourhood, since they were unable to hold the Panionia there, they shifted the festival gathering to a safe place near Ephesus. (*Library* 15.49.1)

The Ionians managed to communicate, even though they did not all speak the same dialect. Herodotus' well-ordered presentation moves from south to north.[161]

Miletus, Myus, and Priene are all in the delta of the Maeander. Priene is located on the northern branch of the great river, and Myus and Miletus on the southern branch.

The next six cities occur in that order going north from Ephesus. The first four are on the coast, but one has to cut across the base of the peninsula to reach Cloazomenae, and Phocaea is located on a peninsula on the north side of the great bay that gives Smyrna access to the sea. Clearly these six cities do not share the geographical unity of the first three and cannot in any sense be considered neighbors. This makes their use of a common tongue all the more strange.

It is understandable that islands should have their own dialects. Erythrae is thirty kilometers directly across the sound from Chios but only twenty-five kilometers from Cloazomenae. Perhaps water was less of a barrier than the easy pass through the mountain range.

It is noteworthy that Herodotus does not claim superiority for any one of the dialects. To their speakers they would have all been Greek, and evidence of "the kinship of all Greeks in blood and speech" (Herodotus 8.144). By the third century B.C.E., however, dialect begins to give way in inscriptions to a form of Greek that is very close to Attic. This is the beginning of Ionic-Attic, which eventually provided Greece with a standard language.[162] By the time of Paul any educated Ephesian could have been understood anywhere in the eastern Roman empire.

THE ROYAL ROAD FROM EPHESUS TO PERSIA

Thus the whole tale of stages is 111. So many resting-stages then there are in the going up from Sardis to Susa. If I have rightly numbered the parasangs of the royal road (*hē hodos hē basileiē*), and the parasang is of 30 stadia length (which assuredly it is), then between Sardis and the kings's abode called Memnonian there are 13,500 stadia, the number of parasangs being 450. If each day's journey be 150 stadia, then the number of days spent [on the road] is 90, neither more nor less.

Thus Aristagoras of Miletus spoke the truth to Cleomenes the Lacedaemonian when he said that the journey inland was three months long. But if any desire a measurement yet exacter, I will give him that too. For the journey from Ephesus to Sardis must be added to the rest. So then I declare that from the Greek sea to Susa (for that is the city called Memnonian) is a journey of 14,040 stages. For there are 540 stadia from Ephesus to Sardis, and thus the three months' journey is made longer by three days. (*History* 5.53-54)

The context of this account of "the royal road" is an attempt by Aristagoras to persuade the king of Sparta to invade Asia Minor and there to reap ever-increasing riches until they came to Susa. "Take that city," Aristagoras said, "and then you need not fear to challenge Zeus for riches" (5.49). Hearing that Susa was three months' march inland, "Cleomenes [520–490 B.C.E.] cut short all the rest that Aristagoras began to tell him about the journey, and bade his Milesian guest depart from Sparta before sunset" (5.50).

It is very much in character for Aristagoras to start the journey from Sardis, because it had been the chief city of Lydia under Croesus, and when he was defeated by the Persians in 546 B.C.E. it became the headquarters of the principal Persian satrapy in the west. The "parasang" was a Persian unit of distance, and presumably Aristagoras used a Persian source.

It is strong evidence of the importance of Ephesus and its facilities that Herodotus selects it as the sea terminus of the royal road, because Smyrna was also a port and much closer to Sardis. Ephesus was in fact the western terminus of the "common highway" described by Strabo (14.2.29; p. 36), which would have been a much better road. The route described by Aristagoras goes unnecessarily far north, since it crosses the river Halys. Only in the region of the Euphrates do the two routes coincide. Had Herodotus been more of a geographer he could have pointed out that from Sardis one could have reached the much easier "common highway" by ascending the valley of the river Kogamos and then dropping down into the valleys of the Maeander and the Lycus through Tripoli on the Maeander and Hierapolis.[163]

For Aristagoras the average day's march was 150 stadia. The stadium was 600 Greek feet. The foot could vary from 295.7 millimeters (11.64 inches) to 330 mm (13.1 inches),[164] so the stadium is roughly the equivalent of 200 meters. Thus 150 stadia is thirty kilometers (18 miles). This is slow daily mileage, and one must assume that Aristagoras was using the Persian calculation of the average movement of a fully equipped army, whose speed could have varied from day to day.

A HARBOR AND HOUSES

> The Ionians, having come to Ephesus with this armament, left their ships at Coressus in Ephesian territory (*en Korēsō tēs Ephesiēs*), and themselves marched inland with a great host, taking Ephesians to guide them on their way. Journeying beside the river Caicus, and crossing thence over Tmolus, they came to Sardis and took it, none withstanding them. (*History* 5.100)

This episode took place in 498 B.C.E., when the same Aristagoras of Miletus decided to profit by the arrival of twenty-five ships from Athens and Eretria by attacking Sardis. He rejected the option of docking at Smyrna because that would have meant a much longer voyage to the north against the prevailing wind. The problem of the location of Coressos has been noted elsewhere (p. 12). Here it is clearly an Ephesian town with a harbor capable of receiving the twenty-five ships. To get to Sardis from Ephesus the Milesians could not have followed the river Caicus, which in fact carved out the valley in which Pergamum is located. Herodotus, or his source, confused it with the river Cayster, from whose headwaters the invaders would have passed through Hypaipa to cross the Tmolus Mountains and drop down the valley of the Pactotus to Sardis.

The Ephesians and their allies did not plunder Sardis because of a mistake of one of their own. According to Herodotus, "The greater part of the houses in Sardis were of reeds, and as many as were of brick, even they had roofs of reeds. So it was that when one of these was set afire by a soldier, the flames spread from house to house all over the whole city" (5.101). If we remember that at this time Sardis was a much more important city than Ephesus, we can be quite sure that the size and quality of the dwellings in Ephesus were not superior to those in Sardis. This makes the construction of the monumental temple of Artemis some fifty years earlier all the more remarkable, and perhaps explains why foreign architects had to be employed. They were "Chersiphron of Cnossus [in Crete] and his son Metagenes" (Vitruvius, 7. pref. 16).

A TRAGIC ERROR

> When the Chians entered the territory of Ephesus on their march, it chanced that they came by night and the women were keeping their Thesmophoria. The Ephesians, never having heard the story of the Chians, and seeing an army invading their country, were fully persuaded that these were robbers come after their women. So they mustered all their force and slew the Chians. (*History* 6.16)

After a battle with Persia the Chians in question had barely gotten their sinking ships ashore at Mycale and were making their way back to Chios overland. Their natural route along the coast would have brought them very close to Ephesus. The Thesmophoria was a pan-Greek women's festival in honor of Demeter, the goddess of all crops and vegetation. It was celebrated in the autumn before the new sowing. In order to ensure that men were completely excluded, the women usually camped out for three days at a little distance from the town or village. The secret of the festival was so well kept that no male historian records any details of the ceremonies. No doubt extreme curiosity ensured that a number of Ephesians were endeavoring to find out what the women were doing, and so noticed the arriving Chians, who were given no time to explain themselves.

IGNATIUS OF ANTIOCH

The reputation of Ignatius, bishop of Antioch-on-the-Orontes, rests on a series of seven letters written while he was being marched across Asia Minor to be thrown to the lions in Rome. They show him to be a wise and fearless leader of a great church at a time of storm and stress. The shining quality of his holiness is not dimmed by the pages of print and must have had a striking impact on those who met him in person. It is thought that he became bishop of Antioch about 69 C.E. and died a martyr on 19 December 107 in the Flavian amphitheatre, the Colosseum, in Rome. The letters would have been written some two or three months earlier.

A LETTER TO EPHESUS

Ignatius, who is also called God-bearer, to the church that is blessed with greatness by the fullness of God the Father, a church foreordained from eternity past to obtain a constant glory which is enduring and unchanging, a church that has been unified and chosen in true suffering by the will of the Father and of Jesus Christ, our God; to the church in Ephesus of Asia, which is worthy of all good fortune. Warmest greetings in Jesus Christ and in blameless joy.

Now that I have received in God your greatly loved name, which you have obtained because of your upright nature, according to the faith and love that is in Christ Jesus our Savior—for you are imitators of God and have rekindled through the blood of God the work we share as members of the same family and brought it to perfect completion. For you were eager to see me, since you heard that I was being brought in chains from Syria because of the name and hope we share, and that I was hoping through your prayer to be allowed to fight the beasts in Rome, that by doing so I might be able to be a disciple.

Since, then, I have received your entire congregation in the name of God through Onesimus, who abides in a love that defies description and serves as your bishop in the flesh—and I ask by Jesus Christ that you love him, and that all of you be like him. For blessed be the one who has graciously granted you, who are worthy, to obtain such a bishop.

(2) But as to my fellow-slave Burrhus, your godly deacon who is blessed in all things, I ask that he stay here for the honor of both you and the bishop. And Crocus as well—who is worthy of God and of you, whom I received as an embodiment of your love—has revived me in every way.

So may the Father of Jesus Christ refresh him, along with Onesimus, Burrhus, Euplus, and Fronto, those through whom I lovingly saw all of you . . .

(6) The more one notices that the bishop is silent, the more he should stand in awe of him. For we must receive everyone that the master of the house sends to take care of his affairs as if he were the sender himself. And so we are clearly obliged to look upon the bishop as the Lord himself. Thus Onesimus himself praises you highly for being so well ordered in God, because all of you live according to the truth and no heresy resides among you. On the contrary, you no longer listen to anyone except one who speaks truthfully about Jesus Christ. . . .

(9) I have learned that some people have passed through on their way from there with an evil teaching. But you did not permit them to sow any seed among you, plugging your ears so as not to receive anything sown by them. . . . And so you are all traveling companions bearing God, bearing the temple, bearing Christ, and bearing the holy things, adorned in every way with the commandments of Jesus. . . .

(21) Pray on behalf of the church in Syria; I am being taken from there to Rome in chains—even though I am the least of those who believe there—since I have been deemed worthy to be found honorable to God. Farewell in God the Father and in Jesus Christ, our mutual hope. (*To the Ephesians* 1-21)

It must have come as a surprise to "the leopards" (*To the Romans* 5), the ten Roman soldiers escorting Ignatius to death in Rome, to discover that their journey through western Asia had become a triumphal procession. Such was the reputation for sanctity of their prisoner that Christians from all over came to greet him. The word probably went out from Laodicea or Hierapolis in the Lycus valley, when Christians there noted that the the prisoner was being herded on the nothern route through Philadelphia and Sardis to Smyrna rather than down the valley of the Maeander to Ephesus.[165]

Onesimus and a delegation from Ephesus thought it well worth their while to tramp the forty miles (64 kilometers) to Smyrna, where Ignatius was being temporarily held. He was delighted to have their support, but he lived with the fear that someone would intervene on his behalf and so deprive him of the crown of martyrdom. His ecstatic cry, "I am God's wheat ground fine by the lions' teeth to become purest bread for Christ" (*To the Romans* 4), reverberated throughout the Christian world and made death for the faith the supreme goal of the believer.

The conditions under which Ignatius was being held throw some light on Paul's imprisonment in Ephesus. Ignatius makes frequent mention of his chains, which was normal Roman procedure (Acts 28:20; 2 Tim 1:16; 2:9) and could take different forms. Even though oppressed by his guards (*To the Romans* 5), he was free to receive visitors and write letters.

When he traveled he could be accompanied by his friends. The Burrhus mentioned here journeyed with him as far as Troas before being sent back with letters (*To the Smyrnaeans* 12). Other committed Christians from Antioch trailed him across Asia Minor to impart the good news that the persecution there had ended, and thereafter remained with him (*To the Philadelphians* 10-11; *To the Smyrnaeans* 10).

Ignatius' effusive compliments to the church in Ephesus stem from the fact that it had been Paul's base for so long; believers there were "fellow initiates with Paul" (§10). His respect "for a church of eternal renown" (§8) is so great that he speaks to them as "my fellow learners" (§3). He assumed that they were inspired by Paul's epistles, which Ignatius himself knew well and to which he frequently refers in his letters.[166] Helmut Koester claims that Ignatius was aware of divisions in the church of Ephesus.[167] This, however, is a mistaken interpretation of the warnings against disunity.[168] At Antioch Ignatius had experienced the evils of heresy and schism, and their suppression became a recurrent theme in his teaching. Ignatius does appear to be familiar with one aspect of life in Ephesus, namely the veneration accorded to Artemis by the procession of her statues and those of others through the whole city from the Magnesian to the Coressian Gate.[169] If this is correct, it underlines once again the continuing vitality of the cult of Artemis at the end for the first century C.E.

Doctrinally it is much more significant that false teachers "from there" passed through Ephesus but were not permitted to establish their heresy in the community (§6 and §9). Where they had come from is not specified, but Philadelphia is the best candidate for J. B. Lightfoot, who further suggests that the teaching in question stemmed from Judaizers who refused to accept the full reality of the humanity of Christ.[170] The hints scattered throughout *To the Ephesians* are confirmed by *To the Trallians* 9-10. Paul would have been gratified, but perhaps also astonished, that the Ephesians had remained faithful to his strongly incarnational christology.

Ignatius' letter is also important as evidence of the evolution of the organization of the church at Ephesus. On his final journey to Jerusalem it is very likely that Paul left Timothy in Ephesus to exercise a leadership role.[171] His failure eventually forced Paul to remove him (2 Tim 1:4) and to replace him with Tychicus (2 Tim 4:12), who had been with Paul in Ephesus some years earlier (Col 4:7). Normally Paul refrained from appointing community leaders, preferring that such people emerge by virtue of the exercise of their Spirit-given gifts. Only then would he recommend their acceptance by the community: e.g., 1 Thess 5:12-13; 1 Cor 16:15-16.

It is highly significant that neither of these Pauline texts mentions a single individual. Both speak of "such people." Yet by the time of Ignatius a single individual, Onesimus, headed the church at Ephesus. One might speculate that, once the difficulties of government by committee had made themselves manifest, Paul's appointment first of Timothy and then of Tychicus at Ephesus was taken as evidence of his mind as to how leadership in the church there should develop.[172] Were this evolution to have taken place in Ephesus it would be natural for its daughter churches to adopt the organizational structure of bishop, priests, and deacons (*To the Magnesians* 2). Obviously there had been a similar but independent development far to the east at Antioch-on-the-Orontes.

Few have resisted the temptation to identify this Onesimus with the ex-slave who was converted by Paul in Ephesus and who became the subject of Paul's letter to Philemon. His age, about which we know nothing, cannot be considered a serious objection. If he was an impetuous teenager in 53 C.E. he would have been about seventy when Ignatius was at Smyrna. A serious case can be made that Onesimus in the course of his episcopate was responsible for the complete collection of the Pauline letters.[173]

The focus of this book on Paul makes it inappropriate to extend our inquiry any further into the post-Pauline period. However, in view of current trends in gospel research, notably the return to the historical credibility of the gospel narratives,[174] it is important to keep in mind how mobile leaders of the early church were. When he was sixty-five, Polycrates, a second-century bishop of Ephesus, claimed to have "conversed with Christians from all parts of the world,"[175] and his contemporary Mileto, bishop of nearby Sardis, made a pilgrimage to Jerusalem. It would be very surprising if Christians from western Asia had not visited Jerusalem before the catastrophe of 66–74 C.E., when the Jews rose against Rome. At this stage eyewitnesses to the ministry of Jesus would have been still alive. Thus it is entirely possible that the words of some of those who had actually been with Jesus were reported and discussed in Asia about the time that the gospels were being written. The implications of this for the assessment of the Johannine tradition (see p. 154) hardly need to be stressed.

FLAVIUS JOSEPHUS

Josephus was born into a priestly family in Jerusalem some time in the winter of 37–38 C.E. He made his first visit to Rome in 64 C.E. to secure the release of some priest friends who had been arrested on a trivial matter, and returned home in triumph. When war with Rome broke out in 66 C.E. he became commander-in-chief of the Jewish rebel forces in Galilee, but survived only a year before being captured. He had the wit to tell the Roman general, Vespasian, that one day he would become emperor. This in fact came to pass in 69 C.E. (presumably to the great surprise of both), and Josephus lived the rest of his life in Rome as a pensioner of the Flavians.

The only one of his four works that concerns us here is *The Antiquities of the Jews* (= *Ant.*). In it his avowed intention is to win respect for the calumniated Jewish people from open-minded Gentiles. One tactic he employs is to quote a series of official Roman documents that demonstrate "that we have formerly been held in great esteem, and have not been prohibited by those governors we were under from keeping any of the laws of our forefathers."[176] No one today doubts the essential authenticity of the thirty-one documents he cites. Of these, seven are addressed specifically to Ephesus and thus attest to the presence of a Jewish community there and illustrate some of the conditions under which they lived.[177] Moreover, these documents show very clearly how the democratic government of the city worked in practice.

EXEMPTION FROM MILITARY SERVICE

Lucius Lentulus, the consul, said, "Those Jews who are Roman citizens and observe Jewish rites and practice them in Ephesus (*politas Rōmaiōn Ioudaious, hiera Ioudaika exhontas kai poiountas en Ephesō*), I released from military service before the tribunal on the 12th day before the Kalends of October in consideration of their religious scruples, in the consulship of Lucius Lentulus and Gaius Marcellus." (*Ant.* 14.228; cf. 240)

The decree is dated 19 September, but the identical decree in *Ant.* 14.234 suggests that it should be 19 July. Lentulus was consul in 49 B.C.E., and the senate had commissioned him to recruit two legions in the province of Asia (Caesar, *Civil War* 3.4). Obviously it was in his interest to have as large a pool as possible of men of military age. Not surprisingly, therefore, he does not offer a blanket exemption from military service. It is restricted by three conditions. For a Jew to be exempt he must be (1) a Roman citizen, (2) known to practice his religion, and (3) domiciled in Ephesus. Few would have qualified.

Many in the east acquired Roman citizenship as a bribe for their support during the civil wars, and the easiest way for a Jew to obtain Roman citizenship at this period was to be the freed slave of a Roman citizen.[178] How many there were cannot be estimated. The second condition excluded those who were Jewish in name only. Jews who betrayed no scruples about what they ate or drank should not be permitted to claim privilege of conscience when called to the army. For the Jewish objection to military service, see below. One might suspect that the third condition was inspired by the fact that the appeal was made by Ephesian Jews (see below), who would be targeted before any of the army recruiters spread out into the province. If they reached their quota in the city there would be no need to go farther afield.

A BIZARRE REPORT

> Titius Ampius Balbus, son of Titus, legate and propraetor, to the magistrates, council and people of Ephesus (*Ephesiōn archousi boulē dēmō*), greeting. Lucius Lentulus, the consul, has exempted at my petition the Jews in Asia from military service. And on making the same request later of Fannius, the propraetor, and of Lucius Atonius, the proquaestor, I obtained my request; and it is my wish that you take care that no one shall molest them. (*Ant*. 14.230)

The request of the Jews was presented to Lentulus by Balbus, who in consequence was present at the staff meeting at which Lentulus made the above declaration (14.229). It is incredible that a subordinate official on his own authority should extend to all the Jews of Asia the very limited exemption accorded by the consul, particularly since two other senior officials could very easily have checked. Different scenarios must be invoked to explain this rather bizarre letter.

The first, and least probable is that Balbus was thinking in terms of his request for a blanket exemption and not of what Lentulus actually accorded. The second is that in writing specifically to Ephesus Balbus intended "the Jews in Asia" to be understood of those resident in the city, but Ephesus could just as easily be understood as representing the whole of Asia, as the next section shows, and no explanation is offered for the omission of the first two conditions laid down by Lentulus. The third and most probable explanation is that Josephus was sloppy in what he recorded.[179]

EXEMPTION FROM MILITARY SERVICE EXTENDED

> In the presidency of Artemon, on the first day of the month of Lenaeon
> [24 January 43 B.C.E.], Dolabella, Imperator (*autokratōr*) to the magistrates,
> council and people of Ephesus (*Ephesiōn archousi boulē dēmō*), greeting.
> Alexander, son of Theodorus, the envoy of Hyrcanus, son of Alexander,
> the high priest and ethnarch of the Jews, has explained to me that his
> co-religionists cannot undertake military service because they may not
> bear arms or march on the days of the Sabbath; nor can they obtain the
> native foods to which they are accustomed. I, therefore, like the governors
> before me, grant them exemption from military service and allow them to
> follow their native customs and to come together for sacred and holy rites
> in accordance with their law, and to make offerings for their sacrifices.
> And it is my wish that you write these instructions to the various cities.
> (*Ant.* 14.225-27)

In 47 B.C.E. Julius Caesar had formally recognized the strong bonds
linking diaspora Jews with the high priest and his successors (*Ant.*
14.196). The high priest at the time was Hyrcanus II. The pressures of
the civil wars no doubt meant that Jews in Asia, and perhaps even in
Ephesus itself, were swept into the Roman army despite any and all
exemptions. Hyrcanus in his capacity as head of the Jewish people took
up the matter with Rome. After Caesar's assassination on 15 March 43,
Dolabella seized the consulship and achieved recognition. Thus it was
up to him to respond to the request of Hyrcanus and, because he needed
friends, he was generous.

Exemption from military service is now accorded to all the Jews in
Asia without any conditions of citizenship or religiosity, and the position
of Ephesus as "the chief city of Asia" (*Ant.* 14.224) is underlined by its
being given the responsibility of communicating the decision of Dolabella
to all the other cities in Asia. Whether Ephesus was thereby given the
authority to enforce the Roman decision is a moot question. This exemption was only one of the privileges Dolabella accorded to Jews. In addition they had the right of assembly for religious reasons and they were
permitted to send the half-shekel temple tax to Jerusalem. Jews could
not sacrifice anywhere but in Jerusalem, and the temple tax paid for the
daily sacrifice offered there on behalf of the entire Jewish people.

AN EPHESIAN DECREE

> Decree of the people of Ephesus (*Psiphisma Ephesiōn*).
> In the presidence of Menophilus, on the first of the month of Artemi-
> sion [24 March], the following decree was passed by the people (*demos*) on
> the motion of the magistrates (*stratēgoi*) and was announced by Nicanor.
> Whereas the Jews in the city have petitioned the proconsul Marcus
> Junius Brutus, son of Pontius, that they might observe their Sabbaths and

do all those things which are in accordance with their native customs without interference from anyone, and the governor has granted this request, it has therefore been decreed by the council and people (*tē boulē kai tō dēmō*) that as the matter is of concern to the Romans, no one shall be prevented from keeping the Sabbath days nor be fined for so doing, but they shall be permitted to do all those things which are in accordance with their own law. (*Ant.* 14.262-64)

Ephesus may have been a self-governing Greek city but, as we saw above, Rome had no compunction about exacting obedience. Here it is clear that the city was sensitive to any "matter that is of concern to the Romans," particularly when it was pointed out by the proconsul. There is no hint that the Jews of Ephesus had been deprived of any of their rights, but in the Roman empire decisions by an official lost their force when he died or was transferred. Thus it was always important for the Jews of a given area to have their traditional rights ratified by the current incumbent.

This was equally important for pagans. An inscription dated to 88–89 C.E. represents a letter from a private citizen of Ephesus to the proconsul of Asia requesting the renewal of a long-established celebration of the mysteries of Demeter.[180]

SECURITY OF THE TEMPLE TAX

Agrippa to the magistrates, council, and people of Ephesus, greeting. It is my will that the care and custody of the sacred monies belonging to the account of the Temple in Jerusalem shall be given to the Jews in Asia in accordance with their ancestral customs. And if any men steal the sacred monies of the Jews and take refuge in places of asylum, it is my will that they be dragged away from them and turned over to the Jews under the same law by which temple-robbers are dragged away from asylum. I have also written to the praetor Silanus that no one shall compel the Jews to give a bond (to appear in court) on the Sabbath. (*Ant.* 16.167-68)

Marcus Vipsanius Agrippa was the son-in-law and viceroy of the emperor Augustus. He was in the east in 16–13 B.C.E., as we shall see below. The circumstances of this letter to Ephesus will become clear in the next section. One issue was particularly sensitive. When Jews had collected money for the half-shekel temple tax (= two Roman denarii or two Greek drachmae) it was stolen from them.

Clearly it was impossible for every Jew to go to Jerusalem to pay the temple tax. Therefore a central collection place was appointed in each area, and the amount of coin was reduced to the smallest volume by being exchanged for metal of the highest value, namely gold (*m. Shekalim* 2.1). The temptation for venal officials is obvious. Those who simply wished to annoy the Jews could argue that the export of such an amount of money could affect the local economy and bring forward as evidence the senatorial decree forbidding the transfer of gold and silver from the empire to a foreign country.[181]

Thus in 59 B.C.E. Lucius Valerius Flaccus was brought to court in Rome for refusing the Jews of Asia permission to export a hundred pounds of gold from Apamea, twenty pounds from Laodicea, a hundred pounds from Adramyttium, and a lesser amount from Pergamum when he was governor of Asia (Cicero, *Pro Flacco* 66-69).

The importance of these figures is that they permit an estimate of the number of Jews in a particular area on the basis that one pound of gold equaled approximately a thousand denarii or drachmae.[182] Thus the twenty pounds of gold confiscated from Laodicea show that there were at least 10,000 adult male Jews in the Lycus valley, the home of the three Pauline churches Colossae, Laodicea, and Hierapolis (Col 4:13), which were founded from Ephesus.

Officials, of course, were not the only potential danger. Smaller fry might steal smaller sums Jews had saved for the tax. Should they seek to cloak themselves in the inviolability of a temple, notably the temple of Artemis in Ephesus, they were to be dragged out and punished. Here we have a perfect illustration of the fact that the right of asylum was not absolute (for details see Strabo, 14.1.23; p. 25).

It is very curious that the criminals should be handed over to the Jews rather than to the secular authorities. It makes sense only if Agrippa thought the thieves were themselves Jews and that, in consequence, it was an internal dispute to be handled by the Jewish community (cf. Acts 18:14-15). If Josephus is correct in hinting that the Jewish community in Ephesus was organized in the same way as that in Alexandria (*Apion* 2.38-39), then it was a *politeuma*. The best definition of this institution is that of E. M. Smallwood: "A *politeuma* was a recognized, formally constituted corporation of aliens enjoying the right of domicile in a foreign city and forming a separate, semi-autonomous civic body, a city within the city; it had its own constitution and administered its internal affairs as an ethnic unit through officials distinct from and independent of those of the host city. It had to be officially authorized by the local ruler or civic body, presumably by a written charter setting out its rights and constitutions, though no example of such a document survives."[183] The Jews of Sardis, according to Josephus, claimed to have had "from the earliest times an association of their own constituted in accordance with their native laws and a place (*topos*) of their own where they decided their affairs and settled internal disputes" (*Ant.* 14.235). It would be surprising if the Jews of nearby Ephesus were not similarly organized.

AGRIPPA AND HEROD IN EPHESUS

Herod the Great sailed across the Mediterranean, along the western coast of Asia Minor, and through the Bosporus to meet Agrippa at Sinope in Pontus. They returned overland via Paphlagonia and Cappadocia and from there "to Great Phrygia and reached Ephesus" (*Ant.* 16.23). It was 13 B.C.E.

> It was also at this time when they were in Ionia that a great multitude of Jews, who lived in its cities, took advantage of their opportunity to speak out freely, and came to them and told them of the mistreatment which they had suffered in not being allowed to observe their own laws and in being forced to appear in court on their holy days because of the inconsiderateness of examining judges. And they told of how they had been deprived of the monies sent as offerings to Jerusalem and of being forced to participate in military service and civic duties and to spend their sacred monies for these things, although the Romans had also permitted them to live in accordance with their own laws. (*Ant.* 16.27-28)

Herod persuaded Agrippa to listen, and arranged for his best friend Nicolas of Damascus to plead the case of the Jews, which he does with extraordinary rhetorical skill (*Ant.* 16.29-57). He attributes the treatment of the Jews in Asia to simple antisemitism: "they feel a hatred for our religion which is undeserved and unauthorized" (*Ant.* 16.45). At the conclusion of the speech, Josephus tells us, "their opponents did not defend themselves by denying that they had done these things but gave the excuse that by merely spreading over their country the Jews were now doing them all kinds of harm" (*Ant.* 16.59).

Such classical antisemitism appears to have had particularly deep roots in Asia. Of the thirty-one Roman documents cited by Josephus as defending the rights of the Jews in Palestine and the diaspora, fully half are directed to Asia or its individual cities. This means that in this region Jewish rights were seriously and regularly violated. "Behind the frequent disputes there seems to have lain, in Asia at least, friction over Jewish civic status, and in the lucrative pastime of devising pretexts for confiscating the tax the Greeks could give practical expression to their hostility."[184]

The contrast with Greece is striking. Even though it was divided into two Roman provinces, Achaia and Macedonia, and had a very sizable Jewish population (Philo, *Gaius* 281), not once did Rome have to intervene to protect the rights of its Jewish inhabitants, at least to judge by the researches of Josephus. Jews did have a tendency both to want to have their cake and eat it, and if such irrationality was irritating to Asians (*Ant.* 12.126), it should have been so equally for Greeks. In evaluating these contrasting situations one must keep in mind the bloody Jewish

uprisings against Rome in Palestine (66–70 and 132–35 C.E.) and in Cyrenaica and Egypt (115 C.E.).

ROME AGAIN CONFIRMS ITS LAWS

> In no way differently did the proconsul Julius Antonius write. To the
> magistrates, council, and people of Ephesus, greeting. When I was admin-
> istering justice in Ephesus on the Ides of February, the Jews dwelling in
> Asia pointed out to me that Caesar Augustus and Agrippa have permitted
> them to follow their own laws and customs. . . . And they asked that I
> confirm by my own decision the rights granted by Augustus and Agrippa.
> Therefore I wish you to know that in agreement with the will of Augustus
> and Agrippa I permit them to live and act in accordance with their ancestral
> customs without interference. (*Ant.* 16.172-73)

This episode is dated to 4 B.C.E. and illustrates the Jews' fear. Despite
imperial edicts in their favor they still felt so insecure that when the son
of Mark Antony took up office as proconsul of Asia they petitioned him
to restate their rights in his own name.

The solution was not permanent. In 2 or 3 C.E. the emperor Augustus
was forced to respond to a petition from the Jews of Asia by an edict
spelling out in precise detail their traditional rights (*Ant.* 16.162-65).
Inscribed on a pillar of the temple of Caesar in Rome, this decree was
communicated to Asia by a letter beginning, "Caius Norbanus Flaccus,
proconsul, to the governors of the Ephesians, greeting" (Philo, *Gaius*
315). Once again Ephesus stands for the whole of Asia.

Ephesus was the seat of the *Koinon* ("Confederacy") of the Greeks
in Asia. This was an annual assembly of delegates from the cities and
tribes in the province of Asia that served as the major avenue of communication between Rome and the province.[185]

In the light of what we have seen above, the existence of synagogues
at Ephesus could have been taken for granted. The epigraphical evidence,
however, is surprisingly sparse.The words *to thysiastērion*, "the altar,"
followed by a menorah suggests a synagogue, as does another inscription mentioning *archisynagogoi* and *presbyteroi*.[186]

MEDICINE IN EPHESUS

The involvement of Jews in the life of the city is confirmed by the
fact that the Jewish community (*[hoi en Ephe]sō Ioudeoi*) set up an epitaph
for a family, the father of which was a "public doctor" (*archiatros*). This
seems to have been a title given to competent physicians attracted to a
city by tax exemptions. The point was just to have them available for
those who could afford to pay; it was not a free civic medical service. As

one might have expected, accusations of overcharging were not uncommon.[187]

Ephesus appears to have been well supplied with medical practitioners. Broughton draws attention to a group of inscriptions from Ephesus that betray the existence of a museum, to which was attached an association of physicians (*to synedrion, hoi en Ephesō apo tou Mouseiou iatroi*). These inscriptions further demonstrate that this association actively stimulated the progress of medical science by means of competitions between senior practitioners in problem-solving, use of instruments, surgery, and composition of a text.[188]

In antiquity a "museum" was a place associated with the muses, the nine goddesses who originally inspired literature, music, and dance, but who later came to be thought of as the forces behind all intellectual pursuits. Thus any center of research and learning could be called a "museum." By far the most celebrated museum was that established by Ptolemy I Soter (366–282 B.C.E.) in Alexandria. It was distinct from the library and housed a group of well-paid scholars dedicated to research and to the dissemination of their results in frequent symposia. Presumably it was in this sort of context that the medical competitions mentioned above took place. At Ephesus professors and lawyers shared the museum with the physicians.[189]

LIVY

Titius Livius was born in Patavium (modern Padua) in 59 B.C.E. and died there at the good age of seventy-five. The purpose of his history was to chronicle Rome's progressive mastery first of all Italy and then of the Mediterranean world. For any given period he normally drew on one principal authority, which he complemented by other reading. His main source for the material that concerns us was the Greek historian Polybius (200–118 B.C.E.). Livy divides his material like an annalist; each chapter records the events of a single year. Even though he was closely tied to his sources, Livy's originality lies in the way he can bring his material to life. He brilliantly evokes atmosphere and emotions. Short, vivid sentences convey the speed and confusion of battle.

THE TEMPLE OF ARTEMIS

> When the king had promoted the grandeur of the state by enlarging the City, and had shaped all his domestic policy to suit the demands of peace as well as those of war, he was unwilling that arms should always be the means employed for strengthening Rome's power and sought to increase her sway by diplomacy, and at the same time to add something to the splendour of the City. Even at that early date the temple of Diana at Ephesus enjoyed great renown. It was reputed to have been built through the cooperation of the cities of Asia, and this harmony and community of worship Servius praised in superlative terms to the Latin nobles, with whom, both officially and in private, he had taken pains to establish a footing of hospitality and friendship. By dint of reiterating the same arguments he finally carried his point, and a shrine of Diana was built in Rome by the nations of Latium conjointly with the Roman People. (*History of Rome* 1.45)

Servius Tullius is conventionally dated 578–535 B.C.E. and called the sixth king of Rome. The earliest sources for the beginnings of Rome are dated to the first century B.C.E. and thus can provide little reliable information regarding events that happened half a millenium earlier. It is not impossible, however, that some elements reflect genuine memory.

At the time of Servius Tullius the temple of Artemis in Ephesus would still have been very new,[190] and one can legitimately wonder just how far its fame had spread. By the time of Livy, of course, it had become one of the seven wonders of the world,[191] and he could well have heard that the temple was build by "all of Asia"[192] and interpreted this as evidence of the unity of the people of Asia. Livy could also safely assume that Servius Tullius, a "tyrant" who had come to power by force,[193] would want to unify the people of Rome behind him, and knew that grandiose public works were a common means to that end. Finally, Livy certainly would have been aware that the temple of Diana on the Aventine hill was of great antiquity. All our author did was to spin these various elements into an uplifting story.

SELEUCID CONTROL OF EPHESUS

> In that same year [196 B.C.E.], after wintering at Ephesus, Antiochus tried to coerce all the cities of Asia into acknowledging the sovereignty which he had once exercised over them. . . . He therefore sent troops from Ephesus to invest Smyrna, and ordered troops at Abydus to leave only a small guard there and march to attack Lampsacus. . . . At the beginning of spring Antiochus left Ephesus with his fleet and sailed to the Hellespont, and ordered his land forces to be transported from Abydus to Chersonesus. (*History of Rome* 33.38-39)

In a long reign, Antiochus III the Great (242–187 B.C.E.) proved himself one of the most dynamic and successful of the Seleucid kings who inherited the eastern part of the empire of Alexander the Great after his death in 323 B.C.E. The Seleucids extended their control into Asia with the defeat in 281 B.C.E. of Lysimachus, who had refounded Ephesus (see Strabo, 14.1.21; p. 17). Antiochus lost control of western Asia in 220 B.C.E. when his viceroy at Sardis proclaimed himself king and independent. It was not until 213 that Antiochus was free to move against Sardis, which he took after a two-year siege. The taste of freedom, however, had not been forgotten, and in 198 B.C.E. Smyrna just north of Ephesus and Lampsacus on the eastern side of the Hellespont (modern Dardanelles) raised the flag of revolt. In no way could they have been a threat to Antiochus, but he was afraid that other cities would follow their example. Thus he sent troops against Smyrna from his headquarters in Ephesus and ordered the garrison of Abydus to march the thirty kilometers (18 miles) north to Lampsacus on the same side of the Hellespont.[194]

It was typical of the time, and much later (cf. 1 Cor 16:6), not to travel in winter, and this was particularly true of sea voyages. Pliny summarized the received wisdom, "spring opens the sea to voyagers," and dated the beginning of spring to February 8 (2.122). Vegetius was more cautious and considered spring to begin a month later.[195] Note the clear implication of the following section: that a fleet was expected to be at sea only during the summer.

Both Abydus and Lampsacus had excellent harbors, but the former was closer to Ephesus. Antiochus' strategy in moving his troops across to Chersonesus (modern Gallipoli) was to prepare for the invasion of Thrace.

THE HARBOR OF EPHESUS

When they reached Samos, Aemilius took over the fleet from Livius and after duly performing the sacrifice in the usual way called a council. There Gaius Livius—for he was the first to be asked his opinion—said that no one could give more loyal advice than the man who, if he were in the same situation, would have done what he advised the other to do. He had it in mind to proceed to Ephesus with the entire fleet, taking along numerous cargo-boats heavily loaded with sand, and to sink them at the mouth of the harbour. The closing of the harbour would involve less difficulty because the mouth of the harbour was like a river, long, narrow, and full of shoals. Thus they would have taken away from the enemy the use of the sea and immobilized his fleet.

This suggestion was approved by no one. King Eumenes asked what came next? . . . For if [the Romans] go away, who doubts that the enemy will raise the sunken hulls and open up the harbour with less trouble than was taken to close it? But if they are to stay none the less, what good does it do to close it? On the contrary, the enemy, enjoying a very safe harbour and a very prosperous city, with Asia supplying their every want, will spend a quiet summer. But the Romans, exposed on the open sea to waves and storms, needing everything, will be continually on guard . . . keeping the enemy blockaded. (*History of Rome* 37.14-15)

This episode took place in 190 B.C.E., just six years after the one reported in the previous section. His campaign in Thrace had brought Antiochus III into conflict with Rome, which began to fear his ambitions. This fear was shared by Eumenes II of Pergamum (196–158 B.C.E.), and an alliance with Rome was the natural outcome. Antiochus' fleet was based at Ephesus under the command of his admiral, Polyxenidas. The suggestion of the retiring Roman commander, Gaius Livius, was designed to deny Antiochus the use of his fleet. Eumenes was very quick to spot its fatal flaw. The Seleucids could remove the sunken ships once the Romans had sailed away.

This, of course, confirms the information that the mouth of the harbor at Ephesus was "narrow and full of shoals." Since it is unlikely that Ephesus had a corps of specialist divers such as those attested for the port of Rome,[196] only ships sunk in very shallow water could be removed. To block a deep harbor entrance, ships would have to be sunk in such a way as to land one on top of the other, a very tricky operation particularly if there was the slightest current. The reaction of Eumenes was based on what must have been common knowledge: that the harbor of Ephesus tended to silt up (see Strabo, 14.1.24; p. 26). Pergamum would have been very conscious of the trade that passed through Ephesus because it was itself far from the sea.

The size of the harbor of Ephesus can be estimated very roughly from the fact that Polyxenidas had under his command eighty-four triremes, three hexeremes, and two hepteremes (37.30.1). These last were at least twice the size of a trireme, which had a length of one hundred fifteen to one hundred twenty feet (38 to 40 meters) and a beam of twelve feet (4 meters).[197] The more rowers to an oar, the greater the beam and consequently the longer the ship. Given that the Roman fleet at Samos would have been able to pounce at very short notice, it seems unlikely that any of these ships would have been anchored in the roads or drawn up on a beach outside the harbor.

If the triremes were docked side by side perpendicular to the quay, which was the normal procedure, and if we allot fifteen feet (5 meters) to each trireme, the eighty-four triremes would have needed at least 1,260 feet (420 meters) of quay. This figure, of course, should be increased if there were also merchant ships in the harbor. Leptis Magna on the Libyan coast, a mid-sized harbor of the Roman period, had 1,200 meters of stone quays embracing a basin of 102,000 square meters (25.2 acres).[198] It would have been about three times bigger than Ephesus, whose basin in consequence can be estimated at 34,000 square meters (8.4 acres). It would easily have accommodated the thirty-five ships of Lysander (Diodorus Siculus, 13.104.3).

Strabo tells us that Attalus II of Pergamum (220–138 B.C.E.) narrowed the mouth of the harbor by building a mole (14.1.24; p. 26), which suggests that the previous harbor simply had two breakwaters roughly parallel to each other and perpendicular to the city quay. On the basis of the figures just mentioned one can suggest that the city quay reached by the Arcadiane was some two hundred meters long and the moles extended out for approximately one hundred seventy meters. At nearby Samos toward the end of the sixth century B.C.E. Polycrates had constructed two moles of massive rough-hewn blocks, one three hundred seventy meters long and the other one hundred eighty meters,[199] which were seen by Herodotus (*History* 3.60).

According to Lionel Casson's list, freighters of average size had a beam varying between four and ten meters.[200] If we think in terms of usable space, the three quays around the basin at any one time could accommodate slightly less than a hundred of the small ships, and perhaps forty-five of the larger ones. Given that the entrance to the harbor was notoriously shallow, it is improbable that Ephesus was used by any of the super-freighters of the period with beams of around forty-five feet

(15 meters).[201] Ephesus may have had a safe harbor, but it was not a big one.

In a subsequent engagement with a fleet under Roman command, Polyxenidas lost forty-two of his ships before fleeing to Ephesus (37.30). In triumph, Aemilius Regillus lined up his ships before the harbor of Ephesus (37.31), and no doubt taunted Polyxenidas to bring out what remained of his fleet. For this victory Aemilius was awarded a tablet fixed above the doors of the temple of the Lares of the Sea in the Campus of Rome some ten years later (40.52).

Having lost his ships, in 189 B.C.E. Antiochus was forced into a land battle at Magnesia near Sipylus that he lost badly, though he managed to escape to Apamea (37.44). The next day the cities adjacent to the battle-field—Thyatira, Magnesia near Sipylus, Tralles, Magnesia on the Maeander, and Ephesus—sent delegates to Scipio Africanus to surrender. Thus "the cities of Asia put themselves under the protection of the consul and under the sovereignty of the Roman people" (37.45.1).

Tralles, Magnesia on the Maeander, and Ephesus paid for the help they had given Antiochus by having the Roman army quartered on them for the following winter (37.47). There were two legions, 10,800 allies of Latin status and 2,200 Roman cavalry (37.39).[202] Naturally, the Roman commanders took up residence in Ephesus.

ASIA AFTER ANTIOCHUS

> The ten commissioners, having looked into the situation of the cities, made different dispositions in different cases. . . . Upon King Eumenes they bestowed, in Europe, the Chersonesus and Lysimachia, the strongholds, villages and lands within the boundaries of Antiochus; in Asia, both Phrygias, the one on the Hellespont, the other which they call the Greater. And they gave back to him Mysia, which King Prusias had taken from him, and Lycaonia and Milyas and Lydia and expressly (*nominatim*) the cities of Tralles and Ephesus and Telmessus. (*History* 38.39.14-16)

Having put themselves under the protection of Rome, the cities of Asia immediately sent envoys to the Senate in Rome in order to secure the best deal possible. Eumenes went in person. The Senate contented itself with establishing the broad lines of a peace settlement, and nominated ten commissioners to determine the precise details on the spot (37.55-56). From our perspective their most important decision (taken in 188 B.C.E.) was to single out Ephesus by name as restored to the Attalids of Pergamum. Its commercial importance to the region might have led its inhabitants to believe that they could be granted full independence. The commissioners, however, felt that Eumenes should be as richly rewarded as possible. Ephesus was to remain tributary to Pergamum until the last Attalid, who was without an heir, willed it to Rome in 133 B.C.E. What Eumenes said in his speech to the Senate regarding the longstanding relations between the Attalids and Rome (37.53) makes this rather extraordinary gesture much more intelligible.

LUKE

Acts 1:1 makes it clear that this is the second part of a two-part work. The close overlap between Luke 24 and Acts 1 means that the first part can only be the Gospel of Luke. Since the gospel must have been written after the fall of Jerusalem in 70 C.E., the double work probably came into being between 80 and 90 C.E., with Acts some time after the gospel. A physician Luke is mentioned by Paul as a companion in adversity (Col 4:14; Phlm 24; 2 Tim 4:11), and tradition ascribes the authorship of the gospel and Acts to him. However, the reporting of certain facts in the life of Paul and the reflection of what purports to be his theology in the speeches of Acts forces the conclusion that its author cannot have known Paul personally.[203] It is not impossible, however, that this Luke provided some material the author used. "Once can only add to this that Luke [the author of Acts] evidently sought further information where he could get it. Some would come from members of the Pauline circle, some at least of whom must still have been accessible when the book was written, some he would obtain from local memory persisting in the towns in which Paul had worked."[204]

RIOT OF THE SILVERSMITHS

About that time there arose no little stir concerning the Way. For a man named Demetrius, a silversmith, who made silver shrines of Artemis, brought no little business to the craftsmen. These he gathered together with the workmen of like occupation, and said, "Men, you know that from this business we have our wealth. And you see and hear that not only at Ephesus but almost throughout all Asia this Paul has persuaded and turned away a considerable company of people, saying that gods made with hands are not gods. And there is danger not only that this trade of ours may come into disrepute but also that the temple of the great goddess Artemis may count for nothing, and that she may even be deposed from her magnificence, she whom all Asia and the world worships." When they heard this they were enraged and cried out, "Great is Artemis of the Ephesians!"

So the city was filled with the confusion; and they rushed together into the theatre, dragging with them Gaius and Aristarchus, Macedonians who were Paul's traveling companions. Paul wished to go in among the crowd, but the disciples would not let him. Some of the Asiarchs also, who were friends of his, sent to him and begged him not to venture into the theatre. Now some cried one thing, some another; for the assembly (*ekklēsia*) was in confusion, and most of them did not know why they had come together.

Some of the crowd prompted Alexander, whom the Jews had put forward. And Alexander motioned with his hand, wishing to defend himself to the people. But when they recognized that he was a Jew, for about two hours they all with one voice cried out, "Great is Artemis of the Ephesians!"

When the Secretary (*grammateus*) had quieted the crowd, he said, "Men of Ephesus, what man is there who does not know that the city of the Ephesians is the temple keeper (*neōkoros*) of the great Artemis, and of the thing that fell from the sky. Seeing that these things cannot be contradicted, you ought to be quiet and do nothing rash. For you have brought these men here who are neither sacrilegious nor blasphemers of our goddess. If therefore Demetrius and the craftsmen with him have a complaint against any one, the courts are open, and there are proconsuls (*anthymatoi*); let them bring charges against one another. But if you seek anything further it shall be settled in the regular assembly (*en tē ennomō ekklēsia*). For we are in danger of being charged with rioting today, there being no cause that we can give to justify this commotion." And when he had said this, he dismissed the assembly. (Acts 19:23-41, RSV adapted)

There is much in this narrative that can be documented from the sources assembled elsewhere in this volume. Artemis was the goddess everyone associated with Ephesus. Her temple there was one of the seven wonders of the ancient world (p. 160). In an age without cameras all pilgrimage sanctuaries developed an industry providing souvenirs for visitors, and the Ephesians in the past had fought for their livelihood when they saw it threatened (Strabo, 14.1.21; p. 18). Pliny the Younger warned the emperor Trajan that Christianity posed a threat to the economy of Bithynia insofar as it might lead to fewer sacrificial animals being bought (*Letters* 10.96.10). The first theater in Ephesus was built some time in the first decades after Asia became a Roman province in 133 B.C.E., but needed expansion in the first half of the first century C.E. "Asiarchs" were a wealthy and influential group in the city at all periods. The "assembly of the people" (*ekklēsia tou dēmou*) did in fact meet in the theater, and was headed by a *grammateus tou dēmou*. The secretary was right to warn of the danger that such an unauthorized assembly would be misinterpreted by the Roman "proconsul" (*anthymatos*), the title of the official who governed the province from its inception. As we shall see in Part 2, the church in Ephesus had a successful missionary outreach "almost throughout all Asia." Finally, Paul confesses to having been in danger of his life at Ephesus (1 Cor 15:32) and in Asia (2 Cor 1:8).

Clearly, therefore, the narrative is solidly rooted in first-century Ephesus. There are, however, some minor problems. Miniature silver models of the temple of Artemis have never been found, though terra-cotta ones are common. Hence it has been suggested that the word Luke found in his source was *neōpoios*, the title of an official elected to supervise the finances of a temple, whose syllables Luke inverted, giving *poiōn naous*, "making shrines."[205] What Demetrius really made were silver statuettes of the goddess, some of which have in fact been found.[206] It is difficult to attribute such a gross error to Luke, and one must remember that the temple, not the statue (as was the case at Olympia and Rhodes; p. 161), was the wonder of the world. Thus while there was certainly a market for statuettes, there would also have been one for replicas of the temple. Their absence from the archaeological record may be just an accident. Absence of evidence is not evidence of absence.

The "thing that fell from the sky" is commonly understood as a statue of Artemis (NRSV, NJB, NAB; RSV "sacred stone") but, while our sources contain many references to the cult statue of the goddess (p. 6), it is never suggested that it was of heavenly origin. One might think of a meteorite. Some of these were venerated as a goddess,[207] but once again this would be an element alien to the traditions concerning Artemis.

The plural "proconsuls" cannot be taken as proof of historical igno-rance. Of course there was never more than one proconsul at any given time, but here the rhetorical use of the plural of category was inspired by the very natural reference to "courts" in which the proconsul presided. If one finished his tour of duty, his successor would take care of unfin-ished business.

The one possible non-historical element in the story is the identifica-tion of Ephesus as "the temple keeper (*neōkoros*) of the great Artemis." In the light of present knowledge this title is attested for the first time on a coin of the time of Nero,[208] who came to power in 54 C.E., the year that Paul left Ephesus. It is not impossible that the title was in circulation when Paul was there, but it does seem more probable that it came into general use only when the emperor Domitian (81–96 C.E.) granted Ephesus its first imperial neocorate title in 89 C.E. (Tatian, p. 137). Ephesus had sought the Roman title eagerly because other cities of Asia flaunted it competitively, but to give the same title to Artemis would have been a subtle affirmation of the Greek identity of the city to which Rome could not object.

However accurate the background may be, the story contains so many loose ends and contradictions that its credibility as an actual event is greatly impaired. Demetrius takes the first critical action, but then disappears from the scene without pushing his case. Where is Paul? at home, as the message of the Asiarchs seems to imply? or outside the theater, as the action of his disciples suggests? It is also curious that his companions were taken, when Demetrius was yelling Paul's name as the leader. Then, without any preparation, Jews appear on the scene, and select a spokesman, who says nothing!

What we have in this episode is a perfect illustration of Luke's literary technique. He does not want merely to tell a story, but to permit his readers to become spectators of the event. He creates each scene with broad strokes of bright color, laid on with a speed that leaves his readers with a vivid impression of the central point but no clear memory of the details. If we ignore the niggling details of the previous paragraph, what do we take away from the story? quite simply the victory of Christianity over the most important goddess in the eastern part of the Roman empire. Her most devoted followers confess their fear of her fall, and this is confirmed by the anger of the crowd. Nonetheless, the authorities recognize Christians to be peaceful; they operate by persuasion, not by force. It is not Christians but their opponents who are a threat to public order. Thus in effect Paul's leadership is praised by all Ephesus. His success is proclaimed by some, whereas his method is acknowledged by others. A triumphant victor, he can now leave the vanquished city for unconquered lands.

This picture is definitely not historical.[209] The great inscription of C. Vibius Salutaris, which is dated to 104 c.e., records the sums of money he laid out to guarantee that a procession of statues through the city would take place at least once every two weeks throughout the year.[210] This was a private initiative, but the purpose of the inscription was to give publicity to the fact that the procession was formally approved by the "council" (*boulē*) and the "assembly" (*dēmos*). Thus it became a project of the city as a whole and was further ratified by the Roman governor. The organization of the procession and the route it followed were designed to reinforce the identity of the city through the evocation of its Ionian, Macedonian, and Roman past and present. But out of the thirty-one statues in the procession, nine represented Artemis,[211] and the procession, which traversed the entire center of the city, both began and ended in her temple. There could hardly be a more forceful demonstration of the respect in which the goddess continued to be held and of the popular belief in her ability to protect Ephesus and to assure its prosperity.

PAUSANIAS

Not much is known about Pausanias beyond the facts that he was a medical practitioner from Magnesia near Sipylum in Ionia who spent some twenty years in Greece (in the Roman province of Achaia) during and after the reign of Hadrian (117–38 C.E.) and thereafter wrote an account, *Guide to Greece*, of the pre-150 B.C.E. antiquities he so much admired. His purpose was not to give all the details of a site but to highlight the elements in it that were worth seeing. He expected local guides to provide fuller information. He visited everything he talks about, did his homework thoroughly, and archaeology confirms that he made few mistakes.

HOME IS BEST

The land of the Ionians has the finest possible climate, and sanctuaries such as are to be found nowhere else. First because of its size and wealth is that of the Ephesian goddess, and then come two unfinished sanctuaries of Apollo, the one in Branchidae, in Milesian territory, and the one at Clarus in the land of the Colophonians. Besides these, two temples were burnt down by the Persians, the one of Hera in Samos and that of Athena at Phocaea. Damaged though they are by fire, I found them a wonder. (*Guide* 7.5.4)

Ionia has other things to record besides its sanctuaries and its climate. There is, for instance, in the land of the Ephesians the river Cenchrius, the strange mountain of Pion, and the spring Halitaea. (*Guide* 7.5.10)

The boastful tone is that of a true Ionian patriot. The size and wealth of the temple of Artemis are regularly mentioned. It is rather surprising to find Pausanias describing the two celebrated sanctuaries of Apollo at Didyma and Clarus as "unfinished." Peter Levi, however, comments apropos of Didyma, "The temple itself belongs to the late fourth century; it stood in an open court planted with bay trees, and had the tallest, slimmest columns in the history of Greek architecture. Work seems to have continued there for over three hundred years and in the end to have been abandoned rather than finished."[212] Many will no doubt have had the same experience of builders! The Persian destruction is dated to 494 B.C.E.

Pausanias' remarks make it certain that he had traveled throughout his homeland. In order to get to Samos he must have passed through

Ephesus, either to take ship from there or to reach a harbor farther down the coast.

The river Cenchrius owed its celebrity to its place in the story of the birth of Artemis, which was the foundation myth of Ephesus (see Strabo, 14.1.20; p. 15). The adjective he employs to describe Mount Pion (modern Panayir Dagh) is fully justified by its highly appropriate nickname Lepre Akte, "the leprous escarpment" (Strabo, 14.1.4; p. 10).

THE FOUNDATION OF EPHESUS

The sanctuary of Apollo at Didyma, and his oracle, are earlier than the immigration of the Ionians, while the cult of Ephesian Artemis is far more ancient still than their coming. Pindar, however, it seems to me, did not learn everything about the goddess, for he says that this sanctuary was founded by the Amazons during their campaign against Athens and Theseus. It is a fact that the women from the Thermodon, as they knew the sanctuary from of old, sacrificed to the Ephesian goddess both on this occasion and when they had fled from Heracles; some of them earlier still, when they had fled from Dionysus, having come to the sanctuary as suppliants.

However, it was not by the Amazons that the sanctuary was founded, but by Coresus, a son of the soil, and Ephesus, who is thought to have been a son of the river Cayster, and from Ephesus the city received its name.

The inhabitants of the land were partly Leleges, a branch of the Carians, but the greater number were Lydians. In addition there were others who dwelt around the sanctuary for the sake of its protection, and they included some women of the race of the Amazons. But Androclus the son of Codrus (for it was he who was appointed king of the Ionians who sailed against Ephesus) expelled from the land the Leleges and Lydians who occupied the upper city (*tēn anō polin*). Those, however, who dwelt around the sanctuary had nothing to fear. They exchanged oaths of friendship with the Ionians and escaped warfare.

Androclus also took Samos from the Samians, and for a time the Ephesians held Samos and the adjacent islands. But after the Samians returned to their own land, Androclus helped the people of Priene against the Carians. The Greek army was victorious, but Androclus was killed in the battle. The Ephesians carried off his body and buried it in their own land, at the spot where his tomb is pointed out at the present day, on the road leading from the sanctuary past the Olympieum to the Magnesian gate. On the tomb is a statue of an armed man. (*Guide* 7.2.6-9; cf. 7.4.2-3)

The only justification for this excursus on Ionia in a work purporting to describe all the monuments of the Archaic and Classical periods in mainland Greece is that Pausanias was himself an Ionian. It occurs at the beginning of his treatment of Achaea (the central section of the north coast of the Peloponnese) because Ion of Thessaly had ruled Achaea before being summoned to help Athens in its war with Eleusis. He died there, but the Ionians he had brought with him stayed on in Athens and, Pausanias tells us, made up the greater part of the colonizing expedition to the west coast of Asia Minor.

The association of the Amazons with the famous temple of Ephesus is treated fully in the commentary on Strabo, 11.5.3-4 (p. 7). Pausanias, however, is the only one to compile a list of their defeats and failures.

The simplest explanation of the attribution of the founding of Ephesus to Coresus and Ephesus is that it was a legendary justification for the two oldest place-names in the lower Cayster valley. Coressus was a harbor village that was absorbed by Ephesus (see Strabo, 14.1.4; p. 10). Given the importance of the river for the fertility of the valley and the prosperity of the port, it is not surprising that Ephesus should be presented as a river god, albeit one that does not appear anywhere else in Greek mythology.

A more plausible explanation for the origin of the word "Ephesus" is provided by Peter Scherrer.[213] An inscription of Mursilis II (1321–1295 B.C.E.), Hittite king of Hattusha (modern Boghazkōy), says: "I went across into the Land of the Arzawa and went into Apasa, the city of [King] Uhhaziti. Uhhaziti offered me no resistance but fled before me and went across the sea to the islands and there he remained." Clearly it is a question of an expedition to the center of the western coast of Asia Minor, which would mean that the land of the Arzawans was approximately the territory of the Ephesians. Thus "Ephesus" could well derive from "Apasa."

It is curious, however, that for Pausanias, Cayster should be associated with Coresus, who is explicitly identified as a human being. Graves reads the name as Cresus, which he translates as "Cretan" and interprets as pointing to an original Minoan colony.[214] Elsewhere Pausanias says that "the first Greeks to arrive there [Colophon] came from Crete when the Carians still occupied the country" (7.3.1). Colophon is just across the bay from Ephesus, and its inhabitants (see below, 1.9.7) were forcibly transferred to Ephesus when Lysimachus refounded the city (see Strabo, 14.1.21; p. 17).

Accounts of the colonization of Ephesus by the Ionians are also given by Strabo (14.1.21; p. 17) and by Athenaeus (361d-e; p. 47). They draw on different sources that do not always agree.

The leader of the expedition, for example, is not mentioned by Athenaeus, but Pausanias is supported by Strabo in naming him Androclus, who was a son of the king of Athens. Similarly, Athenaeus mentions no military action against the occupants, but Pausanias and Strabo agree that there was, while disagreeing about their identity. For the latter they are Carians and Leleges, whereas for the former they are Leleges and

Lydians. The confusion probably arose from the fact that the traditional border between Lydia, which is east of Ionia, and Caria was the valley of the river Maeander. It was so porous that by definition it was ill defined. The Leleges were non-Greek villages in Caria.[215]

Much more interesting is the distinction Pausanias makes between the foreign inhabitants of "the upper city" and those who dwelt around the sanctuary. He appears to confuse a number of elements. He claims that a sanctuary existed before the Ionian invasion and that it was dedicated to Artemis. Archaeology has shown that there was a pre-Ionian temple on the site, but it is thought to have been dedicated to Cybele and Demeter rather than to Artemis.[216] In consequence, there must have been indigenous worshipers nearby, but this idea has to be kept separate from the movement of the Ionians to take up residence around the new sanctuary they built and dedicated to Athena (Strabo, *Geography* 14.1.21; p. 17).

From the perspective of those living around the sanctuary "the upper city" can only be the adjacent hill of Ayasoluk, which is eighty-seven meters above sea level. One can see good grounds for a battle if the Ionian reconaissance party on the island of Syrie (modern Kourou-Tepe) (see Athenaeus, 361d-e; p. 47) noticed the Lydians and/or Carians moving into Ayasoluk. The Ionians had decided to recommend colonization of the fertile Marnas valley, and now they were faced with competition, which they immediately saw off.

If Pausanias is much less precise than either Athenaeus or Strabo regarding the site of the Ionian settlement, he mentions three places in the city that he visited in the second century C.E. The Magnesian Gate is located in the middle of the east wall of Lysimachus (fig. 5, p. 183). What is visible today, however, dates only from the second half of the first century B.C.E.[217] *The* sanctuary can only be the Artemision, whose position is also well known. The processional route from one to the other ran on the east side of Panayir Dagh (see Philostratus, *Lives of the Sophists* 2.23; 605; p. 173). Excavations in this area have brought to light no traces of a large building, and the ground would not have been suited to one.[218]

The archaeologists identify a building in the northwest corner as the official provincial temple for the emperor Hadrian as Zeus Olympius, which was constructed sometime after 130 C.E.[219] Thus it would have been in existence when Pausanias visited Ephesus. Thomas argues that this is the one to which Pausanias refers in order to indicate that the route he took from the Artemision went around the west side of the Panayir Dagh.[220] Should this in fact be the case it is surprising that he should mention the Magnesian Gate, because within the city he would have first encountered many more impressive monuments, notably the theater.

Thus the location of the tomb of Androclus becomes even more problematic.[221] One may doubt when precisely this monument was erected, but Androclus enjoyed a revival in popularity from the time of Augustus. He appears on coins, in statuary form, in mosaics and reliefs, none of which can be dated to the Hellenistic period.[222] As Rome put its imprint ever more firmly on Ephesus through the great building boom under Augustus, the Ephesians harked back nostalgically to what they believed were their superior origins.

HELLENISTIC EPHESUS

> Lysimachus founded also the modern city of Ephesus (*tēn nun polin*) as far as the coast, bringing to it as settlers people of Lebedos and Colophon, after destroying their cities. (*Guide* 1.9.7)

> Of those who were transported to Ephesus only the people of Colophon fought against Lysimachus and the Macedonians. The grave of those Colophonians and Smyrnaeans who fell in the battle is on the left of the road as you go to Clarus.
>
>   The city of Lebedus was razed to the ground by Lysimachus simply in order that the population of Ephesus might be increased. The land around Lebedus is a happy one. In particular its hot baths are more numerous and more pleasant than any others on the coast. Originally Lebedus also was inhabited by the Carians, until they were driven out by Andraemon the son of Codrus and the Ionians. The grave of Andraemon is on the left of the road as you go from Colophon, when you have crossed the river Claon. (*Guide* 7.3.4-5)

In Strabo's account of the refounding of Ephesus by Lysimachus (14.1.21; p. 17) nothing is said of any forcible transfer of population. Colophon and Lebedos are on the north coast of the bay on whose east coast lies Ephesus. They were both Ionian foundations. The military activity of another son of Codrus is recorded above (7.2.6-9). The report of the destruction of the two cities is considered to be an exaggeration or misunderstanding. The population transfer, however, cannot be discounted. It was common in the Hellenistic period for rulers to insert new settlers into a city old or new in order to kick-start trade and commerce. Thus Antiochus III the Great (242–187 B.C.E.) moved Jews from Babylon into Phrygia and Lydia,[223] and one of his successors, Antiochus IV Epiphanes (175–164 B.C.E.), placed Greek and Jewish settlers in Tarsus to increase the productivity of the oriental population.[224]

THE TEMPLE OF ARTEMIS

> All cities worship Artemis of Ephesus, and individuals hold her in honour above all the gods. The reason, in my view, is the renown of the Amazons, who traditionally dedicated the image, also the extreme antiquity of this sanctuary. Three other points as well have contributed to her renown, the

size of the temple, surpassing all buildings among men, the eminence of the city of the Ephesians and the renown of the goddess who dwells there. (*Guide* 4.31.8)

In Olympia there is a woollen curtain, adorned with Assyrian weaving and Phoenician purple, which was dedicated by Antiochus, who also gave as offerings the golden aegis with the Gorgon on it above the theatre at Athens. This curtain is not drawn upwards to the roof as is that in the temple of Artemis at Ephesus, but it is let down to the ground by cords. (*Guide* 5.12.4)

Another figure of Strife is in the sanctuary of Ephesian Artemis. Calliphon of Samos included it in his picture of the battle at the ships of the Greeks. (*Guide* 5.19.2)

Not only have I seen this armor depicted by Polygnotus, but in the temple of Ephesian Artemis Calliphon of Samos has painted women fitting on the *gyala* of the corselet of Patroclus. (*Guide* 10.26.6)

I have stated in an earlier part of my work [8.14.8] that two Samians, Rhoecus, son of Philaeüs, and Theodorus, son of Telecles, discovered how to found bronze most perfectly and were the first casters of that metal. I have found extant no work of Theodorus, at least no work of bronze. But in the sanctuary of Ephesian Artemis, as you enter the building containing the pictures, there is a stone wall above the altar of Artemis called Goddess of the First Seat. Among the images that stand upon the wall is a statue of a woman at the end, a work of Rhoecus, called by the Ephesians Night. A mere glance shows that this image is older, and of rougher workmanship, than the Athena in Amphissa. (*Guide* 10.38.6)

But when the Attic ships were captured at Aegospotami the Samians set up a statue of Lysander at Olympia, and the Ephesians set up in the sanctuary of Artemis not only a statue of Lysander himself, but also statues of Eteonicus, Pharax, and other Spartans quite unknown to the Greek world generally. But when fortune changed again, and Conon had won the naval action of Cnidus and the mountain called Dorium, the Ionians likewise changed their views, and there are to be seen statues in bronze of Conon and of Timotheus both in the sanctuary of Hera in Samos and also in the sanctuary of the Ephesian goddess in Ephesus. It is always the same. The Ionians merely follow the example of all the world in paying court to strength. (*Guide* 6.3.15-16)

Pausanias' extravagant praise of Ephesus occurs as a throw-away parenthesis in a discussion concerning the veneration of Laphrian Artemis in Messenia, which is in the southwest corner of the Peloponnesus. It is easy to detect the pride of an Ionian, and this perhaps explains the strong element of hyperbole in his words. The hesitation ("traditionally") in what is said of the Amazons was probably a bow to the full-blown skepticism of Strabo (11.5.3-4; p. 7), but Pausanias was not prepared to abandon ancestral beliefs completely.

It seems likely that the Antiochus who offered the temple veil to Olympia, perhaps the closest Greece came to a national sanctuary, was the extreme philhellene Antiochus IV Epiphanes of Syria (175–164 B.C.E.). In that case the veil may have come from the Jewish temple in Jerusalem, which he had plundered in 169 B.C.E.; it is explicitly mentioned as part of his booty (1 Macc 1:22). Once again it gave Pausanias an opportunity to make a connection with what he believed to be the greatest temple in the world. If he mentions the practice of dropping the curtain at Olympia, it was because it was unique. Many other temples could have been cited to make this point, but the one that immediately came to his mind was that of his homeland.

It is difficult to decide whether the statue or the painting of Strife was in the temple of Artemis, because Levi translates, "Conflict stands between them [the figures of Hector and Ajax carved in relief on the side of a chest], extremely ugly to look at. Calliphon of Samos made Conflict like this, in his painting of the battle at the Greek ships, in the sanctuary of Ephesian Artemis."[225] Levi's interpretation is perhaps to be preferred because the next quotation from Pausanias (10.26.6) appears to refer to another element in the same painting.[226] The archaic armor of Patroclus was made of two bronze pieces, one covering the chest and sex, the other intended to protect the back (10.26.6). Help was necessary to buckle the two parts together. Homer relates the battle at the ships in Book 13 of the *Iliad*.

The painting must have been a votive offering to the temple of Artemis. There were many others. Pliny mentions two great paintings of Apelles, "Alexander the Great holding a Thunderbolt" and "Heracles with Face Averted" (35.36.79-97), and it is probable that the extremely archaic panel picture of Artemis at Ephesus by the woman painter Timarete (35.40.147) formed part of the temple collection.

In contrast to sacrifice, which destroyed the offering, the deposition in a sanctuary of something enduring both removed it from the owner and gave it to the god. The gift did not have to be intrinsically valuable. It often marked the passage from one stage of life to another. Thus children dedicated toys, retiring priests or priestesses a statue, and retiring craftsmen their tools.[227] When Alexander of Cythera gave up his musical career he offered his "psaltery" to Artemis (Athenaeus, 183c; p. 49).

It is all the more helpful, therefore, for Pausanias to confirm the natural assumption that provision was made somewhere in the sanctuary grounds for the storage of votive offerings. He specifically mentions a picture gallery. Perhaps it stood in the area where Pliny locates the statue of "Hecate," namely, "in the precinct behind the temple of Diana" (36.4.32). This statue certainly stood in the open, because the guardians had to warn visitors of the danger to their eyes of the reflected light.

It is clear from Pausanias, however, that the building housing the paintings also contained statues, perhaps even those mentioned in the final tart quotation above. On Lysander at Ephesus see Plutarch, *Lysander* 3.2-3 (p. 123). Conon was an Athenian admiral who escaped from the defeat at Aegospotami (405 B.C.E.). After a period in exile he reemerged as a Persian fleet commander in 397 B.C.E., and after a victorious campaign definitively crushed the Spartans at Cnidus in 394 B.C.E. Timotheus was his son.

For the archaic temple of Artemis to have been destroyed by fire (Strabo, 14.1.22; p. 20) there must have been much flammable material in the temple building proper. Presumably the gifts of particularly generous benefactors were given central positions.

PLINY THE ELDER

Gaius Plinius Secundus, called Pliny the Elder to distinguish him from his nephew, Gaius Plinius Caecilius Secundus, was born about 23 C.E. and died heroically on 24 August 79, when an expedition to study the eruption of Mount Vesuvius turned into a rescue mission and his ships were trapped on a lee shore. His death of asphyxiation on the beach at Stabiae is movingly described by his nephew (*Letters* 6.16).

Despite serving in a number of high offices under the emperor Vespasian (69–79 C.E.), Pliny never ceased to read, study, and record. He wrote much, but his greatest achievement is the thirty-seven volumes of his *Natural History*, which alone survives. To a modern reader the name is misleading, for in his preface Pliny says that for him nature is life (13). A more exact title, therefore, might be "Everything under the Sun." Later in the preface he claims to have collected twenty thousand noteworthy facts from some two thousand authors, and experts consider this "a severe underestimate."[228] The *Natural History* (= *NH*) is in fact an encyclopedia of all the knowledge (animal, vegetable, and mineral) available in the first century C.E.

THE SITE OF EPHESUS

On the coast [of Ionia] is Matium and Ephesus built by the Amazons, previously designated by many names—that of Alope at the time of the Trojan War, later Ortygia and Amorges. It was also called Smyrna Trachia and Haemonion and Ptelea.

It is built on the slope of Mount Pion, and is watered by the Cayster, which rises in the Cilbian range and brings down the water of many streams, and also drains the Pegasaean Marsh, an overflow of the river Phyrites. From these comes a quantity of mud which advances the coastline and has now joined the island of Syrie on to the mainland by the flats interposed.

In the city of Ephesus is the spring called Callippia, and a temple of Diana surrounded by two streams, both called Selinus, coming from different directions. (*NH* 5.31.115)

This text illustrates the best and the worst of Pliny, all-embracing scope accompanied by a certain sloppiness of judgment. He must have found the ancient names of Ephesus somewhere in his vast reading, but

"Alope," "Amorges," "Haemonion," and "Ptela" are found nowhere else. The fact that Ephesus was once called "Smyrna Trachia" also attracted the attention of Strabo, who devised a credible reason (14.1.4; p. 10). "Ortygia," however, was never predicated of Ephesus. It was the name of the grove near Ephesus in which Artemis and Apollo were born (see Strabo, 14.1.20; p. 15).

The Amazonian origin of Ephesus was a commonplace in Pliny's world, but he should have been much more critical of the historicity of the myth, as Strabo was (see 11.5.43; p. 7).

From what Pliny says of the city itself it is clear that he never visited it. Mount Pion is the Panayir Dagh, but there were as many buildings on the Bulbul Dagh, and the principal monumental structures of the city were all in the valley between the two mountains. An even more serious mistake is to put the temple of Diana (the Roman name of Artemis) within the city. Archaeology has shown (cf. Strabo, p. 21) that it was well outside the city to the north of the rivers Marnas and Selinus. Pliny is correct, however, in noting a second river Selinus on the far side of the Artemision, and in what he says of the volume of mud brought down by the Cayster. Syrie (modern Kourou-Tepe) used to be an island in quite a large bay and was probably the base of the pioneering Ionian colonists (see Athenaeus, 361d-e; p. 47).

LAW AT EPHESUS

Ephesus, the other great luminary of Asia, is the centre for the Caesarienses, Metropolitae, Upper and Lower Cilbiani, Mysomacedones, Mastaurenses, Briullitae, Hypaepeni and Dioshieritae. (*NH* 5.31.120)

When the new Roman province of Asia was organized in 129 B.C.E. by Manius Aquillius the cities were grouped into circuits (*dioceseis* or *conventus*) for judicial purposes. A complete list is given by Pliny (5.25.95-33.126). In all, twenty-three cities formed the judicial circuit of Ephesus.[229] Just before speaking of Ephesus, Pliny had dealt with Smyrna, which must be the other "luminary of Asia." Understandably Pliny names the inhabitants rather than the cities themselves, because it was individuals who had to go to Ephesus for judgment there by the governor. The latter's edict defined for the whole province the principles on which justice would be administered; these in general conformed to the edicts published in Rome.[230] It goes without saying that citizens of Ephesus had better access to the governor, who was resident there, than the inhabitants of the other twenty-two cities of his jurisdiction, which he visited only periodically. Naturally only the most serious cases were submitted to him, notably those involving Roman citizens and the ultimate penalties, capital punishment and banishment.

Greeks were notably litigious, and the governor could not possibly have handled all the disputes arising out of trade, commerce, and land tenure, to mention only the most obvious problem areas. In consequence, there must have been courts with purely local jurisdiction, even though they are not documented.[231] The one hint of how they might have been administered appears in a letter of Cicero asserting that he had implemented in Cilicia many wise provisions of Quintus Municius Scaevola, called "Pontifex," who had been governor of Asia in 94–93 B.C.E., "including that one which the natives (*Graeci*) regard as their charter of liberty, that cases between natives (*Graeci*) should be tried under their own laws."[232]

STAIRCASE IN THE TEMPLE OF ARTEMIS

Even on account of its size the vine used in early days rightly to be reckoned as belonging to the class of trees. In the city of Populonium is to be seen a statue of Jupiter made of a single vine-stalk that has resisted decay for many ages; and similarly a bowl at Marseilles; the temple of Juno at Metapontum has stood supported by pillars of vine-wood. And even at the present day (*nunc*) we ascend to the roof of the temple of Diana at Ephesus by a staircase made from a single vine, grown it is said at Cyprus, inasmuch as vines grow to an exceptional height in that island. And no other timber lasts for longer ages. (*NH* 7.38.125)

The fact that Pliny should have inquired as to the origin of the vine from which the staircase in the temple of Artemis at Ephesus was cut betrays a welcome hint of skepticism. A little farther on (36.21.95-97; p. 116) he will tell us that the external columns of the temple of Artemis were sixty Greek feet high, which is equivalent to twenty meters. To this we should add at least two meters to reach roof level. This is the equivalent of a five-story building. It would indeed have been a most unusual vine (a) to have grown so high, and (b) to have been of a uniform diameter all the way up so as to permit the carving of steps.

Moreover, why would anyone have gone to the trouble of seeking out such a vine merely to provide an access to the roof that was used only by workmen? None of the reconstructions of the temple of Artemis show a roof walkway that could have been used by visitors to admire the view, nor is anything similar reported for any other temple of antiquity.

The columns of the temple in Metapontum (modern Metaponto) in southern Italy would demand a great number of vines of the same unusual size. This increases the improbability. The vine does not appear in Vitruvius' detailed discussion of building timber (*On Architecture* 2.9). Nor is wood ever mentioned in his discussion of temple columns.

TIMBER IN THE TEMPLE OF ARTEMIS

It is believed that ebony lasts an extremely long time, and also cypress and cedar, a clear verdict about all timbers being given in the temple of Diana at Ephesus, inasmuch as though the whole of Asia was building it, it took 120 years to complete.

It is agreed that the roof is made of beams of cedar, but as to the actual statue of the goddess there is some dispute, all the other writers saying that it is made of ebony, but one of the people who have recently seen it and written about it, Mucianus, who was three times consul, states that it is made of the wood of the vine, and has never been altered even though the temple has been restored seven times; and that this material was chosen by Endoneus. Mucianus actually specifies the name of the artist, which for my part I find surprising, as he assigns to the statue an antiquity that makes it older than not only Father Liber but Minerva also. He adds that nard is poured into it through a number of apertures so that the chemical properties of the liquid may nourish the wood and keep the joins together— as to these I am rather surprised that there should be any—and that the folding doors are made of cypress wood, and the whole of the timber looks like new wood after having lasted nearly 400 years. It is also worth noting that the doors were kept for four years in a frame of glue. Cypress was chosen for them because it is the one kind of wood which beyond all others retains the polish in the best condition for all time. (*NH* 16.79.213)

The logic of the first paragraph is not as clear as one would wish. That the value of ebony, cypress, and cedar should be shown by their selection for use in one of the most celebrated buildings of the ancient world is self-evident. The reference to the time it took to erect the temple is meaningless. Why emphasize that these timbers lasted for one hundred twenty years when a little farther down Pliny says that the timber has lasted nearly four hundred years?

Cedar is an entirely appropriate choice for roof beams because this tree produces excellent long timber. Solomon used it for the temple in Jerusalem (1 Kings 5:20). What is said of the doors implies that planks of cypress were held together with glue.

From the absolute way that Pliny speaks of the statue of Artemis one must presume that he is referring to the archaic statue that was a feature of the original temple and apparently survived all its vicissitudes. In this case it seems a little improbable that it should have been made of ebony. The word is derived from the Latin ebenus and the Greek *ebenos*, both of which come from the Egyptian *hebni*. This alone shows that this tree is not native to Europe or Asia. According to Strabo it is found only in India (15.1.37) and Ethiopia (17.2.2). Perhaps at some point the reputation of the statue was enhanced by claiming that it was made of a rare and therefore valuable wood, even though all the known statues made of ebony are very small. It was principally used in Egypt as a veneer and inlay.[233] It is also possible that the wood of the original (whatever it was) darkened with age and multiple anointings and thus was mistaken for ebony.

This may be one of the reasons why Pliny opted for the minority opinion of Licinius Mucianus, whose character is sketched with some acerbity by Tacitus (*Histories* 1.10). Clearly, however, his report created problems for Pliny. The previous section (above) showed that Pliny believed that there were very large wild vines and that their wood was hard and resistant. Why, then, should the statue not have been carved from a single block of wood? And why should it have needed to be kept moist in order to avoid disintegration?

While agreeing with Pliny regarding the ceiling, Vitruvius had a different opinion as to the wood of the statue: "In the temple at Ephesus, the image of Diana, the coffers (*lacunaria*) of the ceiling also, are made of these trees," namely cedar (*On Architecture* 2.9.13).

ARTISTS AND EPHESUS

> Euphranor the Isthmian distinguished himself far before all others in the 104th Olympiad [364–361 B.C.E.]. . . . There is a celebrated picture by him at Ephesus, "Odysseus Feigning Madness" and yoking an ox with a horse, with men in cloaks reflecting, and the leader sheathing his sword. (*NH* 35.40.129)

> By the Athenian Niceas [the Younger] . . . at Ephesus is the tomb of a megabyzus or priest of Diana of Ephesus. (*NH* 35.40.132)

> Ctesicles won notoriety by the insult he offered to Queen Stratonice, because she did not give him a honourable reception he painted a picture of her romping with a fisherman with whom gossip said that she was in love, and put it on exhibition at Ephesus Harbour, himself making a hurried escape on shipboard. The Queen would not allow the picture to be removed, the likeness of the two figures being admirably expressed. (*NH* 35.40.140)

> There have also been women artists: Timarete the daughter of Micon who painted the extremely archaic panel picture of Artemis at Ephesus. . . . (*NH* 35.40.147)

> The "Hercules" of Menestratus is greatly admired, and so too is the "Hecate" in the precinct behind the temple of Diana (*in templo Dianae post aedem*) at Ephesus. In studying this statue people are warned by the sacristans (*aeditui* = temple wardens) to be careful of their eyes, so intense is the glare of the marble. (*NH* 36.4.32)

> Apelles of Cos surpassed all the painters that preceded him and all who were to come after him; he dates in the 112th Olympiad [332–329 B.C.E.]. He singly contributed almost more to painting than all the other artists put together, also publishing volumes containing the principles of painting.

His art was unrivalled for graceful charm, although other very great painters were his contemporaries. Although he admired their works and gave
high praise to all of them, he used to say that they lacked the glamour that
his work possessed, the quality denoted by the Greek word *charis*, and that
although they had every other merit, in that alone no one was his rival.

He also asserted another claim to distinction when he expressed his
admiration for the immensely laborious and infinitely meticulous work
of Protogenes; for he said that in all respects his achievements and those
of Protogenes were on a level, or those of Protogenes were superior, but
that in one respect he stood higher, that he knew when to take his hand
away from a picture—a noteworthy warning of the frequently evil effects
of excessive diligence.

The candour of Apelles was however equal to his artistic skill. He used
to acknowledge his inferiority to Melanthius in grouping, and to Asclepi-
odorus in nicety of measurement, that is in the proper space to be left
between one object and another.

A clever incident took place between Protogenes and Apelles. Protogenes lived at Rhodes, and Apelles made a voyage there from a desire to
make himself acquainted with Protogenes's works, as that artist was hith-
erto only known to him by reputation. He went at once to his studio. The
artist was not there, but there was a panel of considerable size on the easel
prepared for painting, which was in the charge of a single old woman. In
answer to his enquiry, she told him that Protogenes was not at home, and
asked who it was she should report as having come to see him. "Say it was
this person," said Apelles, and taking up a brush he painted in colour
across the panel an extremely fine line. When Protogenes returned the old
woman showed him what had taken place. The story goes that the artist,
after looking closely at the finish of this, said that the new arrival was
Apelles, as so perfect a piece of work tallied with nobody else. He himself,
using another colour, drew a still finer line on the top of the first one.
Leaving the room, he told the attendant to show it to the visitor if he returned and said that this was the person he was in search of. And so it
happened, for Apelles came back, and, ashamed to be beaten, cut the lines
with another in a third color, leaving no room for any further display of
minute work. Hereupon Protogenes admitted he was defeated, and flew
down to the harbour to look for the visitor. And he decided that the panel
should be handed on to posterity as it was, to be admired as a marvel by
everybody, but particularly by artists.

I am informed that it was burnt in the first fire which occurred in
Caesar's palace on the Palatine [4 c.e.]. It had been previously much admired by us, on its vast surface containing nothing else than the almost
invisible lines, so that among the outstanding works of many artists it
looked like a blank space, and by that very fact attracted attention, and
was more esteemed than every masterpiece there.

Moreover it was a regular custom with Apelles never to let a day of
business be so fully occupied that he did not practise his art by drawing
a line, which has passed from him into a proverb. Another habit of his was
when he had finished his works to place them in a gallery in the view of

passersby, and he himself stood out of sight behind the picture and listened to hear what faults were noticed, rating the public as a more observant critic than himself.

It is said that he was found fault with by a shoemaker because in drawing a subject's sandals he had represented the loops in them as one too few. The next day the same critic was so proud of the artist's correcting the fault indicated by his previous objection that he found fault with the leg. But Apelles indignantly looked out from behind the picture and rebuked him, saying that a shoemaker in his criticism should not go beyond the sandal—a remark that has also passed into a proverb.

In fact he also possessed great courtesy of manners, which made him more agreeable to Alexander the Great, who frequently visited his studio— for, as we have said, Alexander had published an edict forbidding any other artist to paint his portrait. But in the studio Alexander used to talk a great deal about painting without any real knowledge of it, and Apelles would politely advise him to drop the subject, saying that the boys engaged in grinding the colours were laughing at him. So much power did his authority exercise over a king who was otherwise of an irascible temper.

And yet Alexander conferred honour on him in a most conspicuous instance. He had such an admiration for the beauty of his favourite mistress, named Pancaspe, that he gave orders that she should be painted in the nude by Apelles. Then discovering that the artist, while executing the commission, had fallen in love with the woman, he presented her to him, great-minded as he was and still greater owing to his control of himself, and of a greatness proved by this action as much as by any other victory, because he conquered himself, and presented not only his bedmate but his affection also to the artist, and was not even influenced by the feelings of his favourite in having been recently the mistress of a monarch and now belonging to a painter. Some persons believe that she was the model from which the Aphrodite Anadyomene (Rising from the Sea) was painted.

It was Apelles also who, kindly among his rivals, first established the reputation of Protogenes at Rhodes. Protogenes was held in low esteem by his fellow-countrymen, as is usual with home products, and when Apelles asked him what price he set on some works he had finished, he had mentioned some small sum, but Apelles made him an offer of fifty talents for them, and spread it about that he was buying them with the intention of selling them as works of his own. This device aroused the people of Rhodes to appreciate the artist, and Apelles only parted with the pictures to them at an enhanced price.

He also painted portraits so absolutely lifelike that, incredible as it sounds, the grammarian Apio has left it on record that one of those persons called "physiognomists," who prophesy people's future by their countenance, pronounced from their portraits either the year of the subjects' death hereafter or the number of years they had already lived.

Apelles had been on bad terms with Ptolemy in Alexander's retinue. When this Ptolemy was King of Egypt, Apelles on a voyage had been driven by a violent storm into Alexandria. His rivals maliciously suborned the king's jester to convey to him an invitation to dinner, to which he came.

Ptolemy was very indignant, and paraded his hospitality-stewards to say which of them had given him the invitation. Apelles picked up a piece of extinguished charcoal from the hearth and drew a likeness on the wall, the King recognizing the features of the jester as soon as he began the sketch.

He also painted a picture of King Antigonus who was blind in one eye, and devised an original method of concealing the defect, for he did the likeness in "three-quarter," so that the feature that was lacking in the subject might be thought instead to be absent in the picture, and he only showed the part of the face that he was able to display as unmutilated. Among his works are also pictures of persons at the point of death.

But it is not easy to say which of his productions are of the highest rank. His "Aphrodite Emerging from the Sea" was dedicated by his late lamented majesty Augustus in the shrine of his father Caesar; it is known as the *Anadyomene*. This, like other works, is eclipsed yet made famous by the Greek verses which sing its praises. The lower part of the picture having become damaged, nobody could be found to restore it, but the actual injury contributed to the glory of the artist. This picture, however, suffered from age and rot, and Nero when emperor substituted another for it, a work by Dorotheus.

Apelles had also begun on another Aphrodite at Cos, which was to surpass even his famous earlier one. But death grudged him the work when only partly finished, nor could anybody be found to carry on the task in conformity with the outlines of the sketches prepared.

He also painted "Alexander the Great holding a Thunderbolt" in the temple of Artemis at Ephesus, for a fee of twenty talents in gold. The fingers have the appearance of projecting from the surface and the thunderbolt seems to stand out from the picture—readers must remember that all these effects were produced by four colours [cf. 35.36.50]. The artist received the price of this picture in gold coin measured by weight [of the panel?] not counted.

He also painted a "Procession of the Magabyzus," the priest of Artemis of Ephesus, a "Clitus with Horse" hastening into battle, and an armour-bearer handing someone a helmet at his command. How many times he painted Alexander and Philip it would be superfluous to recount.

His "Habron at Samos" is much admired, as is his "Menander King of Caria" at Rhodes, likewise his "Antaeus," and at Alexandria his "Gorgosthenes the Tragic Actor," and at Rome his "Castor and Pollux with Victory and Alexander the Great," and also his figure of "War with Hands Tied Behind with Alexander Riding in Triumph in his Chariot." Both of these pictures his late lamented majesty Augustus with restrained good taste had dedicated in the most frequented parts of his forum. The emperor Claudius, however, thought it more advisable to cut out the face of Alexander from both works and substitute portraits of Augustus.

The "Heracles with Face Averted" in the temple of Diana is also believed to be by his hand—so drawn that the picture more truly displays Heracles' face than merely suggests it to the imagination—a very difficult achievement. He also painted a "Nude Hero," a picture with which he challenged Nature itself.

There is, or was, a picture of a "Horse" by him painted in a competition, by which he carried his appeal for judgement from mankind to the dumb quadrupeds; for perceiving that his rivals were getting the better of him by intrigue, he had some horses brought and showed them their pictures one by one; and the horses only began to neigh when they saw the horse painted by Apelles; and this always happened subsequently, showing it to be a sound test of artistic skill.

He also did a "Neoptolemus on Horseback" fighting against the Persians, an "Archelaus with his Wife and Daughter" and an "Antigonus with a Breastplate" marching with his horse at his side. Connoisseurs put at the head of all his works the portrait of the same king seated on horseback, and his "Artemis in the Midst of a Band of Maidens Offering a Sacrifice," a work by which he may be thought to have surpassed Homer's verses describing the same subject [*Odessey* 6.102ff.]. He even painted things that cannot be represented in pictures—thunder, lightning and thunderbolts, the pictures known respectively under the Greek titles of "Bronte," "Astrape," and "Ceraunobolia."

His inventions in the art of painting have been useful to all other painters as well, but there was one which nobody was able to imitate. When his works were finished he used to cover them over with a black varnish of such thinness that its very presence, while its reflexion threw up the brilliance of all the colours and preserved them from dust and dirt, was only visible to anyone who looked at it close up, but also employing great calculation of lights, so that the brilliance of the colours should not offend the sight when people looked at them as if through muscovy-glass and so that the same device from a distance might invisibly give sombreness to colors that were too brilliant. (*NH* 35.36.79-97)

Pliny is mistaken in thinking that Apelles came from the island of Cos. He was in fact born in Colophon, just across the bay from Ephesus, but like many other young artists realized that he had a better chance of financial success in a big city, and so spent his working life in Ephesus (Strabo, 14.1.25; p. 29). Pliny's error may be due to the fact that two of his greatest paintings had been hung "in the Asclepieium [of Cos], a temple exceedingly famous and full of numerous votive offerings, among which is the 'Antigonus' of Apelles. And 'Aphrodite *Anadyomene*' [Rising from the Sea] used to be there, but it is now dedicated to the deified Caesar in Rome, Augustus thus having dedicated to his father the female founder of his family. It is said that the Coans got a remission of 100 talents of the appointed tribute for the painting" (Strabo, 14.2.19). Of course, Apelles also died in Cos while painting a second Aphrodite, probably in the early third century B.C.E. His work, however, lived on into the first century C.E., as the barbarism of Claudius attests, but by then some paintings were showing signs of age.

The one-eyed Antigonus (382–301 B.C.E.) was one of Alexander's generals, who after the latter's death briefly ruled territory stretching from the Aegean Sea to the Hindu Kush and died as king of Macedonia

(306–301). The model for "Aphrodite Rising from the Sea" was reputed to be Alexander the Great's ex-mistress, Pancaspe. Just these two pictures underline how closely Apelles was involved with Alexander's inner circle. He painted Alexander and his father innumerable times, and also another of his generals, Neoptolemus. One might speculate that his quarrel with a third general, Ptolemy I of Egypt, arose because Apelles refused to paint him.

There are a number of problems in this sketch. Philip II of Macedon (382–336 B.C.E.) died two years before Alexander arrived in Asia in 334 B.C.E. Had Apelles traveled to Macedon to paint him there, and thus won the appreciation of Alexander before the latter's arrival in the East? If Apelles painted Alexander and so many members of his court, he must have worked with incredible speed, because Alexander did not tarry long in the west. In November 333 B.C.E. he won the decisive battle against Persia at Issus in Cilicia, having crossed the whole of Asia. Perhaps Apelles made quick sketches of his different subjects that he later developed into detailed portraits, as David Roberts later did of historical sites in the Holy Land.

The extent to which Apelles was a figure in the public eye, not only in his native Asia but also in Greece and Rome, is graphically illustrated by his association with two proverbs: *Nulla dies sine linea*, "No day without a line," i.e., "Practice makes perfect," and *Ne sutor ultra crepidam*, "A cobbler should stick to his last." His paintings were much appreciated in Rome, several being in the imperial collections, and elsewhere in the Greco-Roman world.

Pliny tells us that two paintings—"Alexander the Great Holding a Thunderbolt" and "Heracles with Face Averted"—were to be found in the temple of Artemis in Ephesus. They had not been bought by the temple because of their beauty or as an investment. Their fame and great value made them very appropriate votive offerings. Temples thus became the first public galleries, where great art could be appreciated by those who could never afford it.

Unfortunately nothing is known about the woman painter Timarete. She is one of only five female painters mentioned by Pliny (35.40.147-48). The way their achievements are formulated makes it clear that it was she, and not her father, who painted the extremely archaic panel picture of Artemis at Ephesus.

THE FIVE AMAZONS

The most celebrated artists have also come into competition with each other, although born at different periods, because they had made statues of Amazons. When these were dedicated in the temple of Artemis of Ephesus, it was agreed that the best one should be selected by the vote of the

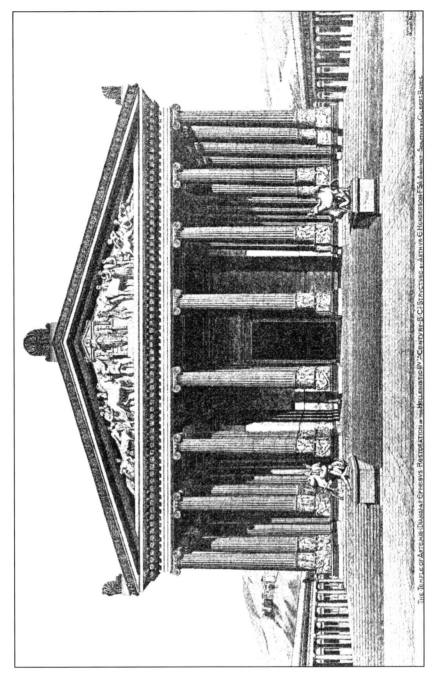

Figure 3
Arthur Henderson's Reconstruction of the Hellenistic Temple of Artemis at Ephesus

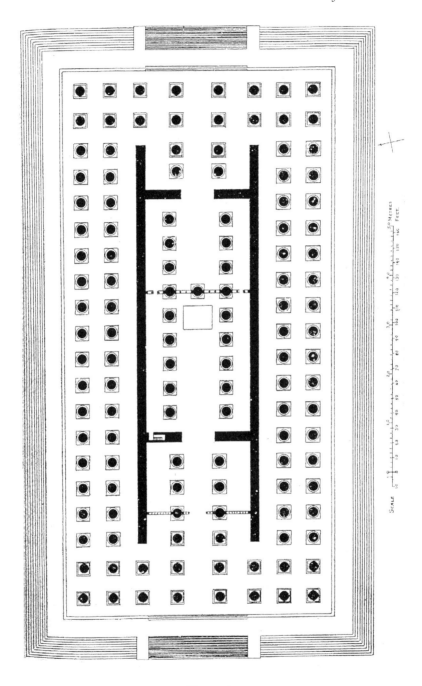

Figure 4
Arthur Henderson's plan of the Hellenistic Temple of Artemis at Ephesus

artists themselves who were present. It then became evident that the best was the one which all the artists judged to be the next best after their own: this is the Amazon of Polycleitus, while next to it came that of Pheidias, third Cresilas's, fourth Cydon's and fifth Phradmon's. (*NH* 34.19.53)

This short paragraph has given rise to a lively debate, notably because of a desire to identify the bronze statues with the five types of Amazons to be seen in various museums. All the artists used to be dated to the fifth century B.C.E., but it now seems that Phradmon worked in the fourth century.[234] This makes a historical competition impossible and increases the probability of the hypothesis that the order of the winners simply corresponded to the arrangement of the statues on a single plinth. It was a simple way of explaining to visitors why so many statues of the same subject were displayed together.

The credit for a plausible attempt to recreate the history of the group of Amazons must go to Brunhilde Ridgway.[235] On grounds of pose, iconography, and style she postulates that one, or perhaps two, statues belonged to the archaic temple of Artemis and should be dated 440–430 B.C.E. When the temple was rebuilt after the fire of 356 B.C.E. a third statue was added, perhaps at the instigation of Alexander the Great, to symbolize the rebirth of the great sanctuary. (On the association of Amazons with the foundation of the temple of Artemis see Strabo, 11.5.3-4; p. 7.) The two final statues, Ridgway suggests, were added by Augustus to emphasize the antiquity of the sanctuary, whose temenos he had modified in 5 B.C.E. by inserting a temple to himself.

THE TEMPLE OF ARTEMIS

Of grandeur as conceived by the Greeks a real and remarkable example still survives, namely the Temple of Diana at Ephesus, the building of which occupied all Asia Minor for 120 years. It was built on marshy soil so that it might not be subject to earthquakes or be threatened by subsidences. On the other hand, to ensure that the foundations of so massive a building would not be laid on shifting, unstable ground, they were underpinned with a layer of closely trodden charcoal, and then with another of sheepskins with their fleeces unshorn.

The length of the temple overall is 425 feet, and its breadth 220 feet. There are 127 columns, each constructed by a different king and 60 feet in height. Of these, 36 were carved with reliefs, one of them by Scopas. The architect in charge of the work was Chersiphron.

The crowning marvel was his success in lifting the architraves (*epistylia*) of this massive building [or possibly: such massive architraves] into place. This he achieved by filling bags of plaited reed with sand and constructing a gently graded ramp which reached the upper surfaces of the capitals of the columns. Then, little by little, he emptied the lowest layer of bags, so that the fabric gradually settled into the right position.

> But the greatest difficulty was encountered with the lintel itself (*in limine ipso*) when he was trying to place it over the door, for this was the highest block and it would not settle on its bed. The architect was in anguish as he debated whether suicide should be his final decision. The story goes that in the course of his reflections he became weary, and that while he slept at night he saw before him the goddess for whom the temple was being built. She was urging him to live because, as she said, she herself had laid the stone. And on the next day this was seen to be the case. The stone appeared to have been adjusted merely by dint of its own weight. The other embellishments of the building are enough to fill many volumes, since they are in no way related to natural forms. (*NH* 36.21.95-97)

The function of "real" in the first line is to contrast this actual building with such legendary wonders as the hanging garden of Thebes in Egypt (36.20.94). Details of the construction and decoration show that it was built over a considerable period, which goes some way to confirming Pliny's "120 years."[236]

John T. Wood's excavations (1870–74) brought to light the two huge superposed temples known from the literary record. The subsequent excavation by David G. Hogarth added a new element by revealing that they had been erected on the ruins of much older sanctuaries. If these had become the nesting place of quails, it would be natural to think of the site as chosen by Artemis, whose symbol they were.[237] This meant that the first large temple had to be erected there, even though the site was already showing signs of becoming marshy as the mud washed down by the river Cayster caused silting in the valley of the river Marnas. Credit for the technique employed for drying out the ground is given to Theodorus, son of Rhoecus from Samos. "He it was who advised laying charcoal embers under the foundations of the temple in Ephesus; for, as the ground was very damp, the ashes being free from woody fibre would retain a solidity which is actually proof against moisture."[238] This brilliant individual is also credited with inventing the set square, lathe, lever, and the lock and key (Pliny, 7.56.198). It goes without saying that the builders of the first temple had to be extra careful in balancing their construction. They had to bring all sides up together. Extra weight at either end, for example, would mean uneven sinking and cause the foundations to crack.

The floating effect was in fact protection against the earthquakes that occured frequently in the area; a list of those mentioned in our sources is given by T. Robert S. Broughton.[239] Pliny himself recalls: "The greatest earthquake in human memory occurred when Tiberius Caesar was emperor, twelve Asiatic cities being overthrown in one night" (2.86.200). This was in 17 C.E. Ephesus does not appear in the list given by Tacitus (*Annals* 2.47), but is mentioned in conjunction with this event by Jerome's translation of the *Chronicle* of Eusebius (II, p. 146). According to Broughton one occurred in Ephesus "before 30 [C.E.]."[240] The date was in fact 23 C.E., and significant damage was done to the stoa of Pollio in the State Agora (cf. p. 188) and to the porticos of the *Tetragonos Agora*, "the square marketplace" (cf. p. 197).

Elsewhere Pliny speaks of the archaic temple of Artemis:

> It was in the earlier temple of Diana at Ephesus that columns were for the first time mounted on moulded bases and crowned with capitals, and it was decided that the lower diameter of the columns should be one-eighth of their height, and that the height of the moulded bases should be one-half of the lower diameter, and that the lower diameter should exceed the upper diameter by a seventh. (*NH* 36.56.179)

Pliny's account here, however, would seem to be pointless unless he was describing the Hellenistic temple of his day. The two, however, were identical in size. "The new floor was raised 7.5 feet above the old yet the new walls stood exactly over the old, as shown by the limestone foundations, and column was placed over column, as exemplified by the bases still standing one above another, and other foundations indicate the same procedure."[241]

The platform of this second temple was 425 feet long and 220 feet wide. It is unlikely that the lines of the platform and those of the steps going up to it (which had to be an odd number according to Vitruvius, *On Architecture* 3.4.4) were absolutely horizontal, because "if it is constructed exactly on the level, it will appear somewhat hollowed to the eye"; thus these lines curved upward from each end toward the center (Vitruvius, 3.4.4). This must also have been true of the sides of the roof. The Ionian foot measured thirteen inches. In meters the dimensions of the platform together with the steps leading up to it were 142 x 73. The latter figure has been confirmed archaeologically. Therefore Pliny's figure for the length should be accepted.[242]

Vitruvius tells us of the arrangement of the columns: "The dipteros [type of temple] has eight columns front and back, but around the building it has two rows of columns, like the Doric temple of Quirinius [at Rome], and the Ionic temple of Diana at Ephesus, set up by Chersiphron" (3.2.7). Thus the long sides each had two rows of twenty columns and the short sides each had two rows of eight columns. This accounts for ninety-six columns. The disposition of the other thirty-one columns is a matter of some debate, but plausible suggestions have been made.[243]

If the height of the columns was sixty Ionian feet (20 meters), how thick were they? The proportion of eight to one given above by Pliny is confirmed by Vitruvius (4.6-7; p. 140). One-eighth of twenty meters is two and a half meters, and this was the diameter of the columns.[244] The thirty-six that were sculpted presumably stood at the east and west ends, where the entrances were. The sum of the two rows of eight columns at either end is thirty-two. The other four were the two outermost columns in the *pronaos* and the *posticum*. How exactly they were carved is a matter of guesswork. The most natural assumption is that life-sized figures were sculpted immediately above the base.[245]

The capitals, of course, were Ionic with a spiral (*volute*) at each corner.[246] On these were laid the architraves, which were six meters long and probably a meter square. Pliny indicates how they were moved into position but gives no hint of the vast labor involved. The lintel was nine meters long, because the center two columns at the east and west end were more widely spaced than the others to give dignity to the entrance.

The simple pitched roof was covered with terracotta tiles of two types, flat pan-tiles with raised outer edges and ridged cover-tiles that bridged the gap. In order to blur the monotony of a long roofline the ends of the cover-tiles were ornamented with heads or floral palmettes (*antefixes*). Similarly the angularity of the gable (pediment) at the west and east ends was softened by *acroteria*, normally huge symmetrical floral designs at the three points of the triangle.

Some ancient coins depict three openings in the pediment. The center door could be seen over the surround wall of the great altar some thirty meters to the west, and it is thought that a statue of Artemis was placed there at the time of sacrifice to create an epiphany of the goddess.[247] How these openings fitted into the sculptures of the pediment, which would have been normal and are shown in other coins, is not explained.[248]

In 263 C.E., according to the *Scriptores Historiae Augustae*, "The Scythians—they are a portion of the Goths—devastated Asia, and even plundered and burnt the temple of the Moon at Ephesus, the fame of which building is known throughout all nations" (*The Two Gallieni* 6.2; cf. Zozimus 1.28.1). The temple can only be that of Artemis. To Romans she was Diana, whose name comes from a root meaning "the bright one," and who was originally a moon goddess.[249] This destruction had wide ramifications. It destroyed the morale of the devotees of Artemis. She could not protect her most hallowed sanctuary. It also ruined the economy of the city, which depended to a great extent on the temple as the bank of Asia (p. 64).

The long history of the Artemision came to an end only in the fifth century C.E., when pagan temples were destroyed as a matter of Christian policy. Many elements from the Artemision were reused in the nearby basilica of St. John, which was erected by the emperor Justinian (527–565) on Ayasoluk.[250] From the sixth century C.E. onward this ridge effectively became Ephesus, as people drifted away from the increasingly malarial valley between the Bulbul Dagh and the Panayir Dagh.[251]

PLINY THE YOUNGER

Born about 61 C.E., Gaius Plinius Caecilius Secundus was brought up by his uncle, Pliny the Elder. He did not inherit his uncle's taste for research, but in the midst of a busy legal practice he contented himself with depicting the daily life of his world in a series of carefully crafted letters with a strong moral component. He also served the state in a series of appointments, and not just the posts in the usual *cursus*. He proved himself a civil administrator of exceptional competence, and that is why the emperor Trajan employed him when the province of Bithynia was in urgent need of financial reform. The tenth book of Pliny's letters consists solely of epistles to Trajan seeking rulings on specific problems. They are a major source of information on Roman provincial government. Pliny died ca. 112 in the course of his mission to Bithynia.

TRAVEL NORTH OF EPHESUS

Pliny to the Emperor Trajan
I feel sure, Sir, that you will be interested to hear that I have rounded Cape Malea, and arrived at Ephesus with my complete staff, after being delayed by contrary winds. My intention now is to travel on to my province partly by coastal boat and partly by carriage. The intense heat prevents my travelling entirely by road, and the prevailing Etesian winds make it impossible to go all the way by sea. (*Letters* 10.15)

Pliny to the Emperor Trajan
I kept in excellent health, Sir, throughout my voyage to Ephesus, but I found the intense heat very trying when I went on to travel by road, and developed a touch of fever which kept me at Pergamum. Then, when I had resumed my journey by coastal boat, I was further delayed by contrary winds, so that I did not reach Bithynia until 17 September. (*Letters* 10.17A)

Both of these letters were written in late summer of 110 C.E. when Pliny was *en route* to the south coast of the Black Sea to take up his appointment as governor of Bithynia. It must have been August when he left Rome, which was late for a departing official. Letter 10:18, however, makes it clear that Pliny had been chosen for "a special mission" to resolve administrative and financial problems in Bithynia.

In recounting the mundane details of his voyage he was playing on the well-known reputation of Trajan (98–117) as courteous, friendly, and forbearing. In addition one can perhaps detect a desire to win favor by suggesting that everything he did was completely above board and could be told in detail to the emperor. Reprehensible as this might be, the details he provides give us an insight into the travel conditions in an area traversed several times by Paul and his agents. On his first visit to Europe Paul came down through Mysia from the high country and crossed from Troas to Neapolis (Acts 16:11). He would have traveled in the other direction from Macedonia *en route* to Jerusalem with the collection (Acts 20:6-38), and on his farewell visit to Ionia (2 Timothy). Ephaphroditus, who like Pliny became ill, traveled from Philippi to Ephesus and back (Phil 2:25).

By his mention of Cape Malea Pliny might have been hinting to Trajan how brave he was not to have taken the conventional route across the isthmus of Corinth. Any traveler in the ancient world would have known the proverb "when you double Cape Malea forget your home" (Strabo, 8.6.20). Since the time of Homer (*Odyssey* 9.80) it had become traditional to emphasize the dangers of the strait between Cape Malea, the southeastern tip of the Peloponnese, and the island of Cythera. In fact the channel was eight kilometers (five miles) wide and free of rocks. The only risk was the delay caused by contrary winds, and many captains were prepared to take that chance rather than pay the transshipment taxes that made Corinth wealthy. Flavius Zeuxis of Hierapolis in the Lycus valley had it carved on his tombstone that "as a merchant he had rounded Cape Malea 72 times on voyages to Italy."[252]

If Pliny went to Ephesus he and his staff must have taken deck passage on a merchantman. Once in the Aegean a Roman warship would have cut across the base of the triangle and angled much more sharply northeast toward the Hellespont (the modern Dardanelles). This is confirmed by Pliny's mention of "a coastal boat," a small trader that sought a safe harbor every evening. What Pliny says about meeting contrary winds when trying to sail north in the Aegean is borne out by modern navigation manuals. Josephus reports that when Herod the Great was near Lesbos "a north wind caught him there and prevented his ships from putting out to sea. He therefore waited over in Chios several days."[253]

Pliny does not say so, but his decision to go at least part of the way by road from Ephesus must have been based on what he heard about sailing up the Hellespont and the Bosphorus to gain access to the Black Sea. A huge volume of water pours south down the Bosphorus and out through the "darkly swirling" Hellespont. Only an exceptionally strong south wind, which is very rare, permitted an ancient boat to sail upstream.[254] In *The Jason Voyage*, Tim Severin gives a graphic description of trying to maneuver such a boat against the hostile speed of a three- to four-knot current. Few, if any, merchant ships of the period would have attempted it. If Herod the Great and Marcus Agrippa took their ships through to the Black Sea[255] it was because their crews were under military discipline, had reserve rowers, and were commanded by iron-willed masters.

AN APPEAL TO CAESAR

Pliny to Cornelianus
I was delighted to be summoned by the Emperor [Trajan] to act as his assessor at Centum Cellae (the name of this place). Nothing could give me more pleasure than to have first-hand experience of our ruler's justice and wisdom, and to see his lighter moods, in the sort of country environment where these qualities are easily revealed. There were several types of cases which tested his judicial powers in various ways.

The first was that of Claudius Aristo, the leading citizen of Ephesus (*princeps Ephesiorum*), popular for his generosity and politically harmless, but he had roused the envy of people of a vastly different character who had suborned an informer against him. He was accordingly cleared of the charge and acquitted. (*Letters* 6.31.1-3; cf. 10.81)

If Claudius Aristo was politically harmless, it would appear that his grandiose title *princeps Ephesiorum* was no more than a gesture of municipal gratitude for his benefactions to Ephesus. His efforts to improve the water supply were particularly appreciated.[256] Naturally this stimulated the envy of detractors, who tried to bring him down. If he was tried by Trajan himself he must have exercised his right as a Roman citizen to appeal to the emperor, just as Paul had done some fifty years earlier (Acts 25:11). This meant that the whole proceeding—trial, verdict, and sentence—was removed from the lower court in Ephesus and transferred to the highest court in the empire.[257]

PLUTARCH

Plutarch came from a prominent and wealthy family of Chaeroneia, a small town located about thirty-five kilometers (twenty-two miles) due east of Delphi in central Greece. The date of his birth is estimated at 46 or 47 C.E., and he died around 120 C.E. His studies at the Platonic Academy in Athens (about 66 C.E.) made him one of the best-educated men of his age. His life of study, lecturing, and writing was interrupted only by the demands of civic and religious duty. His immense literary production is classified under two headings. The *Moralia* comprise twenty-eight ethical, religious, physical, and political studies whose paragraphs are given successive numbers with alphabetical subdivisions. The *Parallel Lives* are biographies of fifty Greek and Roman soldiers and statesmen. The historicity of the anecdotes is a matter of some debate. Each should be judged on its own merits.

A MORAL LESSON

The goddess Artemis at Ephesus grants to debtors when they take refuge in her sanctuary protection and safety from their debts, but the protecting and inviolable sanctuary of Frugality is everywhere wide open to sensible men. (*Moralia* 828D)

This is typical of Plutarch's wide knowledge and moral concern. That the temple of Artemis at Ephesus should pop into his mind when he wants to make the point that debt is the enemy of liberty is important evidence of its worldwide reputation. He could be sure that its tradition of asylum was well known. It should be noted, however, that the action of the debtor was to give himself time to find the money to pay his debts. Asylum did not relieve him of the obligation to repay what he owed.

LYSANDER AT EPHESUS

When Lysander came to Ephesus he found the city well disposed to him and very zealous in the Spartan cause, although it was then in a low state of prosperity and in danger of becoming utterly barbarized by the admixture of Persian customs, since it was enveloped by Lydia, and the king's generals made it their headquarters.

He therefore pitched his camp there, and ordered the merchant vessels from every quarter to land their cargoes there, and made preparations for the building of triremes. Thus he revived the traffic of their harbours, and the business of their market, and filled their houses and workshops with profits, so that from that time on, and through his efforts, the city had hopes of achieving the stateliness and grandeur which it now enjoys. (*Parallel Lives: Lysander* 3.2-3)

Antiochus, as if in bold mockery of Lysander, put in to the harbour of Ephesus with two triremes, and rowed ostentatiously past his ships, as they lay drawn up on shore, with noise and laughter. Lysander was incensed, and launching at first only a few of his triremes, pushed him back. Then seeing that the Athenians were coming to the rescue, he manned others, and at last the action became general. Lysander was victorious. (*Parallel Lives: Lysander* 5.1; see also *Alcibiades* 35.5-6)

Ephesus had been in Persian hands since the defeat of Croesus, king of Lydia, by Cyrus the Great in 546 B.C.E. Thus when Athens interfered in western Asia in the late fifth century B.C.E. by encouraging the rebellion of two satraps, Pissouthnes and Amorges, Persia acted on the principle that "the enemy of my enemy is my friend" and entered into an alliance with Sparta.[258] Lysander, a Spartan admiral, was appointed to Ephesus in 408 or 407 B.C.E. where, funded by Cyrus the Younger, he won victory over victory against Athens (see Didorus Siculus, 13.104.3). He was so succesful that he was worshiped as a god on Samos, the first living Greek to be given divine honors.[259]

It was typical of Lysander's good sense that he should take pains to get the Greeks of Ephesus (who claimed Athenian origins) on his side not by bribing them, but by increasing their prosperity in such a way that they could share the credit. His fleet easily forced mariners to land their cargoes in Ephesus, whence they were distributed inland. By inaugurating shipbuilding, he both created a new industry and increased his own sea power. The trireme was a long narrow warship, manned by two hundred men, whose principal weapon was a bronze ram fixed on the prow. It took its name from the fact that it was rowed by groups of three men sitting one above the other. It is noteworthy that Plutarch speaks of "harbors" because at this stage Ephesus in fact had two harbors, the Sacred Harbor and the Harbor of Coressus (see Strabo, 14.1.24; p. 26).

While Lysander did much good for Ephesus, the city also changed him, though perhaps not for the better. According to Aelian,

When Lysander the Spartan had lived in Ionia he is said to have rejected Lycurgus' rules of behaviour which were burdensome, and to have adopted very luxurious habits. The Attic courtesan Lamia remarked, "The lions of Greece turn into foxes at Ephesus." (*Historical Miscellany* 13.9)

Tradition gave Lycurgus the credit for laying down the laws and customs that were the framework of the austere "good order" (*eunomia*) of Sparta.

Lamia's remark is thought to be the adaptation of a proverb; see Aristophanes, *Peace* 1189-90.

Antiochus was the deputy of Alcibiades, the Athenian admiral, and in the absence of his superior made a silly gesture that cost Athens dearly. Once again Plutarch describes the scene at Ephesus exactly. There would have been no room for the merchantmen had Lysander moored his warships in the two small harbors. The best way to have them ready for instant action was to ground their bows on the coastline, which was then much closer to the city.

ASYLUM IN EPHESUS

> And it is astonishing that Alexander had time to write so many letters for his friends . . . and one to Megabyzus about a house-slave who had taken refuge in a sanctuary, bidding him, if possible, entice the slave outside the sanctuary and then arrest him, but not to lay hands on him in the sanctuary. (*Parallel Lives: Alexander* 42)

Since the title of Megabyzus is specific to the priest(s) of the temple of Artemis in Ephesus (Strabo, 14.1.23; p. 24), it must be the sanctuary in question. Presumably it was while Alexander was in Ephesus that his attendant escaped and sought asylum there. Such scrupulous respect for the inviolability of the temple is a little unusual in such a high-handed personality, but it becomes understandable if the episode occurred just at the moment when Alexander was trying to acquire glory by becoming the major benefactor of the restored temple (Strabo, 14.1.22; p. 20). On the status of runaway slaves in asylum temples, see Cicero (p. 57).

SULLA PUNISHES ASIA

> Sulla now laid a public fine upon Asia of 20,000 talents, and utterly ruined individual families by the insolent outrages of the soldiers quartered upon them. For orders were given that the host should give his guest four tetradrachms every day, and furnish him, and as many friends as he might wish to invite, with a supper, and that a military tribune should receive 50 drachmas a day and two suits of clothing, one to wear when he was at home, and another when he went abroad. (*Parallel Lives: Sulla* 25.2)

Having been given command in the war against Mithridates VI Eupator in 87 B.C.E., Lucius Cornelius Sulla chased him out of Greece and followed him to Asia, where he forced him to surrender in 85 B.C.E. He rewarded the cities of Asia that had resisted Mithridates. The punishment mentioned here fell on those that had sided with him, and Ephesus is singled out for particular notice (Appian, *Mithridatic Wars* 12.9.61; p. 42). There is no more graphic illustration of what it was like to have enemy soldiers billeted in private homes. Sulla had 40,000 troops in Asia (Appian, *Civil Wars* 1.79) with a full complement of officers for eight legions. Thus if they were quartered in enemy cities for six months it would have cost the population 120,000,000 drachmae (= $9,600,000,000), not counting what had to be paid for food, lodging, and clothing.[260]

When one adds to this what Brutus and Cassius, and then Mark Antony, took out of Asia (see Appian, *Civil Wars* 5.1.4; p. 43), it becomes clear why Augustus had to pour money into the province to aid its recovery (Dio Cassius, *Roman History* 54.7.5). He got to know the situation at first hand during his visit in 20–19 B.C.E.[261] Ephesus benefited by major construction projects that brought cash into the local economy (see part 2, ch.1).

A SWIFT CROSSING

> Having put to sea with all his ships from Ephesus, on the third day (*tritaios*) he came to anchor in Piraeus. (*Parallel Lives: Sulla* 26.1)

Despite his success against Mithridates, Sulla was relieved of his command for political reasons. His crossing of the Aegean was but the first step in his march on Rome.

The exact route followed by Sulla's ships will never be known, but it is easy to plot a plausible line. If he left the islands of Samos, Ikaros, and Mykonos to port, then sailed north of Syros and south of Keos, he would have had a clear run northwest to Piraeus.[262] The distance is only 210 nautical miles (390 kilometers), and if he sailed from dawn the first day to dusk on the third day, the crossing with favorable winds would have taken about sixty hours, which means a speed of 3.5 knots. This was well within the capacity of warships even when sailing with supply ships in a fleet.[263] On the Chios-Samos section of Paul's journey to Jerusalem (Acts 20:14-15) the merchant ship in which he had taken passage thrashed along at an above-average 5.7 knots.

These figures permit us to estimate how long it would have taken first Timothy and then Paul to get from Ephesus to Corinth when time was of the essence.[264] If the ship landed at Piraeus it was a further two days walk to Corinth (Dio Chrysostom, *Oration* 6.6), but if the ship went directly to Cenchreae, the eastern port of Corinth, the crossing would take only a day longer than Sulla's. Hence Paul and Timothy could have reached Corinth well within a week.

BUYING FAVORS

> Lucullus, after filling Asia full of law and order, and full of peace, did not neglect the things which minister to pleasure and win favour, but during

his stay at Ephesus gratified the cities with processions and triumphal festivals and contests of athletes and gladiators. (*Parallel Lives: Lucullus* 23.1)

Lucius Licinius Lucullus was Sulla's most trusted officer and served as proquaestor in the east. When Mithridates VI Eupator rebelled for the third time in 74 or 73 B.C.E. he pushed him out of Pontus into Armenia and thus restored peace to western Asia. Naturally Ephesus was his base. His strategy to win over Ephesus and other cities was not at all as intelligent as that of Lysander (see above). Circuses were a crude bribe to win loyalty, but if it worked in Rome, why not elsewhere?

ANTONY TAXES EPHESUS

Antony left Lucius Censorinus in charge of Greece and, crossing over into Asia [in 41 B.C.E.], laid hands on the wealth there. Kings would come often to his doors, and wives of kings, vying with one another in their gifts, and their beauty, would yield up their honour for his pleasure. . . . When Antony made his entry into Ephesus, women arrayed like Bacchus, and men and boys like Satyrs and Pans, led the way before him, and the city was full of ivy and thyrsus-wands and harps and pipes and flutes, the people hailing him as Dionysus Giver of Joy and Beneficent. For he was such, undoubtedly, to some, but to the greater part he was Dionysus Carnivorous and Savage. For he took their property from well-born men and bestowed it on flatterers and scoundrels. . . .

But finally when he was imposing a second contribution on the cities, Hybreas, speaking in behalf of Asia, plucked up courage to say, "If you can take a contribution twice in one year, you have power to make summer come for us twice, and harvest time twice." These words were rhetorical, it is true, and not unpleasant for the high spirit of Antony. But the speaker added in plain and bold words that Asia had given him 200,000 talents. "If you have not received this money," he said, "demand it from those who took it. But if you did not receive it, and have it not, we are undone." This speech made a powerful impression on Antony, for he was ignorant of most that was going on, not so much because he was of an easy disposition, as because he was simple enough to trust those about him. (*Parallel Lives: Antony* 24.3)

Marcus Antonius was born in 83 B.C.E., and rode high on the coattails of Julius Caesar. After the murder of his patron in 43 B.C.E. he and Octavian hunted down the assassins, Brutus and Cassius, and defeated them decisively at Philippi in 42 B.C.E. They agreed that Octavian should return to take charge in Italy while Mark Antony would reorganize the east. Ephesus was the obvious choice for his principal base when he landed in Asia in 41 B.C.E. His reputation as a general made it impossible for the inhabitants to do anything but welcome him. His celebrated charm worked in his favor, but Plutarch rightly hints at a much darker side to his character.

The unscrupulously rapacious side of Mark Antony had already made itself evident during the proscription of the Triumvirate at Rome in 43–42 B.C.E. Many were executed, not for their crimes but for their wealth. Now Ephesus, which represented the whole of Asia, was his new victim, and he stripped the city to the bone. He demanded of the province of Asia ten years' tribute in one. Entreaties such as we have here caused him to reduce his demand to nine years' tribute in two years. For what this would have meant in today's terms see Appian, *Civil Wars* 5.1.4 (p. 43).

PREPARATIONS FOR WAR

> Antony heard of this [an offer from Octavian] while he was tarrying in Armenia. At once he ordered Canidius to take 16 legions and to go down to the sea. But he himself took Cleopatra with him and came to Ephesus. It was there that his naval force was coming together from all quarters, 800 ships of war with merchant vessels, of which Cleopatra furnished 200, besides 20,000 talents, and supplies for the whole army during the war. (*Parallel Lives: Antony* 56.1)

Antony's success in the east had made it clear to Octavian that he had a rival for absolute power. Thus he did everything to undermine Antony's position in Rome. Antony retorted by annexing Armenia in 34 B.C.E., a victory he celebrated with Cleopatra VII (69–30 B.C.E.) in Alexandria in a way that gave the impression that it was a Roman triumph. The resentment this caused in Rome meant that a decisive clash could no longer be avoided.

Antony started to build up his forces. He did not know where Octavian would strike, but ships were the most efficient way to move troops around the eastern Mediterranean. That he chose to assemble his fleet at Ephesus underlines its tremendous strategic importance. Its harbors, however, were far too small to accommodate all his ships. Cleopatra bet the wealth of Egypt on his side and did not stint her support. Merchant vessels were necessary as supply ships to the fleet.

Plutarch records that, while the preparations for war were going on, Antony hosted a great party on Samos. "While almost all the world around was filled with groans and lamentations [at the thought of war], a single island for many days resounded with flutes and stringed instruments, theatres there were filled, and choral bands were competing with one another" (56.4). This gave Octavian time to build up his strength, and he defeated Antony in the sea battle of Actium on 2 September 31 B.C.E., thereby making himself sole master of the world.

WEIRD STORIES

Brennus, king of the Gauls (*Galatōn basileus*), when he was ravaging Asia came to Ephesus and fell in love with a maiden, Demonicē. She promised to satisfy his desires and also to betray Ephesus, if he would give her the Gauls' bracelets and feminine ornaments. But Brennus required his soldiers to throw into the lap of the avaricious woman the gold which they were wearing. This they did, and she was buried alive by the abundance of gold. This Cleitophon relates in the first book of his *Gallic History*. (*Moralia* 309B)

Aristonymous of Ephesus, the son of Demostratus, hated women and used to consort with an ass. In due time the ass gave birth to a very beautiful maiden, Onoscelis by name. So Aristocles in the second book of his *Strange Events*. (*Moralia* 312D)

These two stories come from a work entitled *Parallel Stories*, whose attribution to Plutarch is widely denied, though it is printed in the Loeb edition. It seems to be a parody of his famous *Parallel Lives* in which he compared and contrasted eminent Roman and Greek statesmen and generals. The anonymous author of *Parallel Stories* simply paired the weirdest tales on the same theme that he could find in genuine Greek and Latin works.

Another name for the Gauls in question is Galatians. A population explosion forced them out of their tribal lands north of the Pyrenees. Brennus in fact led them in their abortive attempt to settle in Greece in 279 B.C.E., but committed suicide during the retreat northward. Thus he could not have been their leader when they crossed the Hellespont into Asia the following year. After decades of struggle to claim land in Asia they were defeated by Attalus I of Pergamum in 230 B.C.E., and by the Romans in 189 B.C.E. They then settled down in central Anatolia and were the Galatians to whom Paul wrote.

The name of the woman in the second story means "the girl with an ass's legs." In the parallel Roman story a man copulates with a mare and the result is again a beautiful girl, but she becomes the goddess who protects horses.

SENECA

Lucius Annaeus Seneca was born in southern Spain about the same time that Jesus Christ was born in Bethlehem. As a child he was brought to Rome, where he received a first-class rhetorical education that he deployed into a growing reputation as a speaker and writer. He was appointed tutor to the twelve-year-old Nero in 49 C.E., and when the latter became emperor in 54 C.E. Seneca's role changed to that of political advisor. He retired in 62 C.E. and devoted himself to philosophy and writing. In 65 C.E. he was forced to commit suicide because Nero suspected that he had been involved in an unsuccessful plot against him.

THE POPULATION OF EPHESUS

> The human soul is a great and noble thing. It permits of no limits except those which can be shared even by the gods. First of all, it does not consent to a lowly birthplace, like Ephesus or Alexandria, or any land that is even more thickly populated than these, and more richly spread with dwellings. (*Letters* 102.21)

It is typical of Seneca to sharpen his point regarding the spirituality of the soul by contrasting it, not with the body, which would have been banal, but with densely populated cities. He could not evoke Rome because he wanted to use the adjective "lowly." Thus he was forced to look elsewhere, and what could be more appropriate than two well-known cities that had been conquered by Rome. His association of Ephesus with Alexandria betrays his conviction that they were roughly the same size. How big were their populations?

A figure for Alexandria is provided by Diodorus Siculus:

> Alexandria in general has grown so much in later times that many reckon it to be the first city of the civilized world, and it is certainly far ahead of all the rest in elegance and extent and riches and luxury. The number of its inhabitants surpasses that of those in other cities. At the time when we were in Egypt, those who kept the census returns of the population said that its free residents were more than 300,000, and that the king received from the revenues of the country more than 6000 talents. (*Library of History* 17.52.5)

Diodorus probably visited Egypt between 60 and 56 B.C.E.[266] The figure he gives for the number of residents is considered to reflect the size of the total population. Jews, for example, would have been counted separately only after the imposition of a special tax in 72 C.E. following the failure of the First Revolt against Rome.[267]

If "Ephesus," "Alexandria," and "any land" in Seneca's text are understood to be gradations on a rising scale of magnitude, the implication is that the population of Ephesus did not quite equal that of Alexandria.[268] Thus we might suggest that the inhabitants of Ephesus numbered some 225,000, which is in fact the estimate of Broughton.[269] This figure can be verified only if satisfactory answers are provided to two questions: (1) What was the inhabited area? and (2) What was the density of population?

Ludwig Bürchner estimated the area circumscribed by the wall of Lysimachus at 415 hectares (= 4,150,000 square meters = 1000.5 acres).[270] Not all of this space, however, was occupied by housing. There were great public buildings and spaces in the city center, and the steep angle of the slope makes it improbable that houses went all the way up the Bulbul Dagh to the line of the wall. Thus it seems preferable to accept Josiah Russell's estimate of the habitable area as 345 hectares (3,450,000 square meters = 832 acres).[271]

Very different estimates of population density have been put forward. A number of excavated ancient cities around the Mediterranean are calculated to have had an average of forty to fifty inhabitants per thousand square meters.[272] In 1918 the Old City of Jerusalem averaged fifty-one per thousand square meters. Using this figure, the population of Ephesus would have been between 138,000 and 172,500, with a preference for the higher figure. Russell, however, works with a density factor of 14.8 per thousand square meters, which gives a population of only about 51,060. This figure strikes me as far too low. Without providing any arguments Michael White opts for a population of more than 180,000, but this includes outlying village districts in the Cayster valley.[273]

The size of Pergamum was roughly equivalent. In the late second century C.E. Galen (5.49), a native son, estimated its population to be 40,000 male citizens, which came to a total of 120,000 when wives and slaves were included. By adding the young of both sexes up to the age of eighteen, Stephen Mitchell proposes a figure of between 180,000 and 200,000.[274]

IMMIGRANTS TO EPHESUS

It has been calculated that in ancient cities deaths slightly exceeded births.[275] Thus the population of a city would shrink unless the loss was offset by immigration. It goes without saying that significant growth depended on substantial immigration.

Nothing is known about the influx of artisans and laborers into Ephesus because they left no record. The upper classes were another matter, and a most interesting study has been done of those permanent residents of Ephesus (as opposed to temporary residents such as Roman officials) who are identified in 106 inscriptions as of foreign origin.[276] Not all can be dated, but sixteen are attributed to the first century C.E., forty to the second century, fifteen to the third century, and three to the fourth century.

If we analyze the inscriptions from the first century a little more closely an interesting picture emerges. Ten have the triple names of a Roman citizen, and they come from Samothrace, Ancyra, Lydia, Tralles and Nysa, Hypeipa, Teos and Italy, Teos, Caria, Asia, and Xantos. Those who do not have Roman names are two sculptors, Agatharkos from Samos and Boetos from Carthage, a Publius from Aphrodisias, three brothers who happened to die in Ephesus Metrodora, Demetrius and Dionysius Symmachus from Paros in Achaia, and a certain Euthenos who appears to have been a Scythian.

The family from Ancyra is of particular interest. Ancyra was the chief town of the Tectosages, one of the three Celtic tribes, which after a rather violent beginning in Anatolia, "by voluntary cession received the present Galatia or Gallo-Graecia, as it is called" (Strabo, 12.5.1-2). The head of the family was C. Antius Aulos Julius Quadratus, whose inscription is dated in the last decade of the first century C.E. He was of Galatian royal ancestry, but the family eventually became citizens of Ephesus. The names of his descendants and relatives regularly appear as occupants of prominent offices in the city for the next century.[277]

If aristocratic Galatian families migrated to the western coast of Asia—in addition to Ephesus, Celtic names are attested in Priene, Smyrna, and Pergamum[278]—we can be sure that many of the lower classes also did. The landscape of Galatia encouraged emigration. All descriptions emphasize its desolate character. It is chill, bare, bleak, "treeless" (*axylon*), dead steppe, dusty and hot and arid in summer, snow-covered in winter.[279] Its meagre pastoral resources could not support an expanding population, which is why the Galatians had to leave the region of the Pyrenees in the first place (Strabo, 4.1.13). It would be most surprising, therefore, if Ephesus, among other coastal cities, had not exercised a strong pull on enterprizing or bored young people from central Anatolia. In Greek romantic novels of the second century C.E. Ephesus appears "not as a land of sojourn, but as the desired destination: bustling and glamorous."[280] One has only to think of the numbers of Irish peasants (another group of Celts) who headed for New York in the nineteenth and twentieth centuries. The envoys who brought word to Paul in Ephesus of the troubles in his churches in Galatia might have been encouraged in their long trek westward by the thought of hospitality from friends or relatives in Ephesus.

Children of well-off families were attracted to western Asia by the quality of instruction available in its schools. According to Philostratus, "while Scopelian taught at Smyrna, Ionians, Lydians, Carians, Macedonians, Aeolians also and Hellenes from Mysia and Phrygia flocked thither to his school."[281] An inscription from Ephesus lists among the students of a professor of rhetoric two from Rhodes and one each from Hierapolis, Nicaea, Antioch, Cilbium, Phocaea, Caunnus, and Ancyra.[282] The last named, of course, is in Galatia.

TACITUS

P. Cornelius Tacitus was born about 56 C.E. and rose steadily through the ranks of state functionaries under the Flavian emperors. His most senior appointment was as Proconsul of Asia for 112–113, when he would have resided in Ephesus. He is thought to have begun work on the *Histories* around 105 C.E. and to have completed the work some five years later. When first published it covered Roman history from 69 to 96 C.E., but only the material dealing with the first year has survived. His next publication was the *Annals*, but instead of moving forward into the second century he went back to the reign of Tiberius and then dealt with his successors up to and including Nero.

A RIVAL TO THE TEMPLE OF ARTEMIS

> On the return journey Germanicus made an effort to visit the Samothracian Mysteries, but was met by northerly winds, and failed to make the shore. So, after an excursion to Troy and those venerable remains which attest the mutability of history and the origin of Rome, he skirted the Asian coast once more, and put in at Colophon, to consult the oracle of Apollos at Claros. Here there is no priestess, as at Delphi, but a male priest, chosen from certain families, usually from Miletus. He is told only the number and names of his clients, and then descends into a cave, drinks water from a sacred spring, and—though generally illiterate and ignorant of metre—produces a set of verses on whatever the visitor had in mind. Rumor had it that the oracle of Claros (in the cryptic fashion of oracles) foretold Germanicus' early death. (*Annals* 2.54)

Germanicus, the son of the emperor Tiberius, clearly was an enthusiastic tourist, as were other Romans.[283] Aeneas was a member of the royal house of Troy who escaped before the final conflagration. Poseidon prophesied that he and his children would rule over the Trojans (*Iliad* 20.307). According to Virgil (*Aeneid* 3), Aeneas became the founder of Rome, which was now the master of Asia, to which Troy belonged.

From the acropolis at Colophon-on-the-Sea there is a fine view across the bay to Ephesus. Some two kilometers (1.2 miles) inland a wooded depression enshrines the temple of Apollo at Claros, the great rival of the temple of Artemis at Ephesus. Its attraction lay not in its splendor but in its divinely inspired answers to questions. From the third century B.C.E. onward it was the most important oracular site in Asia Minor. Germanicus' visit was a tribute also paid by many other eminent personalities. The fact that he died the following year (*Annals* 2.72) boosted the popularity of Claros so much that it came to rival Delphi.[284]

Tacitus' description of the procedure of consultation is not entirely correct. Inscriptions from the site furnish a more accurate picture. No oracle was a mind-reader, and more than one temple official was involved. On selected nights clients were led in procession to the temple, where they handed over written questions to the priests. The latter carried them underground and communicated the requests to the *thespiōdos*. He drank from the sacred spring beneath the cella and gave his responses to the *prophētēs*, who wrote them down in verse and passed them to the suppliants.[285]

THE RIGHT OF ASYLUM AT EPHESUS

Tiberius, however, while tightening his grasp on the solid power of the principate, vouchsafed to the senate a shadow of the past by submitting the claims of the provinces to the discussion of its members. For throughout the Greek cities there was a growing laxity, and impunity, in the creation of rights of asylum. The temples were filled with the dregs of the slave population; the same shelter was extended to the debtor against his creditor and to the man suspected of a capital offence; nor was any authority powerful enough to quell the factions of a race which protected human felony equally with divine worship. It was resolved, therefore, that communities in question should send their charters and deputies to Rome. . . .

The Ephesians were the first to appear. "Apollo and Diana," they stated, "were not, as commonly supposed, born at Delos. In Ephesus there was a river Cenchrius, with a grove Ortygia; where Latona, heavy-wombed and supporting herself by an olive-tree which remained to that day, gave birth to the heavenly twins. The grove had been hallowed by divine injunction; and there Apollo himself, after slaying the Cyclopes, had evaded the anger of Jove. Afterwards Father Liber, victor in the war, had pardoned the suppliant Amazons who had seated themselves at the altar. Then the sanctity of the temple had been enhanced, with the permission of Hercules, while he held the crown of Lydia. Its privileges had not been diminished under the Persian empire. Later they had been preserved by the Macedonians, last by ourselves."

[Similar statements are made by the representatives of Magnesia-on-the-Maeander, Aphrodesias, Stratonicia, Hierocaesarea, and Cyprus].

Deputations from other states were heard as well; till the Fathers, weary of the details, and disliking the acrimony of the discussion, empowered the consuls to investigate the titles, in search of any latent flaw, and to refer the entire question back to the senate. Their report was that—apart from the communities that I have already named—they were satisfied that there was a genuine sanctuary of Aesculapius at Pergamum; other claimants relied on pedigrees too ancient to be clear. . . .

> The senate, accordingly, passed a number of resolutions, scrupulously complimentary, but still imposing limit. And the applicants were ordered to fix the brass records actually inside the temples, both as a solemn memorial and as a warning not to lapse into secular intrigue under the cloak of religion. (*Annals* 3.60-63)

In the commentary on Strabo, 14.1.23 (p. 25), which deals with asylum in the temple of Artemis in Ephesus, attention was drawn to the possibility of abuse of this right. In the early first century C.E. such abuses had become so scandalous that the emperor Tiberius (14–37 C.E.) felt himself obliged to intervene. Suetonius exaggerates in reporting that "Tiberius abolished the traditional rights of sanctuary throughout the Empire" (*Tiberius*, 37). He did in fact abolish some, but only after an inquiry by the Senate in 22 C.E., when he summoned representatives of the great Greek sanctuaries to Rome to prove that their institutions traditionally had the right of asylum.

An invitation to speak first acknowledged the primacy of Ephesus. In order to beat back the strong challenge of Delos to be most closely associated with Artemis, its representatives developed its case along two distinct lines, the mythological and the legal.

The foundation myth of the birth of Artemis at Ortygia is recounted more fully by Strabo (14.1.20; p. 15). Latona is simply the Latin form of the Greek Leto. The choice of Artemis to be born in the immediate vicinity of Ephesus obviously conferred on that area unusual sanctity. This, then, is confirmed by the behavior of three gods, who of course are given their Latin names, Jove (= Jupiter = Zeus), Father Liber (= Bacchus = Dionysus) and Hercules (= Heracles). It was a powerful argument in favor of the temple of Artemis that the supreme god and the most unruly and unpredictable of all the gods, in addition to the reliable Heracles, should have respected its inviolability.

How much ice the mythological argument would have cut with cynical senators is anyone's guess. The representatives of Ephesus moved to much more solid ground in drawing attention to the attitude of the secular authorities at three different periods. When Cyrus the Great defeated Croesus, king of Lydia, in 546 B.C.E. Ionia became part of the Persian empire. This situation continued until 334 B.C.E. when Alexander the Great of Macedon overthrew the Persians and assumed control in Asia. After his successor Lysimachus died, about 280 B.C.E., two other of Alexander's generals, Ptolemy and Seleucus (and their descendants), forcefully disputed control of Ionia. Rome acquired Asia in 133 B.C.E. under the will of Attalus III of Pergamum. Presumably the Ephesian delegates were able to produce documents supporting their case for the right of asylum from each of the three regimes: Persian, Macedonian, and Roman.

EMPEROR WORSHIP

To divert criticism Tiberius attended the senate with frequency, and for several days listened to the deputies from Asia debating which of their communities was to erect his temple. Eleven cities competed, with equal ambition but different resources. With no great variety each pleaded national antiquity, and zeal for the Roman cause in the wars with Perseus, Aristonicus, and other kings.

Hypaepa and Tralles, together with Laodicea and Magnesia, were passed over as inadequate to the task. Even Ilium, though it appealed to Troy as the parent of Rome, had no significance from the glory of its past.

Some little hesitation was caused by the statement of the Halicarnassians that for 1200 years no tremors of earthquakes had disturbed their town, and the temple foundations would rest on living rock.

The Pergamenes were refuted by their main argument; they already had a sanctuary of Augustus, and the distinction was thought ample. The state worship in Ephesus and Miletus was considered to be already centered on the cults of Diana and Apollo respectively.

The deliberations turned, therefore, on Sardis and Smyrna [which both produced arguments ranging from the mythical to recent support for Rome]. The Fathers accordingly, when their opinion was taken, gave Smyrna the preference. (*Annals* 4.55-56)

Tacitus admirably captures the fierce competitiveness of the Greek cities of Asia for honor and glory. This was characteristic of their relationships at all periods. The war against Perseus of Macedonia in 168 B.C.E. is of no interest here, but Ephesus resisted the attempt by Aristonicus to subvert the testament of Attalus III of Pergamum in 130 B.C.E. (see Strabo, 14.1.38; p. 33). The five cities first dismissed were too small to have the resources to support an imperial temple. The originality and audacity of the argument of Halicarnassus no doubt produced a moment of stunned silence before the assembly passed on to more serious matters. Augustus had already accorded a temple in his honor to Pergamum in 29 B.C.E. (see Dio Cassius, 51.20.6; p. 62). A second was not thereby excluded, and Pergamum in fact received a second imperial temple late in the reign of Trajan. In this case, however, the vote went to Smyrna. The year was 26 C.E.

The defeat must have been particularly galling for Ephesus, which knew itself to be superior to Smyrna in every way. None of the classical authors mentions Ephesus' acquisition of the long-sought honor of having a temple dedicated to a reigning emperor. However, a temple complex adjoining the State Agora on the east yielded inscriptions referring to "a common temple of the emperors of Asia in Ephesus" in addition to colossal imperial statues. The temple was originally erected in honor of Domitian (81–96 C.E.) and his predecessors.[286] This earned Ephesus the title *neōchoros*. Thereafter in all official inscriptions Ephesus called itself *neōchoros tōn Sebastōn*.[287] It was the first city in Asia to use this formula as a title. It was soon claimed also by Pergamum, whose right to it was much older.[288] The term *neōchoros* originally designated the office of "temple warden," i.e., someone with special responsibilities in the temple of a particular deity. When transferred to a city the title implied that the whole urban area was entirely at the service of the god. It also, of course, suggested that the city in return enjoyed the special favor of the god, which was a way of enhancing the status of the city in the intense civic competition for superiority among the cities of Roman Asia. It goes without saying that the emperor was both more accessible and more generous than any other god. The immediate byproduct of an imperial honor was economic advantage. It attracted visitors who were an important source of local revenue.

After Domitian was assassinated, the senate decreed a *damnatio memoriae*, "that all inscriptions referring to him must be effaced, and all records of his reign obliterated" (Suetonius, *Domitian*, 23). His name was systematically hammered out of inscriptions in Ephesus, with the exception of those referring to the temple, which were transformed into the name of his upright father Vespasian.[289] Thus by a pious fraud did Ephesus manage to retain the treasured title of *neōchoros tōn Sebastōn*.

VITRUVIUS

Since Marcus Vitruvius Pollio dedicated his *On Architecture* to the emperor Augustus (31 B.C.E.–14 C.E.), its composition is dated to the years 30–20 B.C.E., when Augustus had emerged from the civil wars in Rome as the undisputed master of the world. Thus Vitruvius would have been born some fifty years earlier. His father was a small farmer who somehow found the money to give his talented son a good standard education before he specialized in architecture. Vitruvius was swept into the army during the civil wars, and occasional remarks hint that he served as an architect on Caesar's military staff. Augustus later rewarded him with an annual stipend, which gave him the leisure to write *On Architecture*. It is a synthesis of his own practical experience and the discoveries of his predecessors in engineering and architecture that remained an influential manual for some fifteen hundred years. It won him an appointment as an architect in the bureau responsible for the water supply of Rome.

THE FOUNDATION OF IONIA

Afterwards the Athenians, in accordance with the responses of Apollo, and by the general assent of all Greece, founded 13 colonies in Asia at the same time. They appointed chiefs in the several colonies, and gave the supreme authority to Ion, the son of Xuthus and Creusa (whom Apollo, in his responses at Delphi, had declared to be his son). He led the colonies into Asia and seized the territory of Caria. There he established the large cities of Ephesus, Myus (which was long ago swallowed up by water, and whose holy places and voting rights the Ionians turned over to the Milesians), Priene, Samos, Teos, Colophon, Chios, Erythrae, Phocaea, Clazomenae, Lebdos, and Melite.

This Melite, because of the arrogance of its citizens, was destroyed by a war declared by these cities in joint deliberation. Afterward in its place the city of Smyrna was received into the Ionian League, thanks to the good offices of King Attalus and Queen Arsinoë.

These cities drove out the Carians and Leleges and named that region of the earth from their leader Ion, and establishing there sanctuaries of the immortal gods, they began to build temples in them. (*On Architecture* 4.1.4-5)

For all Vitruvius' care and precision he here slips up, mentioning thirteen colonies but giving only twelve names. Moreover, he claims that the final city was Melite, and that it was replaced by Smyrna. The only Melite in the *Barrington Atlas* is on mainland Greece, and none of the other three lists of Ionian colonies mentions Smyrna. Instead, they have Miletus. Herodotus attempts to explain why there are twelve cities and twelve only (*History* 1.145), but groups them by dialect (*History* 1.142; p. 70) so that no hint of precedence is implied. Both Strabo (14.1.3) and Velleius Patercullus (*Compendium*) list Ephesus first and Miletus second, but the other ten cities occur in no particular order. Strabo gives the names of the founders of the individual colonies, which are omitted by Vitruvius. Velleius somehow ignores Teos.[290]

HEIGHT AND WIDTH IN COLUMNS

First, to Panionian Apollo they established a temple as they had seen it in Achaia. Then they called it Doric because they had first seen it built in that style.

When they wished to place columns in that temple, not having their proportions, and seeking by what method they could make them fit to bear weight, and in their appearance to have an approved grace, they measured a man's footstep and applied it to his height. Finding that the foot was the sixth part of the height in a man, they applied this proportion to the column. Of whatever thickness they made the base of the shaft they raised it along with the capital to six times as much in height. So the Doric column began to furnish the proportion of a man's body its strength and grace.

Afterwards also seeking to plan a temple of Diana in a new kind of style, they changed it to a feminine slenderness with the same measurement by feet. And first they made the diameter of the column the eighth part of it, so that it might appear taller. Under the base they placed a convex moulding as if a shoe. At the capital they put volutes, like graceful curling hair, hanging over right and left. And arranging cymatia and festoons in place of hair, they ornamented the front, and over all the trunk (i.e., the shaft), they let fluting fall, like the folds of matronly robes. Thus they proceeded to the invention of columns in two manners; one manlike in appearance, bare, unadorned; the other feminine.

Advancing in the subtlety of their judgments and preferring slighter modules, they fixed seven measures of the diameter for the height of the Doric column, nine for the Ionic. This order, because the Ionians made it first, was named Ionic. (*On Architecture* 4.1.5-8)

The temple of Diana (= Artemis) in question can only be that in Ephesus, as is confirmed by the following citation. This text fills out what is said by Pliny (36.21.95-97; p. 116) regarding the construction of the temple. The stylistic evolution traced here is considered to be historical.[291]

BOOKS ON THE TEMPLE OF ARTEMIS

> Subsequently Silenus published a work upon Doric proportions; Rhoecus and Theodorus on the Ionic temple of Juno which is at Samos; Chersiphron and Metagenes on the Ionic temple of Diana which is at Ephesus (*On Architecture* 7 pref. 12).

As the next section shows, Chersiphron and his son Metagenes were the architects of the original temple of Artemis. According to Athenaeus (525c), Democritus of Ephesus wrote two books *On the Temple of Ephesus*. Such publicity would have greatly enhanced the stature of the temple of Artemis as one of the seven wonders of the world (p. 160). These books may have aided the researches of those who wrote about the temple much later, e.g., Strabo (p. 20) and Pliny the Elder (p. 116), in addition to Vitruvius himself.

ARCHITECTS OF THE TEMPLE OF ARTEMIS

> In four places temples have been erected and finished with marble, whence their names are current and most renowned. Their fine character and the skilful management of their design gains a high regard among the chefs-d'oeuvre of religion. First of all the temple of Diana at Ephesus was planned in the Ionic style by Chersiphron of Cnossus and his son Metagenes. After-wards Demetrius, a temple-warden of Diana and Paeonius of Ephesus are said to have completed it. At Miletus the same Paeonius and Daphnis of Miletus built for Apollo in the Ionic style. (*On Architecture* 7 pref. 16)

"Temple-warden" here translates *ipsius Dianae servos*, not *neōkoros* as might have been expected. Nothing is known of Demetrius and Paeonis. What precisely did they do? Ingrid Rowland and Thomas Howe interpret "completed" as meaning that they rebuilt the temple after it was destroyed in the fire of 356 B.C.E. (p. 20).[292] This, however, would be a rather curious use of the verb. Hence the activity of Demetrius and Paeonis should rather be understood in the light of Strabo's assertion: "As for the temple of Artemis, its first architect was Chersiphron; and then someone else made it larger" (14.1.22), i.e., the design was altered in the course of the 120 years it took to complete the temple (Pliny, p. 116). Physical evidence confirms that changes were in fact made.[293]

The translation of the last phrase is not entirely accurate. The original refers to "Milesian Apollo," whose colossal Ionic dipteral temple was located at Didyma, some sixteen kilometers (ten miles) south of Miletus. Its history is very similar to that of the temple at Ephesus. Both were founded in the first half of the sixth century B.C.E. The temple of Apollo was destroyed by the Persians in 494, and that of Artemis by fire in 356 B.C.E. Both were rebuilt in the time of Alexander the Great (356–23 B.C.E.).

The other two marble temples are on mainland Greece at Eleusis and Athens.

INTERIOR DECORATING

> Marble (*marmor*) is not found of the same kind in all regions. In some places, blocks occur with shining flakes, as of salt. And these being crushed and ground are of use. But where there are no such supplies, marble-rubble, or splinters as they are called, which the marble workers throw down from their benches, are crushed and ground. This material when sifted the plasterers use in their work. Elsewhere, for example, between the boundaries of Magnesia and Ephesus, there are places where it is dug up ready for use, and need not be ground nor sifted. It is as fine as if it had been crushed by hand and sifted. (*On Architecture* 7.6.1)

From the context, which deals with interior decoration, it is clear that Vitruvius is not concerned with marble as such, but with marble dust, which produces the finest plaster. According to Varro, the interior of a pigeon tower should be "covered with the smoothest possible plaster made of marble dust, and the exterior is also plastered around the windows, so that no mouse or lizard can crawl into the pigeons' nests" (*On Agriculture* 3.7.3-5). If the best marble dust was easily available so close to Ephesus, one can be quite sure that it was employed lavishly in public monuments and the wealthier homes.

VERMILION

> I will now go on to describe the treatment of vermilion. It is said to have been discovered in the Cilbian Fields of Ephesus. . . . When it is extracted under the blows of iron tools it sheds copious tears of quicksilver. (*On Architecture* 7.8.1)

"Vermilion" here translates *minium*, which is sulphide of mercury. Vermilion is in fact "a bright red pigment consisting of mercuric sulfide" (*Webster's Dictionary*). Red mercuric sulfide is also called "cinnabar." According to Pliny "the best cinnabar is found in the Cilbian territory beyond Ephesus, where the sand is of the scarlet colour of the kermes-insect. . . . The Greek name for it is '*miltos*,' and they call *minium* 'cinnabar' (*milton vocant Graeci miniumque cinnabarim*)" (33. 37-38.114-115). Pliny further quotes Theophrastus to the effect that cinnabar was discovered accidentally by an Athenian named Callias in 405 B.C.E. when trying to extract gold from the red sand found in silver mines (33.37.113). The clue that he had found something remarkable was probably the quicksilver that squirted out at him.

According to Strabo, "Contiguous on the east to the Cayster Plain, which lies between the Mesogis and the Tmolus, is the Cilbian Plain"

(13.4.13). The Mesogis and the Tmolus are the mountain ranges that limit the Cayster Plain on the south and north respectively. The Cilbos is a tributary of the Cayster not far from its headwaters.[294]

What Pliny says reflects a time when Ephesus seems to have had a lucrative monopoly on the production of an indispensable commodity. Vermilion gave bright color to frescoes, and quicksilver was essential for gilding silver and bronze. According to Vitruvius, however, "The workshops that used to be in the Ephesian mines have now been transferred to Rome because this type of vein has since been discovered in regions of Spain, and from those mines the raw material is brought to Rome and processed by contractors" (7.9.3). Ships could sail from Spain to Rome without any difficulty, whereas cargoes from Ephesus had either to risk Cape Malea at the tip of the Peloponnese, which increased insurance premiums, or be transshipped across the isthmus of Corinth, which increased labor costs.

ARCHITECTS' FEES

> In the renowned and spacious Greek city of Ephesus, a law is said to have been made of old by the forefathers of the citizens, in harsh terms but not unjust. For when an architect undertakes the erection of a public work, he estimates at what cost it will be done. The estimate is furnished, and his property is assigned to the magistrate until the work is finished. On completion, when the cost answers to the contract, he is rewarded by a decree in his honour (*decretis et honoribus ornatur*). If not more than a fourth part has to be added to the estimate, the state pays it, and the architect is not mulcted. But if more than a fourth extra is spent in carrying out the work, the additional sum is extracted from the architect's property. Would that the Gods had impelled the Roman people to make such a law not only for public, but also for private buildings! (*On Architecture* 10 pref. 1).

It is unfortunate that Vitruvius does not tell us when and under what conditions the city fathers of Ephesus introduced a law designed to make cost overruns the responsibility of the careless architect. It must have been the consequence of a public project costing far more than the original estimate. The law makes sensible provision for unforeseen eventualities and obviates the risk of having an architect decamp by securing a lien on his property as soon as he signed the contract.

MOVING MARBLE FOR THE TEMPLE OF ARTEMIS

> It is quite germane to our subject to describe an ingenious contrivance of Chersiphron. When he desired to bring down the shafts of the columns from the quarries to the temple of Diana at Ephesus, he tried the following arrangement. For he distrusted his two-wheeled carts, fearing lest the wheels should sink down in the yielding country lanes because of the huge

loads. He framed together four wooden pieces of four-inch timbers; two of them being cross pieces as long as the stone column. At each end of the column, he ran in iron pivots with lead, dovetailing them, and fixed sockets in the wood frame to receive the pivots binding the ends with wood cheeks. Thus the pivots fitted into the sockets and turned freely. Thus when the oxen were yoked and drew the frame, the columns turned in the sockets with their pivots and revolved without hindrance.

Now when they had thus brought all the shafts, and set about bringing the architraves, Metagenes, the son of Chersiphron, applied the method of conveying the shafts to the transport of the lintels. For he made wheels about 12 feet in diameter, and fixed the ends of the architraves in the middle of the wheels. In the same way he fixed pivots and sockets at the ends of the architraves. Thus when the frames of four-inch timber were drawn by the oxen, the pivots moving in the sockets turned the wheels, while the architraves being enclosed like axles in the wheels (in the same way as the shafts) reached the building without delay. (A similar machine is used when rollers level the walks in the palaestrae). This expedient would not have been possible unless, to begin with, the distance had been short. It is not more than 8 miles from the quarries to the temple, and there are no hills but an unbroken plain. . . .

I will make a small digression and describe how these quarries were discovered. Pixodarus was a shepherd who lived in this neighbourhood. Now when the citizens of Ephesus planned to build a temple of marble and decided to obtain marble from Paros, Proconnesus, Heraclea, and Thasos, Pixodarus was driving his sheep and was pasturing them in the same place. And the two rams, butting together, overran one another, and in the rush, one of them struck a rock with his horns and a chip of the whitest color was thrown down. So Pixodarus is said to have left his sheep on the hills and to have run with the chip of marble to Ephesus at the time when there was a great discussion about the matter. Thus the citizens decreed him divine honours and changed his name. Instead of Pixodarus he was to be named Evangelus. And to this day every month the magistrate sets out to that place and sacrifices to Evangelus. If he omits to do so he is subject to a penalty. (*On Architecture* 10.2.11-12, 15)

If, as seems likely, Vitruvius had read the book that the architect of the temple of Artemis had written about his achievement (see above 7 pref. 12), it would have been the source of his knowledge of the modes of transport. Perhaps Chersiphron even included drawings similar to the excellent ones provided by Rowland and Howe.[295]

Chersiphron and Metagenes had to face two distinct problems: (1) how to transport exceptionally large *round* blocks of marble, and (2) how to transport *rectangular* blocks of marble. The solution to the first problem was no doubt suggested by the stone rollers used to level the walks in the palaestrae. The great weight of the circular block was made irrelevant by resting it on the road, where it turned within a simple wooden frame anchored to the center of the ends by iron pins. Towing ropes were attached to the frames and were pulled by oxen.

Normally columns would have been transported to the building site in the form of their component drums, which were roughly the same height as their diameter. Four bosses were left sticking out of the rough disc. Ropes could be attached to these to lift the drum into a wagon and subsequently to its position on the column.[296] Then the bosses were trimmed off and the columns fluted.

The term used by Vitruvius is *scapus* (Greek *skapos*), which is translated by "shaft." Strictly speaking the "shaft" is the part of an Ionic column between the base and the capital.[297] Unfortunately in Vitruvius it is not always clear whether he is using *scapus* to mean a "shaft" or a "drum."[298] In the present instance, however, it can only mean "shaft," because otherwise the discussion regarding the mode of transport would be meaningless, "Drums" were moved every day all over the Roman empire without any fuss. Vitruvius wants to suggest that the shafts of the Artemision were monoliths, i.e., were cut from a *single block* of marble, which when it left the quarry must have been over twenty meters long and three meters in diameter (cf. p. 118). This is why their transport posed a unique problem that had to be solved in a creative way.

There was also another difficulty Vitruvius does not mention. Very few, if any, of the greatest cities of the period had thoroughfares whose width exceeded twenty meters. Certainly no rural roads were that wide. Thus a special road had to be laid out from the quarry to the temple. This made it possible to ensure that the road was as flat as possible. Given the weight of the shaft, even the slightest downslope would have been a danger to the towing oxen, and the drivers had to be alert to put down wooden wedges as soon as the shaft began to move of its own accord, and so ease it down the slope.

What happened when the shafts reached the site was extremely sophisticated and demanded a high degree of skill on the part of the masons. The shafts delivered from the quarry would have been several centimeters larger than necessary all the way round. This was to compensate for chips or flaking *en route*. Once the shaft had been erected on its base, it was cut back to the desired diameter and then fluted. This was a purely decorative measure; it added nothing to the strength of the column. An Ionic column had twenty-four flutes (a groove or curved section) separated by a smooth band (Vitruvius, 3.5.14). The columns, however, did not taper along a straight line but swelled slightly (*entasis*) halfway up (Vitruvius 3.3.13). Finally, only the center columns at both ends were symmetrically vertical. The outer faces of the rest were inclined slightly inward (Vitruvius 3.5.4). Without these subtle refinements the visual effect would have been quite different. The columns would have looked concave and would have appeared to lean dangerously outward. As Vitruvius comments dryly, "Where the eye deceives us, reasoning must compensate" (3.3.11).

Vitruvius complicates the visualization of the solution to the second problem by throwing in the example of the palaestrae rollers, which is completely irrelevant in this context because it operates on the principle of the first solution. The architraves (6 x 1 x 1 meters), on the contrary, could not roll. What Metagenes did was to build a wheel at each end so that the architrave served as the axle. The towing ropes were attached to pitons driven into the center of the ends of the architrave. Clearly the wheels had to have precisely the same diameter. Otherwise the contraption would have gone round in circles. Any downslope, however slight, was a much greater danger for this configuration, and an efficient braking system must have been devised. It is a pity that Vitruvius does not tell us how the wheels were built around the architrave, which would have had to be lifted and maintained strictly horizontal during the operation, or how the wooden wheels were constructed to carry the weight of almost sixteen metric tons.

One would have expected Vitruvius to criticize rather than admire these two modes of transport, because they are showy rather than really effective. The architraves could have been moved much more easily on rollers, and so could the columns, provided that one portion was left flat until it reached the building site so that it could not move off the rollers.

Since the ceremony honoring Pixodarus continued into the first century C.E. ("to this day"), one wonders whether Paul knew that he was not the first to "evangelize" Ephesus (Acts 18:19). Pixodarus was the first "bringer of good news" (*Evangelus*) when he announced that there was a marble quarry not more than eight Roman miles (7.6 miles; 12.3 kilometers) from the city. Three of the alternatives being considered by the city fathers were islands in the Aegean and the Sea of Marmara. Had these famous quarries been used, not only would costs have soared because of the need to use maritime transport, but the blocks could not have been as big as those moved overland. There are too many Heracleas to be sure which one is in question, but there can be little doubt that it presented few advantages.

POETS AND NOVELISTS

ACHILLES TATIUS

Virtually nothing is known about the career of Achilles Tatius. He was apparently a native of Alexandria. A papyrus page from Oxyrhynchus shows that his romantic novel *The Adventures of Leucippe and Clitophon* was in circulation in the late second century C.E. "It can hardly antedate AD 150."[299] It is a classical love and adventure story: boy meets girl, boy loses girl, boy finds girl and they live happily ever after. Leucippe is born in Byzantion and Clitophon in Tyre. The former arrives in Tyre as a refugee with her family. For Clitophon it is love at first sight. She responds, but because their respective families have different marriage plans for them, they elope. On the way from Beirut to Alexandria they are shipwrecked and washed ashore at Pelusium. After various adventures up the Nile, they eventually get to Alexandria. On a visit to the island of Pharos, Leucippe is kidnapped by pirates. Clitophon gives chase in a naval ship. When they get too close Leucippe is beheaded and her body dumped in the sea, whence it is recovered and buried by Clitophon in Alexandria.

Melite, a wealthy Ephesian widow at large in Alexandria, is consumed with love for Clitophon. He refuses to have sex with her in the country in which he lost Leucippe, but promises to marry her when they return to her home in Ephesus. His virtue is severely tested on the voyage, but he remains faithful to Leucippe. On a visit to Melite's country house he is recognized by a female slave, who is in fact Leucippe. She had not been the girl beheaded. Their reunion is complicated by the arrival of Melite's husband Thersander. The report of his death had been premature. Thersander accuses Clitophon of adultery, and Melite discovers that her slave is the Leucippe about whom she had heard too much.

Clitophon lands in the municipal jail, and Thersander kidnaps Leucippe in the hope that she will return his love. She rebuffs him, and to afflict Clitophon he gets word to him that she was murdered at the orders of Melite. Leucippe, however, manages to escape. At his court appearance Clitophon claims to have killed Leucippe himself in order to be executed and so be one with her in death. He is in fact condemned to death, but a stay of execution is imposed by the arrival of an embassy from Byzantion headed by Leucippe's father, Sostratos, who is also Clitophon's uncle. When he recognizes his nephew, Clitophon is released into the custody of the priest of Artemis.

LEUCIPPE SEEKS THE PROTECTION OF ARTEMIS

Now quite near to the country house [where she had been imprisoned] was the temple of Artemis. So Leucippe ran thither, and there clutched hold with her hands of the shrine within it. The shrine was anciently forbidden to free matrons, but open to men and maidens. If any other woman entered it, death was the penalty of her intrusion, unless she were a slave with a legal complaint against her master. Such a one was permitted to come as a suppliant to the goddess, while the magistrates decided the case between her and the master. If the master were found to have committed no offense against her, he used to take the serving-girl back, after taking an oath that he would bear no malice against her on account of her flight. But if the sentence were given for the servant, then she stayed there as the goddess's slave. (*Leucippe and Clitophon* 7.13.2-3)

One of the temple servants comes to tell the priest of Artemis that a young woman has taken sanctuary. From his description Clitophon and Sostratos recognize that she can be none other than Leucippe, and they rush to the temple. There they are challenged by Thersander, who brutally assaults Clitophon. He, in response, protests vigorously.

CLITOPHON CLAIMS ASYLUM

Now, whither are we to flee from violence? What is to be our refuge? To which of the gods are we to have recourse if Artemis cannot protect us? We are assaulted in her very temple. We are beaten before the sanctuary-veil. . . . Even evil-doers have a refuge in the safety of the sanctuary. But I, who have offended against no man, and had taken up the position of Artemis' suppliant, am struck before her very altar, with the goddess, oh shame, looking on. (*Leucippe and Clitophon* 8.2.1-2)

Thersander is dragged away howling that the virginity of Leucippe would be tested by the ordeal of the pan-pipes.

THE TEST OF VIRGINITY

After inventing his pipes Pan hung up the instrument, shutting it up in a cave. Some time after he made a gift of the whole spot to Artemis, making a compact with her that it should be entered by no woman who was no longer a virgin. If therefore any girl is accused of being of doubtful virginity, she is sent by public decree to the door of the grotto, and the pan-pipes (*syrinx*) decides the ordeal for her. She goes in, clad in the proper dress, and the door is closed behind her.

If she is in reality a virgin, a clear and divine note is heard, either because there is some breeze in the place which enters the pipes and makes a musical sound or possibly because it is Pan himself who is piping. And after a short time the door of the grotto opens of its own accord, and out comes the virgin with a pine wreath on her head

But if she has lied about her virginity, the pan-pipes are silent, and a groan comes forth from the cave instead of a musical sound. On the third day after, a virgin priestess of the temple comes and finds the pan-pipes lying on the ground, but there is no trace of the woman. (*Leucippe and Clitophon* 8.6.11-14)

When the court comes to order the next day Thersander accuses the priest of Artemis of having exceeded his authority by setting Clitophon free.

THE MEANING OF ASYLUM

And now, most reverend and worthy priest, what have you to say? In what part of divine law is it written that, when men are condemned by the government and its executive officers and given over for death or chains, you should rescue them from their sentence and have their chains struck off them, arrogating to yourself higher powers than those of presiding judges and courts of law? . . . Better still, claim a position above mankind altogether. Have worship paid to you along with Artemis, for it is her honor that you have usurped. She alone has had the power until now, of affording asylum to those who fly to her for help. And that only before the court has pronounced its verdict. The goddess has never loosed a criminal from his chains or rescued a condemned felon from his deserved fate. Her altars are for the unfortunate, not for the guilty. But now you take it upon yourself to strike the shackles from the prisoner and acquit the condemned, thus setting yourself above the goddess. (*Leucippe and Clitophon* 8.8.6-10)

Leucippe, of course, passes the test with flying colors, and Melite emerges successful from her ordeal. Fearing that he might be stoned by the crowd, Thersander flees, and is subsequently condemned to perpetual banishment. The happy couple sails from Ephesus to Byzantion, where they are married and enjoy their honeymoon in Tyre.

Clearly for the author Ephesus is Artemis and Artemis is Ephesus. This would have been the perception of Greeks living in a Roman world. Foreign domination impacted every aspect of their lives through the exactions of the Roman tax-collectors. The deep resentment this caused is reflected in this story by the complete absence of anything Roman. Blocking out the reality that the great monuments of Ephesus were built by Romans, the readers of the novel in Asia escaped into a golden age. The reputation of the city as *the* place of asylum had been established during a prolonged period of political turbulence in the third and second centuries B.C.E. It had been a time of perpetual danger, particularly for Ephesus, which had chosen the wrong side on several occasions, and the temple of Artemis became a symbol of serenity and security. The happy ending to the story of Clitophon and Leucippe could not have been achieved so succinctly and effectively without the intervention of the goddess to proclaim the innocence of the two women. It was the happy ending dreamt of by those battered by fate.

What is said about the use and abuse of asylum in the temple of Artemis is by and large correct. The two ordeals are another matter. No historical source associates Pan with the sanctuary of Artemis. Perhaps the author got the idea for his story of the pan-pipes from the fact that Alexander of Cythera dedicated his stringed instrument (*psaltērion*) to the temple of Artemis when he retired (Athenaeus, 183c; p. 49). None of the classical dictionaries contains an entry for "ordeal," so one must assume that it did not form part of Greco-Roman religion.

RESCUE AT SEA

> After that I swam for the rest of the day, though I no longer cherished any hope of being saved. I was already worn out and had given myself up to fate, when I saw a ship bearing towards me from straight in front. And so lifting up my hands as well as I could, I entreated and prayed for their pity by gestures. They, either taking compassion on me or because the wind so impelled them, came quite close by me, and one of the sailors flung me a rope without the vessel pausing in her course. I caught hold of it, and so they dragged me from the very gates of death. (*Leucippe and Clitophon* 5.9.3)

This episode occurred much earlier in the story. I include it because of its relevance to an experience of Paul. The speaker here is Clinias, a friend of Clitophon, who has been thrown into the sea in a fight with pirates and is rescued by a ship sailing to Sidon. Even if it is purely fictional, its understatement gives depth and meaning to Paul's terse "Three times I have been shipwrecked; a night and a day I have been adrift at sea" (2 Cor 11:25). Merchant ships of the period had very little maneuverability, and Clinias was quite lucky that the ship was coming straight at him. Had it been a hundred yards to one side or the other it is unlikely that he would have been noticed, because the freeboard was so low. And if he was seen, it is improbable that the captain would have done anything. In the time it would have taken to lower the mainsail, or to brail it up, Clinias would have been far behind. No captain would have considered turning and sailing back against the wind. In ships of the period it would have been impossible to do so. Moreover, time was money and life was cheap. To hang on to a rope trailing from a moving ship would almost have pulled Clinias' arms from their sockets when the strain came on suddenly. But he knew that to let go meant certain death.

This is one way in which Paul could have been rescued. Alternatively, he might have been lucky enough to find himself in a current that swept him onto one of the hundreds of islands in the Greek archipelago. It would have taken patience and fortitude to wait to see what would happen as the island moved slowly closer. Then he would have had to survive the landing. He could have been carried by gentle waves onto a sandy beach with low dunes behind. But if he was unlucky he could have been battered by heavy surf on a narrow, stony beach backed by steep cliffs.

In either scenario it is a wonder that Paul ever took ship again. But he lived through that experience not once but three times, and was still prepared to take ship for Rome, on a voyage that ended in another shipwreck (Acts 27:1-44).

ACTS OF JOHN

The *Acts of John* was written in Egypt not long after the middle of the second century C.E., probably by a new convert from paganism to Christianity.[300] His goal is to proclaim Jesus as the true God, but he does so in such a way as to throw serious doubt on the reality of Jesus' humanity (§93). Thus the book was condemned by the church as docetic.

The association of John the evangelist with Ephesus is stated unequivocally for the first time around 180 C.E. by Irenaeus of Lyons (ca. 130–200): "John, the Lord's disciple, who leaned on his breast, published the gospel himself as he was staying in Ephesus."[301] Some ten years later Polycrates, bishop of Ephesus, recorded that John was buried there.[302] This latter testimony is nonetheless important because Polycrates was born "no later than AD 130 into a family of prominent Christian leaders long resident in the province of Asia and who must have known local tradition in the church of Ephesus well."[303] Nothing in the canonical Johannine literature demands Ephesus as its place of composition, but equally nothing contradicts it. The late-second-century tradition is consistent, but its origins remain obscure.

To attract readers, and to entertain those who were already believers, the author of the *Acts of John* draws heavily on the novelistic motifs that appear in the romances of Achilles Tatius and Xenophon of Ephesus in this volume. The *Acts of John* tells of the ministry of John the evangelist in Ephesus as the fast-moving story of a great adventure. It is not history, but what a young and inexperienced apostle would like his difficult ministry to be. It is an exercise in wishful thinking. Every word of the minister is heeded. Every action is effective. Every desire is satisfied, e.g., bedbugs leave the room on John's orders and return to the bed when he leaves the inn in the morning (§60-61). Nonetheless, one or two details are significant.

In the story John travels from Palestine to Miletus, where a vision orders him to Ephesus. The incident of the temple of Artemis takes place during his sojourn there. John then accepts an invitation to preach in Smyrna, which cannot bear to be left out. Subsequently he goes to Laodicea, presumably the one in the Lycus valley, whence he returns to Ephesus where he dies.

THE TEMPLE OF ARTEMIS

Two days later there was the dedication-festival of the idol-temple. So while everyone was wearing white, John alone put on black clothing and went up to the temple. They seized him and tried to kill him. But John said, "You are mad to lay hands on me, a man who serves the one true God. And he went up on a high platform, and said to them. . . . So saying he uttered this prayer, "O God, who art God above all that are called gods; yet rejected until this day in the city of the Ephesians; who put me in mind to come to this place, of which I never thought; who convicts every form of worship by converting men to yourself; at whose name every idol takes flight, and every demon and every unclean power; now let the demon that is here take flight at your name, the deceiver of this great multitude; and show your mercy in this place for they have been led astray."

And while John was saying this, of a sudden the altar of Artemis split into many pieces, and all the offerings laid up in the temple suddenly fell to the floor, and its goodness was broken, and so were more than seven images. And half the temple fell down, so that the priest was killed at one stroke as the roof came down. . . . And the people rising from the ground went running and threw down the rest of the idol temple. (*Acts of John* 38-44)[304]

The mystique of the temple of Ephesian Artemis was still vital throughout the Roman empire in the second century c.e. When our Egyptian author wanted to highlight the greatest obstacle to the spread of Christianity in Ephesus, it was this temple that immediately came to mind. The reputation of the goddess was such that her victory was a foregone conclusion. But if her temple fell down it meant that she could no longer protect her home, and therefore her followers were left bereft. They should turn to the God of John, who manifested his power in miracles and who inspired fear in the demon that was the reality of Artemis.

Eric Junod and Jean-Daniel Kaestli argue correctly that the author of the *Acts of John* knew nothing about the temple of Artemis except its reputation.[305] No one aware of the topography of Ephesus would speak of "going up" to the temple from the city. If anything, the Artemision was slightly downhill from the Coressian Gate. It did have a high podium (see Philostratus, *Life of Apollonius of Tyana* 4.2-3; p. 169), and contained valuable offerings. But these were features of temples everywhere. Moreover, our author gives the impression that the altar was within the temple, whereas in fact it was outside to the west.[306]

ACTS OF PAUL

Ephesus also plays a role in the *Acts of Paul*. This work is attributed to a presbyter in Asia who wrote shortly before the end of the second century C.E.[307] If we are to judge from the importance he gives Iconium, he may have been a native of that city. The narrative is similar to that of the *Acts of the Apostles* in that Paul is depicted as traveling from city to city in Syria, Asia, Macedonia and Achaia, but differs radically in its report of Paul's preaching. In addition to conversion to Christ, the *Acts of Paul* makes the apostle insist on a life of complete celibacy as the only one appropriate for believers. Inevitably this drew on him the wrath of the husbands and lovers of the women who responded to his message. Thus the *Acts of Paul* embodies many of the same novelistic features as the *Acts of John*: frustrated love, flamboyant gestures, dramatic escapes, and frequent journeys. Its unique feature is that it offers the sole description of Paul. The historical value of the *Acts of Paul* is nil. Its purpose was to draw believers away from pagan romances (such as those by Achilles Tatius and Xenophon of Ephesus) by satisfying their craving for the spectacular and the marvelous through inventing legends about Christian heroes and heroines. Edification was, after all, a form of truth.

THE DESCRIPTION OF PAUL

> He saw Paul coming, a man small of stature, with a bald head and crooked legs, in a good state of body, with eyebrows meeting and a nose somewhat hooked, full of friendliness; for now he appeared like a man, and now he had the face of an angel. (*Acts of Paul* 3.3)[308]

By modern standards this is not a flattering description. In consequence some scholars have been tempted to take it at face value, because they could not imagine why the author of the *Acts of Paul* would want to disparage his hero.[309] The portrait, however, must be judged by the canons of the age. The world in which Paul and the author lived was a verbal one. Effective response in public debate demanded the ability to sum up the personality of an opponent quickly. One had to know instantaneously what sort of arguments would appeal to him. Facts and logic would cut no ice with a sentimentalist. Manuals of physiognomy appeared to meet this need. They purported to instruct their readers on how to deduce character traits from physical features.[310]

The first modern scholar to use these manuals to interpret the description of Paul concluded from the reference to his bandy legs that the intention was to present Paul as a general.[311] This is perhaps a little too specific. Bandy legs normally suggested that the person was firmly planted, and thus was a sign of sturdy common sense; he was highly realistic. Such qualities are no doubt desirable in a general, but also in many other walks of life. A hooked nose indicated magnanimity, generosity of spirit. Distances between body parts were shorter in small men who, in consequence, were thought to be quick and agile both mentally and physically.[312] In consequence, a large forehead (high brow) indicated a sluggish mind, and a small forehead (low brow) a nimble mind. Level eyebrows suggested gentleness.[313] Baldness betrayed genuine humanity, because neither animals nor angels go bald.[314] Clearly the portrait of Paul in the *Acts of Paul* is highly idealized. It could not be more complimentary, and thus is all of a part with its fictionalized account of Paul's triumphal progress across Asia.

THE BAPTIZED LION

One incident in the *Acts of Paul* struck the popular imagination forcibly and became the best-known feature of the book. At a meeting in the house of Prisca and Aquila in Ephesus, Paul tells how once on his way to Jericho he heard the roaring of "a great and terrible lion," and fell to prayer.

> But when I finished praying, the beast had cast himself at my feet. I was filled with the Spirit and looked upon him, and said to him, "Lion, what do you want from me?" He said, "I wish to be baptized." I glorified God, who had given speech to the beast and salvation to his servant. . . . I took the lion by his mane and in the name of Jesus Christ immersed him three times. When he came up out of the water he shook his mane and said to me, "Grace be with you!" And I said to him, "And likewise with you!" The lion then ran off to the country rejoicing (for this was revealed to me in my heart). A lioness met him, and he did not yield himself to her but ran off.[315]

The lion not only requested and submitted to baptism, but thereafter renounced sex. He was in all respects a perfect Christian! Not surprisingly, this provoked raised eyebrows in antiquity, and in an unexpected number of modern studies.[316]

Subsequently, in response to a tumult raised by the goldsmiths, the governor of Ephesus, having scourged Paul, condemns him to the beasts. After some time in prison, where he converts the wife of the governor, Paul is brought out and thrown into the stadium.

> When the governor had taken his place he ordered a very fierce lion, which had but recently been captured to be let loose against him. . . . But the lion looked at Paul and Paul at the lion. Then Paul recognized that this was the lion which had come and been baptized. And borne along by faith, Paul said, "Lion, was it you whom I baptized?" And the lion in answer said to Paul, "Yes." Paul spoke to it again, and said, "And how were you captured?" The lion said with one voice, "Even as you were, Paul." As Hieronymus [the governor] sent many beasts, that Paul might be slain, and against the lion archers, that it too might be killed, a violent and exceedingly heavy hail-storm fell from heaven, although the sky was clear, so that many died and all the rest took to flight. But it did not touch Paul or the lion. (*Acts of Paul* 7)[317]

It is not difficult to find the roots of this story. In 1 Corinthians, Paul asked rhetorically "What do I gain if, humanly speaking, I fought with beasts at Ephesus?" (15:32). In his last letter he says, apropos of an episode in Rome, "I was rescued from the lion's mouth" (2 Tim 4:17). No good storyteller wishing to glorify his hero would have been bothered by the facts that the two sayings referred to different occasions and that Paul was obviously speaking metaphorically.[318] They provided a golden opportunity to devise a Christian story that would surpass the celebrated pagan one of Androclus and the lion.[319]

According to Aulus Gellius (ca. 123–160 C.E.), Androclus was a fugitive Roman slave who, when seeking refuge in a cave in Africa, was approached by a lion with a badly swollen paw. Androclus removed the splinter that had been causing the trouble. The gratitude of the great animal became apparent only years later, when he was one of the beasts to which Androclus was thrown in the Circus Maximus in Rome. Instead of eating his benefactor, the lion caressed him, and thereafter followed him around like a dog.[320] In the *Acts of Paul* not only is the protagonist a Christian, but so is the baptized lion, who is more wonderful than his pagan counterpart in that he can talk.

THE FEMINIST LIONESS

In order to underline that Christianity was altogether superior, the author of the *Acts of Paul* also provided a feminist version of the good lion story. While in Iconium Paul converts Thecla, and takes her with him to Antioch. Now committed to total celibacy, she there rebuffs the advances of a certain Alexander, who in frustration has the governor condemn her to the arena.

> When the beasts were led in procession, they bound Thecla to a fierce lioness, and the queen Tryphaena followed her. And as Thecla sat upon her back, the lioness licked her feet and all the crowd was amazed. . . . Thecla

was taken out of Tryphaena's hand and stripped, and was given a girdle and flung into the stadium. And lions and bears were set upon her, and a fierce lioness ran to her and lay down at her feet. And the crowd of women raised a great shout. And a bear ran upon her, but the lioness ran and met it, and tore the bear asunder. And again, a lion trained against men, which belonged to Alexander, ran upon her. And the lioness grappled with the lion, and perished with it. And the women mourned the more, since the lioness which had helped her was dead. . . . But as other more terrible beasts were let loose, the women cried aloud, and some threw petals, others nard, others cassia, others amomum, so that there was an abundance of perfumes. And all the beasts let loose were overpowered as if by sleep, and did not touch her. (*Acts of Paul and Thecla* 33-35)[321]

The differences between this and the Paul story are evident. Thecla does nothing to benefit the lioness; the latter does not speak and does not survive the encounter in the stadium. The glory of Thecla must not distract from the glory of Paul. It is thought that the various animals, which do not appear in the Paul story, represent pagan gods and goddesses—the bear, for example, was associated with Artemis—who are vanquished by the spiritual authority of Thecla.[322] Subsequently Thecla is commissioned by Paul as an apostle (§41), and proclaims the word of God in Iconium and Seleucia, the port of Antioch, before dying a peaceful death.

ANTIPATER OF SIDON

Nothing is known of this Greek epigammatist, but since he lamented the destruction of Corinth by the Roman general Lucius Mummius in 146 B.C.E. (*Greek Anthology* 7.439; 9.151) he is usually ascribed to the second half of the second century B.C.E.

WONDERS OF THE WORLD

I have set eyes on the wall of lofty Babylon, on which is a road for chariots, and the statue of Zeus by the Alpheus, and the hanging gardens, and the Colossos of the Sun, and the huge labor of the high pyramids, and the vast tomb of Mausolus, but when I saw the the house of Artemis that mounted to the clouds, those other marvels lost their brilliancy, and I said, "Lo, apart from Olympus, the Sun never looked on aught so grand!" (*Greek Anthology* 9.58)

The list given by Antipater of Sidon is generally reckoned to be the oldest canon of the seven wonders, but what became the technical term, "wonders of the world" (Greek *hepta theamata*, "sights"; Latin *septem miracula*, "wonders"), is not used.

Strabo describes the two wonders of Babylon:

Babylon too lies in a plain; and the circuit of its wall is 385 stadia. The thickness of the wall is 32 feet . . . and the passage on top of the wall is such that four-horse chariots can easily pass one another; and it is on this account that this and the hanging garden are called one of the Seven Wonders of the World. The garden is quadrangular in shape, and each side is four plethra in length. It consists of arched vaults, which are situated, one after another, on checkered, cube-like foundations. The checkered foundations, which are hollowed out, are covered so deep with earth that they admit of the largest of trees, having been constructed of baked brick and asphalt—the foundations themselves and the vaults and the arches. The ascent to the uppermost terrace-roofs is made by a stairway. And alongside these stairs there were screws, through which the water was continually conducted up into the garden from the Euphrates by those appointed for this purpose. For the river, a stadium in width, flows through the middle of the city, and the garden is on the bank of the river. (*Geography* 16.1.5)

These two wonders should be dated to the city's age of glory when it was the capital of the Neo-Babylonian empire (605–539 B.C.E.).

Alpheus is the largest river in the Peloponnese, and flows past Olympia to the Ionian Sea. Strabo describes

> the image of Zeus made by Phidias of Athens, son of Charmides. It was made of ivory and was so large that, although the temple was very large, the artist is thought to have missed the proper symmetry, for he showed Zeus seated but almost touching the roof with his head, thus giving the impression that if Zeus arose and stood erect he would unroof the temple. (*Geography* 8.3.30)

Phidias was active 465–425 B.C.E., and played a major role in the construction of the Parthenon at Athens, which was basically a showcase for his other famous statue, Athena. It stood almost twelve meters (thirty-eight feet) tall. The visible parts of her body were veneered in ivory to represent white skin. Her garments were plated with over a ton of beaten gold, and precious stones made her eyes glow.[323] Phidias' statue of Zeus was of the same *chryselephantine* ("gold and ivory") type, but even taller, though seated. Evidently it did not impress Strabo, and the hint of a lack of perfection may perhaps explain why he does not consider this statue of Zeus one of the seven wonders. It made a completely different impression on Pausanias:

> I know the recorded measurements of the height and breadth of Zeus at Olympia, but I find myself unable to commend the measurers since the measurements they give fall a long way short of the impression this statue has created in those who see it, who say that even the god himself bore witness to the art of Phidias. When the statue was completely finished, Phidias prayed to the god to make a sign if the work pleased him, and immediately a flash of lightening struck the pavement at the place where the bronze urn was still standing in my time. (*Guide* 5.11.9)

The huge statue of Helius, the sun god, at Rhodes does find a place on Strabo's list:

> The best of these are, first, the Colossus of Helius, of which the author of the iambic verse says, "seven times ten cubits in height, the work of Chares the Lindian." But it now lies on the ground, having been thrown down by an earthquake and broken at the knees. In accordance with a certain oracle, the people did not raise it up again. This, then, is the most excellent of the votive offerings (at any rate, it is by common agreement one of the Seven Wonders). (*Geography* 14.2.5)

Strabo mentions the Colossus in the context of a list of votive offerings. Its sculptor, Chares of Lindos, was active around 300 B.C.E., which makes the Colossus the most recent of the Seven Wonders. The bronze statue was thiry-two meters (105 feet) tall and stood on a hill overlooking the city, not astride the entrance to the harbor. The earthquake that caused its destruction is dated to 228 or 226 B.C.E.[324] In writing *tōn goun hepta theamatōn homologeitai,* "it is by common agreement one of the Seven Wonders," Strabo offers a valuable clue as to how the canon of the Seven Wonders came into being.

Strabo also explicitly lists the Pyramids in Egypt, "two of these are numbered among the seven wonders of the world" (17.1.33), and the tomb, "Then to Halicarnassus, the royal residence of the dynasts of Caria, which was formerly called Zephyra. Here is the tomb of Mausolus [d. 353 B.C.E.], one of the Seven Wonders, a monument erected by Artemisia [d. 351 B.C.E.] in honor of her husband" (14.2.16). But for a description of the latter we have to go to Pliny:

> Bryazis, Timotheus and Leochares . . . were the artists chiefly responsible for making the structure one of the Seven Wonders of the World. On the north and south sides it extends for 63 feet, but the length of the façades is less, the total length of the façades and sides being 440 feet. The building rises to a height of 25 cubits and is enclosed by 36 columns. . . . Above the colonnade is a pyramid as high again as the lower structure and tapering in 24 stages to the top of its peak. At the summit there is a four-horse chariot of marble, and this was made by Pythis. The addition of this chariot rounds off the whole work and brings it to a height of 140 feet. (NH 36.4. 30-31)

The notes to the Loeb edition question the accuracy of Pliny's "sixty-three feet" and "twenty-five cubits." The correct figures and other supplementary ones have emerged from excavation. The tomb-chamber was encased in a high podium measuring thirty by thirty-six meters, which was crowned by a stepped pyramid. Freestanding sculptures thronged the steps of the podium, which was surmounted by an Amazon frieze.[325]

It is curious that Vitruvius, while offering a detailed description of the town of Halicarnassus (2.8.10-15), does not mention the Mausoleum. Nonetheless he lists a series of artists whose "outstanding skill in their art propelled the fame of their work to a place among the seven wonders of the world" (7. preface 13). They are the same as those mentioned by Pliny as having worked on the Mausoleum.

For Antipater only Olympus, the home of the gods, might surpass the splendor of the temple of Artemis (= Diana) at Ephesus. The details of the building are supplied by Strabo (14.1.22; p. 20) and Pliny (36.21.95-97; p. 116), and have been dealt with in those contexts. (See also figures 3 and 4).

If we analyze the contents of the canon of the Seven Wonders we find "a wall, a statue, gardens, pyramids, a temple, another statue, a tomb" (*Greek Anthology* 8.177)—or in other words four structures, two statues, and a garden. No common denominator leaps to the mind.

When one recalls that after the death of Alexander the Great in 323 B.C.E. two of his generals, Ptolemy and Seleucus, inherited Egypt and

Babylon respectively, it is clear that the wonders are scattered throughout the world Alexander created. The statue of Zeus is at the western extremity, the two wonders in Babylon at the eastern limit, and the four others in between, three in Asia and one in Egypt. The list of the seven wonders might be a travel poster to encourage Greeks to appreciate their heritage.

Educated Greeks did in fact travel, and so did cultivated Romans under their influence. Herodotus (ca. 484–424 B.C.E.) tells us that Solon of Athens (d. ca. 560 B.C.E.) went to Egypt and Lydia "for the sake of seeing" (*The Histories* 1.30). At least for the upper classes such tourism seems to have become a fashionable form of entertainment about the fourth century B.C.E., and it was both fueled and supported by a recognized genre of travel literature,[326] which culminated in the second century C.E. with *The Guide to Greece* by Pausanias. The impact of this tradition on Romans who could afford to indulge their curiosity is nowhere better illustrated than in the visit to Greece by Aemilius Paulus in 167 B.C.E. Livy begins his account thus: "It was now about the season of autumn; Paulus decided to take advantage of the beginning of this season by traveling around Greece to visit the places which have become so famous by report that they are taken on hearsay as more impressive than they prove to be when actually seen" (*History of Rome* 45.27). Livy then follows him through Delphi, Lebadia, Chalcis, Aulis, Oropus, Athens, Corinth, Sicyon, Argos, Epidaurus, Sparta, and Olympia. For each site he gives a hint of what Paulus saw, but apropos of Olympia he writes, "he saw many sights which he regarded as well worth a visit; but he was moved in the depth of his soul when he gazed on what seemed like the very person of Jupiter" (45.28).

The reference is to the statue of Zeus, one of the Seven Wonders. Livy (59 B.C.E.–17 C.E.), of course, was not with Paulus to see and record his emotion. The basis of his account, therefore, can only be what he knew to be the standard reaction to the sight of the famous statue. An exceptional response, which happened repeatedly in personal experience and was so recorded in texts, which then conditioned further spectators, must have been the basis for the canon of the Seven Wonders. Strabo, as we have seen above, explicitly mentions "by common agreement" (14.2.5). Everyone said they were the greatest.

But what actually impressed the visitors? What aspect of the object captivated them? Were all seven wonders statues, one might think of their exceptional beauty. The same might be true of a garden, but certainly not of a wall. The only feature common to all seven wonders is their sheer size. This is explicitly noted for the two statues and the temple of Artemis, and self-evident for the rest. Their very bigness, it would appear, enhanced their other qualities. A lifesize statue, for example, was so common that all could perceive the problems inherent in creating a much greater one. The Colossus of Rhodes was sixteen times lifesize, and Zeus at Olympia cannot have been much smaller. To succeed on such a scale commanded admiration. Thus technical competence in creation must have been one of the components of a wonder of the world. This aspect is also particularly marked in the construction of the hanging gardens of Babylon and of the temple of Artemis in Ephesus.

Rome made its first decisive intervention in Greece in 229 B.C.E., and thereafter consolidated its position, consistently moving ever farther east. For Greeks who resented the ever-increasing influence of Rome the canon of the Seven Wonders must have been a great sop to their self-esteem. If they were unhappy with the present, they could at least take pride in the glories of their past.[327] It would have been refreshing to remind the Romans where true greatness lay. The Roman reaction unambiguously shows that the Seven Wonders got under their skin.

Iulius Frontinus (35–104 C.E.) contemptuously dismissed "the idle pyramids or the useless, though famous works of the Greeks."[328] Pejorative adjectives alone, however, would not have sufficed. He had to find something Roman to praise as superior to any of the Seven Wonders. Not surprisingly, given that he was *curator aquarum*, he selected "the array of indispensable structures carrying so many waters," namely the aqueducts of Rome.

His contemporary, Martial (40–104 C.E.) opted for the Colosseum, the Flavian Amphitheatre, which the emperor Titus (79–81 C.E.) dedicated in June of 80:

> Let barbarous Memphis speak no more of the wonder of her pyramids, nor Assyrian toil boast of Babylon; nor let the soft Ionians be extolled for Trivia's temple; let the altar of many horns say naught of Delos; nor let the Carians exalt to the skies with extravagant praise the Mausoleum poised in empty air. All labour yields to Caesar's Amphitheatre. Fame shall tell of one work in lieu of all. (*Epigrams* 1.1)

Martial's list lacks the statues of Zeus and Helius, presumably because they could not be compared to a monumental building. He also introduces a false element by including the altar that Apollo constructed of the horns of the beasts slain by his sister Diana. The classical list contained only human achievements. Do we catch a fawning hint that Titus was more than a man?

"Trivia" does not mean "trifles, unimportant matters," but probably reflects confusion between the temple of Artemis (= Diana) in Ephesus. of which he was supposed to be writing, and her temple at Aricia twenty-five kilometers southeast of Rome, which was located at a "crossways" (*trivia*, "three ways"), and which would have been much more familiar to Martial (*Epigrams* 9.64). According to Graves, "Taurian Artemis has several Greek titles . . . and to the Latins she is Trivia."[329]

The freedom that Martial felt to omit some traditional items, while introducing new ones into the canon, is also attested by Pliny, who for the first time proclaims the fame of the lighthouse of Alexandria, a series of labyrinths, the hanging town of Thebes in Egypt, and the temple of Zeus at Cyzicus on the south side of the Sea of Marmara (36.16.76-23.100), but in typical thin-skinned Roman fashion concludes, "This is indeed the moment for us to pass on to the wonders of our own city, to review the resources derived from the experiences of 800 years, and to show that here too in our buildings we have vanquished the world" (36.24.101). That he had in mind the classical canon of seven wonders is clear from his far-fetched effort to claim that Rome was a "hanging city" (*urbs pensilis*) because of the size and extent of its sewers (36.24.104), and thus superior to "any garden hanging over the waters of Babylon"!

CALLIMACHUS

Callimachus of Cyrene in North Africa was a member of the royal court in Alexandria during the middle of the third century B.C.E. He is reputed to have written more than eight hundred works, but only fragments now survive.

HYMN TO ARTEMIS

> For thee, too, the Amazons, whose mind is set on war, in Ephesus beside the sea established an image beneath an oak trunk, and Hippo performed a holy rite for thee, and they themselves, O Upis Queen, around the image danced a war-dance—first in shields and in armour, and again in a circle arraying a spacious choir. And the loud pipes thereto piped shrill accompaniment, that they might foot the dance together (for not yet did they pierce the bones of the fawn, Athene's handiwork, a bane to the deer). And the echo reached unto Sardis and to the Berecynthian range. And they with their feet beat loudly and therewith their quivers rattled.
>
> And afterwards around that image was raised a shrine of broad foundations. Than shall Dawn behold nothing more divine, naught richer. Easily would it outdo Pytho. Wherefore in his madness insolent Lygdamis threatened that he would lay it waste, and brought against it a host of Cimmerians, who milk mares, in number as the sand; who have their homes hard by the Straits of the Cow, daughter of Inachus. Ah! foolish among kings, how greatly he sinned! For not destined to return to again to Sythia was either he or any of those whose wagons stood in the Caystrian plain, for thy shafts are ever more set as a defence before Ephesus. (*Hymns* 3. lines 237-259)

This hymn is typical of Callimachus' "quizzical learning and virtuoso invention."[330] The association of the Amazons with the foundations of the cult of Artemis (= Diana) at Ephesus was widespread; see Strabo, 11.5.3-4; p. 7. Their queen was Hippolyte (Hippo).

Upis (*Oupis*) is one of Artemis' many names. Athena invented the flute, which was often made from fawn bones. Sardis is some seventy kilometers northeast of Ephesus. One would expect the Berecynthian range to be in that region or perhaps farther east, which may be why the LCL note locates it in Phrygia.[331]

The "shrine," of course, is the temple of Artemis in Ephesus. "Pytho" may be a quirky allusion to the temple of the Pythian Apollo at Delphi, which would be a worthy term of comparison. Lygdamis (overthrown ca. 525 B.C.E.) was tyrant of Naxos,[332] an island in the Cyclades some 180 kilometers southwest of Ephesus. The Cimmerians were driven out of south Russia by the Sythians, and terrorized Ionia ca. 644 B.C.E.[333] Nothing is said of any association with Lygdamis. Did he recruit them as mercenaries? The "cow" (*bous*) is Io, daughter of Inachus, king of Argos, and the straits in question are not the Thracian Bosphorus, on which lies Istanbul, but the Cimmerian Bosporus (modern Straits of Kerch) connecting the Black Sea with the Sea of Azov.[334] The Cayster was the principal river of Ephesus, and ultimately the reason why Ephesus could no longer be described as "beside the sea" (*paralios*); see Pliny, 5.31.115 (p. 104).

PHILOSTRATUS

L. Flavius Philostratus was born about 172 C.E. into a celebrated family on the island of Lemnos. He studied rhetoric in Athens and Rome, where he was commissioned by Iulia Domna, the wife of the emperor Septimius Severus (193–211 C.E.) to write a *Life of Apollonius of Tyana*, a first-century C.E. philosopher and miracle worker. The result is pure hagiography, from a birth accompanied by miracles and portents to a bodily ascent into heaven at the end of his life, after which he appeared to those with doubts about survival after death. In consequence, as the *Oxford Classical Dictionary* reports with admirable brevity, the historical value of the *Life* "is suspect both in sources and details" (1171b).

According to Philostratus, Apollonius spent part of his life in Ephesus, and while no confidence can be placed in what he said and did there, anything about the city itself is likely to be accurate because Philostratus had been a student there, and the credibility of his story would have been compromised by blatant errors regarding the background.

PUBLIC BATHS

> Apollonius said that it was the duty of philosophers of his school to hold converse at the earliest dawn with the gods, but as the day advanced, about the gods, and during the rest of the day to discuss human affairs in friendly intercourse. . . . And when he thought he had enough of such conversation he would be anointed and rubbed, and then fling himself into cold water, for he called hot baths the old age of men. At any rate when the people of Antioch were shut out of them because of the enormities, he said, "The Emperor, for your sins, has granted you a new lease of life." And when the Ephesians wanted to stone their governor (*archōn*) because he did not warm their baths enough, he said to them, "You are blaming your governor because you get such a sorry bath. But I blame you because you take a [hot] bath at all." (*Life* 1.16)

If closing the baths of Antioch-on-the-Orontes punished the citizens for some unknown atrocities, there can hardly be more graphic evidence of the importance of baths in the life of a city. Here a note on terminology is appropriate. Borrowed from Greek, the Latin feminine plural *balneae*, "baths" always denotes public baths, whereas the neuter singular *balneum* always connotes the bath in a private house.[335] In addition to their usefulness for cleansing of the body, the baths were the social centers in which friends met, exchanged gossip, and did deals. Baths in antiquity met the need satisfied by bars and cafés today; they facilitated social contact. Many attended the baths daily and spent the greater part of their leisure time there.

Baths were a public benefaction, and philanthropists competed to build them. Sometimes they were free; otherwise a nominal fee was required. They could be a commercial proposition either to be managed personally or rented out to others. Public baths put personal hygiene on the daily agenda and within the grasp of the poorest. The governor of Ephesus, of course, had the ultimate responsibility for the public baths, and it was the duty of one of his officials, usually the aedile, to supervise them, to check that their heating apparatus worked properly, and to ensure that they were clean and tidy and were properly policed to keep out undesirables.

Technological advances in heating and insulation facilitated the construction of large baths in Rome in the Julio-Claudian period. This eventually had an impact on the architecture of western Asia. The first palatial bath house in that region appeared in Miletus in 43 c.e. Other major cities quickly followed suit. "At Ephesus no less than three great *bathing palaces* . . . occupied over twenty acres of the urban landscape."[336] One of these baths lies at the eastern end of the triple-aisled stoa running along the north side of the State Agora. It differs from the others in being of the asymmetrical ring type.[337] The Varius Bath is to be found at the junction of Bath Street with Curetes Street (Embolos).[338] The Harbor Baths was entered from the great Hellenistic street running from the theater to the harbor.[339] No precise date is assigned to any of these structures. It goes without saying that all the gymnasia listed in the discussion of Xenophon of Ephesus (p. 178) had bathing facilities.

IN THE TEMPLE OF ARTEMIS

> The first discourse which he delivered [in Ionia] was to the Ephesians from the platform of their temple, and its tone was not that of the Socratic school, for he dissuaded and discouraged them from other pursuits, and urged them to devote themselves to philosophy alone, and to fill Ephesus with real study rather than with idleness and arrogance such as he found around him there, for they were devoted to dancers and taken up with pantomimes and the whole city was full of pipers, and full of effeminate rascals, and full of noise. . . . His other discourses he delivered under the trees which grow hard by the cloisters. (*Life* 4.2-3)

The absolute form of the expression means that the temple in question can only be that of Artemis. It was surrounded by a flight of steps climbing up to a terrace seven feet three inches (2.2 meters) above ground level. The platform on which the great columns stood was a further two feet three inches (0.6 meters) above that.[340] Thus if Apollonius spoke from the platform his feet would have been nine feet six inches (2.9 meters) above his audience. He could be seen without difficulty from anywhere in the crowd of listeners.

The marvelous reconstruction drawing by Arthur Henderson (fig. 3, p. 114) shows the cloisters just beyond the foot of the steps leading up to the temple. These would have provided shade for his audience. The trees grew in the open space outside them. Again the protection from the sun would have been welcome.

Apollonius' criticism of the Ephesians sounds more like a rhetorical convention than an actual description. In 8.7.viii (below) he will pass an opposite but equally hyperbolic judgment on the city.

PLAGUE IN EPHESUS

> When the plague (*nosos*) began to rage in Ephesus, and no remedy sufficed to check it, they sent a deputation to Apollonius, asking him to become the physician of their infirmity; and he thought that he ought not to postpone his journey, but said, "Let us go." And forthwith he was in Ephesus, performing the same feat, I believe, as Pythagoras, who was in Thurii and Metapontum at one and the same moment. He therefore called together the Ephesians, and said, "Take courage, for I will today put a stop to the course of the disease (*nosos*)." And with these words he led the population entire to the theatre where the image of the Averting god (*apotropaios*) had been set up. [Apollonius then points out the demon (*daimon*) who caused the disease masquerading as an old beggar, and the Ephesians stone him to death.] Accordingly the statue of the Averting god, namely Hercules, has been set up over where the ghost was slain. (*Life* 4.10; 8.7.ix)

This quotation offers a perfect illustration of the incredible in the life of Apollonius: namely, his instant transfer from Smyrna to Ephesus.

Even though he does not use the Greek technical term (*loimos*), Philostratus is obviously thinking of an infectious epidemic. Such diseases are density-dependent, and in antiquity their frequency increased with the growth of the population. The city, in consequence, was the prime location. Typhus and smallpox were probably the most common causes of epidemics in antiquity.[341] In ancient literature, however, the most prominent diseases are malaria and tuberculosis, and all three types of the former (vivax, falciparum, and quartan) were present in Greece in the fourth century B.C.E.[342] Ephesus would have been particularly vulnerable to malaria because the marshy ground caused by the silting up of the Cayster river would have been a perfect breeding ground for the malarial mosquito.

Philostratus was certainly in a position to know about the plague brought to Ephesus in 165 C.E. by the two Roman legions returning from the victory of Marcus Aurelius and Lucius Verus over the Parthians in Mesopotamia.[343] Ephesus would have been the natural port of embarkation for Rome and the west.

The theater was the obvious place in Ephesus for a large crowd to assemble (Acts 19:29), particularly if they were to see Apollonius. The adjective *apotropaios*, "averting evil" is frequently applied to Apollo, but could of course be predicated of any god. Hence Pausanias' reference to "the Turners-away, the gods to whom they perform the universal Greek ceremonies for the turning away of evil" (2.11.2). Later Apollonius justifies his choice of Hercules: "I chose him to help me, because he is the wise and courageous god, who once purged of the plague the city of Elis, by washing away with the river-tide the foul exhalations which the land sent up under the tyranny of Augeas" (*Life* 8.7.ix). This, of course, is the Labor of the Augean Stables.

It is known that there were statues in the theater at Ephesus, and were one of Hercules/Heracles to be identified as *Apotropaios*, this might have been the spark that triggered an etiological story. Whether Philostratus inherited the story or created it remains unclear, but it struck deep roots and served as the basis for a hero cult offered to Apollonius at Ephesus as late as the fourth century C.E.[344]

From Homer onwards a "demon" served as the explanation of the unexpected in human life, which could be either good or evil. Naturally it was seen as the cause of disease. This belief also appears in the New Testament (e.g., Matt 8:28-34), and in the *Acts of John* (p. 135). It lived on in parallel with the insistence of the Hippocratic school of medicine that illnesses were due to natural causes.[345] Hippocrates of Cos lived in the fifth century B.C.E., but virtually all that is known of him derives from a biography written by a second-century C.E. physician, Soranus of Ephesus.[346]

IN PRAISE OF EPHESUS

Who would desire to deprive Ephesus of its salvation, a city which took its beginnings from that purest of beings Atthis, and which grew in size beyond all other cities of Ionia and Lydia, and stretched itself out to the sea, on the promontory over which she is built, and is filled with studious people, both philosophers and rhetoricians, thanks to whom the city owes her strength, not to her cavalry, but to the tens of thousands of her inhabitants in whom she encourages wisdom. And do you think that there is any wise man who would not do his best in behalf of such a city? (*Life* 8.7.viii)

The only Atthis attested is the son of the mythical king Cranaüs (Strabo, 9.1.18), and this is obviously a mistake for Artemis, the founding goddess of Ephesus (Strabo, 14.1.20; p. 15). Ephesus was certainly the greatest city in western Asia at the time of Philostratus. If he describes it as a "promontory" (*to hyperēin tēs gēs*) this must have meant that the silting up of the Cayster valley had been slower than Pliny the Elder seems to have expected (5.31.115; p. 104) and that the site of the original settlement still projected into the sea (see Strabo, 14.1.4; p. 10). This has been confirmed by the archaeologists: "Recent geological deep drilling in this area has shown that as late as the Augustan era a coastal swamp still existed relatively close to the foot of Panayirdag (Mount Pion); only in about 100 CE did the Ephesians fill this area in order to wrestle new land from the sea."[347]

THE DEATH OF DOMITIAN

> Although this deed [the assassination of the emperor Domitian] was done in Rome, Apollonius was a spectator of it in Ephesus. For about midday when he was delivering an address in the groves of the colonnade, just at the moment when it all happened in the palace at Rome. . . . And with an awful glance at the ground, and stepping forward three or four paces from his pulpit, he cried, "Smite the tyrant, smite him,"—not like one who derives from some looking-glass a faint image of the truth, but as one who sees things with his own eyes, and is taking part in a tragedy. (*Life* 8.26)

The setting for this episode would appear to be the temple of Artemis (see 4.2-3 above). Like most people Apollonius had a poor opinion of Domitian, before whom he had been brought on a variety of charges (7.20), and would not have regretted his demise, which took place in 95 C.E.

This incident is the only one in the life of Apollonius for which there is independent confirmation, and that might give one pause regarding other events. Dio Cassius wrote:

> A certain Apollonius of Tyana on that very day and at that very hour when Domitian was being murdered (as was afterwards accurately determined by events that happened in both places) mounted a lofty rock at Ephesus (or possibly it was somewhere else) and having called together the populace, uttered these words, "Good, Stephanus! Bravo, Stephanus! Smite the bloodthirsty wretch! You have struck, you have wounded, you have slain." This is what actually happened, though one should doubt it ten thousand times over. (*Roman History* 67.18.1)

According to the previous paragraph in Dio Cassius (17.1-2), Stephanus was the first assassin to strike Domitian, and was himself slain in the fracas that followed. Philostratus names him as having wounded Domitian mortally before being killed, but claims that the emperor was dispatched by his bodyguard (8.25).

AN EMPEROR STIMULATES THE ECONOMY

> Hadrian had hitherto favoured Ephesus, but Polemo so completely converted him to the cause of Smyrna that in one day he lavished ten million drachmae on the city, and with this the corn-market was built, a gymnasium which was the most magnificent of all those in Asia, and a temple that can be seen from afar, the one on a promontory that seems to challenge Mimas. (*Lives of the Sophists* 1.25; 531)

The purpose of this note is to exalt the personality of Polemo, who headed a school of rhetoric in Smyrna. Ephesus and Smyrna were perennial rivals (Dio Chrysostom, *Oration* 34.48; 38.47), and this can serve as a good illustration of the intense competition among the cities of Asia for imperial favor. It should not, however, be taken at face value. The truth is that Ephesus had had its share of Hadrian's largesse, and it was now Smyrna's turn. According to Dio Cassius, Hadrian "aided the cities . . . with supreme munificence . . . and he assisted practically all of them, giving to some a water supply, to others harbours, food, public works, money, or various honours, each according to its own need."[348] It was Hadrian's policy to invest in Asia in order to encourage the generosity of local benefactors.[349]

An inscription records that under this scheme Hadrian in 129 C.E. made a major contribution to keeping the harbor of Ephesus open by diverting the course of the river Cayster.[350] The other major project associated with Hadrian is the Olympieion, the colossal temple the Ephesians dedicated to him as Zeus Olympius, the second imperial cult established in Ephesus.[351] Whether he contributed to its construction is unclear. Hadrian was only continuing the economic policy begun by Augustus and maintained by his successors.[352]

A COVERED ROAD TO THE ARTEMISION

> Damianus of Ephesus was himself magnificently endowed with wealth of various sorts, and not only maintained the poor of Ephesus, but also gave most generous aid to the state by contributing large sums of money and by restoring any public buildings that were in need of repair.
>
> Moreover, he connected the temple with Ephesus by making an approach to it along the road that runs through the Magnesian Gate. This work is a portico, a stade in length, all of marble, and the idea of this structure is that the worshippers need not stay away from the temple in case of rain. When this work was completed at great expense, he inscribed it with a dedication to his wife.

> But the banqueting-hall in the temple he dedicated in his own name. In size he built it to surpass all that exist elsewhere put together. He decorated it with an elegance beyond words, for it is adorned with Phrygian marble such as had never before been quarried. (*Lives of the Sophists* 2.23; 605)

In the next paragraph (606) Philostratus claims that he knew T. Flavius Damianus through three personal interviews. At this stage Damianus was a very old man, and Philostratus must have met him in Ephesus. The building achievements of Damianus, therefore, must be attributed to the first half of the second century c.e.

Traces of the portico are visible on the east side of Panayir Dagh, and they were the critical clue that enabled John Turtle Wood to find the Artemision.[353] That is the good news. The bad news is the disagreement between this text and the archaeological evidence. According to Philostratus the length of the portico was only a "stadion" (200 meters), and he emphasizes that this was the completed work. The situation on the ground is much more complex.

It is now known that the portico between the Artemision and the Magnesian Gate was over 2.5 kilometers long and 3.70 meters wide, i.e., over ninety per cent longer than Philostratus says! Barrel vaults of brick were supported by brick pillars on limestone bases.[354] The extraordinary depth (five meters) and strength of the foundations betray the difficulty of constructing a processional road across very marshy land. The real benefaction Damianus offered to pilgrims was to make it possible for them to cross dryshod from the city to the temple. Protection from sun and rain was secondary.

The Austrian archaeologist Dieter Knibbe has found evidence that there were in fact two covered processional roads linking the city to the Artemision. Whether both were built by Damianus is another question. The second ran from the Artemision along the north side of the Panayir Dagh to the Coressian Gate, and this, Knibbe believes, is actually the one of which Philostratus speaks.[355] It is certainly shorter than the other, but once again the figures do not match. The Artemision is 1.3 kilometers in a straight line from the Coressian Gate, i.e., 6.5 stadia, not the single stadion of Philostratus. It is difficult to explain why he was so unobservant of the achievement of one whom he obviously admired, unless his text has been corrupted.

The mention of a banqueting-hall gives another insight into what the precinct of the Artemision looked like. It is not unrelated to the processional route. Processions from the Artemision circled around the Panayir Dagh. The statue of Artemis rode in a four-wheeled carriage. She had been dressed by women of high position to whom inscriptions give the title "adorners of the goddess." After stops along the way for prayer and offerings, all the participants returned to the Artemision for a common meal served in the banqueting hall.[356] Its size reflected the hope of Damianus that the comfort of the new processional route would attract more participants. Apparently devotion to Artemis had declined by the end of the second century C.E. because she had no answer to the crucial question of life after death.[357]

The glory days of such processions were depicted by the great Ephesian artist Apelles in his painting "Procession of the Magabyzus" (Pliny, 35.36.93; p. 111). For a description of such a procession see Xenophon of Ephesus, *An Ephesian Tale* 1.2-3 (p. 177).

HOLIDAYS IN EPHESUS

Almost contemporary evidence of an official effort of the municipal council and citizens of Ephesus to restore the importance of Artemis in the life of the city is furnished by an inscription dated 162–164 C.E. It is inscribed on three sides of a statue base and is in fact made up of three documents related to the same subject, the honor to be accorded to Artemis. The first (A) is an edict of the proconsul, which ratified a decree (B) by the council and people of Ephesus. The third (C) honors the council member who took the initiative. The key phrases of these texts are:[358]

> (A) I make it known by decree that these days shall be holy and the festival holidays will be observed on these days (*tas hēmeras tautas hieras kai tas ep' ekecheirias*).

> (B) Therefore, it is decreed that the entire month Artemision be sacred for all its days, and that on the same (days) of the month, and throughout the year, feasts and the festival and the sacrifices of the Artemisia are to be conducted, inasmuch as the entire month is dedicated to the goddess.

> (C) He obtained festal holidays for the entire month named after the goddess (*ekecheirias eis holon ton epōnymon tēs theou mēna*).

Clearly there would be no point in such legislation, which must have been rooted in immemorial tradition, unless the month-long festival of Artemis, which occured in April, was not being kept in the proper manner. What had gone wrong? *Ekecheiria*, strictly speaking, means a "truce/ armistice" and the connotation is of something not done. Thus Philo found this word appropriate to explain the Jewish sabbath to pagans (*Vita Mosis* 2.21-22, 211). In context, therefore, the term means a time when no work is done, and the same must be true of "holy days."

Some have thought that only legal business was forbidden, but Greg Horsley rightly argues that this is too narrow and points to the fact that "the celebrations of Artemis in the month Artemision included games, festivals, banquets, sacred processions, and sacrifices . . . it probably included Saturnalian elements such as the temporary freeing of slaves and dismissal of schools, elements which ocurred during the *ekecheiria* at nearby Magnesia."[359] Since the upper classes were leisured by definition, the point of the decree must be that no one else should do any work either. How could one enjoy the games or participate in the banquets if one had to work? In other words, the city closed down for a month.

In order to avoid a conclusion that creates so many problems one might be tempted to say that the prohibition of labor applied only to citizens, and that the vast majority of the inhabitants of Ephesus continued to work as usual. But the closing of schools and the temporary release of slaves must mean that teachers and servants were also excused from work. If Juvenal sneered at the Jews for observing "a day of idleness" every week (*Satires* 14.106), what would he have said of the Ephesians, who became "leisured" for thirty days a year?

Even with the best will in the world the idealism of such legislation could hardly have resisted the pressures of practical necessity. Everyone no doubt approved in principle but was fully prepared to make exceptions when good reasons were forthcoming, particularly if they were financial. For example, were ships from Athens or Corinth supposed to wait in the harbor of Ephesus until the end of the festival in order to be unloaded?

Other needs were even more basic. Fish paste (*garum*) could be stored, but where would bread come from if the bakeries were closed? A decree putting the livelihood of the bakers at stake may be why another inscription records "the confusion and uproar (caused) because of the assembling together and insolence of the bakers in the agora."[360] The guild must have had a considerable membership because there was in Ephesus "a place of the bread-mixers" (*topos tōn phyratōn*),[361] where presumably the price of bread was set by the market master.[362]

The approval of the proconsul gave the council of Ephesus much greater authority to punish violators of the work prohibition. One wonders how the decree could have been enforced. Policemen would have had to work! The absence of sanctions is curious. Were the authorities content that their decree would be more honored in the breach than in the observance? In the eyes of the world (and of the goddess?) had they not done their duty?

XENOPHON OF EPHESUS

As was the case with Achilles Tatius, nothing is known of this author beyond the fact that he also wrote a book *Concerning the City of Ephesus*. The best guess for the time of his activity is the second century C.E. His story of the love and adventures of Anthia and Habrocomes exemplifies "the basic pattern of late Greek romance: initial felicity, rudely broken by journey and separation; danger to life, limb, and chastity; rescue by divine agency; and eventual reunion through similar means."[363]

THE PROCESSION OF ARTEMIS

The local festival of Artemis was in progress, with its procession from the city to the temple nearly a mile away (*stadioi de eisin hepta* = seven stadia). All the local girls had to march in procession, richly dressed, as well as all the young men of Habrocomes' age. He was around sixteen, already a member of the Ephebes, and took first place in the procession. There was a great crowd of Ephesians and visitors alike to see the festival, for it was the custom at this festival to find husbands for the girls, and wives for the young men.

So the procession filed past—first the sacred objects, the torches, the baskets, and the incense; then horses, dogs, hunting equipment . . . some for war, most for peace. And each of the girls was dressed as if to receive a lover. Anthia led the line of girls. She was the the daughter of Megamedes and Euippe, both of Ephesus. Anthia's beauty was an object of wonder, far surpassing the other girls'. She was fourteen. Her beauty was burgeoning, still more enhanced by the adornment of her dress. Her hair was golden, a little of it plaited, but most hanging loose and blowing in the wind. Her eyes were quick. She had the bright glance of a young girl, and yet the austere look of a virgin. She wore a purple tunic down to the knee, fastened with a girdle and falling loose over her arms, with a fawnskin over it, a quiver attached, and arrows for weapons. She carried javelins and was followed by dogs. Often as they saw her in the sacred enclosure the Ephesians would worship her as Artemis. . . .

And so when the procession was over, the whole crowd went into the temple for the sacrifice, and the files broke up. Men and women, and girls and boys came together. (*The Ephesian Tale of Anthia and Habrocomes* 1.2-3)

This episode occurs at the very beginning of the story. The procession is the occasion when Anthia and Habrocomes see each other for the first time and fall madly in love. Xenophon was in a position to know what processions in honor of Artemis looked like, and it would have enhanced the credibility of his story to make the background as realistic as possible. Accuracy in details tends to authenticate the narrative. Today procedural police thrillers work on the same principle. The Artemision is in fact just under seven stadia (1.3 kilometers) from the Coressian Gate, and Dieter Knibbe has shown that the two were linked by a processional way.[364] Another longer processional way ran from the Artemision to the Magnesian Gate (see Philostratus, *Lives of the Sophists* 2.23; 605; p. 174).

Traditionally the procession of Artemis was circular. She left her sanctuary to visit her city and returned.[365] Thus it would appear that Xenophon for his own literary purposes preserved only the last part of the returning procession.

Several centuries before this novel was written the *ephēbeia* "increasingly resembled an association for young 'gentlemen,' with a (superficial) intellectual training (notably classes in philosophy, letters, rhetoric, and music are attested) coming to supplement athletics and arms-drill."[366] Membership defined social status and kept the youth of the leisured class occupied. It was based on the gymnasium, which was an essential feature of every Greek city. A number have been excavated in Ephesus. The names, of course, are those employed by the archaeologists.

The East Gymnasium (130 x 107 meters) is sited on the north side of the Magnesian Gate and was probably erected in the second half of the second century C.E. It perfectly illustrates the dual function of the institution. Adjoining the east side of the open-air exercise ground (*palaestra*) is a tiered lecture hall.[367] The late Hellenistic "Upper Gymnasium" lay immediately to the east of the so-called State Agora.[368] A gymnasium dated to the early Roman period is located just beside the theater, from which it takes its name. It faced the eastern end of the Arcadiane, the great Hellenistic street running from the theater to the harbor. The intellectual dimension is not as evident here because all attention is focused on the *palaestra* by the seat-stepped and sloped spectator area running along the wide north side.[369] The original name of the Harbor Gymnasium was probably "Gymnasium of the Emperors." Surrounding the 90 x 90 meter peristyle courtyard on three sides are rooms that served the academic side of the institution. A gate in the fourth side gave access to an unusually large sports field (240 x 200 meters) known in antiquity as "Xystoi."[370] Both of these structures were improved in the second century C.E. but date back to the first century at least. Another gymnasium lies just inside the Byzantine city wall and beside the Stadium. It takes its name from Publius Vedius Antoninus, who rebuilt it in the middle of the second century C.E.[371]

It is disputed whether *ta hiera* means "sacred objects" or "sacrificial victims."[372] The latter is recommended by the reference to the sacrifice that concludes the procession, but statues of the goddess were in fact carried as part of the procession.

It is striking that Anthia's dress and accoutrements in no way resemble the cult statues of Ephesian Artemis that are dated to the second century C.E. These show the goddess with a tall headress, heavily figured necklaces, protuberances above the waistline, and a tight skirt.[373] Anthia, on the contrary, appears as the virgin huntress, which was an integral aspect of the goddess's panhellenic persona. How much significance should be attributed to this shift is debatable. Ephesians would certainly have been aware of Artemis as the virgin huntress, and the choice of garb for Anthia in the procession might simply have been motivated by the difficulty of dressing a very young girl in imitation of the cult statue.

VISIT TO AN ORACLE

> The temple of Apollo in Colophon is not far away. It is ten miles' (*stadiôn ogdoēkonta* = twenty-four stadia) sail from Ephesus. There the messengers from both parties asked the god for a true oracle. They had come with the same question, and the god gave the same oracle in verse to both. (*The Ephesian Tale of Anthia and Habrocomes* 1.6)

After their meeting at the procession, Anthia and Habrocomes go into a decline because they cannot be together. Ultimately both sets of parents ask Apollo for an oracle that would explain the sickness and provide the cure. The only intelligible element to emerge from the response is that the two young people would share the same fate. Hence the families deduce that Apollo wishes them to be married, and then send them off on a honeymoon during which the dire predictions of the oracle come true.

The first value of this citation is that it gives the distance of the normal route from Ephesus to Colophon on the Sea. A straight run northwest across the bay was much shorter than the land route, which meant crossing the swampy mouth of the Cayster. The great oracular sanctuary of Apollos at Claros was some two kilometers inland from Colophon (see Tacitus, *Annales* 2.54; p. 134).

That the parents sent to Claros would seem to suggest that oracles were not given in the Artemision in Ephesus, which would have been a more appropriate source. Given the conditions under which Anthia and Habrocomes first met, the Artemision should have been the first place to seek oracular guidance. If the parents sent instead to Claros, it must be because Ephesian Artemis did not give oracles. This is contested by Richard Oster, but his supporting references do not really prove his point.[374] In Strabo, 4.1.4 (p. 5) the goddess does respond to a request from the Phocaeans, but by appearing in a dream to a third party, Aristarcha.

The date is the sixth century B.C.E., and nothing indicates that such an oracle was ever repeated. Charles Picard, for his part, does not give a list of verbal revelations, but rather a series of three "epiphanies" in which the goddess reveals her power by means of punitive miracles that cause disease.[375]

A small prostyle sanctuary in Ephesus dating from around 400 B.C.E. is identified as an oracular temple dedicated to Apollo.[376] If this is correct, it may be the temple of Didymaean Apollo at Ephesus that Gaius planned to finish.[377] The sole and slender basis for the identification, however, appears to be the fact that the temple was built across a narrow but deep natural fissure, which is often associated with oracular temples. There could, however, be other reasons for the choice of site.

Part 2

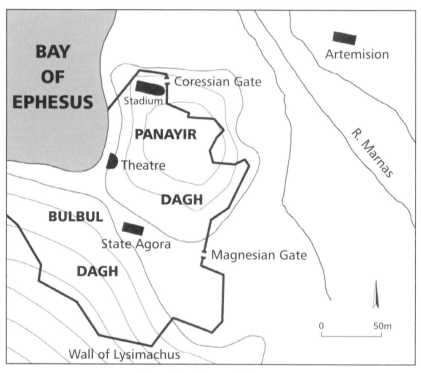

BAY
OF
EPHESUS

Artemision

Stadium

Coressian Gate

R. Marnas

PANAYIR

Theatre

DAGH

BULBUL

State Agora

Magnesian Gate

DAGH

0   50m

Wall of Lysimachus

Figure 5   Roman Ephesus

Chapter One

THE CENTER OF EPHESUS IN 50 C.E.

Recreating the physical framework of Paul's stay in Ephesus presents certain challenges. In *Saint Paul's Corinth* I was able to integrate the results of over a century of archaeological excavations much more easily because Pausanias had written a guidebook to Corinth in the second century C.E. This made it easy to combine texts and archaeology in a very natural way. I could accompany Pausanias as he approached the city from Athens. I could be with him as he strode around the agora commenting on the buildings and statues in the city center and then systematically walked the different roads radiating out from the center. Unfortunately, none of the classical authors who write about Ephesus mentions a single building, with the obvious exception of the Artemision.

Austrian archaeologists have helped to provide what the classical authors ignored. They have been excavating Ephesus for as long as the Americans have been working at Corinth and have brought to light a great number of buildings in the city center. These have been dated with varying degrees of probability, and I intend to concentrate on those that were in existence when Paul lived in Ephesus in the fifth decade of the first century C.E. How would he have reacted to architectural gems with which Augustus, for example, had adorned Ephesus? In order to respond to this question we must first go back to Paul's impressionable years in the Jerusalem of Herod the Great. Its magnificence would color Paul's appreciation of every other city he was to visit.

PAUL IN JERUSALEM

When Herod entered Jerusalem in triumph in the summer of 37 B.C.E. he walked through a sea of ruins. It had taken fifty-five days of relentless pounding by the great catapults of his Roman allies to reduce the city to submission. Herod, however, wasted no time lamenting the past. He looked ahead. He saw clearly what Jerusalem could become. He envisioned a city that would imbue his people with pride, a city that would impress both friends and foes, a city that would express the glory and grandeur he felt was his birthright. Private citizens might rebuild their houses, but he would not merely repair what he had inherited. He intended to build public monuments from scratch in order to signal that a new era had begun.

Herod made his first mark on the city by erecting the fortress Antonia in the mid-thirties B.C.E. He sited it on a spur of rock some distance north of the Temple, whose fortress had been the Baris. The dropoff on all sides meant that it could be no more than 120 meters long and 40 meters wide, yet by skilled engineering he created a building that "from its possession of all conveniences seemed a city, and from its magnificence a palace."[1] Some years later he endowed Jerusalem with a theatre and an amphitheatre.[2] Both were outside the city, the former at Abu Tor and the latter in the Kidron Valley.

Herod's next project was even more grandiose. The old Hasmonean palace located somewhere in the center of the city did not adequately symbolize his glory. It was antiquated and had been repaired after the fighting for the city. So in 23 B.C.E. Herod determined on a new palace and selected a site in the northwest corner, the highest point in the city, which he raised even higher by creating a vast podium on which the buildings stood. In two wings, called the Caesareum and the Agrippeum, were banqueting halls, a hundred guest rooms, porticos, courtyards, pools, and of course the usual service facilities.[3] Three great towers commemorating his brother Phasaelis, his friend Hippicus, and Mariamne, the wife he had murdered, guaranteed the security of the palace. Phasaelis was 45 meters high and comparable to the lighthouse tower at Alexandria, which was one of the seven wonders of the ancient world.[4]

The marble and gold of these magnificent structures blazing in the bright sun stigmatized the old Temple, which had been destroyed and rebuilt twice. It appeared shabby even against the new houses climbing up the hills. Herod refused to countenance mere cosmetic refurbishment. In 20 B.C.E. he revealed his plan to his people, who were stunned by his audacity. It involved doubling the size of the previous Temple and rebuilding everything on a much larger scale. Thus, for example, the height of the building housing the Holy of Holies was increased from thirty to fifty meters and its façade was covered with gold plates. There were two distinct areas, the complex as a whole,[5] and within it the specifically religious area.[6] When finished it was the largest religious institution in the Greco-Roman world. At 140,000 square meters it was much bigger than anything in Rome or Greece; its closest competitor was the temple of Jupiter in Damascus (117,000 m²).[7]

Even though Josephus may tend to exaggerate, there can be no doubt that Herod built the Temple with the greatest possible splendor. Philo, who was an eyewitness,[8] says: "The buildings of it are of most exceeding beauty and magnificence, so as to be universal objects of admiration to all who behold them, and especially to all foreigners who travel to those parts, and who, comparing them with their own public edifices, marvel both at the beauty and sumptuousness of this one."[9] Philo, it will be remembered, was from Alexandria in Egypt, a country that had no dearth of impressive buildings. But he saw Jerusalem from the perspective of a Diaspora Jew, and we can be sure that his reaction was shared by Paul. The grandeur of the Temple became proverbial: "Whoever has not seen Herod's building has never seen anything beautiful."[10] It is significant that this saying was preserved long after the temple had been completely destroyed by the Romans in 70 C.E.

Paul made his first journey to Jerusalem, probably for Passover, around 15 C.E., when he would have been about twenty.[11] On his way south from Tarsus he passed through Antioch-on-the-Orontes. It was the most Romanized city of the East, and in prestige it ranked immediately after Rome and Alexandria. Ever since Pompey had named it as the capital of the new province of Syria in 64 B.C.E. the powerful and wealthy had vied for the honor of increasing its splendor. Tarsus was not a poor city, but Paul had never seen anything like Antioch, and in particular the broad colonnaded avenue, the first of its kind, that bonded the different quarters. It was the gift of the future emperor Tiberius and of Herod the Great. No doubt the proud Jewish community would have made the pilgrims aware of the high-profile contribution of a Jewish king, but its impact on Paul is likely to have been minimal. He had the confidence of a well-off young man with a cosmopolitan education and solid roots in a prosperous and respected Jewish community. It was natural to him that Jews should play their part in the world. If rich pagans could be social benefactors, why not wealthy Jews?

Antioch would not have prepared Paul for Jerusalem. Splendid as Antioch was, it was what he took for granted in a major city, only on a grander scale. Jerusalem had been in his mind and heart since he was a small child. It was mentioned one way or another every Sabbath in the synagogue. He read about it in the Scriptures. It would be surprising had he not built up a mental image of what it looked like. It is rare for the reality to measure up to such images, but sometimes it can surpass them. Paul probably imagined Jerusalem much bigger than it actually was, and no doubt expected to have to search for what was central. Instead, the moment the city came within sight his gaze encompassed it. The reduction in scale intensified the impact. The warmth of the golden radiance reflected off the clean new stone of the Temple, and the towered palace drew him in. The imagery of the psalms and the prophets came alive. Now he "knew" what they were talking about.

This initial impact would have been intensified as he explored the city and became familiar with its details. The caution that had become habitual to one who up to then had lived as part of a minority gave way to a feeling of comfort. No matter how assimilated Diaspora Jews were, bitter experience had taught them that, while their rights were generally acknowledged, they were not always respected. They had to be ever on their guard. It must have taken some time for Paul to assimilate the fact that in Jerusalem he was part of the majority. No longer was he merely tolerated; he belonged. He realized in some indefinable way that he was home.

Now Paul could look at Herod's buildings with fresh eyes. No longer were they just magnificent examples of contemporary architecture. They were the creations of a Jewish king in a Jewish city. They belonged to the Jewish people, and thus in a sense to himself. Only one who has lived as part of a minority can appreciate the sense of pride this instilled. The message Herod intended to send to the world by the display of his generosity—"the Jews are a great people"—found an eager echo in the hearts of all Diaspora Jews who came to Jerusalem. Each new aspect revealed by the subtle modulation of the moving sun reinforced their self-esteem.

There is no reason to think that Paul's first impressions of Herod's buildings would have changed after he joined the Pharisees. Had the king still been alive, Paul no doubt would have come under pressure to moderate his enthusiasm, because the Pharisees had good reason to be critical of the king. But when Paul became a member Herod had been dead for some twenty years and a new political order was in place. Rome had assumed direct control of Palestine in 6 c.e. but left day-to-day administration in the hands of the high priest. Thus the country was run much as it had been since the time of the Babylonian exile. The Pharisees were free to continue their mission of education, and it would not have served their purpose to be critical of their environment. Moreover, they would have seen Herod's buildings with the jaded familiarity of natives. The great structures had been there ever since they were small children, and in adulthood they would have had no incentive to think about them critically. Paul's perspective was completely different. When seen from the perspective of a Diaspora Jew the Temple and the palace were unique and called forth unreserved appreciation. Paul is unlikely ever to have forgotten what he experienced when he first saw the Temple in Jerusalem.

A QUICK VISIT TO EPHESUS

When Paul left Corinth after his founding visit (50–51 c.e.) his destination was Antioch-on-the-Orontes. He had been on the road for five years and there was much to report to the church that had commissioned him as an apostle (Acts 13:1-3). The original missionary plan, to push as far west as possible from Antioch-in-Pisidia, had been aborted for various reasons (Acts 16:6-7; Gal 4:13), but such "failure" was more than counterbalanced by his unplanned successes in Macedonia and Achaia.

At this time Paul also had very clear plans for the future. He knew exactly what had to be done. The need to write 1 and 2 Thessalonians while he was in Corinth had brought home to him that maintenance was an indispensable component of his ministry. He had been forced to the realization that he could not simply found Christian communities and then walk away, leaving them to the tender ministrations of the Holy Spirit. After his departure, converts still needed his nurturing care. Thus he determined that his next base, while virgin territory from a missionary perspective (Rom 15:20), would be so placed as to permit him to keep contact with his foundations. His choice fell on Ephesus. Not only was it roughly equidistant from his churches in Achaia, Macedonia, and Galatia, but as a capital city at the head of an excellent road system and with an important port it offered him superb communications.

Paul first saw Ephesus from the deck of a ship. In the early autumn of 51 C.E., just before the end of the shipping season, he had sailed from Cenchreae in the company of Prisca and Aquila (Acts 18:18-19). They had given him hospitality and work in Corinth (Acts 18:2-3), which had made the start of his ministry there infinitely easier. That had been an accident, but Paul had seen the advantages of making it policy. He planned to leave Prisca and Aquila in Ephesus so that they, not he, would face the daunting challenge of finding work, a place to live, and building a community in a strange city. No doubt Paul justified this decision by claiming that it saved time. On his return from Antioch he anticipated slotting into a smooth-running enterprise that would give him a home and work and, if all went well, a number of converts. He could begin to preach without any delay.

On this occasion Paul saw little of Ephesus. The great bowl of the theatre set into the hill caught his eye from the port, but he was interested only in finding accommodation and workspace for Prisca and Aquila. He had to know where to locate them when he returned in six months' time. The matter was urgent because the end of the sailing season was approaching. If he delayed too long there would be no ships to take him eastward. Since we do not know where they found lodging, we cannot even begin to speculate on the landmarks Paul must have memorized in order to find his way back.

A WALK WITH PAUL THROUGH EPHESUS

When Paul arrived back in Ephesus in the late summer of 52 C.E. he came overland from Galatia, where he preached the collection for the poor (1 Cor 16:1-4), which had been agreed upon in Jerusalem the previous autumn (Gal 2:10). His route brought him west along "the common highway" of Strabo (cf. p. 36), which after passing through the Lycus valley (modern Çürük-su) followed the north bank of the river Maeander (modern Menderes). The road left the broad valley at Magnesia-on-the-Maeander and crossed a low pass from which travelers to Ephesus could see their goal: not the city itself, but the seven-meter-high wall Lysimachus had built on the crest of the Bulbul Dagh in 286 B.C.E. For the last three miles (five km) the arches of a great aqueduct, the *Aqua Troessitica*, marched on Paul's right into the city.

As the plain of the Marnas widened out, Paul's eye would have been caught by the splendor of the Artemision directly ahead (cf. p. 182). He would have been too far away to see any of the details, and he was approaching it side on, but even without knowing its name he must have recognized that it was an extraordinary monument. Its impressive size and beauty were internationally acknowledged by its place in the canon of the seven wonders of the ancient world (cf. p. 160).

Given the culture of the time, the religious character of the building would have been self-evident. For Paul it would undoubtedly have symbolized the forces he must overcome if Ephesus was to become a Christian city. While some might have been overawed, it is extremely unlikely that this made Paul downhearted. He had known the Temple of YHWH in Jerusalem, whose glory surpassed that of the Artemision. The Jewish Temple was bigger and better. For her followers, the wealth of the temple of Artemis might have evoked the power of the goddess, but for Paul she was merely an idol without real existence (1 Cor 8:4). The Temple in Jerusalem, on the contrary, was the home of the one true God, whom Paul venerated as the Father of his Lord, Jesus Christ (Col 1:3), and whose power was regularly and effectively exercised on Paul's behalf, as the extraordinary success of his ministry in Galatia and Greece proclaimed (2 Cor 3:2). Paul also knew that neither Jerusalem nor Ephesus represented the temple of the future, which would be entirely spiritual, composed of those in whose hearts God's Spirit dwelt (1 Cor 3:16; 6:19).

From where Paul was on the road from Magnesia it would have been natural to enter the city by the Magnesian Gate, which gave access to the valley between the Bulbul Dagh and the Panayir Dagh and had been the principal gate of the city ever since Lysimachus had relocated it (cf. p. 17) and erected his great wall, which Paul would have seen climbing the hills on either side. Any gate in a valley bottom is likely to be buried in mud, and the original gate had undergone a number of repairs by the time of Paul's entry. What is visible today postdates his visit.[12]

The State Agora

The numbers in square brackets in the text that follows correspond to those in figure 6, which shows only those buildings that probably existed at the time of Paul.[13] It goes without saying that the names of the

---

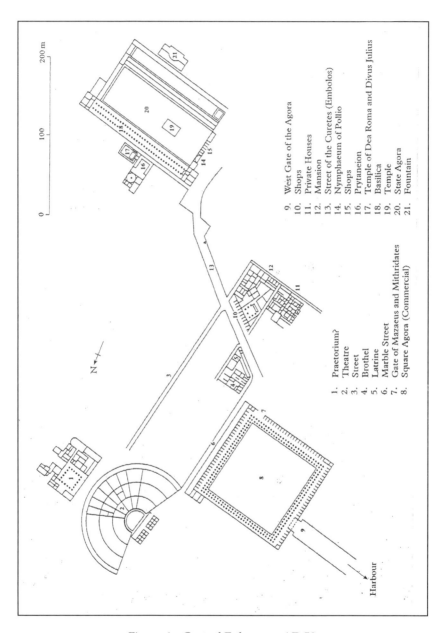

1. Praetorium?
2. Theatre
3. Street
4. Brothel
5. Latrine
6. Marble Street
7. Gate of Mazaeus and Mithridates
8. Square Agora (Commercial)
9. West Gate of the Agora
10. Shops
11. Private Houses
12. Mansion
13. Street of the Curetes (Embolos)
14. Nymphaeum of Pollio
15. Shops
16. Prytaneion
17. Temple of Dea Roma and Divus Julius
18. Basilica
19. Temple
20. State Agora
21. Fountain

Figure 6   Central Ephesus c. AD 50

different structures and buildings are those employed by archaeologists on the basis of their analyses or by people of the area inspired by local legends.

A ten-minute stroll on the colonnaded street inside the Magnesian Gate would have brought Paul to the State Agora [20]. The area has been given this name because the buildings scattered there show that it was the administrative center of Ephesus at least from the time of Augustus. The great open space (160 x 58 m) was paved in 66 B.C.E. by the *agoranomos* Timon.[14] Possibly this was the renovation of an earlier agora dating to the refounding of the city by Lysimachus, but at that stage the edges of the great space were marked only by monuments dedicated by individuals. Porticos first appear in the reign of Augustus. A glance at the topography shows that the agora was artificially leveled.

When Paul came through the Doric gatehouse at the southeast corner of the agora his gaze would have been captured by the forest of columns lining the whole of the north side [18]. Reached by a flight of steps from the agora, this was a magnificent two-story, three-aisled "basilica stoa" erected by C. Sextilius Pollio and his family in 11 C.E.[15] Clearly he followed the advice of Vitruvius that "the sites for basilicas should be chosen next to the forum in the warmest possible location, so that businessmen can meet there without being inconvenienced by bad weather."[16] Here they would have been protected from the cold north and east winds of winter.

The side aisles were 4.70 meters wide and the higher center aisle 6.85 meters. The facade had sixty-seven fluted columns with Ionic capitals. The interior columns apparently were more widely spaced because there the Ionic capitals had projecting bulls' heads to distribute the load of the architraves. Paul, however, would not have seen this stoa in its pristine glory, for it was badly damaged by an earthquake around 23 C.E. In the restoration the number of interior columns was doubled, but they were given Corinthian capitals,[17] which would have detracted somewhat from the aesthetic unity of the structure. This stoa also served as a gallery containing statues of members of the imperial family.

The only building on the great paved expanse of the agora was a small prostyle peripteros temple [19], whose narrow side facing Paul had six columns and its long side ten columns. Various proposals have been made as to its purpose, but it now seems agreed that it had been dedicated to the divine Caesar and Dea Roma in 29 B.C.E.[18] Paul would have given it no more than a glance.

Today the north side of the stoa of Pollio is dominated by a well-restored little theatre. An inscription, however, dates it to the second century C.E.[19] Whether it had a predecessor that Paul might have seen is unclear. Adjoining the theatre on the west is an open courtyard (33 x 28 m) bordered on three sides by colonnades [17]. Once thought to be the temple of Caesar and Dea Roma, it is now identified as a precinct with an altar for the worship of Artemis and Augustus.[20] By putting an Augusteum in the precinct of the temple of Artemis in 6 or 5 B.C.E. the emperor had effectively made himself the "partner" of the goddess. This unparalleled and rather intrusive gesture must have been a continuous irritant to the Greek citizens of Ephesus.

The next building [16], despite its modest size, was the emotional centerpiece of the building program of Augustus. A large peristyle court-yard (26 x 22 m) gave entrance to a colonnaded chamber. Called the Prytaneion (from *prytaneis*, "presidents"), it was the communal hearth of the city. The goddess Hestia was symbolized by the eternal flame that burned there. "The center of Greek life was the domestic hearth, also regarded as a sacrificial altar; and Hestia, as its goddess, represented personal security and happiness and the sacred duty of hospitality."[21] Eventually the hearth of a king became the focal point of the architecture of his palace and the symbol of his responsibility for his people. When democracy replaced monarchy, state or civic hearths were housed in public buildings such as this.[22] On the eight plain columns of the facade were carved the names of the Curetes, who watched over the sacred fire and who celebrated the mysteries of Artemis at Ortygia.[23]

The tradition of hospitality remained primary and at the time of Paul the Prytaneion functioned as a public dining room in which civic hos-pitality was offered, both to honor citizens and to welcome foreign dig-nitaries. As Rome exercised more and more authority the political function of the Prytaneion faded into the background, and its religious role came to the fore. Thus in addition to Hestia, inscriptions show that other deities were worshiped here, notably Ephesian Artemis, Demeter and Kore, Clarian Apollo, Sopolis, and, just to be sure, *pantes hoi theoi*, "all the gods."[24] On a more mundane level the building housed archives and donations and served as law court and social welfare center.[25] The outstanding discovery made during the excavation of the Prytaneion was three Roman-period cult statues of many-breasted Artemis, which are now in the Ephesus museum.[26] Recent excavations have brought to light a first-century C.E. banqueting house adjoining the Prytaneion on the west.[27]

The lane running in front of the Prytaneion, known in antiquity as *Kathodos* ("way down"), would have brought Paul up against the slope of the Bulbul Dagh in a space the archaeologists call Domitian Square. The solid wall to his left supported an extension of the basilica stoa and next to it [14] was the memorial tomb of its builder, Sextilius Pollio. It was much less ornate than the freestanding tower-like monument on the other side of the square honoring C. Memmius, a grandson of the

Roman dictator Sulla. This monument was erected in the third quarter of the first century B.C.E.[28]

The wide street [13] sloping down in front of Paul lost twenty meters vertically in its 210-meter length. The archaeologists now call it Curetes' Street because of the names on the reused drums of the columns, which originally stood in front of the Prytaneion. In antiquity it was known as *Embolos* ("wedge"), presumably because it cut diagonally across the Hippodamian grid of streets with which Lysimachus had endowed the city. A glance at the topography shows that strict adherence to the grid pattern would have been highly unrealistic at this point. At all times a path would have followed the little valley that is the narrowest point between the Bulbul Dagh and the Panayir Dagh. In the Hellenistic period it was widened to create a street whose width varies between 10 meters and 6.8 meters, exclusive of the sidewalks on either side measuring 3.5 to 4.5 meters. These would have been covered, and no doubt those in search of glory would have erected statues between the columns. Little has been excavated until one gets to the far end, but up to Paul's left, just where the slope of the Bulbul Dagh steepens, a two-story round monument would have caught his eye, no doubt only to be dismissed (correctly) as another useless honorific monument.[29]

The Terrace Houses

Paul's attention would have quickened when he came to a cross-roads. To the right a road [3] led up to the back of the theatre, which would not have interested him at all. What he saw to his left was a completely different matter. There may have been other private houses along his way, but these are the only ones to have been excavated [11 and 12]. Perhaps Prisca and Aquila had already found a Phoebe or a Gaius (Rom 16:1-3, 23) who had a house large enough to host the liturgical assembly of the church. But if they had not, it would be his responsibility to find a patron. Experience had taught him that he would not be long tolerated in the synagogue, and Christianity as yet had no right to its own public space. For rooms in which to gather his community he had to rely on the charity of better-off converts.[30]

As he looked up the hill the height of the buildings, the pattern of the red-tiled roofs, and the lack of windows would have told him immediately that these were not cheap apartment-blocks. The lightwells were an unambiguous sign that these were up-market individual private residences. Thus they were just the type of homes that had the space to offer hospitality to his flock.[31]

The eastern *insula* ("city block") was once thought to be the mansion [12] of a wealthy single individual.[32] Now it seems that in the first century B.C.E. it was a collection of six residential units built in pairs on three terraces on the lowest part of the Bulbul Dagh.³³ These were radically modified at the beginning of the second century C.E. when half the *insula* was transformed into the clubhouse of an association and served particularly for banquets.³⁴ This *insula*, in consequence, is of much less interest than its companion on the west side of the three-meter-wide stepped street running up the hill from Curetes' Street.

Throughout the centuries the western *insula* [11] preserved its original plan of pairs of residential units on three terraces.³⁵ It was bordered on the south by a street conforming to the grid pattern that dropped some twenty-six meters to reach Curetes' Street near the Memmius Monument. "According to the examination of the foundations and evaluation of the finds, the entire site was first built upon during a short span of time at the close of the 1st century BC. In most cases it can be shown that the apartments were in use after numerous phases of rebuilding and renovation up to at least the end of the 4th century, and some until the beginning of the 7th century."³⁶ Such longevity says much for the quality of the original construction. The first real damage was caused by the earthquake of 262 C.E. Thus this structure gives us an unrivalled opportunity to visualize the sort of household in which Paul and his community might have celebrated the eucharistic liturgy.

The pair of houses illustrated in figure 7 are typical of those in the western *insula* [11].³⁷ The division between House A at the top of the drawing and House B at the bottom is arbitrary. In reality no certitude is possible. Undoubtedly rooms where the houses met changed ownership over the years as one owner needed more space and the other more cash. It would have been easy to open or block a door. They were entered from the stepped streets climbing the Bulbul Dagh from Curetes' Street.

Internal staircases show that both houses had an upper floor, but this was out of bounds to visitors. Thus the plans show only the ground floors, which contained the public areas. Peter Scherrer underlines the comfort of these houses by drawing attention to aspects that could not be included in the drawings. "As a rule, all apartments had several heatable rooms. In some cases the upper stories were also equipped with hypocaust heating systems. A public utility network provided internal running water and removed the waste of indoor latrines. In addition cisterns and wells dug into the rock ensured a supply of water to individual households. A system of city drains under the stairway alleys [limiting the *insula*] disposed of waste water."³⁸

House A covered roughly 370 square meters. Just inside the entrance the stairs on the right led to the upper story, whereas those on the left descended to a small vestibule. A door to the right gave access to a room whose suspended floor identified it as the hot room of a Roman bath. The nearby furnace was no doubt also connected to the kitchen. The

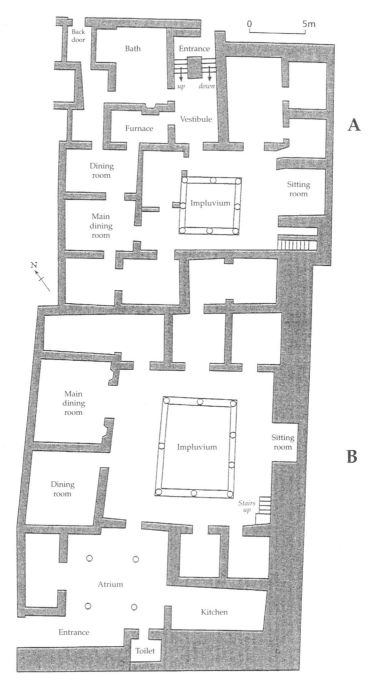

Figure 7   Terrace Houses at Ephesus

light-filled peristyle courtyard (7.5 x 5 m) lay straight ahead, with as its center an almost square shallow pool (*impluvium*), which caught the rain that fell into the lightwell. The pillars surrounding the pool supported the gallery of the upper floor. If we go around the pool clockwise we first encounter the arched entrance to a large chamber (4.25 x 6.5 m) with colorful frescoes on the walls, which gave access to two smaller rooms. Then comes the wide, arched opening of a room (4 x 3.20 m) whose plain walls were probably covered with colorful hangings. Both of these no doubt would have been furnished with chairs or couches, which permitted guests to sit without blocking circulation in the courtyard. In the corner was another staircase to the upper floor. Directly opposite was the entrance to the main dining room (*triclinium*) (3 x 5.5 m) with another, slightly smaller, beside it.

At approximately 650 square meters, House B was appreciably larger. The entrance led into a colonnaded atrium. On the far side the kitchen lay just beyond a latrine. A door to the left gave access to the peristyle courtyard (13 x 14 m). If one followed the beautiful mosaic carpet running along the north side, one passed the main dining room (3 x 3.5 m). The T-shaped mosaic floor makes its function certain; there was no need to put mosaic underneath the dining couches along three of the walls. Just beyond was a long narrow room (3 x 12 m) whose mosaic floor suggests that it was part of the public area, probably a sitting room, as was the very small one (1.1 x 1.5 m) on the other side of the courtyard. Just beyond in the corner were steps to the upper floor.

In these brief descriptions I have not mentioned the frescoes that covered many of the walls, because no date is assigned to them. It would be unreasonable to think that they were not renewed as they discolored with age and/or as fashions changed. If we do not know what precise images adorned the walls at the time of Paul, we can be quiet sure that they were colorful and cheerful.

Houses A and B contain all the architectural features of the classical Roman *domus* "house." The privileged state enjoyed by the occupants and their immediate neighbors can be gauged from the fact that in an official description of the city of Rome from the fourth century c.e. there were only 1,797 "houses" as against 46,602 apartment blocks.[39] Yet these in Ephesus were not the palaces of great magnates. They were the houses of relatively affluent people who could afford space and comfort. Paul would have been very lucky to convert one of the owners; the percentages were certainly not in his favor. But he had done so at Corinth, where Gaius was one of his very first converts (1 Cor 1:14), and he trusted God to aid him here.

Nonetheless, if we look at the public space available in either of these houses from the perspective of Paul as a pastor, problems immediately surface. There is no way of computing the number of believers in Ephesus, but it would be extremely surprising if they were fewer than the converts that Paul made in Corinth. On the basis of the names given in Acts and Paul's letters we can estimate that the minimum number of Christians in Corinth was between forty and fifty.[40] Only a fraction of these could have been accommodated in either of the dining rooms (House A: 16.5 m²; House B: 21.5 m²), even if the guests sat side by side on the couches on which diners normally reclined. The rest of the community had to be accommodated in the sitting areas (House A: 40.4 m²; House B: 46 m²) located off the peristyle courtyard. We must assume, however, that couches, chairs, and tables would have taken up at least half the available space. In consequence it would be surprising if House A could handle twenty sitting guests in comfort. House B had space for slightly more.

Just these elementary calculations highlight how problematic it would be to get all the converts in Ephesus into one place even in these spacious houses.[41] The traditional arrangement of space in the *domus* necessarily imposed a division within the community. Those in the heated dining room would be much more comfortable than those in the sitting rooms, which were exposed to the cold air in the lightwell. Believers were divided into those who got the best and those who received much less.

Since Paul did not write to the church at Ephesus we shall never know whether it developed the problems that plagued the church at Corinth. The class divide there, however, is clear in Paul's bitter criticism of those who had too much to eat and drink: "Do you despise the church of God and humiliate those who have nothing?" (1 Cor 11:21-22). In this instance we can safely assume that the host made sure to invite friends of his social class to arrive early in order to guarantee them places in the dining room, where he entertained them royally. He would then expect the same preferential treatment when his friends in their turn hosted the liturgical assembly. When those who were not as free to dispose of their time (small shopkeepers, slaves) arrived later, they had to be content with chairs (if they were lucky) in cold rooms off the peristyle courtyard. The difference would be accentuated if the host also discriminated in terms of the food he provided. The entire fifth satire of Juvenal is devoted to the humiliation of poor clients at the tables of their wealthy patron; they could see much better dishes being brought to his real friends.[42]

These problems, however, would arise only when the "whole" church came together, e.g., in the case of Gaius of Corinth, "who is host to me and to the *whole* church" (Rom 16:23). Note also that when "the *whole* church is assembled" (1 Cor 14:23) some have to "sit" (14:30). One might assume, in consequence, that this sort of general assembly was unusual, not only because of the difficulty of finding any private space big enough but also because of the problems that developed even when it was available. Nonetheless, it had to happen occasionally, otherwise the unity of the church, whether at Corinth or Ephesus, would have been merely notional. In all probability the normal assembly would have been in sub-units of the community. Groups of ten or so met "in the home of X or Y" (cf. 1 Cor 16:19; Rom 16:5; Col 4:15; Phlm 2). Here I translate *oikos* by "home" rather than "house," which appears in all translations, because "house" can give a very false impression (see above). As far as we know, the majority of first-generation Christians could not have afforded a "house" (cf. 1 Cor 1:26). Their options were very limited. Either they owned or rented a cramped apartment in a block with many others or they lived above their workplace in one of the commercial markets. The latter is likely to have been the case for Prisca and Aquila. Were Paul their guest, he would have slept among the rolls of leather and canvas below.[43] We shall see just this sort of commercial market as we continue to walk with Paul through Ephesus.

The Square Agora and the Theatre

As Paul strolled on he would have noticed on his left an octagonal monument with a polygonal roof, but he is unlikely to have known that it was the tomb of Arsinoë,[44] the youngest sister of the famous Cleopatra VII, who had her murdered in Ephesus by Mark Antony in 41 B.C.E.[45] Just beyond was a U-shaped monument. It was built toward the end of the second century B.C.E. in honor of Androclus, the mythical founder of Ionian Ephesus.[46]

Paul, of course, would not have seen the magnificently reconstructed two-story facade of the Library of Celsus, which has become the trademark of Ephesus in much the same way that the so-called Tower of David symbolizes Jerusalem. It was not built until the first quarter of the second century C.E. Paul, however, would have become familiar with the imposing structure beside it. Inscriptions record that in 3 B.C.E. two imperial freedmen, Mazaeus and Mithridates, erected this three-way gate (*triodos*) [7] in honor of Augustus and his family at the point where the procession glorifying Artemis turned left towards Ortygia, her traditional birthplace.[47]

It also gave entrance to what an inscription identifies as the *Tetragonos Agora*, "the Square Marketplace" [8]. This great area had served the commercial life of Ephesus since the time of Lysimachus, when the ground level in this area was three meters lower, but it received its current dimensions (112 x 112 m) only in the late first century B.C.E., when a complete rebuilding doubled its size.[48] This must have been one of the first fruits of the building program of the emperor Augustus. The agora needed to be rebuilt again after the earthquake of 23 C.E., but it was functioning normally in 43 C.E. when an association of Roman merchants erected there a statue of the emperor Claudius.[49]

The sixty or so shops that surrounded three sides of its periphery provided the sort of space in which Paul, Prisca, and Aquila plied their trade, and perhaps lived.[50] Their main light source was a door that looked out onto a magnificent two-story, two-aisled portico running along all four sides and pierced by gates on the north and west. The latter was the principal entrance [9], and was obviously designed more to impress visitors arriving via the West Road (24 x 160 m) from the harbor than to facilitate the movement of goods. These would have had to be dragged up a flight of ten steps between colonnaded wings.

After a glance at the agora, whose function he understood immediately, Paul went back through the Gate of Masaeus and Mithridates and turned left onto Marble Street [6]. Work may already have begun on a great elevated stoa on the left. Called the Doric Stoa or the Hall of Nero because of an inscription dedicating it to Nero and his mother Agrippina, it would have been completed some time between 54 and 59 C.E.[51] Behind the eastern portico of the street were the usual shops. Multi-story *insulae* climbed the slope of the Panayir Dagh.[52] The accommodation they offered in cramped, noisy apartments was greatly inferior to that of the Terrace Houses [11] we have seen above. These apartment buildings were served by the parallel streets crossing Curetes' Street.

It was once thought that the great theatre [2] had been built by Lysimachus, but the current opinion is that no theatre existed before the first century B.C.E. The foundations may have been laid to celebrate the incorporation of Asia as a Roman province with Ephesus as its capital in 133 B.C.E.[53] The rapid growth of the city stimulated by the building program of Augustus meant that further tiers of seats had to be added in the course of the first century C.E. Thus its precise configuration at the time of Paul, when it was the scene of the riot of the silversmiths, is uncertain.[54] Inscriptions furnish information as to where the city council (*boulē*), the council of elders (*gerousia*), the youth association (*ephebes*), etc. had their reserved seats.[55]

Directly above the theatre is a palatial mansion [1] built around a peristyle courtyard open to the west. Constructed in the Hellenistic period, its prime situation guaranteed that it remained in use into late antiquity.[56] There is no proof that it was the residence (*praetorium*) of the proconsul of Asia, the Roman official who governed the province, but no site could be more appropriate. The view over the city and the harbor was unparalleled and the symbolic value was immense. It dominated the theatre, which was the meeting place of the municipal council (*boulē*) and the assembly of citizens (*ekklēsia*). These could not have been unaware that Rome was looking over their shoulders as they deliberated.[57]

Like visitors today, Paul would have gazed with wonder at the great colonnaded street running west from the theatre to the harbor, where it terminated in a magnificent gate. It gets its present name, the "Arcadian Way," because of a major restoration by the emperor Arcadius (395–408), but it was in fact laid down by one of his predecessors in the first century B.C.E. It was eleven meters wide and three stadia (528 m) long.[58] All the great recreational institutions that line its north side—the Theatre Gymnasium, the Halls of Verluanus, the Harbor Gymnasium and Baths—did not exist at the time of Paul, but it is most improbable that such prime real estate was not built on. Certainly there must have been warehouses lining the quays around the harbor.

The street running north from the theatre, today called Theatre Street, does not fit the Hippodamian grid pattern of the Hellenistic city. This can be taken as a sign of its antiquity, when it was known as *plateia in Coressus*, the "street in Coressus."[59] It runs along the base of Panayir Dagh and would have brought Paul into the oldest part of Ephesus. The little hill on his left is most probably where the first Ionians settled.[60]

If Paul bore to his right at that point he would have passed the stadium, which came into being with the Hellenistic city. Perhaps it reminded him of the site of the Isthmian Games at Corinth, which had provided him with a theological image (1 Cor 9:24-27). During his stay Paul certainly could not have ignored its existence. It might not have attracted the crowds that attended the great pan-Hellenic games in Corinth, but since the fourth century B.C.E. it had hosted the Ephesia, a pan-Ionian festival celebrated each year in the month of Artemisium (April). There were all sorts of contests. "Music was emphasized, and it is not unlikely that the musical program included the type of choral dance described by Aelian [*Hist. An.* 12.9] and performed by maidens in the temple of Artemis: 'The sweet maidens, daughters of Lydia, sport and lightly leap and clap their hands in the temple of Artemis the Fair at Ephesus, now sinking down upon their haunches and again springing up like a hopping wagtail.'"[61] In the second century *Acts of Paul* the stadium is the scene of Paul's fictional encounter with the baptized lion (see p. 158).

The longer Paul lived in Ephesus the more conscious he would have become that the semicircular route he had followed through the city was the Processional Way of Artemis. Periodically her cult statue was carried along those streets with great solemnity both to assert her rights as patroness and to remind the inhabitants of the foundation myth that made Ephesus unique. The proud insistence on the international fame of *their* goddess strengthened civic pride, which the authorities no doubt hoped would overflow into benefactions, be they ever so humble.

Once Paul stepped outside the Coressian Gate the Artemision filled his eye. It was just under a mile (1.3 km) away, and now he was seeing it from the front, as the architect intended. Towering majestically over its *temenos* wall and the covered processional stoa (cf. p. 114), the eight tall columns with their Ionic capitals supported a simple architrave, above which was a frieze decorated by small tooth-like features called *dentils*, on which rested a pediment crowded with sculptured figures. *Acroteria* (probably symmetrical floral designs) on the apex and the two ends softened the angularity of the triangle (cf. fig. 3).

As he contemplated such beauty Paul could not be simply dismissive, as he might have been when he first saw it from afar. Along his way there would have been many signs that forced him to realize the grip Artemis had on the hearts of the people of Ephesus. There had been no such dominant god or goddess at Corinth, and the fragmentation of pagan religion had worked in his favor. Certainly the Greek, Roman and Egyptian deities worshiped at Corinth also had their devotees in Ephesus,[62] but no one challenged the supreme authority of Artemis. Unlike these others, her religion had not been imported by any foreigner, whether Greek, Roman, or Egyptian. Her indigenous origins went back to the dawn of the world. She was local. She had been born there before the Greeks arrived, and her prestige was intertwined with the development of the city throughout all its history. If she was worshiped as far west as the limit of the known world, it was because Ephesians had brought her there (cf. p. 5). Artemis was part of the fabric of Ephesus, and the city was unthinkable without her. Ministry in Ephesus, Paul mused, was going to be very different.

Chapter Two

PAUL'S MINISTRY IN EPHESUS

According to Luke, Paul spent two years and three months (Acts 19:8-10) or three years (Acts 20:31) in Ephesus. The latter figure is obviously a rounding up of the former, whose rather awkward precision recommends its historicity. Moreover, given what Paul accomplished while in Ephesus, it is a very plausible time-span, particularly when it is contrasted with what he achieved during the eighteen months he spent in Corinth (Acts 18:11). Thus if Paul arrived in Ephesus in August of 52 C.E., he would have left in September or October of 54. Before we look at the details, it will be helpful to see in outline what our sources report or hint of his activities during this period.

PAUL'S YEARS IN EPHESUS

Date	Epistles	Acts
Nov. 51	Jerusalem Conference (Gal 2:1).	Jerusalem Conference (15:1-29).
Winter 51–52	Paul in Antioch (Gal 2:11).	Paul in Antioch (15:30; 18:22).
Summer 52	Paul in Galatia (1 Cor 16:1).	Paul in Galatia and Phrygia (18:23).
	Apollos to Corinth (1 Cor 3:6).	Apollos to Corinth (18:24; 19:1).
September 52	Paul arrives in Ephesus (1 Cor 16:8).	Paul in Ephesus for two years and three months (19:8-10) or three years (20:31).
	Judaizers in Galatia (Gal 1:7).	
Winter 52–53	Consolidation of church in Ephesus. Beginning of mission to Asia.	
Spring 53	Epaphras preaches in Lycus valley (Col 1:7; 4:12).	
	Bad news from Galatia. In response Paul writes **Galatians**.	
	Paul writes **Philippians C** (3:2–4:1).	
Summer 53	Money from Philippi (Phil 4:18).	
	Paul writes **Philippians A** (4:10-20).	
	Paul and coworkers arrested (Col 4:10-14; Phlm 23-24).	

Date	Epistles	Acts
	From prison Paul writes **Philippians B** (1:1–3:1 + 4:2-9), **Colossians**, **Philemon**.	
	Paul liberated.	
	Apollos to Ephesus (1 Cor 16:12).	
	Paul writes **"Previous Letter"** to Corinth (1 Cor 5:9).	
	Paul travels to Lycus valley (?) (Phlm 22).	
Winter 53–54	Paul winters in Ephesus.	
April 54	Chloe's people to Corinth and back to Ephesus (1 Cor 1:11).	
	Judaizers from Galatia pass through Macedonia to Corinth.	
May 54	Timothy to Corinth (1 Cor 4:17).	
	Arrival in Ephesus of Stephanas etc. (1 Cor 16:17) with letter (1 Cor 7:1).	
	Paul writes **1 Corinthians**, planning to stay in Ephesus until Pentecost (2 June), then go to Macedonia, Corinth (1 Cor 16:5-6), and Jerusalem (1 Cor 16:3).	Paul plans to go to Macedonia, Achaia, and Jerusalem (19:21).
June 54	Timothy returns to Ephesus.	
		Timothy and Erastus to Macedonia (19:22).
Summer 54	Paul's second visit to Corinth (2 Cor 13:2).	
	Paul returns to Ephesus via Macedonia (2 Cor 1:23–2:1).	
	Titus to Corinth with **"Severe Letter"** (2 Cor 2:4, 13).	
	Paul suffers affliction in Asia (2 Cor 1:8)	Demonstration in Ephesus against Paul (19:23-41).
October 54	Paul to Troas (2 Cor 2:12).	
	Paul to Macedonia (2 Cor 2:23).	Paul to Macedonia (20:1).

HEARING ABOUT APOLLOS

In all probability one of the first topics of conversation between Prisca and Aquila and Paul concerned Apollos, who shortly before had left for Corinth. Apart from two references in Paul's correspondence with

Corinth (1 Cor 3:6; 16:12), our only source regarding this important individual is Acts 18:24-28, which exists in two different versions called the Alexandrian Text and the Western Text. These agree regarding his background and activity (vv. 24-26):

> Now a Jew named Apollos, a native of Alexandria, came to Ephesus. He was an eloquent man, well versed in the Scriptures. He had been instructed in the way of the Lord; and being fervent in spirit, he spoke and taught accurately the things concerning Jesus, knowing only the baptism of John. He began to speak boldly in the synagogue, but when (Priscilla and) Aquila heard him, they took him and expounded the way of God (the Way) more accurately. (RSV)[63]

The two versions disagree, however, on how Apollos got from Ephesus to Corinth (vv. 27-28):

Alexandrian Text	Western Text
	Certain Corinthians residing at Ephesus, who had heard him,
When he wished to cross to Achaia, the brethren encouraged him,	begged him to come home with them.
	When he agreed,
and wrote to the disciples	the Ephesians wrote to the disciples at Corinth
to receive him.	to receive him.
When he arrived	He, having left to reside in Achaia,
He gave great service	gave great service
to those who through grace had believed.	to the churches.
For he powerfully refuted the Jews in public, showing by the Scriptures that the Christ was Jesus.	For he powerfully refuted the Jews in public, showing by the Scriptures that the Christ was Jesus.

The differences are considerable, but it is not difficult to see that the Western Text corrects the Alexandrian Text by neatly tying up its loose ends, namely (1) why did Apollos go to Achaia and (2) where was the main Christian community in Achaia? The first question is answered by the introduction of the invitation by Corinthian business travelers returning home. The double mention of Corinth responds to the second question. In making these insertions, however, the Western Text created another problem. What need had Apollos of a letter of introduction from Ephesus when he was accompanied by members of the Corinthian community, who could vouch for him?

The first part of the story also has its problems. We are told that Apollos "spoke and taught accurately the things concerning Jesus." Yet he had experienced "only the baptism of John." If we accept the latter, he could not have known the Passion and resurrection of Jesus, and so could not have spoken "accurately" about his career. If we look at the two phrases a little more closely, however, it becomes clear that they do not fit well together. "Knowing only the baptism of John" looks like an afterthought. It is simply juxtaposed to what precedes. Were a single author to have written the whole sentence, one would have expected something like "*although* he knew only the baptism of John, *nonetheless* he taught accurately the things concerning Jesus."

The only reasonable hypothesis to explain the tension is to identify "knowing only the baptism of John" as an addition made to justify the need for further instruction by Prisca and Aquila. Why? In order to transform Apollos from a Christian of uncertain origins (note that, unlike those in 19:1-7, he does not need to be baptized) into a guaranteed bearer of the authentic Pauline Gospel. In other words, Apollos has been "domesticated" by Luke in order to force him into a specific pattern of the development of the church (Acts 1:8).

Apollos is described as "eloquent" (*logios*), which means that he was an orator trained to combine ideas and translate them into persuasive speech. The Greek term can also mean "learned, cultured,"[64] and this is certainly implied also because we are told that he was "well versed in the Scriptures." An Alexandrian Jew of this period could hardly have escaped the formative influence of Philo, the great intellectual leader of Alexandrian Jewry, particularly since the latter appears to have been particularly concerned with education and preaching.[65] His supreme achievement was to recast Jewish religious thought into the categories of Greek philosophy in order to make it acceptable to pagans. His life-work was to give Hellenized Jews, such as Apollos, a perspective on the Law that would enable them to accept both it and their ambient pagan culture.

In 1 Corinthians 1–4 Paul deals with divisions within the church. The dominant group is inspired by Philonic ideas regarding the "heavenly man," who despises the physical body, and the "earthly man," who is dragged down by its grossness. Thus they reject the idea of resurrection and consider Jesus a purely spiritual "Lord of Glory" (1 Cor 2:8). They have lost all sense of his historical existence. Such nefarious influence could only have been exercised by someone with the qualities and intellectual background of an Apollos. It is entirely possible, of course, that these Corinthians misunderstood Apollos, just as they had given Paul's own ideas a twist he could not accept. But for Paul the division at Corinth would not have taken place without Apollos.

It goes without saying that Paul knew nothing of this when he arrived in Ephesus, but the more he heard the praise heaped on Apollos the more nervous he became. By using Philo's methods of interpretation, and his philosophical framework, Apollos provided intellectual fulfill-ment for those who desired it by building a rich synthesis of the elements Paul provided but refused to develop. Moreover, Apollos' polished elo-quence made him a religious leader to be proud of. For Apollos the purpose of preaching was to provide food for thought, whereas for Paul it was to stimulate Christlike action.

We can be sure that Paul's reaction to what he learned about Apollos was ambivalent. What his head told him conflicted with what his heart felt. In theory he should have been delighted that Corinth now had a leader whose gifts complemented his own. Paul had planted the seed; why should not God send another to water the crop? In reality Paul resented Apollos. On the personal level he dreaded losing the affection and respect of the Corinthians to an intruder whose brilliance Paul could only think of as superficial pandering to convention. Paul was extremely possessive of his converts.

On a much more serious level Paul feared that speculation about God would replace the following of Christ. As an ex-Pharisee he knew the pleasures of endless debate and discussion. As a Christian he was aware that the self-sacrificing love of the crucified Jesus posed a daunt-ingly unambiguous challenge to believers, which could be avoided by concentrating on the will of God because this could be manipulated subjectively to justify virtually anything.

If Paul worried about what Apollos might do at Corinth, he must also have been concerned about what he had already done in Ephesus. Had his intellect and eloquence introduced an alien element into the nascent community? Had Prisca and Aquila been sharp enough to see what was going on, and authoritative enough to insist on Paul's approach? Paul would discover that the community was in fact divided. A number re-fused his authority, but this became apparent only gradually.

JOHANNITE DISCIPLES OF JESUS

Paul's first winter in Ephesus (52–53 c.e.) was marked by an event that brought him back to the very beginnings of the Jesus movement. Somehow he came into contact with a small group who considered themselves followers of Jesus of Nazareth but had never heard of the Passion, resurrection, or descent of the Holy Spirit. They knew only the baptism of John (Acts 19: 1-7). The tension within the narrative becomes evident when it is recognized that for Luke "believers" and "disciples" always mean "Christians," i.e., those who accepted Jesus as the Messiah. Yet these people had experienced only the baptism of John, and here it is definitely not a later insertion (as it was in the case of Apollos), because Paul requires them to be baptized in the name of the Lord Jesus (v. 5).

The simplest explanation is that these were Ephesian Jews who, while on pilgrimage to Jerusalem, had received a baptism of repentance for their sins at the hands of Jesus. They knew him only as the senior assistant of John the Baptist. When John and Jesus moved their prophetic mission to reform Judaism to the more densely populated west bank of the Jordan, the former as the leader took the more difficult task of preaching to the Samaritans, while Jesus went to the Judeans (John 3:22-24). Both believed that the time was short, and that maximum exposure was imperative.

Thus John baptized at the springs on the eastern slope of Mount Gerizim (as close as he could get to the ruined Samaritan temple on the summit), and Jesus went to the heart of Jewish life, the Temple in Jerusalem. There in a prophetic gesture designed to grab attention he overturned the tables of the moneychangers (John 2:13-16). This was also a summons to return to the pristine truth of the Law, both as regards the frequency and the coinage of the temple tax.[66] This would have been the ideal occasion for Jesus to have come in contact with the Ephesian pilgrims.

Peter could have spoken to Paul in Jerusalem about this period in the life of Jesus because he had shared it, but that meeting was fifteen years ago (Gal 1:18). Paul's questions then, and certainly his preaching since, would have focused on the subsequent period, when Jesus had come to the realization that he was the Messiah.

It was now Paul's task to convince these Ephesian Jews that Jesus was in fact the Messiah for whom they had longed. He would have spoken of the resurrection as the authentication of all that Jesus had said and done, and of the power of the Risen Lord as displayed in the growing numbers of believers.

Once the Ephesians had accepted Jesus as the Christ and had been baptized, Paul would have been eager to hear their memories of a crucial day in their lives a quarter of a century earlier. They must have provided new fragments of information to be fitted lovingly into the portrait of of the historical Jesus he presented in his oral preaching (2 Cor 11:4; Gal 3:1).

Apart from this small group of twelve Jews (Acts 19:7), nothing is known of the composition of the Ephesian community. This is not the view of Helmut Koester, who believes that Rom 16:1-23 was originally an independent letter written to Ephesus. In it Paul salutes twenty-six individuals, twenty-four of whom are named. In addition he mentions three house churches and two groupings of (ex?) slaves, which also may have been house churches. Thus, for Koester, we know as much, if not more, about the composition of the church at Ephesus as we do about Corinth.[67] Unfortunately, Rom 16:1-23 was always an integral part of the letter to the Romans and tells us nothing about Ephesus. It opens with the words "now I commend you," and the particle *de* clearly indicates that 16:1 is not a beginning, but a continuation. Moreover, without 16:1-23 Romans would contain only one of the three elements with which Paul regularly concludes his letters, namely the "peace wish" (15:33). The characteristic "kiss greeting" (16:16) and "final blessing" (16:20b) would be lacking.[68] Finally, nowhere else does Paul greet individuals in a community in which he had ministered. The risk was too great. It would be invidious to accidentally omit anyone.

All that we can say, therefore, is that, since Ephesus was similar to Corinth in so many ways, the two communities must have resembled one another in both size and makeup (1 Cor 1:26-29). Each was the city in microcosm: more Gentiles than Jews, a few relatively wealthy members, the majority tradespeople and slaves, possibly more women than men.

SEPARATION FROM THE SYNAGOGUE

According to Luke it was three months before the Jews reacted negatively to Paul's preaching (Acts 19:8-10). This simple statement gives rise to a series of unanswerable questions. The most obvious, of course, is: why did it take so long for them to perceive the subversive thrust of his message?

But this is only the tip of the iceberg. We must assume that Prisca and Aquila had been preaching in Ephesus for the better part of a year. We must also assume that they tried to make converts, and that they went about it in the Pauline way: Jews first and then Gentiles. Thus they must have started in the synagogue. Why had their preaching of Jesus not gotten them into trouble? And if they had in fact been expelled, why did Paul start again, as if their efforts had counted for nothing?

There are two different versions of Paul's departure from the synagogue in Acts 19:9.

Alexandrian Text	Western Text
But since certain were hardened and disobeyed, speaking ill of the Way before the crowd, withdrawing from them, he separated the disciples, daily arguing in the hall of Tyrannus.	Since certain, therefore, were hardened and disobeyed, speaking ill of the Way before the crowd of pagans. Then Paul, withdrawing from them, separated the disciples, daily arguing in the hall of Tyrannus from the fifth to the tenth hour.

The first difference is the most crucial. According to the Alexandrian text the dispute regarding Paul's teaching remains within the Jewish community, because "the crowd" is most naturally understood of those within the synagogue, i.e., "the congregation" (NRSV). The meaning, then, is that some Jews objected violently to Paul's message while their co-religionists remained passive.

According to the Western Text, however, those who object to Paul's teaching carry their protest outside the synagogue to "the crowd of pagans" (*enōpion tou plēthous tōn ethnōn*). Do we have here a parallel to the situation in Antioch-in-Pisidia where "the Jews incited the women of high standing and the leading men of the city, and stirred up persecution against Paul and Barnabas" (Acts 13:50)? If so, the continuation is to be found in 19:23, "About that time there arose no little stir concerning the Way," which is the beginning of the riot of the silversmiths.[69] Were this the intention of the original report, however, we should expect simply *enōpion tōn ethnōn*.

The awkwardness of the expression in the Western Text suggests that the Alexandrian Text contains the original reading, and that "the pagans" was an editorial addition designed precisely to prepare the final explosion in Ephesus, the riot of the silversmiths. Historically there was just the usual division in the synagogue.

Some confirmation of this hypothesis comes from the fact that the second difference in the two texts is manifestly a Western addition designed to explain how Paul could find an audience in the middle of a working day. If we count from the end of the fifth hour to the end of the tenth hour, the time-span is from noon to 5 p.m. This was the time of the midday meal and siesta. According to Martial,

> until the 5th hour ends
> the city to her various trades attends;
> at 6 o'clock
> the weary workers stop. (*Epigrams* 4.8)[70]

Implicitly we are invited to assume that Paul worked at his trade from dawn to noon and then turned to pastoral work while others rested. His disciples, of course, would also have had to give up their rest period. This is certainly plausible, even if not in the original text. At Thessalonica, where he had no Lydia to support him, Paul worked "night and day" (1 Thess 2:9) at manual labor (1 Cor 4:12).

The formula "he separated (*aphōrisen*) the disciples" is also curious for two reasons: (1) It emphasizes an action of Paul with regard to Jewish (or Judaizing) converts. Elsewhere when Paul leaves a synagogue definitively we are invited to assume that those who accepted his teaching simply followed him (e.g., Acts 13:43). No action on Paul's part was necessary. (2) While *aphorizō* basically means "to separate," this can be understood in two ways: (a) "to take away, to take out," and (b) "to set apart." The two have very different connotations.

If we take the first possibility as the meaning,[71] we discover an explanation for Paul's unusual action because we are forced to suppose that Jews who had been convinced by Paul preferred not to break with the synagogue, and that Paul had to insist that it was "either/or" and not "both/and." If so, this would have been another factor that disturbed the unity of the church at Ephesus.

If we accept the second possibility as the meaning,[72] we have a better link with "disciples" and a very smooth transition to Paul's activity in the hall of Tyrannus, because in this perspective the "setting apart" would be in view of their formation as Christians, e.g., "Come out from them, and be separated from them" (2 Cor 6:17, OT catena).

There are also other problems. Luke tells us that Paul taught "daily" (*kath' hēmeran*) in the lecture hall (*scholē*) of Tyrannus, and Ernst Haenchen correctly comments that he wanted to suggest "unbroken activity" on the part of Paul.[73] Yet we know from his letters that Paul made the "intermediate" vist to Corinth and then the long overland journey to Macedonia and back to the capital of Asia during the two years he was in Ephesus.[74] Did Luke have any detailed knowledge of Paul's movements? Or was Luke merely operating on the basis of "this is what Paul must have done"?

According to Luke it was "Jews from Asia" who were responsible for Paul's arrest in Jerusalem (Acts 21:27-36). They accused him of having brought a pagan, "Trophimus the Ephesian," into the part of the Temple reserved to Jews under pain of death. The garrison in the Antonia fortress had to rescue Paul and his companion from the infuriated mob. Since they recognized Trophimus, it is rightly inferred that these Jews were in fact from Ephesus and were in Jerusalem for one of the pilgrimage feasts, possibly Pentecost.[75] Their hostility may suggest that Paul had had more success among Jews in Ephesus than Luke records. Trophimus had accompanied Paul on his journey with the collection to Jerusalem (Acts 20:4) and was to be with Paul again after the latter's captivity in Rome (2 Tim 4:20).

OTHER EPISODES

Subsequent to what he said regarding Paul's relations with the synagogue in Ephesus, Luke speaks of Paul's miracles (19:11-12), the seven Jewish exorcists (19:13-17), and the burning of the books of magic (19:18-20). Apart from the fact that Paul confesses to having worked "signs, wonders, and mighty deeds" (2 Cor 12:12), it is highly improbable that any of these furnishes reliable historical information regarding Paul's ministry in Ephesus, and so I shall not waste time on them.

It is more profitable to focus on the last line of the synagogue episode: "This went on for two years, so that all the inhabitants of Asia heard the word of the Lord, Jews as well as Greeks" (19:10). The emphasis on the universality ("all") of the mission is of course hyperbole, but once this is discounted the truth is well documented.

MISSIONARY EXPANSION IN ASIA

Even though Paul had chosen Ephesus as his base because of the facility it offered him in keeping in touch with his previous foundations, he did not restrict his activity to maintenance in the twenty-seven months he spent there (Acts 19:8-10). It would have been impossible for him to do so. He was by vocation a missionary (and, incidentally, much more effective in founding churches than in running them), and he believed that churches should reach out to unbelievers.

Two texts reveal his ideal church. "You became an example to all the believers in Macedonia and in Achaia, for not only has the word of the Lord sounded forth from you in Macedonia and Achaia, but your faith in God has gone forth everywhere" (1 Thess 1:7-8). Verbal proclamation ("the word of the Lord") was given power by the quality of their grace-transformed lifestyle ("your faith in God"). "Be children of God without blemish in the midst of a crooked and perverse generation among who you shine as lights in the world, holding forth the word of life" (Phil 2:15-16). The qualitative difference between the church and the world is the proclamation of the good news. Ephesus, in consequence, had to be missionary both existentially and verbally.

The missionary outreach of the church of Ephesus is confirmed by the greetings sent by "the churches of Asia" to Corinth (1 Cor 16:19). Paul himself mentions the names of three of these churches: Colossae, Laodicea, and Hierapolis (Col 4:13). This list, of course, is not exhaustive. Laodicea and Hierapolis were mentioned only because, as neighbors of Colossae in the Lycus valley, they were in danger of being infected by the false teaching that had divided the church at Colossae.

Paul did not evangelize the Lycus valley personally (Col 2:1). The communities there were founded by Epaphras, a native of Colossae (Col 4:12-13), who had been commissioned by Paul (Col 1:7). The choice reflected Paul's evolving missionary strategy. From personal experience in Asia Minor and in Macedonia Paul knew the difficulty of starting from scratch in a strange city. He had found a solution to that problem by sending Prisca and Aquila ahead of him to Ephesus. It was they who carried the burden of loneliness and alienation while they found their feet in an alien environment. No doubt there were many others who were prepared to make the same sacrifice for the Gospel. But, reflected Paul, why not select missionaries who by nature had the advantages that Prisca and Aquila had created for him both in Corinth and Ephesus? The fewer the obstacles, the more efficient the mission.

In Philippi Paul baptized Lydia, a textile merchant from Thyatira, not far north of Ephesus. She, in consequence, became the patron who made it possible for him to preach full time by offering him hospitality (Acts 16:14-15). She would, of course, have to go back to Thyatira to replenish her stock, and Paul could be quite sure that there she would proclaim the Gospel. Her energetic and enterprising character would make her a most effective apostle in an environment she knew well. She was returning to a network of acquaintances rooted in longstanding family, social, and commercial contacts. She had a home and a business. She did not have to look for work or accommodation. She was known and trusted. The respect she had earned guaranteed that there were always at least some sympathetic ears to hear her sermons.

It would be most surprising if Paul did not think of Lydia when he met Epaphras of Colossae (Col 4:12) in Ephesus. We do not know Epaphras' profession, but the assumption must be that he came to Ephesus on business. For the sake of illustrating the principle, let us assume he was a wool merchant, and thus a representative of the dominant industry in the Lycus valley. According to Strabo,

> The country around Laodicea produces sheep that are excellent, not only for the softness of their wool, in which they surpass even the Milesian wool, but also for its raven-black colour, so that the Laodiceans derive splendid revenue from it, as do also the neighbouring Colossians from the colour which bears the same name. (*Geography* 12.8.6)

Strabo's failure to specify the precise color associated with the sheep of Colossae is remedied by Pliny, who tells us that *colossinus* is a purple resembling that of the cyclamen blossom (*NH* 21.51; cf. 25.114).

Inscriptional evidence for the existence of guilds in the woollen industry—wool washers, fullers, dyers, etc.—in the Lycus valley and elsewhere never mentions spinners or weavers. This negative evidence suggests how the wool industry was organized. The spinning and simple weaving were done in the home by women and slaves. Then the wool or woven cloth was brought to skilled workers for finishing. There was a central wool emporium in Laodicea.[76] Clearly middlemen were needed.

The best place to find a market for such high-end commodities was obviously the capital of the province. Among the industries of Ephesus in the imperial period were prosperous guilds of "wool-workers" (*lanarioi*), "wool-dealers" (*eriopōlai*), and "cloak-dealers" (*heimatiopōlai*).[77] It would be very natural, therefore, for Epaphras to visit Ephesus to negotiate a price for the next shearing and to keep an eye on the quality and quantity of the production of the coastal rivals of the Lycus valley, notably Miletus, which produced particularly luxurious wool. Epaphras would have seemed an ideal candidate for Paul to commission as the apostle of the Lycus valley (Col 1:7). Like Lydia, he would return to an area where he was known and respected, to friends who would recognize the sincere conviction with which he preached Christ. In a word, he had everything going for him, something that could not be said were Paul, for example, to send a stranger like Timothy.

Of course, Epaphras could not stay long in Ephesus with Paul. He had a business to run. In consequence, his theological education, and that of others recruited in the same way, was minimal to say the least. This would not have bothered Paul, who did not go in for complications, particularly as regards sophisticated preaching. Presumably he advised them to act as he himself did, namely, (1) preach the crucified Jesus; (2) tell your converts to imitate the self-sacrifice of Christ by loving one another; (3) tell them to preach the Gospel wherever and whenever they could; and (4) make a special effort to acquire a convert with a house large enough to accommodate the liturgical assembly of the community. Paul made the apostolate look simple and easy. But running a business does not really prepare one for inspiring a religious community and, as we shall see, Epaphras was at a complete loss when a doctrinal crisis arose at Colossae.

Since two of the seven churches of the Apocalypse (Rev 2:1–3:22) were Pauline foundations, namely Ephesus and Laodicea-on-the-Lycus, and since a third, Thyatira, was probably founded by Lydia, a Pauline convert in Philippi (Acts 16:14), it seems logical to attribute the creation of communities at Smyrna, Pergamum, Sardis, and Philadelphia to the missionary initiative of Ephesus. To these cities we should probably add Magnesia and Tralles in the Maeander valley.[78] These are not mentioned in the New Testament, but when Ignatius, bishop of Antioch-on-the-Orontes (see p. 74), was being marched through Asia to be thrown to the beasts in Rome he wrote letters to the Christian communities in these two cities, which implies that they had been founded a generation earlier.

The nine cities mentioned were all within a 120-mile (192 km) radius of Ephesus and linked by excellent roads (cf. fig. 1). Colossae, the farthest away, could be reached in a comfortable week's walk.

Paul never wrote to any of these churches. Clearly he had learned not only that he could not do everything but that he did not even have to try. He adopted a policy of delegation, trusting the missionary who had founded a particular church to deal with any maintenance problems that might arise there. No doubt Paul was available for consultation, but he maintained direct contact only with the churches he had founded on his first great journey from Antioch-on-the-Orontes to Corinth. The one exception was his letter to the Colossians, but the circumstances there were exceptional, as we shall see.

CRISIS IN GALATIA

While Paul busied himself with the affairs of the church in Ephesus during the winter of 52–53 c.e., trouble was developing far to the east. At the conference in Jerusalem he had attended as a delegate of Antioch (Gal 2:1-10; Acts 15) it had been decided that Paul's converts from paganism did not first have to become Jews, in the case of men through the rite of circumcision.

James should have been theologically opposed to this decision, but he was forced by political considerations to agree. A rising tide of anti-Semitism in the Roman empire was being actively encouraged by the very authorities who should have protected the Jews.[79] Any alert observer could foresee the inevitable clash between the Jews and the Romans and the equally inevitable result. The Romans would win. But if the Jews were not to be destroyed utterly they must be as united as possible. In consequence, James concluded that this was not the moment to dilute Jewish identity by circumcising a great number of pagan men who would be Jews in name only. Their loyalty would not be to the Jewish people, but to Jesus and Paul, whose message diverged significantly from the consensus of Jewish teaching.

Paul was certainly gratified by James' consent, but he did not realize where its logic was leading. If this was not the moment to dilute Jewish identity, James was equally convinced that it was certainly the time to reinforce the national identity of those Jews who had become Christians. They were but two sides of the same coin. Thus it came as a great shock to Paul when a delegation from James arrived in Antioch-on-the-Orontes and insisted that the Jewish believers there must increase the level of their observation of the Law, particularly with regard to contact with pagans. This meant that table fellowship between Jewish and Gentile believers was no longer possible.

Paul saw this as destructive of the unity of the community, but his opponents only shrugged and pointed out that he was the one who had insisted at Jerusalem that faith *alone* mattered. This, of course, was exactly what Paul had said, but he did not intend to suggest that social contacts between Jewish and Gentile believers were irrelevant. He had no right, however, to expect his interlocutors to be mind-readers who would perceive that what he really meant was "faith working through love" (Gal 5:6). Paul felt that he had been cynically manipulated and betrayed, particularly by the defection of Peter and Barnabas, and decided to break all his links with the church of Antioch.

When Paul headed west out of Antioch after the snow had melted in the high country in the spring of 52 c.e. his heart was heavy with regret. Antioch had been the church that had formed him and given him the responsibility of an apostle, but to remain within its embrace would be to live a lie. He believed that an important portion of his life had come to an end.

Unknown to him, Antioch thought otherwise. Its leaders believed that the churches of Galatia, Philippi, Thessalonica, and Corinth were daughter churches of Antioch. In founding them Paul had been acting as their agent. His repudiation of Antioch did not break the mother-daughter bond, and if Antioch had come to a new understanding of what it meant to be a Christian, then it was its duty to communicate that new truth to what had been Pauline churches, to correct the vision they had inherited from him. The daughter churches had to become much more Jewish in practice.

Thus, once Paul was well on the road to Ephesus, Antioch sent a delegation to follow him. He no doubt had spoken at length of his successes. As a result Antioch knew not only the cities in which he had founded churches, but in all likelihood the names and locations of their leading members. They realized that he would go first to the Galatians and probably spend most of the summer with them. The delegation, in consequence, timed its journey so that it would arrive in Pessinus toward the end of August. The Antiocheans could be sure that Paul would strive to reach Ephesus before the onset of winter.

The Antioch delegation planned to spend the winter in Pessinus. The travel restrictions imposed by winter in the high plateau of Anatolia would guarantee that all those they wanted to see were at home and available. The Greco-Roman world considered the Galatians to be large, unpredictable simpletons, ferocious and highly dangerous when angry, but without stamina and easy to trick, and so the delegation believed that the reconversion of the Galatians had to be done slowly and carefully. Frequent repetition of the Judaizing arguments was probably the best strategy. Any effort to hustle the Galatians was likely to antagonize them, with uncomfortable consequences.

The Judaizing delegation hammered at two points. They attacked Paul personally, and they proposed an alternative Gospel. They insisted that Paul had deformed the message with which he had been entrusted by Jerusalem. He had omitted certain essential elements, they declared, which he knew that pagans would find unpalatable (circumcision, dietary restrictions), in order to be popular and successful. His whole approach was based on deceit.[80]

In contrast to the Pauline Gospel, which focused exclusively on the crucified Christ (1 Cor 2:2), the Antiochean delegation offered an entirely theistic version that was mediated by Abraham.[81] He was the first monotheist, and with him God made a covenant. He promised Abraham that his descendants would be as numerous as the stars, and that in him all the nations would be blessed, provided he accepted circumcision and observance of the feasts. The only importance of Jesus Christ was that he inaugurated the new age in which the blessings promised to the descendants of Abraham would be extended to the Gentiles, of which they, the Galatians, should be proud to be the first fruits. Finally, the delegation insisted, Paul was wrong in not informing them of the 613 precepts of the Law, which would greatly facilitate the moral decisions they had to make. They did not have to worry any longer about doing the right thing. They had only to obey.

There is no doubt that this message appealed to the slow and careful Galatians, but they were too cautious to make a hasty decision, particularly when one was not required. They knew that the Antiocheans were with them until spring, when the snow melted, and afterward until the consequent floods dried up. They also made it clear to the delegation that it was only fair to consult Paul. They would like to hear his response to the issues raised by the Antiocheans. This was not at all what the delegation had in mind. They tried to dissuade the Galatians by harping on Paul's untrustworthiness and the cost of the long journey to Ephesus. The stubbornness of the Galatians here worked in Paul's favor. They would not be moved. To object further, the Antiocheans realized, would seriously weaken their position.

Thus as soon as travel became possible in the late spring of 53 C.E. a small delegation from Galatia set off on the three-week walk to Ephesus. Their arrival was a most disagreeable surprise for Paul. He had had no idea that Antioch thought of his foundations as their daughters, and he found it deeply disturbing that the converts he had won with such pain were even listening to another Gospel. The sense of bewilderment (Gal 5:7), almost of despair (Gal 4:11), is palpable in his response. Moreover, he realized that Galatia was only the tip of the iceberg. If the Antiocheans had followed him to Pessinus, then it was to be expected that they would continue on to Philippi, Thessalonica, and Corinth.

Their plans, in consequence, had to be derailed. He needed to devise a response that would stop the Antiocheans dead in their tracks. Thus he decided not to go to Galatia in person. An acrimonious confrontation descending into personal insults would not serve his purpose. This actually happened in Corinth at a later stage. The only way to get his message across without interruption was to write a letter that, though ostensibly addressed to the Galatians, was in fact directed to the Antiocheans. It would have to achieve two things: to detach the Galatians from the Antiocheans, and also to undermine the convictions of the latter. Paul counted on reestablishing his authority among the Galatians by reducing the intruders to confusion and ultimately to silence.

The sophistication of this two-pronged approach to a highly volatile situation highlights Paul's intellectual prowess. Only someone utterly convinced of his rhetorical skills and literary ability would have attempted to carry out such a delicate strategy by letter.

Did it work? As regards the Galatians we cannot say, because they disappear from Paul's life at this point. There is no hint that they replied to his letter, and he never returned to Pessinus. The letter certainly did not deter the Antiocheans. A year later they turned up in Corinth.

The letter to the Galatians must have been written quickly, because Paul could not detain the delegation very long. They had livings to earn and families to cherish. Once the letter was finished and dispatched one would have expected Paul to warn the churches in Macedonia and Achaia of the danger posed by the Antiocheans. After leaving Galatia Paul's first protracted stay had been in Philippi (Acts 16:12). He knew that was where the Judaizers would go next.

Paul did write immediately to Philippi. The existing letter to the Philippians is in fact a combination of three originally independent letters.[82] One of these (Phil 3:2–4:1) reproduces the broad outline of his letter to the Galatians. The autobiographical material (Phil 3:4-8) is evocative of Galatians 1, but here its function is to show that Paul, once an observant Jew, had found something better in Christianity. The contrast between righteousness acquired by obedience to the Law and that given by God "through the faith/fidelity of Christ" (Phil 3:9 = Gal 2:16) reminds us of Galatians 3–4. Finally, the admonition that salvation is not an immutable given but an ongoing struggle toward a future prize (Phil 3:10-16) is precisely what Paul was trying to say in Galatians 5–6. The broad strokes of this letter suggest that the danger of a Judaizing approach was not actual but imminent. The letter was designed to prepare the minds of the Philippians to refuse the advances of the Antiocheans as energetically as possible. Were Paul in prison when this warning letter was written, a reference to his situation would have been perfectly in place in the evocation of his sufferings in Phil 3:8-11. His silence, therefore, can be taken as suggesting that he had not yet been arrested when he wrote.

No comparable warning letters to Thessalonica and Corinth exist. Perhaps Paul was preparing to write such letters when he was arrested and had to deal with more immediate concerns. It is also possible that in a paragraph that was omitted when the three letters to Philippi were fused into one Paul had told the Philippians to pass on his cautionary letter to Thessalonica and Corinth, as he had told the Colossians and Laodiceans to exchange letters (Col 4:16). Philippi was only three or four days' walk from Thessalonica, which had frequent contacts with Corinth (1 Thess 1:7).

A further possibility is that Paul did in fact write to Thessalonica and Corinth, but these letters were not included when the collection of his letters was made at the end of the first century. In fact, by then it was evident that the Judaizing version of the Gospel would have no success in the west. Vilification of Paul continued for several centuries, but his opponents made no converts in Asia or Europe. The slanders emanated from a group of Christians who were rapidly being marginalized, and who after their expulsion from Jerusalem in 135 C.E. drifted northeast and into oblivion.[83]

COMMUNICATIONS WITH PHILIPPI

Philippi had been Paul's first success in Europe. Why he went there is rather a mystery. His route from Galatia through Mysia had brought him to Troas, which was precisely the sort of city that could multiply his effectiveness as a missionary. It offered such notable advantages in communications that it was rumored that Julius Caesar once thought of making it the capital of the empire.[84] The explanation of Acts that he was summoned to Europe by a man from Macedonia is further refined by the knowledge of the exact status of Philippi revealed in Acts 16:12 ("a city of the first district of Macedonia, and a [Roman] colony"). Such precision is thought to suggest that the author of the "we-passages"[85] was both a citizen of Philippi and "the man from Macedonia."[86] In a word, Paul would have been persuaded to go to Philippi by one of his own entourage.

Be that as it may, Paul certainly established an extraordinarily warm relationship with the church at Philippi. His ministry there was greatly facilitated by the patronage of Lydia (Acts 16:14-15), but what he looked back on with unalloyed pleasure was the collaboration of the converts he made there in the spread of the Gospel. He thanks no other community for "your partnership in the gospel from the first day [in Europe] until now" (Phil 1:5). Nowhere else does he praise two women, Euodia and Syntyche, for having "striven side by side with me in the gospel, together with Clement and the rest of my coworkers, whose names are in the book of life" (Phil 4:3). Collectively the believers "shine as lights in the world, holding forth the word of life" (Phil 2:15-16).

One particularly important initiative taken by the church at Philippi was to subsidize Paul as he continued his ministry elsewhere, first in Thessalonica (Phil 4:16) and later in Corinth (2 Cor 11:9). None of his other foundations appears to have appreciated the fact that the more he became involved with growing numbers of new converts the less time he would have to earn his living. This insight no doubt owed much to the predominance of women in leadership roles in the community at Philippi.

The Philippians, of course, would have known that he was going to Thessalonica when he left them heading west on the Via Egnatia. Sooner or later they would have heard of the trouble that developed with the authorities in Thessalonica and the decision to remove Paul entirely to a completely different jurisdiction by sending him south into the province of Achaia (Acts 17:10-15). Their agents with a further subsidy eventually found him in Corinth. One should not be misled by this simple statement into imagining that their task was an easy one. In antiquity there were no municipal tourist information offices to provide maps. Streets had no names and houses no numbers. Strangers would not know the landmarks by which locals oriented themselves. Success in finding anyone took great persistence.

No doubt the sensible Philippians would have asked Paul where he would be the next time they had a gift for him. It would be unlike Paul to be absolutely sure about something so mundane, and his reply probably took the form of an assurance that he would find some way of letting them know. His warning letter about the Antiocheans, therefore, was a godsend to the church at Philippi. It pinpointed his location. Perhaps money destined for him had been accumulating in the account controlled by "the overseers and their assistants" (Phil 1:1). In any case, the reaction of the Philippians was to dispatch Epaphroditus to Ephesus with a gift for Paul (Phil 2:25; 4:18).

Naturally Paul immediately wrote back to thank them. This originally independent note is now preserved as Phil 4:10-20. In reading it one is somewhat surprised at its self-conscious, defensive tone. His gratitude is evident, but there is more than a hint of resentment (Phil 4:11-12). The well-meant gift was something of an embarrassment.

At first sight this is rather surprising. Paul had already received several pecuniary gifts from the Philippians, and if he resented the implication of his poverty he had had plenty of opportunities to ask them to stop. But he had never done so. Why the difference in his response from Ephesus? The answer is that Paul's circumstances had changed. Just before returning to Ephesus Paul had committed himself to organizing a collection for the poor of Jerusalem (Gal 2:10), and he had preached that charitable act among the Galatians en route to Ephesus. No doubt he had also encouraged the believers at Ephesus to support the project. The instructions he gave the Corinthians, which were based on what he had told the Galatians (1 Cor 16:1-4), would have been equally appropriate in Ephesus.

Now the cause of Paul's embarrassment becomes evident. Acceptance of a personal gift might make it appear that he was appropriating funds given to benefit others. Paul felt that his integrity was at stake. Every official in the ancient world had sticky fingers, and protests arose only when the take was felt to be excessive. One malicious tongue in idle speculation could ruin Paul's reputation. This is why it became important for him to emphasize that he had requested nothing from the Philippians (Phil 4:17) and that he needed no further subsidies (Phil 4:18). These points, obviously, were not made for the sake of the Philippians, who were probably mystified since they had not yet heard of the collection. They were really addressed to the secretary and others who were with Paul when he wrote. This was a neat and effective way to get the real explanation of the Philippian gift into the public domain, and typical of Paul's astuteness when he applied his mind.

Paul then took a further step that he hoped would also serve as a smokescreen. Soon after arriving in Ephesus, Epaphroditus had fallen ill. Paul decided not to wait for him to recover, but set about recruiting a messenger to carry his note of gratitude to Philippi (Phil 2:26). Anyone could see that the matter was not that urgent, and the letter-carrier would have had to abandon his livelihood for the duration of the round trip (at least a month). Thus Paul had to provide a good reason.

Epaphroditus had certainly given him a positive appreciation of the state of the community. Otherwise Paul would have devoted space in his thank-you note to any problems. In Paul's eyes, however, the ethos of the Christian community was supposed to be so radically different from the value-system of society in general that an assessment along the lines of "Everything's OK; nothing to worry about" would not have been satisfying. The need to explain why he needed an independent observer also gave him a new opportunity of impressing the Ephesians with the uniqueness of their situation as believers. He already knew from experience how difficult it was to get this insight across. To those who had spent all their lives in a world characterized above all by divisions, the concept of the church as an organic unity was difficult to assimilate. It was natural for them to see the absence of violence within the church as a positive development. No doubt it was, but Paul wanted them to go much further. They had to realize that the church was the physical presence of Christ in the world (1 Cor 12:12-27). Paul would not have been beyond flattering the Ephesians by suggesting that one of them would have the insight to assess the community at Philippi.

His ploy worked, and someone conveyed Paul's gratitude to the Philippians. The emissary returned to report how saddened they all had been by the news of the illness of Epaphroditus (Phil 2:26), but he also brought word of two problems that the latter had not reported, either because he did not consider them significant or because they had developed subsequent to his departure from Philippi at least six weeks earlier. The leaders of two important house-churches were in dispute to the point where the unity of the church was threatened (Phil 4:2). This was all the more dangerous in that the community was being threatened in some way by pagans, presumably the Roman authorities in the colony (Phil 1:28).

The messenger also brought with him a hymn (Phil 2:6-11) that had been composed in the community as a lapidary synthesis of Paul's christology. The confidence of the Philippians would suggest that it was submitted to Paul for his unreserved approval. There may also have been the intention to suggest that it might be useful to other churches, either in itself or as a model for their own theological inspiration.

IMPRISONMENT

Simply in terms of the travel time necessarily involved, and counting from the departure from Galatia of the delegation to Paul, the events just narrated would have taken the best part of four months. Thus we are now in late July or early August of 53 c.e. At this point Paul was arrested. In the Roman system individuals were held in prison only when under investigation or awaiting execution. If the authorities wanted to keep someone out of circulation they banished him to an island, of which the most notorious was Gyara, the Devil's Island or Alcatraz of the first century.

Since Paul had not been condemned to death, he must have been held for investigation. What had brought suspicion upon him? The governors of senatorial provinces changed every year, and a new proconsul of Asia had taken up office in Ephesus on 1 July.[87] Naturally the locals who hoped for advancement did what they could to curry favor. It takes little imagination to envisage a situation in which a neighbor had come to take an interest in Paul's activities. He would have seemed to be recruiting for something. He spoke to crowds that appeared to get bigger each week. If the group appeared to have no structure, perhaps there was a secret element, which might imply that the movement was subversive. In other words, Paul was a victim of his own success. He was reported to the governor. Since the latter was responsible for the preservation of public order, he could not ignore the warning. Thus Paul was invited "to help the Roman authorities with their inquiries," and they kept him close lest he should disappear.

The form of such precautionary detention was entirely at the discretion of the magistrate, whose decision was determined by his own personality and the nature of the case, but particularly by the amount of influence the prisoner and his friends could bring to bear. The well-connected got better treatment than the poor and strangers. Paul was held in the *praetorium* (Phil 1:3), "Caesar's house" (Phil 4:22), where the emperor's representative lived, and which may well have been the palatial mansion on the hill above the theatre (1 in fig. 6). He was chained in a way that is not specified (handcuffs or leg-irons? to a soldier or to the wall of his cell?), but that must have been burdensome because he frequently mentions his "fetters" (Phil 1:7, 13, 14, 17; Col 4:18; Phlm 10, 13). Even though his movements were restricted, the conditions under which he lived were not too severe. He could receive visitors and stay in touch with his congregation. He could send out messages. His letters to Philippi, Colossae, and Philemon imply that he was given access to a professional secretary. His activities and visitors quickly revealed to those in the Praetorium that he was not a political threat (Phil 1:13).

THE THIRD LETTER TO PHILIPPI

The first letter Paul wrote from prison was to the Philippians (Phil 1:1–3:1 + 4:2-9). His purpose, of course, was to deal with the problems in the church that had been reported to him. In terms of Paul's general theology the most important problem was the threat to the unity of the church posed by the dispute between the two house-church leaders, Euodia and Syntyche. If the church was to be the instrument of salvation in the world it had to offer society something the world had not succeeded in achieving. As Paul saw it, the world was characterized above all by divisions. On the macro level there were great opposed blocks, Jews–Greeks, masters–slaves, and male–female (Gal 3:28). On the micro level there were the anti-social vices that made genuine communication impossible and so isolated individuals behind barriers of fear and suspicion (e.g., Rom 1:29-31). To the world, therefore, the church had above all to offer unity.

It is not surprising, therefore, that when the unity of the church of Corinth was threatened by different groups at Corinth (the followers of Paul, Apollos, and Cephas: 1 Cor 1:12). Paul spent the first four chapters of 1 Corinthians dealing with this problem from several angles. In Philippians, however, Paul first broaches the problem caused by Euodia and Syntyche only at the very end of the letter (Phil 4:2-3). It is not possible to say that perhaps Paul's thought had not yet evolved to the level that appears in 1 Corinthians. In Galatians, which was written before Philippians, he is perfectly clear on unity as the very essence of the church: "you (pl.) are all one person in Christ Jesus" (Gal 3:28). It is much more likely that Paul hesitated about criticizing individuals at Philippi by name. They would have been put to shame when the letter was read in public. He originally thought that a suggestion such as the very generic "(may) you stand firm in one spirit, with one mind striving side by side for the faith of the gospel" (Phil 1:27) or "complete my joy by being of the same mind, having the same love, being in full accord and of one mind" (Phil 2:2) would have sufficed. On reflection, however, he decided that something more specific was needed, and a little later in the letter he commands: "Do not act out of a spirit of rivalry or vain ambition, but in humility count others better than yourselves" (Phil 2:3). Finally he came to the conclusion that the matter was too serious to be left to inferences and that he should be explicit and mention the two women by name.

Paul was intrigued by the Philippian hymn. It was only after it came to his attention that allusions to hymns appear in his letters (Col 3:16; 1 Cor 14:26). The original form of the hymn can be reconstructed as follows from Phil 2:6-11.

I	v. 6a	Who being in the form of God
	v. 6b	Did not claim godly treatment
	v. 7a	But he emptied himself
	v. 7b	Taking the form of a servant.
II	v. 7c	Being born in human likeness
	v. 8a	And being found in shape as a man
	v. 8b	He humbled himself
	v. 8c	Becoming obedient unto death.
III	v. 9a	Therefore God super-exalted him
	v. 9b	And gave him the supreme name
	v. 10a	So that at Jesus' name every knee should bow
	v. 11a	And every tongue confess "Jesus Christ is Lord."

The clarity of the pattern is its own justification. Strophes I and II are constructed on precisely the same model, with the principal verb followed by a reflexive pronoun in the third line. This serves to emphasize that the message of each strophe is identical. It is a very simple one. As the perfect embodiment of the "image (form) of God" (Gen 1:26) Jesus did not have to die, because he was not a sinner. Thus, since he did in fact die, he must have chosen to "empty/humble" himself. The change in structure in Strophe III (the thought of v. 9a is carried on in v. 10a, and that of v. 9b in v. 11a) signals a different aspect. It spells out the reward for such obedience. Jesus is accorded universal veneration and is proclaimed as Lord.[88]

These ideas would have been very congenial to Paul, and he must have taken pride in how well the Philippians had assimilated his teaching. There was one crucial point, however, on which he felt the hymn was inadequate. While giving great importance to the death of Jesus, it did not spell out *how* he died. Thus Paul added at the end of Strophe II, "even death on a cross" (v. 8d). This disturbed the perfect structure of the hymn, but the sacrifice of such beauty did not weigh in the balance against the sacrifice of Christ. Paul firmly believed that if Jesus had chosen to die, and if he had in fact died by crucifixion, then he must have chosen that most horrible of deaths. The intensity of the agony was for Paul the evidence of the immensity of the love Christ had for us. Paul had said in an earlier letter, "He loved me, that is he gave himself for me" (Gal 2:20). Love is self-sacrifice.

TROUBLE IN THE CHURCH AT EPHESUS

We have already had occasion to note two reasons why Paul might be anxious regarding the church at Ephesus. The first was the influence of Apollos, who might have promoted a form of speculation Paul considered a distraction from the real business of living the Christian life. His preaching could have encouraged those with intellectual ambitions to look down on Paul, to treat his message as simplistic, and to view his oratorical style as lacking in polish. The second was the (rather remote) possibility that some convert Jews had wanted to retain their attachment to the synagogue. Their position would have been similar to that of Messianic Jews today, who accept that Jesus is the Christ but do not formally join any church.

A third factor may also have influenced the situation. For the first converts at Ephesus Prisca and Aquila were the founders of the church. The new believers knew perfectly well the sacrifices they had made. In a strange city, without any contacts, they had to establish and build up a business while at the same time pouring their energies into the proclamation of the Gospel. It would be very surprising if a number of these had not resented the arrival of Paul. No matter what praise Prisca and Aquila had heaped on him, he was a latecomer who had avoided the difficulties of the pioneering period. The same sort of thing happened in the history of the Essenes. The movement split when the Zaddokite high priest, who had been dispossessed of his office by Jonathan Maccabaeus, joined the sect and took it for granted that his prestige gave him the right to assume control.[89] For those Essenes who accepted him he was the Teacher of Righteousness, and the erstwhile leader of the movement became the Man of Lies.

These various tensions within the church came to a flash-point when Paul was arrested. One of the unique features of Paul's letter to Philippi from prison (Phil 1:1–3:1 + 4:2-9) is the amount of information he gives us regarding the situation at Ephesus. On the news of his arrest the church split into three groups. A minority was frightened into silence and retreated to evaluate the risks of remaining Christians. The majority (*hoi pleiones*), however, became even more active missionaries. Paul should have been delighted, but he discerned two different motivations. Some preached because they knew it would be what Paul wanted. Others, he believed, preached Christ "from envy and strife," "out of selfish ambition, not sincerely but thinking to afflict me in my imprisonment" (Phil 1:15-17).

What is unusual here is that Paul recognizes that these latter are members of the Christian community in good standing and that their preaching is an authentic proclamation of Christ. There is no question of a doctrinal difference. There is no hint of a false Gospel. The difference between the two groups, therefore, turns on their relationship to Paul personally. At Ephesus there were those who liked him and those who did not. The former, understandably, are praised. The latter are condemned in language whose viciousness cannot be recognized unless we glance at how the terms he employs are used elsewhere in Paul's letters.

"Envy and rivalry" (*phthonos kai eris*) appear only in Rom 1:29 and Gal 5:20-21, both of which are vice-lists describing the "works of the flesh" characteristic of unredeemed humanity. *Phthonos* does not imply any desire for gain, but simply a determination to deprive the other; it is an aggressive intent to do evil without cause, to dirty and to denigrate.[90] It was what motivated those who handed Jesus over to Pilate (Mark 15:10). *Eris* is the will to promote discord, to stir up trouble when there are no real grounds for disagreement.[91] *Eritheia*, "selfish ambition" also occurs in the vice-list in Gal 5:20-21 (also 2 Cor 12:20), and was employed of those who intrigued to win public office exclusively out of a desire to gain fame and money.

To combine just these three terms in condemning those whose only "fault" was that they did not like Paul seems unnecessarily harsh. The apostle is in effect saying that they are not real Christians, an assessment that appears to imply that Paul thought of himself as the emotional touchstone of salvation! This can hardly be considered normal behavior. Paul's response is so exaggerated as to leave him open to the charge of being unbalanced. His temper tantrum carries more than a hint of hysteria. Unfortunately this incident is not unique.

Whereas Paul was seriously worried that the Philippians might be seduced by the Judaizing arguments of the Antiocheans, he is surprisingly nonchalant regarding the "terror" inspired in the community by pressure from outside (Phil 1:28). The suggestion in Phil 1:30 that the Philippians were undergoing what he himself was going through might suggest some sort of persecution by the Roman authorities in the city. He offers no consolation, however, merely telling them that as followers of Christ they should expect to suffer as he did, and that they should count themselves blessed when the opportunity did arrive (Phil 1:29). Evidently he had no qualms about their fortitude. Very probably he saw their suffering as enhancing the existential dimension of the Gospel, as he would say of himself one day in the future, "While we live we are always being given up to death for Jesus, so that the life of Jesus may be manifest in our mortal flesh" (2 Cor 4:11).

As the letter unfolds it becomes clear that this was only Paul's initial response to the threat of persecution. His emotional attachment to the Philippians (Phil 1:8) meant that their persecution weighed upon him to the point that he became desperate for knowledge of how they were faring. Once again this led to an intemperate outburst. Obviously he sought a volunteer from among the believers at Ephesus, but no one agreed to go except Timothy. For his own personal reasons, however, Paul did not want to release Timothy, and he lashed out at the rest of the community. "They all seek their own interest, not that of Jesus Christ" (Phil 2:21). Such an uncharitable interpretation is definitely uncalled for.

With perfectly good reason the Ephesians could have pointed out (a) that he could send Timothy, (b) that Ephaphroditus was going to Philippi shortly (Phil 2:25) and could send back news, and (c) that they were engaged in a fruitful apostolate in Ephesus and there was no need to break it off just to justify Paul's desire for information; on the contrary, was it not extremely selfish of him to prefer his own consolation to the spread of the Gospel?

Naturally Paul did not see things that way. That he should experience severe tension while being investigated by the Roman authorities is perfectly understandable, particularly if he thought his life was at stake (Phil 1:21-25). His reaction in Phil 2:21, however, betrays a willfulness that could not bear to be thwarted. His self-absorption is so great that he even identifies his personal, selfish needs with those of Jesus Christ. If there were other outbursts of this type as he tried to establish his authority at Ephesus, the natural reluctance of some to accept his leadership becomes more intelligible.

One must also wonder what the Philippians made of the conflicting signals Paul sent them. On the one hand he preached the importance of unity in the community and beseeched Euodia and Syntyche to resolve their differences. On the other hand he told them to imitate his example (Phil 4:9) while at the same time revealing his contempt for those at Ephesus who did not like him. At best this can hardly be considered good pastoral leadership.

LETTERS TO THE LYCUS VALLEY

In fairness, however, it must be said that the immature side of Paul's character, which he betrayed in Philippians 1–2, did not remain in evidence for very long. Shortly after the dispatch of this letter he wrote others to the Colossians and to Philemon that are models of sensitive and effective pastoral concern. The initial part of his imprisonment at Ephesus must have been a particularly low moment in the life of Paul.

As we have seen above, Paul did not personally evangelize the churches of the Lycus Valley (Colossae, Laodicea, and Hierapolis). Their existence was to the credit of Epaphras of Colossae, who had encountered Paul while on business in Ephesus and returned home a Christian apostle. Following Paul's advice to recruit early a convert who had a house large enough to host the nascent community, Epaphras won over Philemon, who may not have been the richest man in the valley but who had a house big enough to receive guests (Phlm 22), and who could afford at least one slave. Onesimus was his name, which betrayed his servile condition because it meant "Useful."

Onesimus had done something to offend Philemon, perhaps even something that caused him financial loss (Phlm 18), and, fearing retribution, he fled. He was not simply trying to escape, although that would not have been too difficult. There was no police force to track down runaway slaves (see Cicero, p. 57). Onesimus knew that he would not be considered a fugitive if he sought out a friend of his master. In that case the law understood that the slave's purpose was to find a mediator who would plead for mitigation of whatever punishment was coming to him. Even though at this stage Onesimus was not a Christian, he must have heard Epaphras and Philemon speak of Paul with reverence. This persuaded him to head for Ephesus. It was only a week's walk away, and that would allow time for tempers to cool. It must have taken Onesimus considerable time and effort to find where Paul was being held. The fact that it was the *praetorium* did not deter him, even though he must have been aware of the danger stemming from his ambiguous status. The warmth of his reception by Paul swept away whatever barriers had blocked the preaching of Epaphras from reaching his heart, and he became a believer (Phlm 10).

Paul immediately did what Onesimus asked of him. He wrote a letter on his behalf in which he asked for the errant slave to be treated as a "beloved brother" (Phlm 16) and dropped a rather strong hint that he would like Onesimus released into his sevice (Phlm 13). In keeping with the purpose of the letter, it is couched in the second person singular because the decision is Philemon's alone. Yet the letter is addressed not to Philemon alone, but to Philemon, Apphia, Archippus, and "the church in your (sing.) house" (Phlm 1-2) and concludes with a request: "I am hoping through your (pl.) prayers to be granted to you (pl.)" (Phlm 22).

Here we catch a glimpse of the manipulative side of Paul's character, but it is done so smoothly that any thought of censure quickly gives way to admiration. He could be a very skilled politician and had a definitely jaundiced view of human nature. By addressing the letter to the whole community he ensured that it would be read aloud in public, and he counted on the sympathy of the majority to sway Philemon to grant him his request. It would be hard for Philemon to refuse what his enthusiastic neophyte converts felt was reasonable. Christians, after all, were expected to love their neighbors.

Before this letter could be sent, Epaphras arrived in Ephesus to report trouble in the church of Colossae, and possibly also that of Laodicea, that he felt incompetent to handle. False teaching had made such inroads into the community that Archippus, one of the leadership group in the house church of Philemon (Phlm 1), had gone over to the enemy (Col 4:17). The situation was beyond the skills of a businessman. He saw no alternative but to have recourse to Paul, even though that meant a financial sacrifice of at least two weeks' absence from work. Epaphras also doubted his ability to explain the false teaching adequately to Paul. It was infinitely more complicated than any of the theology Paul had taught him. Thus he decided to bring with him to Ephesus others who were concerned about the problem and who could clarify different points.[92]

It must have come as a considerable shock to Epaphras to find that Paul was not at his usual residence, perhaps in the Square Market (cf. p. 198), but was lodged in the *praetorium* awaiting the pleasure of the pro-consul. It would have come as an even greater and more disagreeable shock to find himself and his delegation imprisoned with Paul. The Roman authorities had begun to take a benign view of Paul's activities (Phil 1:13), assuming them to be local and not threatening to public order. A group of six arriving from the far eastern side of the province put the Jesus movement in a very different perspective. A delegation of such size implied a membership both prosperous and numerous in one remote area. Were there others throughout the province, and how many? Was there any subversive intent in an operation that seemed to shun public-ity? No sensible administrator could afford to let the Colossians loose until the matter had been completely clarified.

No doubt six voices spoke at once when Paul asked what the trouble was, and it is unlikely that any two versions were identical. Eventually, however, a pattern emerged. Some in the community were exhibiting an unhealthy interest in a type of mystical-ascetic speculation emanating from the Jewish synagogue. They were being led to believe that fasting from food and drink, coupled with strict observance of the Jewish feasts, could produce a mystical ascent to heaven that climaxed in a vision of angels worshiping at the throne of God.[93] This, of course, was something much more entertaining and impressive than the rather dull loving your neighbor on which Epaphras insisted. It offered the Colossians a chal-lenging goal to which they could aspire, and that when achieved would redound to their prestige. They would have something to boast about for the rest of their lives. This sort of thing would have been anathema to Paul, not only because it provided an excuse to avoid assuming the burdens of Christian living but above all because it ignored Christ completely.

It was not difficult for Paul to see the damage this sort of speculation could do if it were permitted to pass unquestioned. His policy regarding delegation demanded that he instruct Epaphras, who was responsible for the churches of the Lycus valley, how to deal with the problem. But the latter had also been imprisoned. He was not free to return. That left Paul with no alternative but to write letters to Colossae and Laodicea.

This was a challenge he had not yet encountered. Thus far he had written one letter to the Galatians and several to the Philippians, but these were communities in which he had lived and worked. He knew everyone who would hear the letter read in public and could be sure that their sympathies were with him. He knew how to approach them, and they knew his style and could read between the lines. Although Paul had tramped through the Lycus valley and could visualize the environment of the two cities, he had never met any of the believers at either Colossae or Laodicea (Col 2:1). Apart from what he could pick up from Epaphras he had no idea of what they were like or how their minds worked. It would be an extremely delicate task to find a way to convince them to return to the authentic Gospel. Then fate favored him.

When Paul asked the Colossian delegation, "And how does Christ fit into all this?" they responded by producing a hymn that, they claimed, crystallized the thinking of the false teachers about Christ. It is easily reconstructed from Col 1:15-20.

I	v. 15a	He who is the image of the invisible God
	v. 15b	Firstborn of all creation
	v. 16a	For in him were created all things
	v. 16f	All things through him and to him were created.
II	v. 18b	He who is the beginning
	v. 18c	Firstborn from the dead
	v. 19	For in him all the Fullness was pleased to dwell
	v. 20a	And through him to reconcile all things to him.

As in the case of the Philippian hymn, the perfection of the pattern is its own guarantee. The exact structure of the lines in the first strophe is repeated in the corresponding lines of the second strophe. Such precision cannot be accidental.

Paul would have been stunned when he read this hymn. It exalted the Savior by giving him cosmic significance. How could one object to the honor of such glorification? Paul, however, immediately saw that it effectively marginalized Christ by robbing him of his terrestrial reality. He was no longer a human being who could and should be imitated. The hymn made Christ an object of contemplation for the passive and theological debate for the active. The former gazed in admiration while confessing their inability to understand. The latter were fascinated by the ambiguity and ambivalence of the hymn, which offered material for interminable discussion. The inability of centuries of scholarship to come to a consensus regarding the meaning of the hymn is the best evidence that its purpose was simply to titillate the intelligence. It was not designed to convey an unambiguous message.

Paul must have been immediately tempted to tear up the hymn while vociferously dismissing it as rubbish. Then he saw that he could use it to hoist its author(s) with their own petard. The hymn gave Christ a role in the creation and reconciliation of "all things." Paul might have attacked this statement by asking precisely *how* Christ as a human being, who was himself a creature, could have done either. But that would have led him into precisely the sort of speculation that the false teachers at Colossae would have welcomed with pleasure. Thus he laid down the ground rules by saying in effect, "Without agreeing, I accept your starting-point, but you then must accept the conclusions that flow logically from that premise." In his letter Paul quotes the hymn, but destroys its perfect arrangement by making the insertions he considers necessary to bring out what he saw as its necessary implications.

Paul's argument in these corrections is a simple one. "All things" permits no exceptions; it is universal. Therefore, it must include angels of all kinds (and when he quotes the hymn in his reply he adds the names in Col 1:16bcd). Therefore they are inferior to Christ, who brings them into being. And since angels are also englobed in the "all things" that need reconciliation (thus Paul adds "whether on earth or in heaven," v. 20b, when he cites the hymn) some, if not all, of them must be sinners, and so cannot effectively intercede with God for humans. Angels, in consequence, are far inferior to Christ and both irrelevant and useless as far as human beings are concerned.

Here we see Paul at his best. Without wasted words, with the skill of a trained orator, he formulates an unanswerable objection, because it necessarily follows from the premise his opponents themselves have formulated. With the minimum of force he pricks the bubble of their cosmic speculation, permitting the hot air that gave it lift to escape into the vacuity whence it came.

Then Paul continues, in effect: "Since you have introduced the idea of reconciliation, I will answer the question HOW, which you avoid. It is brought about by Jesus Christ 'making peace by the blood of his cross'" (and Paul inserted these words in the copy of the hymn in his letter, v. 20c). Paul had made an identical addition to the Philippian hymn in order to remind his readers once again of the love Christ showed for humanity and the price he paid to reconcile it with God (Gal 2:20).

Paul was too good a teacher, and too shrewd a leader, to be content with demolishing the false teachers' understanding of Christ. He could not leave his readers with a negative, nor could he simply repeat what Epaphras had told them. He had to give the Colossians something new about Christ to occupy their reflection. This imperative forced Paul to think about Christ in a way he had not done before, and thus he came to an insight that would be central to his future theology. It was in pressure situations like this that Paul became really creative. The process was the antithesis of the leisurely speculations of a scholar in his office slowly drawing out the implications of a fundamental principle. The need to react to changing circumstances conditioned the evolution of Paul's theology. He had to be stimulated and challenged, but his mind was instinctively consistent and each new insight enhanced the burgeoning synthesis.

The issue of the unity of the church was pushed to the forefront of Paul's mind by the division of the community at Philippi, and now again at Colossae. He had already come to the conviction in writing to the Galatians that believers "are all one person in Christ Jesus" (Gal 3:28). But what did that mean? He needed a vivid image to convey to believers their true relationship to one another. And he thought of the human body.

It is impossible that he should have borrowed this concept from the Greek philosophic view of the state or a city as the body politic because, as we have seen, he saw society as characterized above all by divisions. It is much more likely that the idea came to him from contemplation of the ex-votos that accumulated in the healing temples of the eastern Mediterranean. These ceramic representations of the various parts of the body that had been cured caused him to ask: what is the difference between that copy of an arm and a real one? The answer, of course, is that an arm is truly an arm only as long as it belongs to a living body. From there it was but an easy step to thinking of the Christian community as a body. As in a living thing the church's various members, while different in terms of their spirit-given gifts (1 Corinthians 12–14), share a common being. The foot or the hand do not exist independently; each participates in the existence of the whole. In consequence, divisions within the church endangered not only its identity and mission, but its very existence. If a body is dismembered it no longer exists as a person.

The first explicit formulation of this fundamental insight occurs in Colossians and, because christology was such an issue at Colossae, Paul goes even further by combining it with a definition of the relationship of Christ to his church, which also appears here for the first time. In order to draw cosmic speculation down into ecclesiology Paul introduces these two ideas in the form of an insertion between the two strophes of the Colossian hymn, which proclaims that Christ "is the head of the body, that is, the church" (Col 1:18a). But what precisely is meant by "head" (*kephalē*)? The Greek term has two connotations, both of which appear subsequently in Colossians. In saying that Christ is "the head of all rule and authority" (2:10) Paul means that he has "power over" all angelic beings. This sense of *kephalē*, however, is rare in Greek and is not used apropos of the church. The alternative meaning of *kephalē* is "source," which survives in English only in the phrase "the head of a river," i.e., its headwaters. This is the sense used in describing Christ's relation to the church. He is "the head from whom the whole body, nourished and knit together through its joints and ligaments, grows with a growth that is from God" (Col 2:19).

The problems with which Paul had to deal in Galatians and Colossians originated in Judaism, but in tone and atmosphere these are completely different letters. One can only admire Paul's versatility and sureness of touch. In Galatians he had to offer precise, closely reasoned replies to a carefully thought out critique of his person and Gospel. The false teaching at Colossae had virtually no intellectual roots. It floated in a fantasy world. Paul had to restore a sense of reality. He exposed the beguiling speech of the false teaching as "empty deceit," mere "shadow" in contrast to the "substance" of Christ (Col 2:4, 6, 17).

LETTERS TO LAODICEA AND TO EPHESUS?

In his letter to Colossae Paul mentions that he had also written a letter to the neighboring city of Laodicea (Col 4:16), which of course would have been threatened by the same false teaching (Col 2:1). They were only some eight miles (13 km) apart. This letter, unfortunately, has been lost. A document entitled *To the Laodiceans* appeared very early and enjoyed considerable popularity by being included in the Latin Bible between the sixth and fifteenth centuries, but the arrival of critical scholarship only served to confirm the judgment of the Muratorian Canon (ca. 200 C.E.) that it is a very crude and pointless forgery. It is nothing but a patchwork of Pauline words and phrases, mostly drawn from Philippians.[94]

Recently a very plausible theory was put forward claiming that a great part of the letter to the Laodiceans is preserved in the canonical epistle to the Ephesians. This is the logical conclusion to be drawn from the observation that Ephesians "combines in almost equal proportions Pauline and non-Pauline vocabulary, style, forms, settings, purposes and theology."[95] Ephesians, however, contains nothing that can be connected specifically with Laodicea.

There are two ways around this objection. The first and simplest solution is that the authentic letter now buried in Ephesians was not addressed to Laodicea but to another Pauline foundation. This, however, would imply that Paul wrote to a community just for the sake of writing, which would be so unusual as to make the hypothesis implausible.

This forces us to look seriously at a second possibility: namely, that the editor who produced Ephesians excised from a letter to the Laodiceans everything that evoked the teaching that had once troubled the churches of the Lycus valley. This might seem to be an unforgivable liberty to take with an apostolic letter, but if we look at the situation from the perspective of the editor of Ephesians things appear in a different light.

If the editor wanted to use a genuine Pauline letter as the vehicle to carry the apostle's message to a new and different generation its specificity had to be eliminated in order not to distract from what the editor really wanted to say in his additions. This is not pure speculation. The manuscript tradition of the Pauline letters provides abundant evidence of efforts to remove the specifics that for some scribes appeared to detract from the universal importance of the letters. This is particularly evident in the way copyists treated Romans. Here it must suffice to refer to the seminal article of Nils Alstrup Dahl.[96]

To justify himself the editor of Ephesians could have claimed that Paul's critique of the Colossian heresy had served its purpose. The attitudes he condemned had died out in the Lycus valley. The false teaching was no longer a threat. Moreover, the editor well knew that his elimination of Paul's arguments against that teaching did not mean that they were lost forever. Those who for whatever reason might be interested in how the apostle had dealt with the problem had only to read Colossians, which had been preserved intact.

What was the purpose of the expanded edition, and to whom was it addressed? John Muddiman maintains that its destination was Ephesus, and that its purpose can be derived from the the gospel and epistles of John, which were written there. They witness to the fact that Christian unity was under threat in western Asia toward the end of the first century. Muddiman thinks specifically of Johannine Jewish Christians who, after being expelled from the synagogue, hesitated to join Pauline house-churches where some Gentile members may have been tempted to repudiate the Jewish roots of Christianity. Ephesians was designed to reassure them. "Ephesians marks the beginning of that process of re-judaizing Gentile Christianity, the rediscovery of its roots in Jewish salvation-history, worship, scripture and creation theology, that was to preserve it from the threats from Marcionite and Gnostic heresy as the second century proceeded."[97]

Rightly, I think, Muddiman excuses the editor of any intention to defraud. The basis of Ephesians was a genuine Pauline letter, and the editor probably believed that most, if not all, of what he added originated with Paul in one way or another. The purpose of Ephesians was to make the apostle's authentic voice heard again. The awareness of the need for such a clarion call in Ephesus suggests that the editor was of that city. Muddiman astutely notes: "A pseudepigraphical letter is not sent; it 'comes to light' or is 'discovered,' and for this reason its provenance is likely to be the same as its destination."[98] How Ephesians emerged on the scene is frustratingly obscure. It won acceptance, presumably, because there were those who desperately wanted to believe its message. No doubt the editor knew that there were other Christians who thought like him but who needed a prod to make them activists in the cause of church unity. Ephesians, he hoped, would be the catalyst.

There is much here that is speculative, but it is important to recognize that Pauline and Johannine churches coexisted in Ephesus toward the end of the first century. It would be completely abnormal had they traveled on perfectly parallel paths without any interaction. In fact, to see Pauline influence in the Fourth Gospel one has only to read the section on the vine and the branches (John 15:1-6) and compare it with Paul's vision of the church as an olive tree (Rom 11:17-24). But this would take us too far afield and into an Ephesus Paul never knew.

A FREE MAN AGAIN

The time Paul spent in prison in Ephesus was in many ways the most intensively creative period of his life. Amid the tension caused by the complete uncertainty regarding his fate after the the arrival of the delegation from Colossae he had the resilience to generate new theological ideas. This intellectual ferment, however, does not appear to have survived his liberation. There would be no evidence of further insights for the better part of a year, until another crisis blew up.

In his letters from prison he had made promises to the Philippians (Phil 2:24) and to the Colossians (Phlm 22) that he would visit them when he was freed. The two visits could not be accomplished on the same journey. Philippi lay due north of Ephesus and Colossae due east. It is certain that he did not go immediately to Philippi, because a visit there was still on his agenda in the late spring of 54 C.E. (1 Cor 16:5). Did he go to the Lycus valley? Even after winter had set in it would have been an easy, even pleasant, journey. He would have been less than human had he not been intensely interested in finding out what his letters to Colossae and Laodicea had achieved. It would have seemed natural to follow up with a personal visit just in case the letters had not had the impact he desired. However, he knew that he would soon receive a report from Tychicus, the bearer of the letters (Col 4:7-8). If things continued to go badly he could be sure that Epaphras would quickly appear on his doorstep. Hence a visit to the Lycus valley probably did not rank high on his list of things to do. Moreover, he had a number of good reasons to stay in Ephesus.

Recent events in Philippi and Colossae had confirmed his conviction that he needed to be available to nurture his foundations through crises great and small. He had chosen Ephesus as his base for that very reason, and if he traveled away from it he would be that much more difficult to find.

There is no reason to think that the opposition to Paul that is revealed in Phil 1:15-17 vanished once he was released from prison. This group had shown that they could not only survive without him but carry on an effective ministry. Strengthened by their success, they would have grown into a cohesive group. Paul could not have whipped them into line by issuing orders. Such a procedure would have been completely alien to one of his most fundamental principles, namely that precepts produce only goodness by compulsion (Phlm 8, 14), a fragile facade of compliance unrelated to personal choice. He could also have seen how foolish he would look by attempting to oblige people to like him! Thus his only option was to win them over, a process that would take time and could not be delayed. In effect he had to say, as he had done when he wanted a favor from Philemon, "for love's sake I prefer to appeal to you" (Phlm 9). This would have been his main concern during the winter of 53–54 c.e. when the weather restricted travel.

Finally, there was the arrival of Apollos from Corinth before the end of the sailing season in the early autumn of 53 c.e. (1 Cor 16:12). No doubt Paul was eager to meet one whom he had thought of as a potential rival for the affections of his converts there, and to assess him personally. His experiences with Philippi and Colossae would have led Paul to ask searching questions regarding the life of the community at Corinth. He had now been out of touch with them for two full years. Knowing their energy and commitment, he also knew that anything could have happened.

Unfortunately we do not have access to Apollos' full report, but Paul felt it imperative to respond by letter to one detail. There was at least one member of the Corinthian community who was a Christian only in name. He had made not the slightest effort to change his behavior from what had been normal when he was a pagan. Paul was convinced that one bad apple could infect all the others and so ordered the believers at Corinth to have no contact with immoral people.

This letter (see 1 Cor 5:9) has been lost. Why it was not preserved with the rest of the Corinthian correspondence is anyone's guess. Perhaps it was considered too specific to be of general interest when the letters were collected, or the editor may have thought that the essence of its message was preserved in 1 Cor 5:9-13. The fact that Paul had to return to the matter brings to light a serious flaw in his pastoral technique. He tended to believe that his hearers and readers would understand what he *meant*, even though his literal words could be interpreted in another way without distortion. Very frequently, in consequence, his own sloppy formulation was the cause of problems in his churches. His converts often believed that they were doing what he asked of them, but that was not always what he intended them to do.

In the present instance, instead of telling the Corinthians what precisely to do with the specific individual who was causing the trouble, Paul stated a general principle: "Christians should not associate with immoral people," trusting (rather naïvely) that the Corinthians would come to the particular conclusion he intended. Not unreasonably, however, the Corinthians said that everyone is immoral in one way or another, and so to avoid them completely one would have to go and live on another planet. But, since this is manifestly impossible, one should just carry on as before, until Paul clarified his meaning, which he eventually did: "Drive out the wicked person from among you" (1 Cor 5:13).

CONSTERNATION CAUSED BY CORINTH

The last months of Paul's stay in Ephesus were dominated by the affairs of the church at Corinth. Once the sailing season began in late April of 54 C.E. Chloe, a wealthy businesswoman in Ephesus, sent a number of employees to Corinth. As soon as the cargo ships began to move, new goods became available, and the first in made the most profit. Chloe's plan no doubt was to buy a choice selection of the new goods from the west that had arrived in Corinth, and to get back to Ephesus before her competitors. The situation, I imagine, was similar to the intense competition to be the first clipper ship to reach London with the fresh crop of tea from India or China. That cargo commanded much higher prices than the tea brought by ships that arrived later.

This opportunity to get news of the church in Corinth justified Paul's selection of Ephesus as his base. It was precisely what he had in mind when he made that choice. He knew that there he could find travelers going in all directions who would either carry his letters for him or provide the security of a group for members of his own entourage. Not a single road in the Roman empire, even close to Rome, was totally secure, and Paul evokes the situation with the brevity of great skill, "on frequent journeys, in danger from rivers, danger from robbers . . . danger in the city, danger in the wilderness, danger at sea" (2 Cor 11:26). To travel with others minimized the element of risk but did not remove it completely.

At this stage, having dealt with the teething problems of communities in Thessalonica, Galatia, Philippi, Colossae, Laodicea, and Ephesus, Paul had a pretty realistic picture of the sorts of things that could go wrong in a nascent church. It would be most surprising if he did not give Chloe's people some sort of idea of the things to look out for. In particular he would have asked them to inquire how his first letter (1 Cor 5:9) had been received.

The voyage from Ephesus to Cenchreae, the eastern port of Corinth, could have taken as little as three days.[99] So Chloe's people would have been back in Ephesus in two or three weeks. The report they brought about the situation of the church at Corinth disturbed Paul greatly. If it was correct, everything that could possibly go wrong had in fact happened. Just as in Ephesus the community was divided, except at Corinth there were three factions (1 Cor 1:12). This, however, was less titillating than the facts that a man was living with his stepmother with the full support of the community (1 Cor 5:1-8), and that intercourse with prostitutes was considered unobjectionable (1 Cor 6:12-20). Chloe's people judged the liturgical assembly as particularly worthy of censure. The leader was a male homosexual with a magnificent feminine hairdo, and at the eucharist the wealthy section of the church got such special treatment that they had had too much to eat and drink by the time the small shopkeepers and slaves arrived hungry and thirsty after a hard day's work.

Paul could hardly believe his ears. The report was so bizarre that he suspected exaggeration. Certainly it was not the sort of thing on which he could rely unconditionally. He quickly came to the conclusion that it was imperative either to go himself or to send someone to check out the situation in Corinth. For two reasons he chose not to go himself. He needed to be available to other churches, who would expect to find him in Ephesus. And he had the perfect emissary in Timothy, who was both experienced and deeply imbued with Paul's ideas and standards (Phil 2:20). Moreover, some years earlier he had reported on a troubled situation in Thessalonica (1 Thess 3:6).

As not infrequently happens, while Timothy was en route to Corinth a delegation from Corinth comprised of Stephanas, Fortunatus, and Achaicus arrived in Ephesus (1 Cor 16:15-17). They were the bearers of a letter (1 Cor 7:1) in which were set out a series of problems on which the Corinthians wanted his opinion. The community was split on issues such as the appropriateness of sex in marriage (1 Cor 7:1-11), the legitimacy of eating meat offered to idols (1 Corinthians 8–10), the correct hierarchy of spiritual gifts (1 Corinthians 12–14), and the physical resurrection of Christ (1 Corinthians 15).

While happy to be consulted, Paul was deeply perturbed both by the issues the Corinthians saw as problems and by those they did not see fit to mention. Their letter, for example, said nothing about divisions in the community or about its liturgical practices. If these were not seen as problems by the Corinthians, then something very serious was wrong with their perception of what Christianity was all about. Paul did not have to wait for Timothy to check the facts. The delegation could respond to all his questions, and no doubt they did so with perfect frankness and a certain amount of pride.

They believed that they had done precisely what Paul had asked of them, "work out your salvation with fear and trembling" (Phil 2:12).

Contrary to the paralyzing prudence of the Galatians, the Corinthians had eagerly accepted the responsibility of deciding in detail what it meant to be a Christian on the basis of the general principles Paul had given them. They had confidence in their intelligence and the courage to put their conclusions into practice. Good will, Paul now ruefully recognized, was not enough. There were all sorts of reasons why the Corinthians should have gotten things wrong, but it would be very surprising if Paul admitted even to himself that the guidance he gave them might have been susceptible of misinterpretation.

As a qualified orator Paul had been trained to get to the root of conflictual situations. His instinct was not to treat all the issues raised by the letter from Corinth and the report of Chloe's people as separate and unrelated problems, but to look for a common thread that could be traced to a single source. He needed to get behind the symptoms to the real disease. This would have been all the more imperative in the present situation in that the sheer quantity of errors set Corinth apart from all his other foundations. No other church had ever made so many mistakes. What could possibly explain the difference at Corinth?

It did not take long for the thought of Apollos to pop into Paul's mind. He had been instinctively uneasy when Prisca and Aquila first told him of Apollos' departure for Corinth. The latter had stayed there a year and had never visited any of the other Pauline churches. Perhaps his teaching was the factor that made Corinth different? This led Paul to question the delegation very closely regarding what Apollos had done at Corinth. To supplement their answers, of course, he had Apollos himself, who was now resident at Ephesus.

As the discussion went on it became clear to Paul that most, if not all, of the trouble at Corinth stemmed from one group, which had been strongly influenced by Apollos but undoubtedly had misinterpreted his teaching in much the same way that Paul himself had been misrepresented. It is clear from 1 Cor 16:12 that Paul had no problem with Apollos personally. This group, which for convenience can be called the Spirit-people (*pneumatikoi*), had so inadequately appropriated Apollos' version of Philo's teaching on the "heavenly man" and "earthly man" that they can be held responsible for the problems dealt with in thirteen of the sixteen chapters in 1 Corinthians.[100]

This confirmed Paul's bias against speculative theology. One had only to look at the fruits it produced. He had always thought it unnecessary. Now he knew it to be positively harmful. It turned out to be most unfortunate that Timothy was not available at just this moment because, as 2 Corinthians shows, he would never have permitted Paul to adopt the strategy he employed in writing 1 Corinthians. In his absence Paul selected Sosthenes as co-author (1 Cor 1:1). This would be an improbable choice were he not the Sosthenes who was beaten before Gallio by other

Jews at Corinth for his mismanagement of the case against Paul (Acts 18:17). Subsequently, like Crispus, another *archisynagogos* (Acts 18:8), he had become a Christian, and somehow ended up in Ephesus. Paul selected him rather than Titus, for example, presumably because he knew the community at Corinth intimately, at first as a Jew hostile to Christians and then as a believer. Perhaps because he felt flattered to be chosen, Sosthenes made no effort to restrain Paul as he developed his strategy for dealing with the Spirit-people.

Paul refused absolutely to make the slightest effort to understand what the Spirit-people were trying to do. Their aspirations were irrelevant. The idea of entering into a dialogue that would guide them to the truth was anathema to him. He was so angry that he simply wanted to lash out and punish. It would be nice to think that his fury was fueled exclusively by concern for the truth, but it is more likely that it embodied a strong personal sense of injury. The Spirit-people had preferred Apollos' message to his, and evidently contrasted him unfavorably with Apollos. If Paul did not offer them "wisdom" (as Apollos had; 1 Cor 2:6) might it not be that he was incapable of the lofty religious insights that are integral to genuine religious authority? Was Paul's refusal to use rhetoric really rooted in principle (1 Cor 2:2)? Was not oratorical incompetence a more likely explanation for his rather inarticulate, simple message? Such wounding questions go a long way to explaining Paul's desire to hurt the Spirit-people in return. He wanted to crush, not reform.

In 1 Cor 2:6-16 Paul's vengeance takes the form of a cruel intellectual game. What he does is to take some of the key terms in the lexicon of the Spirit-people and give them completely different meanings. His intention was to mystify them and thereby reduce them to confused silence when the letter was read aloud at Corinth. He could be sure that the Spirit-people came from the educated leisured class, who were envied for their lifestyle and despised for their intellectual pretensions. They would also have been a tiny minority (1 Cor 1:26), and Paul was counting on the sniggers and sneers of the rest as the Spirit-people whispered to each other in consternation. They were not so smart after all!

Paul is even more brutal in the savage questions of 1 Cor 4:7: "Who sees anything different in you? What have you that you did not receive?" In other words, you personally are nothing, and you have never achieved anything. It is hard to believe that a pastor could condemn brothers and sisters in Christ so harshly. But Paul does not stop there. He goes on to mock them mercilessly by taking their spiritual language literally, thereby transforming their legitimate aspirations into absurd social attainments: "Without us you have become kings! And would that you did reign so that we might share the rule with you!" (1 Cor 4:8). Here the true orator surfaced in Paul, and he knew perfectly well what he was doing. What mattered was scoring an effective point, not truth and decency. Once again he counted on the malicious laughter and contemptuous looks of the majority.

Timothy was still in Corinth when the delegation returned with the letter, and he would have been profoundly shocked at Paul's lack of sensitivity. His attack was so unmerited and intemperate that even the Paul party is unlikely to have gloated in victory. Any decent Christian would have been repelled by the total lack of charity or comprehension in his demolition of the Spirit-people. Timothy could see that Paul's venom had done him serious damage in the eyes of the community. His judgment was henceforth suspect, and he could no longer expect automatic support.

For the Spirit-people it went much deeper. They had been completely alienated by their public humiliation and became Paul's implacable enemies. Knowing that they could not reach him directly, they determined to attack him indirectly by frustrating his ambitions for the church in Corinth. And they had arms immediately to hand. Having traveled from Galatia via Philippi and Thessalonica, the Antiochean delegation at last arrived to claim Corinth as a daughter church of the Judaizing community of Antioch. Once the Spirit-people heard of their opposition to Paul they welcomed them with open arms. The two groups had little in common, but stranger alliances have been forged against a common enemy.

Timothy was deeply disturbed by the thought that part of the community was prepared to pay serious attention to the Antiocheans. He returned to Ephesus as quickly as he could, and broke the news to Paul. The latter's depression can easily be imagined. It must have been one of the worst moments in his life. He knew the strength of the Judaizers' arguments, and Timothy had made him fully aware that he could not count on any residual loyalty among the Corinthians. Moreover, unlike the slow-moving Galatians, they were used to making up their minds quickly and independently. In this instance Paul decided against writing a letter. The Corinthians were so hostile that they might tear it up before reading it in public.

The situation was complicated by another factor. In his letter Paul had told the Corinthians that he intended to leave Ephesus after Pentecost, which in 54 c.e. fell on June 2,[101] and to go first to Macedonia. Then he would travel south to Corinth in the late summer, and if the sailing season had ended he would winter with them (1 Cor 16:5-6). The purpose of this visit to Philippi and Thessalonica might have been simply to check on his foundations. But he may have been concerned particularly about the Antiochean Judaizers. They were backtracking him, and so after Galatia they would have headed for Macedonia. Paul's rather leisurely plans for the summer would suggest that he felt he had plenty of time to reinforce the resistance to the Antiocheans, which had begun with one of his letters to Philippi (Phil 3:2–4:1).

Timothy's report from Corinth galvanized Paul. If the Judaizers were already in Corinth it meant that they had *already* passed through Philippi and Thessalonica. Thus instead of one problem (Corinth) to worry about, he now had three. Paul could have decided to maintain his original plan and gone to Macedonia to salvage what he could from the wreckage left by the Antiocheans. But then he would have been playing catch-up, and the caliber of the church at Philippi in particular gave him the faint hope that at least some of his Macedonian converts would have resisted the seduction of the Judaizers. The impact of 1 Corinthians had made even residual loyalty at Corinth suspect, and the opportunity to confront the Judaizers in person could not be neglected. Confident in his great oratorical skills, Paul was sure he would win any competition. But Philippi and Thessalonica could not be ignored. Thus Paul decided to split his forces. He would go to Corinth alone and send Timothy, his closest collaborator, and Erastus to Macedonia to deal with the situation there (Acts 19:21).

Paul reached Corinth in June or July of 54 C.E. His arrival came as a surprise because he was expected much later. What happened then is not entirely clear. All our knowledge of the event is indirect. It has to be deduced by incidental references in 2 Cor 2:1-13 and 7:6-16.[102] The established facts are: (1) a single Christian made a serious personal attack on Paul and (2) the Corinthian community refused to take sides and remained neutral.

It is easy to fill out the picture. Paul was attacked by the leader of the Antiochean delegation who, knowing the humor of the Corinthians, left aside the question of his Judaizing Gospel and developed the criticism of Paul that had been one of his major tools in Galatia. There he had focused on the accusation that Paul misrepresented the Gospel with which he had been entrusted. He preached merely his own ideas, not the common Gospel. Now, in addition, he could point to Paul's ill-treatment of the Spirit-people. Would any decent Christian, let alone one who claimed to be a religious leader, have treated brothers and sisters in Christ so harshly and unforgivingly? No doubt Paul pressed the Corinthians to reject the intruder out of hand. He had no place among them, whereas he, Paul, had begotten them in Christ (1 Cor 4:15).

The neutrality of the Corinthians is perfectly understandable. They had nothing with which to defend Paul. They did not know his antecedents or the terms of his commission, and what affection they might have had for him had been alienated to a great extent by his behavior. A very human desire to exact revenge might simply have taken the form of an assertion that no one should be condemned without a fair hearing This, of course, is precisely what Paul wanted to avoid. He knew the seductive power of the Judaizers' arguments. He also could see that the conditions were not propitious for a continued debate. Hence he proposed a breathing-space, a cooling-down period. He would make a visit to Macedonia, and when he returned to Corinth the whole matter could be discussed in a calmer atmosphere (2 Cor 1:16).

It is not difficult to imagine Paul's frame of mind as he tramped north across the great double plain of Thessaly, which in summer is one of the hottest places in Europe. His grip on Corinth was anything but secure. He might have lost Philippi and Thessalonica. And he did not know what had happened in Galatia. With good reason he felt that his world was collapsing around him. His life's work was crumbling into dust. His three-week depression lifted, however, as soon as he got to Thessalonica. The Antiochean delegation had reached Corinth so quickly because they had received short shrift in Macedonia. Once it became evident that they were hostile to Paul and his Gospel they were hustled away from Philippi, and then again from Thessalonica. The churches Paul saw as closest to his ideal (1 Thess 1:6-8; Phil 2:14-16) had proved worthy of his trust.

Paul's sense of relief must have been enormous. No doubt his first instinct would have been to roar back to Corinth in triumph and to humiliate the Antiocheans by flaunting their failure. Moreover, he could use the fidelity of the Macedonian churches to stigmatize the ambivalence of their Corinthian brethren. Now he would take his revenge on those who had refused him the respect and obedience due their father in Christ.

Fortunately Timothy was still in Macedonia and succeeded in turning Paul from such a disastrous course of action. Timothy's moderation shamed Paul's intemperate approach, and the apostle gradually came to his senses. Together the two decided that it would be best to extend the cooling-off period by returning to Ephesus and from there to write an irenic letter to Corinth. It would enable Paul to get his point across calmly without any possibility of interruptions. This, of course, meant another change of travel plans—and the breaking of his promise to come back to Corinth from Macedonia—which subsequently would be the basis for a charge of inconsistency against him at Corinth (2 Cor 1:16-17). Be that as it may, it seemed the lesser of two evils to Paul and Timothy. They would have reached Ephesus some time around the middle of August, 54 C.E.

Unfortunately the letter that Paul immediately wrote to Corinth has not survived. It must have been one of the most extraordinary products of Paul's oratorical skills. We can catch a hint of its tone by what he says about its reception in 2 Cor 2:1-13 and 7:6-16. The letter had to be very carefully crafted. He had to be firm and clear in revealing how deeply wounded he had been by the treachery of the community in not supporting him against the Antiocheans (hence the name the "Severe Letter"). He had to shock them sufficiently to crack the carapace of their complacency. But on the other hand, he could not risk alienating them further. Assurances of his abiding affection had to moderate effective reproofs without eviscerating them. Every word was calculated and weighed. The delicacy of the decisions made the writing an agonizing business. As Paul himself said, "I wrote you out of much affliction and anguish of heart and with many tears" (2 Cor 2:4).

One factor, however, simplified the process of composition. Paul did not have to try to refute the Judaizers. He had decided to send the letter with Titus (2 Cor 2:13; 7:6). Not only had Titus missed the fracas in Corinth, but a unique qualification made him the most suitable emissary. He had been with Paul at the meeting in Jerusalem (Gal 2:1-3), where it was decided that no Gentile converts made by the missions of Antioch had to be circumcised. His first-hand knowledge of the views of the mother church, therefore, could be deployed to refute all claims by the Antiocheans and to correct any distortions in their portrait of Paul.

By the time the letter was ready to be dispatched the end of the sailing season was fast approaching. Paul could not know how long it would take Titus to get to Corinth, or the duration of his mission there. Titus, for his part, could not hurry the assimilation of Paul's message, nor could he dictate how the Corinthians would come to terms with it. It was entirely possible that the ships would have ceased to move by the time Titus was ready to report back. Hence Paul instructed him to return by the much longer land route through Macedonia.

This condemned Paul to a long period of anxiety. It would be several months at least before he could get news from Titus, who would have to cover just over a thousand kilometers (676 miles). Paul could hardly have known that his own time in Ephesus was coming to an end and that the turmoil of his departure would prove a most effective distraction. In his account of the riot of the silversmiths (see p. 92) Luke is so concerned to give the impression that Paul was not forced out of Ephesus that one immediately suspects this is exactly what happened.

We have already had occasion to note the hostility to Paul within the community at Ephesus, but it is unlikely that mere dislike would have made Paul feel that his life was at risk. His reference to fighting with wild beasts at Ephesus (1 Cor 15:32) must be understood metaphorically. Nonetheless it points to a significant danger, coming from outside the church, which is confirmed by the further allusion to "many adversaries" (1 Cor 16:9). Clearly Paul had something weighing on his mind.

Presumably this last was the cause of "the affliction we experienced in Asia," a trial so grave that "we despaired of life itself; indeed, we felt that we had received a sentence of death" (2 Cor 1:8b-9). The formulation suggests Paul's conviction that his days were numbered rather than a judicial condemnation. The way it is presented indicates that it had happened fairly recently and that the Corinthians were being informed for the first time (2 Cor 1:8a). We are forced to assume that a sudden increase in the intensity of the hostility surrounding Paul eventually forced him to abandon Ephesus not long after the dispatch of Titus to Corinth.

This permits us to see his instructions to Titus in a new light, because on leaving Ephesus Paul went north to Troas, where he began a new ministry (2 Cor 2:12-13). Titus would have had to pass through there on his way from Macedonia to Ephesus. If there was any consolation in this move for Paul, it was that once again he had the opportunity to do what he did best: to found a church.[103]

EPHESUS MUCH LATER

Paul's departure from Ephesus in the autumn of 54 C.E. was the end of his ministry there, but he was to have two contacts with it in later years, the first on his journey to Jerusalem with the collection for the poor and the second when he had to take Timothy's place briefly at the head of the community.

At the end of the winter of 55–56 C.E. Paul dispatched the letter to the Romans from Corinth and then turned to the task of getting the collection to Jerusalem. The obvious choice would have been to go by boat, as he had always done in the past when going east. Instead he opted to make a long swing around the northern end of the Aegean. In the light of the evidence we have, the only justification for this much longer and more dangerous journey was Paul's conviction that he might not survive his visit to Jerusalem (Rom 15:30-31). He wanted to visit his foundations one last time.

Paul's experience of trying to say farewell to the community at Troas was so traumatic (Acts 20:6-13) that he found himself emotionally drained. He decided that he did not have the strength to repeat it at Ephesus, where he knew so many more people. Therefore he commanded the elders of the church there to meet him in Miletus (Acts 20:17). They could transmit his goodbyes to the church in which he had spent more years than any other. He could not bring himelf to bid them farewell formally. He could only hope that they would understand what he meant by hinting that his future was uncertain (Acts 20:22) and that henceforward they had complete responsibility for the church at Ephesus (Acts 20:28). They should also have picked up a clue when Paul insisted on leaving Timothy at Ephesus. The reasons he gave to placate his closest friend and collaborator no doubt differed from his real motive. He was convinced that he might die in Jerusalem and he did not want Timothy to suffer the same fate. They were so closely identified as missionary partners that to accuse one was to condemn both. In depriving himself of his strongest support Paul lived the self-sacrificing love he preached.

A lot of water had flowed under the bridge by the time Paul again met Timothy in Ephesus. Paul had escaped the mob in Jerusalem only by being arrested by the Romans. He had spent two years in captivity in Caesarea before being sent to be judged by the emperor in Rome (Acts 27–28). On his release from prison there he had attempted a mission in Spain (Rom 15:24), which proved to be a failure; this can be dated to the summer of 62 C.E. The only place in the east in which he had unfinished business was Illyricum (Rom 15:19). His ministry there had been interrupted by the need to go to Corinth in the autumn of 55 C.E. Paul probably spent a year or so in Illyricum, and with the advent of summer he headed east along the Via Egnatia, passing through Thessalonica and Philippi before crossing over to Troas. At that point the heat of summer was beginning to tell, and he left his heavy winter cloak and some documents with Carpus (2 Tim 4:13) before beginning the long walk south to Ephesus (210 miles; 350 km).

It had been ten years since Paul last saw Ephesus, and no doubt he wondered what changes had taken place. There would, of course, have been new buildings, but the changes that interested him would have been in the church and in its leader, Timothy.[104] He was particularly curious as to how the latter had developed. The joy of their reunion was short-lived. Paul could not hide from himself that Timothy had not lived up to his expectations. There was no doctrinal failure. It was not that he was no longer orthodox, or that he had permitted false teaching to infiltrate the church. By Paul's admittedly high standards Timothy simply was not sufficiently energetic, courageous, or involved; he was not fulfilling his ministry. In particular Timothy had not blocked the development at Ephesus of a group whose foolish and inexpert research gave rise to "godless chatter" (2 Tim 2:16).

Cruel as it seemed, Paul felt he had no alternative but dismiss Timothy and take charge himself. The realization that he had failed Paul reduced Timothy to tears (2 Tim 1:4), but Paul certainly made his departure as easy as possible. In all probability he charged him with a mission to report on some of the churches that had been founded from Ephesus. The mother church had the right and duty of challenge should the daughter church not maintain standards. Perhaps Timothy went to the Lycus valley or even as far as Galatia. Paul had been out of touch with these churches for over ten years, to the best of our knowledge.

Paul's assumption of control did not work out well. There had always been opposition to him at Ephesus (Phil 1:14-18), and the central problem was one that he was constitutionally incapable of dealing with. He was completely out of sympathy with the intellectual aspirations of the researchers and debaters. In his irritation he dealt with them in the same inappropriate way that he had confronted the Spirit-people in Corinth, and with the same disastrous result. "All who are in Asia turned away from me" (2 Tim 1:15). The hyperbole intensifies the note of dejection, almost of despair. The opposition to Paul might even have spread to the daughter churches of Ephesus.

Even though Paul had not learned how to handle those who treat every issue as an opportunity for discussion, his intermediate visit to Corinth had taught him when to cut his losses. Timothy had been right in not letting him return to Corinth from Macedonia; the "Severe Letter" had won a positive result from the Corinthians and set their relationship on a new basis. Paul now had the humility to admit that successful leadership of the church at Ephesus demanded qualities he did not have. His presence there was only making things worse. His response was to withdraw to Miletus, some fifty miles (80 km) to the south (2 Tim 4:20), having decided to send Tychicus to take over at Ephesus (2 Tim 4:12).

For Paul it must have been a melancholy departure from a city in which he had done his most creative theological work. In writing Galatians he had focused for the first time on Jesus as a unique individual and took the first steps in developing his highly distinctive christology. It was on that occasion, too, that he had his first insight into the relation between believers among themselves and with Jesus. This insight he was able to take a crucial step further in Colossians, and to develop fully in 1 Corinthians. This last letter is a kaleidescope of fresh theological ideas. The problems that appeared in Corinth and the issues they raised gave Paul the opportunity to draw together, and to relate to one another, the fruits of his reflections during the years he spent in Ephesus.

NOTES

FOREWORD, pages xiii–xv

1. *Greek Anthology* 9.424.
2. For a list see Christine Thomas, "At Home in the City of Artemis," 116–17 in Helmut Koester, ed., *Ephesos, Metropolis of Asia*, Harvard Theological Studies 41 (Cambridge, MA: Harvard University Press, 2004).
3. Notably his *Bible Studies: Contributions Chiefly from Papyri and Inscriptions to the History of the Language, the Literature, and Religion of Hellenistic Judaism and Primitive Christianity* (Edinburgh: T&T Clark, 1901); *Light from the Ancient East: The New Testament Illustrated by Recently Discovered Texts of the Graeco-Roman World*, trans. Lionel R. M. Strachan (London: Hodder & Stoughton, 1910; repr. Grand Rapids: Baker Book House, 1978).
4. For Deissmann's involvement with Ephesus see Albrecht Gerber, "Gustav Adolf Deissmann (1866–1937): trailblazer in biblical studies, in the archaeology of Ephesus, and in international reconciliation," *Buried History* 41 (2005): 29–42.
5. So, for example, Gustaf Dalman, *Sacred Sites and Ways: Studies in the Topography of the Gospels* (London: S.P.C.K., 1935).
6. Witness the proliferation of national archaeological schools in Jerusalem at this period (American, British, French, German). See Neil Asher Silberman, *Digging for God and Country: Exploration, Archaeology and the Secret Struggle for the Holy Land (1799–1917)* (New York: Knopf, 1982).

PART 1, pages 5–7

1. *Barrington Atlas of the Greek and Roman World*, ed. Richard Talbert (Princeton: Princeton University Press, 2000), map 56 D4.
2. Antoine Hermary, "The Greeks in Marseilles and the Western Mediterranean," in *The Greeks beyond the Aegean*, ed. Vassos Karageorghis (New York: Onassis Foundation, 2003), 6.
3. Gocha Tsetskhladze, "Greeks beyond the Bosphorus," in *The Greeks beyond the Aegean*, ed. Karageorghis, 131.
4. Hemary, "The Greeks in Marseilles," 64.
5. See the *Barrington Atlas* maps 25 and 27.
6. *Oxford Classical Dictionary* (1996), 1440a.
7. Ernst Kuhnert, "Ephesia," in *Paulys Real-encyclopädie der Classischen Altertumswissenschaft*, ed. Georg Wissowa (Stuttgart: J. B. Metzger, 1905), 5:2753–2773, at 2763.
8. Ibid., 2764.
9. Peter Scherrer, ed., *Ephesus: The New Guide* (Istanbul: Ege Yayinian, 2000), 210–13.

10. Christine Thomas, "At Home in the City of Artemis: Religion in Ephesos in the Literary Imagination of the Roman Period," in *Ephesos, Metropolis of Asia: An Interdisciplinary Approach to its Archaeology, Religion, and Culture,* ed. Helmut Koester, Harvard Theological Studies 41 (Cambridge, MA: Harvard University Press, 2004), 86 n. 12.

11. Lynn Di Donnici, "The Images of Artemis and Greco-Roman Worship: A Reconsideration," *Harvard Theological Review* 85 (1992): 389–415.

12. For the origins of the myth see Robert Graves, *The Greek Myths* (London: Penguin, 1960), 1:355.

13. *Oxford Classical Dictionary* (1996), 70a.

14. See the *Barrington Atlas*, maps 56 and 61.

15. *Oxford Classical Dictionary* (1996), 685b.

16. Ibid., 1157.

17. Ibid., 355.

18. Scherrer, *New Guide*, 186–87, though see 60.

19. See the map in Moses I. Finley, ed., *Atlas of Classical Archaeology* (London: Chatto & Windus, 1977), 200.

20. Scherrer, *New Guide*, 188.

21. Georges Radet, *Ephesiaca. 1. La topographie d'Éphèse. 2. La colonisation d'Éphèse par les Ioniens* (Bordeaux: Feret, 1908), 10–11.

22. Scherrer, *New Guide*, 186.

23. Wilhelm Alzinger, "Ephesos vom Beginn der römischen Herrschaft in Kleinasien bis zum Ende der Principatzeit: Archäologischer Teil," in *Aufstieg und Niedergang der Römischen Welt* II.7.2, 811 n. 1.

24. Guy Rogers, *The Sacred Identity of Ephesos* (London: Routledge, 1991), 108.

25. Friedrich W. Blass, Albert Debrunner, and Robert W. Funk, *A Greek Grammar of the New Testament and Other Early Christian Literature* (Cambridge: Cambridge University Press; Chicago: University of Chicago Press, 1961), §442.9.

26. Scherrer, *New Guide*, 146.

27. *Oxford Classical Dictionary* (1996), 1417b.

28. Henry G. Liddell, Robert Scott, and Henry Stuart-Jones, *A Greek-English Lexicon* (Oxford: Clarendon Press, 1966), 248b.

29. Richard Oster, "The Ephesian Artemis as an Opponent of Early Christianity," *Jahrbuch für Antike und Christentum* 19 (1976): 39.

30. Liddell, Scott, and Jones, *A Greek-English Lexicon*, 248.

31. Pausanias, *Guide to Greece* 9.2.3; see Graves, *Greek Myths*, 1:86.

32. Ovid, *Metamorphoses* 6.333-35.

33. Graves, *Greek Myths*, 1:55.

34. *Oxford Classical Dictionary* (1996), 1079b.

35. See the map by A. Schindler in Kuhnert, "Ephesia," *PW* 5:2773.

36. Graves, *Greek Myths*, 1:57.

37. Rogers, *The Sacred Identity of Ephesos*, 145–46.

38. Ibid., 150 n. 15.

39. Oster, "The Ephesian Artemis," 30–37.

40. *Oxford Classical Dictionary* (1996), 1369b.

41. Charles Picard, *Éphèse et Claros. Recherches sur les sanctuaires et les cultes de l'Ionie du nord.* Bibliothèque des Écoles Françaises d'Athènes et de Rome 123 (Paris: Boccard, 1922), 64.

42. *Oration* 60.3; see Thomas, "At Home in the City of Artemis," 97.

43. See Pausanias, *Guide to Greece*, 7.2.7, and the commentary in Peter Levi, *Pausanias: Guide to Greece* (London: Penguin, 1971), 1:232.

44. Picard, *Éphèse et Claros*, 52–53.

45. Dieter Knibbe, "Via Sacra Ephesiaca: New Aspects of the Cult of Artemis Ephesia," in *Ephesos, Metropolis of Asia*, ed. Helmut Koester, 148.

46. David Magie, *Roman Rule in Asia Minor to the End of the Third Century after Christ* (Princeton: Princeton University Press, 1950), 921 n. 13.

47. Scherrer, *New Guide*, 68.

48. Oster, "Ephesus as a Religious Center under the Principate, I. Paganism before Constantine" *Aufstieg und Niedergang der Römischen Welt* II.18.3, 1728.

49. Ibid., 1701–2.

50. Ibid., 1702.

51. Magie, *Roman Rule in Asia Minor*, 545.

52. Susan Woodford, *The Parthenon* (Cambridge: Cambridge University Press, 1981), 17.

53. Bernard McDonagh, *Turkey: The Aegean and Mediterranean Coasts*. Blue Guide (London: A. & C. Black; New York: W. W. Norton, 1989), 265.

54. Woodford, *The Parthenon*, 33.

55. This ban was respected by Cicero (*De divinatione* 1.23.47), Plutarch (*Alexander* 3.5), and Lucian (*Passing of Peregrinus* 22).

56. Horace L. Jones, *The Geography of Strabo*, vol. 6, LCL 223 (London: Heinemann; Cambridge, MA: Harvard University Press, 1940), 227 n. 4, but the reference there given to Vitruvius 1.1.4 is incorrect.

57. Thomas, "At Home in the City of Artemis," 90.

58. Liddell, Scott, and Jones, *A Greek-English Lexicon*, 1086a.

59. Ernst Kuhnert, "Ephesia," *PW* 5:2759.

60. Liddell, Scott, and Jones, *A Greek-English Lexicon*, 697b.

61. Oster, "Ephesus as a Religious Center," 1722.

62. Kuhnert, "Ephesia," *PW* V, 2758.

63. Liddell, Scott, and Jones, *A Greek-English Lexicon*, 984a bottom.

64. Kent J. Rigsby, *Asylia: Territorial Inviolability in the Hellenistic World*. Hellenistic Culture and Society 22 (Berkeley: University of California Press, 1996), 3.

65. Ibid., 10.

66. Greg Horsley, *New Documents Illustrating Early Christianity* IV (North Ryde, N.S.W.: Ancient History Documentary Research Centre, Macquarie University, 1987), 168.

67. Magie, *Roman Rule in Asia Minor*, 470.

68. Rigsby, *Asylia*, 392.

69. Thomas, "At Home in the City of Artemis," 102.

70. Radet, *Ephesiaca*, 19.

71. Scherrer, *New Guide*, 178.

72. Ibid.

73. Richard Oster, "Ephesus," *Anchor Bible Dictionary* (New York: Doubleday, 1992), 2:543.

74. Heinrich Zabehlicky, "Preliminary Views of the Ephesian Harbour," in *Ephesos, Metropolis of Asia*, ed. Helmut Koester, 205.

75. Greg Horsley, *New Documents Illustrating Early Christianity* V (North Ryde, N.S.W.: Ancient History Documentary Research Centre, Macquarie University, 1989), 95–114.

76. Horsley, *New Documents* IV, 170.

77. Horsley, *New Documents* V, 108–9.

78. Horsley, *New Documents* IV, 7.

79. T. Robert S. Broughton, "Roman Asia," in *An Economic Survey of Ancient Rome* IV, ed. Tenney Frank (Baltimore: Johns Hopkins University Press, 1938), 842.

80. Diogenes Laertius, 6.2.77; Plutarch, *Alexander*, 14.

81. *Oxford Classical Dictionary* (1996), 1635b.

82. *Barrington Atlas*, map 61 at the very top of E2.

83. Horsley, *New Documents* IV, 105.

84. *Oxford Classical Dictionary* (1996), 1275b.

85. Robert Scherk, *Rome and the Greek East to the Death of Augustus* (Cambridge: Cambridge University Press, 1984), 86, ll. 22–24.

86. Horsley, *New Documents* IV, 129.

87. Horsley, *New Documents* V, 105.

88. Scherrer, *New Guide*, 188.

89. Suetonius, *Gaius Caligula*, 21.

90. *Oxford Classical Dictionary* (1996), 1142a.

91. Rogers, *The Sacred Identity of Ephesos*, 60.

92. Ibid., 94.

93. Broughton, "Roman Asia," 814.

94. Horsley, *New Documents* IV, 49–55.

95. *Antiquities of the Jews* 14.225, 230.

96. Rogers, *The Sacred Identity of Ephesos*, 101.

97. Anthony D. Macro, "The Cities of Asia Minor under the Roman Imperium," in *Aufstieg und Niedergang der Römischen Welt* II.7.2 (1980), 662.

98. David H. French, "The Roman Road System of Asia Minor," in *Aufstieg und Niedergang der Römischen Welt* II.7.2 (1980), 707.

99. There are excellent maps of the changed coast in McDonagh, *Turkey*, 297–98.

100. There is a good plan in Ingrid D. Rowland and Thomas N. Howe, *Vitruvius: Ten Books on Architecture* (Cambridge: Cambridge University Press, 1999), 195.

101. *Oxford Classical Dictionary* (1996), 467b.

102. For both locations see the *Barrington Atlas* map 61, E2 and H2.

103. *Barrington Atlas* map 61.

104. *Barrington Atlas* map 56.

105. Ibid.

106. *Barrington Atlas* maps 61 and 65.

107. French, "Roman Roads," 707.

108. *Barrington Atlas* maps, 65, 62, 63, and 64.

109. *Oxford Classical Dictionary* (1996), 130.

110. Ibid., 666.

111. Ibid., 1283.

112. Ibid., 990b.

113. S. R. Llewelyn, *New Documents Illustrating Early Christianity* VIII (North Ryde, N.S.W.: Ancient History Documentary Research Centre, Macquarie University; Grand Rapids: Eerdmans, 1988), 58.

114. *Oxford Classical Dictionary* (1996), 1275b.

115. Arnold H. M. Jones, *The Cities of the Eastern Roman Provinces* (Oxford: Oxford University Press, 1971), 59.

116. Stephen Mitchell, *Anatolia: Land, Men, and Gods in Asia Minor* (Oxford: Clarendon Press, 1995), 1:30.

117. Horsley, *New Documents* IV, 168.

118. *Oxford Classical Dictionary* (1996), 189.

119. See Plutarch, *Lives: Antony* 56.1 (p. 128).

120. Magie, *Roman Rule in Asia Minor*, 406–7.

121. Ibid., 471.

122. Broughton, "Roman Asia," 583–84.

123. Ibid., 815.

124. See Plutarch, *Lives: Antony* 24.3 (p. 127).

125. *Antiquities of the Jews* 15.89.

126. Scherrer, *New Guide*, 124.

127. *Oxford Classical Dictionary* (1996), 202.

128. Radet, *Ephesiaca*, 21–22.

129. So Strabo, 14.1.3 (p. 9) and Pausanias, 7.2.8 (p. 97).

130. *Oxford Classical Dictionary* (1996), 355.

131. Ibid., 144.

132. Ibid., 1116.

133. Ibid., 86.

134. *PW* V, 2772–73.

135. The route is shown in detail in the *Barrington Atlas* maps 61, 65, 62, 63, and 66.

136. *Oxford Classical Dictionary* (1996), 1275.

137. Peter Lampe, "Keine 'Sklavenflucht' des Onesimus," *Zeitschrift für die Neutestamentliche Wissenschaft* 76 (1985): 135–37.

138. Llewelyn, *New Documents* VIII, 11–12.

139. Rigsby, *Asylia*, 10.

140. Llewelyn, *New Documents* VIII, 14, 35.

141. Scherrer, *New Guide*, 80.

142. Appian, *Mithridatic Wars* 12.3.21 (p. 39).

143. See Tacitus, *Annals* 4.55-56 (p. 137).

144. *Oxford Classical Dictionary* (1996), 619.

145. Jerome Murphy-O'Connor, *Paul: His Story* (Oxford: Oxford University Press, 2004), 225.

146. *Oxford Classical Dictionary* (1996), 195.

147. Ibid., 338.

148. Mitchell, *Anatolia* 1:219b.

149. Rogers, *The Sacred Identity of Ephesos*, 59.

150. *Oxford Classical Dictionary* (1996), 470a.

151. *Jewish War* 6.282.

152. Marty Stevens, *Temples, Tithes, and Taxes: The Temple and the Economic Life of Ancient Israel* (Peabody, MA: Hendrickson, 2006), 137.

153. Ibid., 160.

154. Broughton, "Roman Asia," 889–90.

155. Ibid., 559–60.

156. Pliny, 34.19.58; Strabo, 13.1.30.

157. Broughton, "Roman Asia," 679.

158. Stevens, *Temples, Tithes, and Taxes*, 129.

159. Michael White, "Urban Development and Social Change in Imperial Ephesos" in *Ephesos, Metropolis of Asia*, ed. Helmut Koester, 41.

160. This natural feature runs from south to north for some 500 meters, rising to a height of 87 meters. Its southern tip is about 300 meters from the Artemision. The name is a Turkish corruption of *Hagios Theologos*, "Holy Theologian," the name given to Saint John the Evangelist; see Procopius, *Buildings*, 5.1.4-6. The ridge housed the remnants of Ephesus from the sixth century c.e. onward (Scherrer, *New Guide*, 34).

161. *Barrington Atlas*, maps 61 and 56.

162. *Oxford Classical Dictionary* (1996), 654a.

163. *Barrington Atlas*, maps 56, 62, and 65.

164. *Oxford Classical Dictionary* (1996), 943a.

165. J. B. Lightfoot, *The Apostolic Fathers*, Part II/2, *Ignatius and Polycarp* (London: Macmillan, 1889), 2.

166. *To the Ephesians* contains clear allusions to Rom 8:5, 8 (§8); 1 Cor 3:16 (§15); 1 Cor 6:9 (§16); and 1 Cor 1:20, 23 (§18).

167. So Helmut Koester, "Ephesos in Early Christian Literature," in *Ephesos, Metropolis of Asia*, ed. Koester, 134.

168. Ignatius himself warns against reading too much into his letters: "I am not writing these things, my beloved, because I have learned that some of you are behaving like this" (*To the Magnesians* 11; see *To the Trallians* 8).

169. Lightfoot sees an allusion to the procession paid for by Gaius Vibius Salutaris in §9 of *To the Ephesians* (*Apostolic Fathers*, Part II/2, 17 and 54–55).

170. *Apostolic Fathers*, Part II/2, 241.

171. Murphy-O'Connor, *Paul His Story*, 211.

172. This, at least, is the interpretation of Eusebius, *History of the Church* 3.4.5.

173. Jerome Murphy-O'Connor, *Paul the Letter-Writer* (Collegeville, MN: Liturgical Press, 1995), 130.

174. E.g., J.D.G. Dunn, *Christianity in the Making*, vol. 1, *Jesus Remembered* (Grand Rapids and Cambridge, UK: Eerdmans, 2003); Richard Bauckham, *Jesus and the Eyewitnesses: The Gospels as Eyewitness Testimony* (Grand Rapids and Cambridge, UK: Eerdmans, 2006).

175. Eusebius, *History of the Church* 5.24.7.

176. *Antiquities of the Jews* 16.174.

177. For a convenient synoptic presentation see Christiane Saulnier, "Lois Romains sur les Juifs selon Flavius Josèphe," *Revue Biblique* 88 (1981): 196–98.

178. Adrian N. Sherwin-White, *The Roman Citizenship*, 2nd ed. (Oxford: Clarendon Press, 1973), 309, 322–26.

179. On the veracity of Josephus see in particular Shaye J. D. Cohen, *Josephus in Galilee and Rome: His Vita and Development as a Historian*, Columbia Studies in the Classical Tradition 8 (Leiden: Brill, 1979), 181.

180. Horsley, *New Documents* IV, 94.

181. Edith M. Smallwood, *The Jews under Roman Rule from Pompey to Diocletian: A Study in Political Relations*, SJLA 20 (Leiden: Brill, 1981), 126.

182. Ibid., 126 n. 21.

183. Ibid., 225.

184. Ibid., 143.

185. Jakob A. O. Larsen, *Representative Government in Greek and Roman History* (Berkeley: University of California Press, 1955).

186. Horsley, *New Documents* IV, 231.

187. Horsley, *New Documents* II, 10–19; *New Documents* IV, 231–32.

188. Broughton, "Roman Asia," 851.

189. Ibid., 854–55.

190. Herodotus, *History* 1.92 (p. 69).

191. Antipater of Sidon, *Greek Anthology* 9.58 (p. 160).

192. So Pliny, 16.79.213 and 36.21.95 (p. 116).

193. *Oxford Classical Dictionary* (1996), 1323a.

194. *Barrington Atlas*, map 51 G-H4.

195. *Epitoma rei militaris* 4.39.

196. Lionel Casson, *Ships and Seamanship in the Ancient World* (Princeton: Princeton University Press, 1971), 370.

197. Ibid., 82, 107.

198. Ibid., 368.

199. Ibid., 362.

200. Ibid., 189–90.

201. Ibid., 184–89.

202. For what billeting involved, see Appian, *Mithridatic Wars* 12.9.61 (p. 42).

203. Werner G. Kümmel, *Introduction to the New Testament* (London: SCM, 1975), 181–83.

204. Charles Kingsley Barrett, *The Acts of the Apostles: A Shorter Commentary* (London: T&T Clark, 2002), xxxiii; cf. 247.

205. Edward L. Hicks, "Demetrius the Silversmith," *Expositor* Series IV 1 (1890): 401–22.

206. Ernst Haenchen, *The Acts of the Apostles: A Commentary* (Philadelphia: Westminster, 1971), 572.

207. Justin Taylor, *Les Actes des deux apôtres* VI. *Commentaire historique (Act. 18,23-28,31)*. Études bibliques, n.s. 30 (Paris: Gabalda, 1996), 54.

208. White, "Urban Development and Social Change," 37.

209. Rick Strelan, *Paul, Artemis, and the Jews in Ephesus*, BZNW 80 (New York: Walter de Gruyter, 1996).

210. Rogers, *The Sacred Identity of Ephesos*, 83.

211. Ibid., 110.

212. Levi, *Pausanias* 1.241.

213. Scherrer, *New Guide*, 29

214. Graves, *Greek Myths* 1:355.

215. *Oxford Classical Dictionary* (1996), 664b.

216. Anton Bammer, *Das Heiligtum der Artemis von Ephesos* (Graz: Akademische Druck und Verlagsanstalt, 1984), 259.

217. Scherrer, *New Guide*, 68.

218. Knibbe, "Via Sacra Ephesiaca," 148.

219. Scherrer, *New Guide*, 184.

220. Thomas, "At Home in the City of Artemis," 109 n. 79.

221. A large honorific monument in the form of a U-shaped fountain was erected to him on Curetes' Street (Embolos) toward the end of the second century B.C.E. (Scherrer, *New Guide*, 126).

222. Rogers, *The Sacred Identity of Ephesos*, 107–8; Oster, "Ephesus as a Religious Center," 1682–84.

223. Josephus, *Antiquities of the Jews* 12.147-53.

224. William Ramsay, *The Cities of Saint Paul: Their Influence on his Life and Thought, The Cities of Eastern Asia Minor* (London: Hodder & Stoughton, 1907), 165–86.

225. Levi, *Pausanias* 2.253.

226. Ibid., 1.475.

227. *Oxford Classical Dictionary* (1996), 1612b.

228. Ibid., 1197.

229. Jones, *Cities of the Eastern Roman Provinces*, 77–79. The cities mentioned here lie in the Cayster and Maeander valleys. But there were others. South of Ephesus on the coast were Phygela and Marathesium, and to its north the coastal towns of Colophon, Lebedus, and Teos (*Barrington Atlas*, maps 56 and 61).

230. Cicero, *Atticus letter* 115; 6.1.15.

231. Macro, "Cities of Asia Minor," in *Aufstieg und Niedergang der Römischen Welt* II.7.2 (1980), 670.

232. Cicero, *Atticus letter* 115; 6.1.15.

233. Alfred Lucas and J. R. Harris, *Ancient Egyptian Materials and Industries* (London: E. Arnold & Co., 1948), 434–35.

234. Brunhilde Ridgway, "A Story of Five Amazons" *American Journal of Archaeology* 78 (1974): 9.

235. Ridgway, "Story of Five Amazons," with the reconstruction drawing in fig. 14 on plate 4.

236. Erich Winter, "Towards a Chronology of the Later Artemision at Ephesos," *American Journal of Archaeology* 84 (1980): 241.

237. Graves, *Greek Myths*, 1:57.

238. Diogenes Laertius, *Lives of Eminent Philosophers* 2.103.

239. Broughton, "Roman Asia," 601–02.

240. Ibid., 601.

241. Arthur Henderson, "The Temple of Diana at Ephesus," *Journal of the Royal Institute of British Architects* 41 (1933): 769.

242. Ibid., 770.

243. Arthur Henderson, "The Hellenistic Temple of Artemis at Ephesus," *Journal of the Royal Institute of British Architects* 22 (1915): 131; Henderson, "The Temple of Diana," 769.

244. There are fine illustrations of the proportions in Rowland and Howe, *Vitruvius*, 214, fig. 56.

245. The various possibilities are illustrated in Anton Bammer and Ulrike Muss, *Das Artemision von Ephesos. Das Weltwunder Ioniens in archäischer und klassischer Zeit* (Mainz: von Zabern, 1996), 50, fig.55.

246. Rowland and Howe, *Vitruvius*, 205, fig. 49.

247. Bammer and Muss, *Artemision*, 60.

248. E.g., ibid., 14, fig. 7.

249. *Oxford Classical Dictionary* (1996), 463a.

250. Procopius, *Buildings* 5.1.4-6. I have found it impossible to determine the origins of the oft-repeated legend that eight columns of the Temple of Artemis were used in Justinian's rebuilding of the Hagia Sophia in Constantinople. The credibility of the story is undermined by the fact that they would all have been fluted, which would have looked rather odd *inside* a building. It is possible, of course, that the fluting had been trimmed off.

251. Scherrer, *New Guide*, 34.

252. *Corpus Inscriptionum Graecarum* 3920.

253. *Antiquities of the Jews* 16.17.

254. Procopius, *Buildings* 5.1.7-12.

255. *Antiquities of the Jews* 16.20.

256. Horsley, *New Documents* IV, 50.

257. On such trials in general see James H. Oliver, "Greek Applications for Roman Trials," *American Journal of Philology* 100 (1979): 543–58.

258. Simon Hornblower, "Greece: The History of the Classical Period," in *The Oxford History of the Classical World*, eds. John Boardman, Jasper Griffin, and Oswyn Murray (Oxford: Oxford University Press, 1986), 145.

259. *Oxford Classical Dictionary* (1996), 901a.

260. Broughton, "Roman Asia," 517.

261. Ibid., 711.

262. *Barrington Atlas*, map 57.

263. Casson, *Ships and Seamanship*, 292–96.

264. Murphy-O'Connor, *Paul: His Story*, 167–69.

265. Broughton, "Roman Asia," 585.

266. *Oxford Classical Dictionary* (1996), 472b.

267. Smallwood, *Jews under Roman Rule*, 222 n. 12.

268. Ludwig Bürchner, "Ephesos," in *Paulys Real-encyclopädie der Classische Alter-tumswissenschaft* V/2, ed. Georg Wissowa (Stuttgart: J. B. Metzler, 1905), 2797.

269. Broughton, "Roman Asia," 813.

270. Bürchner, "Ephesos," 2799.

271. Josiah Russell, *Late Ancient and Medieval Population*, TAPA 48.3 (Philadelphia: American Philosophical Society, 1958), 80–81.

272. Magen Broshi, "La population de l'ancienne Jérusalem," *Revue Biblique* 82 (1975): 6.

273. White, "Urban Development and Social Change," 43.

274. Mitchell, *Anatolia* 1:243–44.

275. Tim Parkin, *Demography and Roman Society* (Baltimore: Johns Hopkins University Press, 1992), 89.

276. White, "Urban Development and Social Change," 57–79.

277. Ibid., 62.

278. Mitchell, *Anatolia* 1:57.

279. For details see Mitchell, *Anatolia* 1:143–49.

280. Thomas, "At Home in the City of Artemis," 83.

281. *Lives of the Sophists* 1.21; 518.

282. Broughton, "Roman Asia," 854.

283. Livy, *History* 45.28.

284. Picard, *Éphèse et Claros*, 121.

285. *Oxford Classical Dictionary* (1996), 335a.

286. Scherrer, *New Guide*, 92.

287. Dieter Knibbe, "Ephesos vom Beginn der römischen Herrschaft in Kleinasien bis zum Ende der Principatzeit: Historischer Teil," in *Aufstieg und Niedergang der Römischen Welt* II.7.2, 772–73.

288. Steven Friesen, "The Cult of the Roman Emperors in Ephesos: Temple Wardens, City Titles, and the Interpretation of the Revelation of John," in *Ephesos, Metropolis of Asia*, ed. Helmut Koester, 235.

289. Knibbe, "Ephesos vom Beginn der römischen Herrschaft," 775.

290. There are a number of conflicting accounts regarding the Ionian foundation of Ephesus. See Athenaeus (*Deipnosophistai* 361d-e; p. 47), Strabo (*Geography* 14.1.21; p. 17), and Pausanias (*Guide* 7.2.6-9; p. 97).

291. Rowland and Howe, *Vitruvius*, 213, who in fig. 56 offer fine illustrations of the proportions.

292. Ibid., 267.

293. Erich Winter, "Towards a Chronology of the Later Artemision at Ephesos," 241.

294. *Barrington Atlas*, map 56, G5.

295. Rowland and Howe, *Vitruvius*, fig. 122.

296. A photograph of a typical example is given in Woodford, *The Parthenon*, 20.

297. Woodford, *The Parthenon*, 15.

298. René Ginouves, *Dictionnaire méthodique de l'architecture grecque et romaine* (Rome: École Française, 1992), 2:78.

299. *Oxford Classical Dictionary* (1996), 7.

300. Eric Junod and Jean-Daniel Kaestli, "Le dossier des 'Actes de Jean': état de la question et perspectives nouvelles," in *Aufstieg und Niedergang der Römischen Welt* II.25.6, 4353.

301. *Against Heresies* 3.1.2.

302. Eusebius, *History of the Church* 5.24.2.

303. Richard Bauckham, *Jesus and the Eyewitnesses: The Gospels as Eyewitness Testimony* (Grand Rapids and Cambridge, UK: Eerdmans, 2006), 438.

304. Edgar Hennecke and Wilhelm Schneemelcher, *New Testament Apocrypha* (London: Lutterworth, 1965), 2:236–37.

305. "Le dossier des 'Actes de Jean,'" 4354 n. 243.

306. Scherrer, *New Guide*, 52.

307. Tertullian (ca. 160–225), *De Baptismo* 17.

308. Hennecke and Schneemelcher, *New Testament Apocrypha* 2:354.

309. For example, Frederick F. Bruce, *Paul, Apostle of the Free Spirit* (Exeter: Paternoster Press, 1977), 468.

310. Elizabeth C. Evans, "Roman Descriptions of Personal Appearance in History and Biography," *Harvard Studies in Classical Philology* 46 (1935): 43–84; Evans, "The Study of Physiognomy in the Second Century C.E.," *Transactions and Proceedings of the American Philological Association* 72 (1941): 96–108.

311. Robert M. Grant, "The Description of Paul in the *Acts of Paul and Thecla*," *Vigiliae Christianae* 36 (1982): 1–4.

312. Abraham J. Malherbe, "A Physical Description of Paul," in *Christians among Jews and Gentiles: Essays in Honor of Krister Stendahl on his Sixty-Fifth Birthday*, eds.

George W. E. Nickelsburg and George W. MacRae (Philadelphia: Fortress Press, 1986), 170–75.

313. Pliny, *Natural History* 11.275–76.

314. Ibid., 11.131.

315. Hennecke and Schneemelcher, *New Testament Apocrypha* 2:388–89.

316. Bruce M. Metzger, "St. Paul and the Baptized Lion," *Princeton Seminary Bulletin* 39, no. 2 (November 1945): 11–21; Wilhelm Schneemelcher, "Der getaufte Löwe in den *Acta Pauli*" in his *Gesammelte Aufsätze zum Neuen Testament und zur Patristik*, ed. Walther Bienert and Knut Schäferdiek. Analecta Vlatadōn 22 (Thessaloniki: Patriarchal Institute for Patristic Studies, 1974), 182–203; Hendrik J. W. Drijvers, "Der getaufte Löwe und die Theologie der *Acta Pauli*," in *Carl-Schmidt-Kolloquium an der Martin-Luther-Universität 1988,* ed. Peter Nagel, Wissenschaftliche Beiträge 9 (Halle: Martin-Luther-Universität, 1990), 181–89; Tamás Adamik, "The Baptized Lion in the *Acts of Paul*," in *The Apocryphal Acts of Paul and Thecla*, ed. Jan N. Bremmer, Studies on the Apocryphal Acts of the Apostles 2 (Kampen: Kok Pharos, 1996), 60–74.

317. Hennecke and Schneemelcher, *New Testament Apocrypha* 2:372–73.

318. Abraham J. Malherbe, "The Beasts at Ephesus," *Journal of Biblical Literature* 87 (1968): 71–80.

319. The author would almost certainly have known of the martyrdom of Ignatius of Antioch, who was thrown to the lions in the Coliseum in Rome in 107 C.E. (see his *To the Romans* 4).

320. *Attic Nights* 5.14. Aulus Gellius attributes the story to the *Aegyptiaca* of Apion, who claims to have been present when the miraculous event took place. He was an eminent first-century C.E. Egyptian who headed the school of Alexandria, and who also lectured in Rome (*Oxford Classical Dictionary* [1996], 121a). Two other stories of lions rewarding men who helped them are given by Pliny, *Natural History* 8.21.56-57.

321. Hennecke and Schneemelcher, *New Testament Apocrypha* 2:362.

322. Elizabeth Esch, "Thekla und die Tiere oder: Die Zähmung der Widerspenstigen," in *Aus Liebe zu Paulus? Die Akte Thekla neu aufgerollt*, ed. Martin Ebner, Stuttgarter Bibelstudien 206 (Stuttgart: Katholisches Bibelwerk, 2005), 171–72.

323. There is a photograph of an excellent reproduction in John Boardman, Jasper Griffin, and Oswyn Murray, eds., *The Oxford History of the Classical World* (Oxford: Oxford University Press, 1986), 305.

324. *Oxford Classical Dictionary* (1996), 318.

325. Ibid., 939.

326. Ibid., 1535a and 1548a.

327. "The frustration of the local élites of Asia minor with their constricted political life found relief in the activities of the contemporary intelligentsia, who collectively reveal a nostalgia for the glorious days of the Greek past. When the oratory and historiography of the first two centuries C.E. are examined, an archaism both of language and theme is discerned" (Macro, "Cities of Asia Minor," in *Aufstieg und Niedergang der Römischen Welt* II.7.2 [1980], 694).

328. *De aquis urbis Romae* 1.16.

329. Graves, *Greek Myths*, 2:74.

330. *Oxford Classical Dictionary* (1996), 277.

331. The only mountain of that name in the *Barrington Atlas* is a small range in northwestern Crete (map 60, B2).

332. *Oxford Classical Dictionary* (1996), 1031.

333. Ibid., 331.

334. *Barrington Atlas* map 84, B3.

335. Carcopino, *Daily Life in Ancient Rome*, 277.

336. Mitchell, *Anatolia* 1:217, emphasis supplied.

337. Scherrer, *New Guide*, 74.

338. Ibid., 120.

339. Ibid., 176.

340. Arthur Henderson, "The Hellenistic Temple of Artemis at Ephesus," *Journal of the Royal Institute of British Architects* 22 (1915): 130.

341. *Oxford Classical Dictionary* (1996), 1188b.

342. Ibid., 468b.

343. Knibbe, "Via Sacra Ephesiaca," 146–47.

344. Lactantius, *Divinae Institutiones* 5.3.14.

345. Owsei Temkin, *Hippocrates in a World of Pagans and Christians* (Baltimore; Johns Hopkins Press University, 1991), 73.

346. *Oxford Classical Dictionary* (1996), 710.

347. Stefan Karwiese, "The Church of Mary and the Temple of Hadrian Olympius," in *Ephesos, Metropolis of Asia*, ed. Helmut Koester, 313.

348. *Roman History* 69.5.2.

349. White, "Urban Development and Social Change," 55.

350. Zabehlicky, "Preliminary Views of the Ephesian Harbour," 205.

351. Karwiese, "The Church of Mary," 313–15.

352. Broughton, "Roman Asia," 711–12.

353. Radet, *Ephesiaca*, 7.

354. Scherrer, *New Guide*, 62.

355. Knibbe, "Via Sacra Ephesiaca," 149–50.

356. Ibid., 153.

357. Ibid., 148.

358. Horsley, *New Documents* IV, 75–76.

359. Ibid., 77.

360. Ibid., 10.

361. Broughton, "Roman Asia," 825.

362. Ibid., 879–80.

363. Graham Anderson, "Xenophon of Ephesus, *An Ephesian Tale*," in *Collected Ancient Greek Novels*, ed. Bryan P. Reardon (Berkeley: University of California Press, 1989), 125.

364. Knibbe, "Via Sacra Ephesiaca," 149–50.

365. Picard, *Éphèse et Claros*, 326–29.

366. *Oxford Classical Dictionary* (1996), 527b.

367. Scherrer, *New Guide*, 70.

368. Ibid., 74.

369. Ibid., 162.

370. Ibid., 176.

371. Magie, *Roman Rule in Asia Minor*, 632.

372. Thomas, "At Home in the City of Artemis," 85 n. 10.

373. Scherrer, *New Guide*, 213.

374. Oster, "Ephesus as a Religious Center," 1724.

375. *Éphèse et Claros*, 362–64.

376. Scherrer, *New Guide*, 188.

377. Suetonius, *Gaius Caligula*, 21.

PART 2, pages 183–192

1. Josephus, *Jewish War* 5.241.

2. Josephus, *Antiquities of the Jews* 15.268.

3. Josephus, *Jewish War* 5.176–83.

4. Ibid., 5.169.

5. Described in Josephus, *Antiquities of the Jews* 15.380–425.

6. Described in Josephus, *Jewish War* 5.184–247.

7. Ross Burns, *Damascus: A History* (London and New York: Routledge, 2006), 64.

8. Emil Schürer, *The History of the Jewish People in the Age of Jesus Christ* III/2 (Edinburgh: T&T Clark, 1987), 818.

9. *De specialibus legibus* 1.73.

10. *b. Baba Batra* 4a; *b. Taʿanit* 23a.

11. Jerome Murphy-O'Connor, *Paul: A Critical Life* (Oxford: Clarendon Press, 1996), 52.

12. Peter Scherrer, ed., *Ephesus: The New Guide* (Istanbul: Ege Yayinin, 2000), 66–68.

13. Comprehensive lists synthesizing the dates assigned to buildings by the archaeologists are provided by Guy Rogers, *The Sacred Identity of Ephesos* (London: Routledge, 1991), 87, and by Michael White, "Urban Development and Social Change in Imperial Ephesos" in *Ephesos, Metropolis of Asia*, ed. Helmut Koester, (Cambridge, MA: Harvard University Press, 2004), 52–54.

14. Rogers, *Sacred Identity of Ephesos*, 87.

15. Scherrer, *New Guide*, 80.

16. *On Architecture* 5.1.4.

17. Scherrer, *New Guide*, 80.

18. Scherrer, *New Guide*, 80; Dio Cassius, *Roman History* 51.20.6 (p. 62).

19. Scherrer, *New Guide*, 87.

20. Ibid., 83.

21. Robert Graves, *The Greek Myths* (London: Penguin, 1960), 1:73.

22. *Oxford Classical Dictionary* (1996), 701a.

23. Strabo, *Geography* 14.1.20 (p. 15).

24. Richard Oster, "Ephesus as a Religious Center under the Principate, I. Paganism before Constantine," in *Aufstieg und Niedergang der Römischen Welt* (1990) II.18.3, 1689–91.

25. Stephen G. Miller, *The Prytaneion: Its Function and Architectural Form* (Berkeley: University of California Press, 1978).

26. Scherrer, *New Guide*, 86. On these cult statues see p. 7 above.

27. Scherrer, *New Guide*, 86.

28. Ibid., 96.

29. Ibid., 98.

30. For the level of wealth of individuals in the Pauline communities see Steven Friesen, "Poverty in Pauline Studies: Beyond the So-called New Consensus," *Journal*

for the Study of the New Testament 26 (2004): 323–61, who proposes a seven-step poverty scale (p. 341). The highest level reached by Paul's followers is "moderate surplus resources," the examples of which are Gaius and possibly Chloe (p. 357).

31. These houses are studied from the perspective of what they reveal of social relations by Michele George, "Domestic Architecture and Household Relations: Pompeii and Roman Ephesos," *Journal for the Study of the New Testament* 27 (2004): 15–23. Her conclusions are vague in the extreme.

32. Wilhelm Alzinger, "Ephesos vom Beginn der römischen Herrschaft in Kleinasien bis zum Ende der Principatzeit: Archäologischer Teil," in *Aufstieg und Niedergang der Römischen Welt* (1980) II.7.2, 824.

33. See the plan in Scherrer, *New Guide*, 104–5.

34. Ibid., 100.

35. The clearest plan of the whole complex is given in Friedmund Hueber, *Ephesos. Gebaute Geschichte* (Mainz: von Zabern, 1997), 55, Fig. 65.

36. Scherrer, *New Guide*, 108.

37. For plans and detailed descriptions see Selahattin Erdemgil, et al., *The Terrace Houses in Ephesus* (Istanbul: Hitit Color, 1988), from which all measurements are scaled.

38. Scherrer, *New Guide*, 110.

39. Jerome Carcopino, *Daily Life in Ancient Rome* (London: Penguin, 1941), 34–35.

40. Murphy-O'Connor, *Paul: A Critical Life*, 277–78.

41. In his article "Rich Pompeiian Houses, Shops for Rent, and the Huge Apartment Building in Herculaneum as Typical Spaces for Pauline House Churches," *Journal for the Study of the New Testament* 27 (2004): 27–46, David Balch entirely ignores the problems posed by getting the "whole" church into a *single* internal space. Naturally he gives no measurements of the rooms of which he speaks.

42. Jerome Murphy-O'Connor, *St. Paul's Corinth* (Collegeville, MN: Liturgical Press, 2002), 184–85.

43. See the illustration in David Macaulay, *City: A Story of Roman Planning and Construction* (Boston: Houghton Mifflin, 1974), 107.

44. Scherrer, *New Guide*, 124.

45. Appian, *Civil Wars* 5.1.9 (p. 45).

46. Scherrer, *New Guide*, 126; Strabo, *Geography* 14.1.3 (p. 9).

47. Scherrer, *New Guide*, 134; Strabo, *Geography* 14.1.20 (p. 15).

48. There is a detailed plan in Hueber, *Ephesos. Gebaute Geschichte*, 71, Fig. 91.

49. Scherrer, *New Guide*, 140–44.

50. For a description of similar workshops in Corinth see Murphy-O'Connor, *St. Paul's Corinth*, 194–95.

51. Scherrer, *New Guide*, 142.

52. Ibid., 156.

53. Scherrer, *New Guide*, 158; Strabo, *Geography* 14.1.38 (p. 33).

54. Luke, *Acts of the Apostles* 19:23-41 (p. 92).

55. Scherrer, *New Guide*, 160.

56. Ibid., 170.

57. Rogers, *Sacred Identity*, 102–3.

58. Scherrer, *New Guide*, 172.

59. Ibid., 164.

60. See the commentary on Strabo, *Geography* 14.1.4 (p. 10).

61. Irene Arnold, "Festivals of Ephesus," *American Journal of Archaeology* 76 (1972): 18.

62. Oster, "Ephesus as a Religious Center," 1990.

63. There is nothing in this text to confirm Helmut Koester's claim that Apollos had founded a community in Ephesus before the arrival of Paul, Prisca, and Aquila ("Ephesos in Early Christian Literature," in *Ephesos, Metropolis of Asia*, ed. Koester, 126, 131).

64. Ceslas Spicq, *Notes de Lexicographie Néo-testamentaire*, OBO 22/1 (Fribourg: Éditions universitaires; Göttingen: Vandenhoeck & Ruprecht, 1978), 1:500–502.

65. Schürer, *History of the Jewish People* 3:818.

66. Jerome Murphy-O'Connor, "Jesus and the Money Changers (Mark 11:15-17; John 2:13-17)," *Revue Biblique* 107 (2000): 42–55.

67. "Ephesos in Early Christian Literature," in *Ephesos, Metropolis of Asia*, ed. Helmut Koester, 122–24.

68. Harry Gamble, *The Textual History of the Letter to the Romans* (Grand Rapids: Eerdmans, 1977), 89, who has been followed by all modern commentators.

69. Justin Taylor, *Les Actes des deux Apôtres VI. Commentaire historique (Act. 18,23-28,31)*, EBib n.s. 30 (Paris: Gabalda, 1996), 30–31.

70. Ronald Hock, *The Social Context of Paul's Ministry* (Philadelphia: Fortress Press, 1980), 82 n. 58.

71. With Walter Bauer, William F. Arndt, F. Wilbur Gingrich, and Frederick W. Danker, *A Greek-English Lexicon of the New Testament and Other Early Christian Literature* (Chicago: University Press, 1979), 127a.

72. Marie-Émile Boismard and Arnaud Lamouille, *Les Actes des deux apôtres*. EBib n.s. 13 (Paris: Gabalda, 1990), 2:312.

73. Ernst Haenchen, *The Acts of the Apostles* (Philadelphia: Westminster, 1971), 559.

74. Ibid., 561.

75. Ibid., 615.

76. T. Robert S. Broughton, "Roman Asia" in *An Economic Survey of Ancient Rome*, ed. Tenney Frank, (Baltimore: Johns Hopkins University Press, 1938), 4:821.

77. David Magie, *Roman Rule in Asia Minor to the End of the Third Century after Christ* (Princeton: Princeton University Press, 1950), 47.

78. This commonsense hypothesis also occurred to J. B. Lightfoot, who goes a step further and suggests that Magnesia was evangelized by Tychicus (Acts 20:2; Col 4:7; 2 Tim 4:12) because the name seems to have been particularly common there (*Apostolic Fathers* II/2, 102).

79. Murphy-O'Connor, *Paul: A Critical Life*, 138–41.

80. Frederick F. Bruce, *The Epistle of Paul to the Galatians* (Exeter: Paternoster Press, 1982), 26.

81. J. Louis Martyn, *Galatians: A New Translation with Introduction and Commentary*, AB 33A (New York: Doubleday, 1998), 302–6.

82. Murphy-O'Connor, *Paul: A Critical Life*, 215–20.

83. Murphy-O'Connor, *Paul: His Story* (Oxford: Oxford University Press, 2004), 235–36.

84. Suetonius, *Caesar* 79.3.

85. On this "Travel Document" see Werner G. Kümmel, *Introduction to the New Testament* (London: SCM, 1975), 176–77.

86. Peter Pilhofer, *Philippi*, vol. 1. *Die erste christliche Gemeinde Europas*, WUNT 87 (Tübingen: J.C.B. Mohr, 1995), 157–58.

87. Murphy-O'Connor, *St. Paul's Corinth*, 164–65.

88. For the justification of this interpretation see my "Christological Anthropology in Philippians 2:6-11," *Revue Biblique* 83 (1976): 25–50, and my "The Origins of Paul's Christology: From Thessalonians to Galatians" in *Christian Origins: Worship, Belief and Society*, ed. Kieran O'Mahoney, JSNTSup 241 (London: Sheffield Academic Press, 2003), 124–32.

89. For details see my "The *Damascus Document* Revisited," *Revue Biblique* 92 (1985): 239–41.

90. Spicq, *Notes de lexicographie*, 919–21; cf. 291.

91. Spicq, *Notes de lexicographie*, 288–91.

92. Jerome Murphy-O'Connor, "Greeters in Col 4:10-14 and Phlm 23-24," *Revue Biblique* 114 (2007) 416–26.

93. Thomas J. Sappington, *Revelation and Redemption at Colossae*, JSNTSup 53 (Sheffield: Journal for the Study of the Old Testament Press, 1991), 170.

94. Edgar Hennecke and Wilhelm Schneemelcher, *New Testament Apocrypha* (London: Lutterworth Press, 1965), 2:128–32.

95. John Muddiman, *A Commentary on the Epistle to the Ephesians*, Black's New Testament Commentary (London and New York: Continuum, 2002), 20.

96. "The Particularity of the Pauline Epistles as a Problem in the Ancient Church," in *Neotestamentica et Patristica. Eine Freundesgabe Herrn Professor Dr Oscar Cullmann zu seinem 60. Geburtstag überreicht*, ed. W. C. van Unnik, NovTSup 6 (Leiden: Brill, 1962).

97. Muddiman, *Ephesians*, 39.

98. Ibid., 45.

99. Plutarch, *Sulla* 26.1 (p. 126).

100. For details see my *Paul: A Critical Life*, 280–82.

101. Robert Jewett, *Dating Paul's Life* (London: SCM, 1979), 48.

102. The best reconstruction is that of C. K. Barrett, "*Ho adikesas* (2 Cor. 7,12)," in *Verborum Veritas. Festschrift für Gustav Stählin*, eds. Otto Böcher and Klaus Haacker, (Wuppertal: Brockhaus, 1970), 149–57.

103. Like many who fragment 2 Corinthians into a series of shorter letters, Helmut Koester claims that 2 Cor 2:4–7:4 and chapters 10–13 were also written from Corinth ("Ephesos in Early Christian Literature" in *Ephesos, Metropolis of Asia*, ed. Koester, 121–22). The majority of scholars rightly divide 2 Corinthians into only two letters (chs. 1–9 and chs. 10–13), which were written in Macedonia after Paul had left Ephesus.

104. From 2 Timothy it is clear that Paul had been out of touch with Timothy for some considerable time. Their relationship was so close that a significant reason must be postulated for their separation. My suggestion (see above) was that Paul had left Timothy in Ephesus on his way to Jerusalem in order to keep him out of danger. This is, of course, entirely speculative, but something in the same order of gravity is indispensable. There may be a historical reminiscence in 1 Tim 1:3, where the author presents Paul as having left Timothy in (or sent him to) Ephesus while he himself went somewhere else.

BIBLIOGRAPHY

Alzinger, Wilhelm. *Augusteische Architektur in Ephesos*. Sonderschriften des Österreichischen Archäologischen Instituts 16. Vienna: Österreisches Archäologisches Institut im Selbstverlag, 1974.

———. "Ephesos vom Beginn der römischen Herrschaft in Kleinasien bis zum Ende der Principatzeit: Archäologischer Teil," in *Aufstieg und Niedergang der Römischen Welt* II.7.2 (1980), 811–30.

Anderson, Graham. "Xenophon of Ephesus, *An Ephesian Tale*," in Bryan P. Reardon, ed., *Collected Ancient Greek Novels*. Berkeley: University of California Press, 1989, 125–69.

Arnold, Irene. "Festivals of Ephesus," *American Journal of Archaeology* 76 (1972), 17–22.

Balch, David. "Rich Pompeiian Houses, Shops for Rent, and the Huge Apartment Building in Herculaneum as Typical Spaces for Pauline House Churches," *Journal for the Study of the New Testament* 27 (2004), 27–46.

Bammer, Anton. "Amazonen und das Artemesion von Ephesos," *Revue archéologique* n.s. 1 (1976), 91–102.

———. *Das Heiligtum der Artemis von Ephesos*. Graz: Akademische Druck und Verlagsanstalt, 1984.

Bammer, Anton, and Ulrike Muss. *Das Artemision von Ephesos. Das Weltwunder Ioniens in archäischer und klassischer Zeit*. Mainz: von Zabern, 1996.

Barrington Atlas of the Greek and Roman World. Richard Talbert, ed. Princeton and Oxford: Princeton University Press, 2000.

Bauckham, Richard. *Jesus and the Eyewitnesses. The Gospels as Eyewitness Testimony*. Grand Rapids: Eerdmans, 2006.

Bennett, Florence. *Religious Cults Associated with the Amazons*. New York: Columbia University Press, 1912.

Boardman, John, Jasper Griffin, and Oswyn Murray, eds. *The Oxford History of the Classical World*. Oxford: Oxford University Press, 1986.

Boismard, Marie-Emile, and Arnaud Lamouille. *Les Actes des deux Apôtres* II. Etudes bibliques n.s. 13. Paris: Gabalda, 1990.

Broshi, Magen. "La population de l'ancienne Jérusalem," *Revue Biblique* 82 (1975), 5–14.

Broughton, T. Robert S. "Roman Asia," in Tenney Frank, ed., *An Economic Survey of Ancient Rome* IV. Baltimore: Johns Hopkins University Press, 1938, 499–916.

Bruce, Frederick F. *Paul, Apostle of the Free Spirit*. Exeter: Paternoster Press, 1977.

———. *The Epistle of Paul to the Galatians*. Exeter: Paternoster Press, 1982.

Bürchner, Ludwig. "Ephesos," in *Paulys Real-encyclopädie der Classische Altertumswissenschaft* V, ed. Georg Wissowa. Stuttgart: J. B. Metzler, 1905, 2773–2822.

Burns, Ross. *Damascus. A History*. London and New York: Routledge, 2006.

Carcopino, Jerome. *Daily Life in Ancient Rome. The People and the City at the Height of the Empire*. London: Penguin, 1941.

Casson, Lionel. *Ships and Seamanship in the Ancient World*. Princeton: Princeton University Press, 1971.

Dahl, Nils A. "The Particularity of the Pauline Epistles as a Problem in the Ancient Church," in W. C. van Unnik, ed., *Neotestamentica et Patristica. Eine Freundesgabe Herrn Professor Dr Oscar Cullmann zu seinem 60. Geburtstag überreicht*. NovTSup 6. Leiden: Brill, 1962, 261–71.

Di Donnici, Lynn. "The Images of Artemis and Greco-Roman Worship: A Reconsideration," *Harvard Theological Review* 85 (1992), 389–415.

Dohrn, Tobias. "Altes und Neues über die ephesischen Amazonen," *Jahrbuch des Deutschen Archaeologischen Instituts* 94 (1979), 112–26.

Erdemgil, Selahattin, et al. *The Terrace Houses in Ephesus*. Istanbul: Hitit Color, n.d.

Esch, Elizabeth. "Thekla und die Tiere oder: Die Zähmung der Widerspenstigen," in Martin Ebner, ed., *Aus Liebe zu Paulus? Die* Akte Thekla *neu aufgerollt*. Stuttgarter Bibelstudien 206. Stuttgart: Katholisches Bibelwerk, 2005, 159–79.

Evans, Elizabeth C. "Roman Descriptions of Personal Appearance in History and Biography," *Harvard Studies in Classical Philology* 46 (1935), 43–84.

———. "The Study of Physiognomy in the Second Century A.D.," *Transactions and Proceedings of the American Philological Association* 72 (1941), 96–108.

Filson, Floyd. "Ephesus and the New Testament," *Biblical Archaeologist* 8 (1945), 73–80.

Finley, Moses I., ed. *Atlas of Classical Archaeology*. London: Chatto & Windus, 1977.

Fleischer, Robert. *Artemis von Ephesos und verwandte Kultstatuen aus Anatolien und Syrien*. Études préliminaires aux religions orientales dans l'empire romain (EPRO) no. 35. Leiden: Brill, 1973.

Fletcher, Banister. *A History of Architecture on the Comparative Method*. London: Batsford, 1931.

French, David H. "The Roman Road System of Asia Minor," in *Aufstieg und Niedergang der Römischen Welt* II.7.2 (1980), 698–729.

Friesen, Steven, "The Cult of the Roman Emperors in Ephesos: Temple Wardens, City Titles, and the Interpretation of the Revelation of John," in Helmut Koester, ed., *Ephesos. Metropolis of Asia. An Interdisciplinary Approach to its Archaeology, Religion, and Culture*, Harvard Theological Studies 41. Cambridge, MA: Harvard University Press, 2004, 229–50.

———. "Poverty in Pauline Studies: Beyond the So-called New Consensus," *Journal for the Study of the New Testament* 26 (2004) 323–61.

Gamble, Harry. *The Textual History of the Letter to the Romans*. Grand Rapids: Eerdmans, 1977.

Gerber, Albrecht. "Gustav Adolf Deissmann (1866–1937): trailblazer in biblical studies, in the archaeology of Ephesus, and in international reconciliation," *Buried History* 41 (2005), 29–42.

George, Michele. "Domestic Architecture and Household Relations. Pompei and Roman Ephesos," *Journal for the Study of the New Testament* 27 (2004) 7–25.

Ginouves, René. *Dictionnaire méthodique de l'architecture grecque et romaine.* Rome: École Française, 1992, 2:78.

Grant, Robert M. "The Description of Paul in the *Acts of Paul and Thecla,*" *Vigiliae Christianae* 36 (1982), 1–4.

Graves, Robert. *The Greek Myths.* London: Penguin, 1960.

Haenchen, Ernst. *The Acts of the Apostles. A Commentary.* Trans. Bernard Noble and Gerald Shinn, under the supervision of Hugh Anderson; trans. rev. R. McLean Wilson. Philadelphia: Westminster, 1971.

Henderson, Arthur. "The Hellenistic Temple of Artemis at Ephesus," *Journal of the Royal Institute of British Architects* 22 (1915), 130–34.

———. "The Temple of Diana at Ephesus," *Journal of the Royal Institute of British Architects* 41 (1933), 767–71.

Hennecke, Edgar, and Wilhelm Schneemelcher. *New Testament Apocrypha* I–II. London: Lutterworth, 1965.

Hermary, Antoine. "The Greeks in Marseilles and the Western Mediterranean," in Vassos Karageorghis, ed., *The Greeks Beyond the Aegean.* New York: Onassis Foundation, 2003, 59–77.

Hicks, Edward L. "Demetrius the Silversmith," *Expositor* ser. IV, 1 (1890) 401–22.

Hock, Ronald. *The Social Context of Paul's Ministry. Tentmaking and Apostleship.* Philadelphia: Fortress Press, 1980.

Hornblower, Simon. "Greece: The History of the Classical Period," in John Boardman, Jasper Griffin, and Oswyn Murray, eds., *The Oxford History of the Classical World.* Oxford: Oxford University Press, 1986, 124–55.

Horsley, Greg. *New Documents Illustrating Early Christianity* II. North Ryde, N.S.W.: Ancient History Documentary Research Centre, Macquarie University, 1982.

———. *New Documents Illustrating Early Christianity* IV. North Ryde, N.S.W.: Ancient History Documentary Research Centre, Macquarie University, 1987.

———. *New Documents Illustrating Early Christianity* V. North Ryde, N.S.W.: Ancient History Documentary Research Centre, Macquarie University, 1989.

Hueber, Friedmund. *Ephesos. Gebaute Geschichte.* Mainz: von Zabern, 1997.

Jones, Arnold H. M. *The Cities of the Eastern Roman Provinces.* Oxford: Oxford University Press, 1971.

Junod, Eric, and Jean-Daniel Kaestli. "Le dossier des 'Actes de Jean': état de la question et perspectives nouvelles," in *Aufstieg und Niedergang der Römischen Welt* II.25.6 (1988), 4293–4262.

Karwiese, Stefan. "The Church of Mary and the Temple of Hadrian Olympius," in Helmut Koester, ed., *Ephesos. Metropolis of Asia. An Interdisciplinary Approach to its Archaeology, Religion, and Culture.* Harvard Theological Studies 41. Cambridge, MA: Harvard University Press, 2004, 311–19.

Knibbe, Dieter. "Ephesos: A. Historisch-epigraphischer Teil," in *Paulys Realencyclopädie der classischen Altertumswissenschaft. Supplement Band,* ed. Konrat Ziegler. Stuttgart: Druckenmüllerverlag, 1970, 12:248–97.

———. "Ephesos vom Beginn der römischen Herrschaft in Kleinasien bis zum Ende der Principatzeit: Historischer Teil," in *Aufstieg und Niedergang der Römischen Welt* II.7.2 (1980), 748–810.

———. "Emperor Worship at Ephesus," in *Aufstieg und Niedergang der Römischen Welt* I.18.3 (1990), 1659–60.

————. *Ephesus. Geschichte einer bedeutenden antiken Stadt und Portrait einer modernen Großgrabung im 102. Jahr der Wiederkehr des Beginnes österreichischer Forschungen (1895–1997).* Frankfurt: Peter Lang, 1998.

————. "Via Sacra Ephesiaca. New Aspects of the Cult of Artemis Ephesia," in Helmut Koester, ed., *Ephesos. Metropolis of Asia. An Interdisciplinary Approach to its Archaeology, Religion, and Culture.* Harvard Theological Studies 41. Cambridge, MA: Harvard University Press, 2004, 141–55.

Kuhnert, Ernst. "Ephesia," in *Paulys Real-encyclopädie der Classischen Altertumswissenschaft* V, ed. Georg Wissowa. Stuttgart: J. B. Metzger, 1905, 2753–2773.

Kümmel, Werner Georg. *Introduction to the New Testament.* Trans. Howard Clark Kee. London: SCM Press, 1975.

Lampe, Peter. "Keine 'Sklavenflucht' des Onesimus," *Zeitschrift für die neutestamentliche Wissenschaft* 76 (1985), 135–37.

Larsen, Jakob A. O. *Representative Government in Greek and Roman History.* Sather Classical Lectures 28. Berkeley: University of California Press, 1955.

Llewelyn, S. R. *New Documents Illustrating Early Christianity* VIII. North Ryde, N.S.W.: Ancient History Documentary Research Centre, Macquarie University; Grand Rapids: Eerdmans, 1988.

Levi, Peter. *Pausanias. Guide to Greece.* London: Penguin, 1971.

Lightfoot, Joseph Barber. *The Apostolic Fathers.* London: Macmillan, 1889.

Lucas, Alfred, and J. R. Harris. *Ancient Egyptian Materials and Industries.* London: E. Arnold & Co., 1948.

Macaulay, David. *City. A Story of Roman Planning and Construction.* Boston: Houghton Mifflin, 1974.

Macro, Anthony D. "The Cities of Asia Minor under the Roman Imperium," in *Aufstieg und Niedergang der Römischen Welt* II, 7, 2 (1980), 659–97.

Magie, David. *Roman Rule in Asia Minor to the End of the Third Century after Christ.* Princeton: Princeton University Press, 1950.

Malherbe, Abraham J. " A Physical Description of Paul," in George W. E. Nickelsburg and George W. MacRae, *Christians among Jews and Gentiles. Essays in Honor of Krister Stendahl on his sixty-fifth birthday.* Philadelphia: Fortress Press, 1986, 170–75.

Martyn, J. Louis. *Galatians: A New Translation with Introduction and Commentary.* AB 33A. New York: Doubleday, 1998.

Meeks, Wayne A. *The First Urban Christians. The Social World of the Apostle Paul.* New Haven: Yale University Press, 1983.

Mitchell, Stephen. *Anatolia. Land, Men, and Gods in Asia Minor.* I. *The Celts in Anatolia and the Impact of Roman* Rule; II. *The Rise of the Church.* Oxford: Clarendon Press, 1995.

McDonagh, Bernard. *Turkey. The Aegean and Mediterranean Coasts.* Blue Guide. London: A. & C. Black; New York: W. W. Norton, 1989.

Miller, Stephen G. *The Prytaneion. Its Function and Architectural Form.* Berkeley: University of California Press, 1978.

Moule, C.F.D. *The Epistles to the Colossians and to Philemon.* The Cambridge Greek Testament Commentary. Cambridge: Cambridge University Press, 1968.

Muddiman, John. *A Commentary on the Epistle to the Ephesians.* Black's New Testament Commentary. London and New York: Continuum, 2001.

Murphy-O'Connor, Jerome. "Christological Anthropology in Philippians 2:6-11," *Revue Biblique* 83 (1976), 25–50.

———. "The *Damascus Document* Revisited," *Revue Biblique* 92 (1985), 223–46.

———. *Paul the Letter-Writer. His World, His Options, His Skills*. Collegeville, MN: Liturgical Press, 1995.

———. *Paul. A Critical Life*. Oxford: Clarendon Press, 1996.

———. "Fishers of Fish, Fishers of Men," *Bible Review* 15/3 (1999) 22–27, 48–49.

———. "Jesus and the Money Changers (Mark 11:15-17; John 2:13-17)," *Revue Biblique* 107 (2000), 42–55.

———. *St. Paul's Corinth. Texts and Archaeology*. Collegeville, MN: Liturgical Press, 2002.

———. "The Origins of Paul's Christology: From Thessalonians to Galatians," in Kieran O'Mahoney, ed., *Christian Origins. Worship, Belief and Society*. JSNTSup 241. London: Sheffield Academic Press, 2003, 113–42.

———. *Paul. His Story*. Oxford: Oxford University Press, 2004.

Oliver, James H. "Greek Applications for Roman Trials," *American Journal of Philology* 100 (1979), 543–58.

Oster, Richard. "The Ephesian Artemis as an Opponent of Early Christianity," *Jahrbuch für Antike und Christentum* 19 (1976), 24–44.

———. *A Bibliography of Ancient Ephesus*. ATLA Bibliography Series 19. Metuchen, NJ: ATLA; London: Scarecrow Press, 1987.

———. "Ephesus as a Religious Center under the Principate, I. Paganism before Constantine," in *Aufstieg und Niedergang der Römischen Welt* II.18.3 (1990), 1661–1728.

———. "Ephesus," in David Noel Freedman, editor-in-chief, *The Anchor Bible Dictionary*. New York: Doubleday, 1992, 2:542–49.

Parkin, Tim. *Demography and Roman Society*. Baltimore: Johns Hopkins University Press, 1992.

Picard, Charles. *Éphèse et Claros. Recherches sur les sanctuaires et les cultes de l'Ionie du nord*. Bibliothèque des Écoles Françaises d'Athènes et de Rome 123. Paris: E. de Boccard, 1922.

Pilhofer, Peter. *Philippi*. Vol. 1. *Die erste christliche Gemeinde Europas*. Wissenschaftliche Untersuchungen zum Neuen Testament 87. Tübingen: J.C.B. Mohr, 1995.

Radet, Georges. *Ephesiaca. 1. La topographie d'Éphèse. 2. La colonisation d'Éphèse par les Ioniens*. Bordeaux: Feret, 1908.

Ramsay, William. *The Cities of Saint Paul and their Influence on his Life and Thought: The Cities of Eastern Asia Minor*. London: Hodder & Stoughton, 1907.

Reardon, Bryan P., ed. *Collected Ancient Greek Novels*. Berkeley: University of California Press, 1989.

Ridgway, Brunhilde. "A Story of Five Amazons," *American Journal of Archaeology* 78 (1974), 1–17.

Rigsby, Kent J. *Asylia. Territorial Inviolability in the Hellenistic World*. Hellenistic Culture and Society 22. Berkeley: University of California Press, 1996.

Rogers, Guy. *The Sacred Identity of Ephesos. Foundation Myths of a Roman City*. London: Routledge, 1991.

Rowland, Ingrid D., and Thomas N. Howe, eds. *Vitruvius. Ten Books on Architecture*. Cambridge: Cambridge University Press, 2001.

Russell, Josiah. *Late Ancient and Medieval Population.* Transactions of the American Philological Association 48.3. Philadelphia: American Philosophical Society, 1958.

Sappington, Thomas J. *Revelation and Redemption at Colossae.* JSNTSupp 53. Sheffield: JSOT Press, 1991.

Saulnier, Christiane. "Lois Romains sur les Juifs selon Flavius Josèphe," *Revue Biblique* 88 (1981), 161–98.

Scherk, Robert. *Rome and the Greek East to the Death of Augustus.* Cambridge: Cambridge University Press, 1984.

Scherrer, Peter, ed. *Ephesus. The New Guide.* Istanbul: Ege Yayinin, 2000.

———. "Ephesus Uncovered. From Latrines to Libraries," *Archaeological Odyssey* 4/2 (March–April 2001), 26–37.

Schürer, Emil. *The History of the Jewish People in the Age of Jesus Christ (175 B.C.–A.D. 135).* Trans. T. A. Burkill, et al. Rev. and ed. by Geza Vermes and Fergus Millar. Vol. 3. Edinburgh: T&T Clark, 1987.

Severin, Tim. *The Jason Voyage. The Quest for the Golden Fleece.* London: Arrow, 1986.

Smallwood, E. Mary. *The Jews under Roman Rule from Pompey to Diocletian. A Study in Political Relations.* Studies in Judaism in Late Antiquity 20. Leiden: Brill, 1981.

Spicq, Ceslas. *Notes de lexicographie néo-testamentaire.* Orbis Biblicus et Orientalis 22/1-2. Fribourg: Éditions Universitaires; Göttingen: Vandenhoeck & Ruprecht, 1978.

Staniforth, Max. *Early Christian Writers.* London: Penguin, 1968.

Stevens, Marty. *Temples, Tithes, and Taxes. The Temple and the Economic Life of Ancient Israel.* Peabody, MA: Hendrickson, 2006.

Strelan, Rick. *Paul, Artemis, and the Jews in Ephesus.* BZNW 80. New York: Walter de Gruyter, 1996.

Taylor, Justin. *Les Actes des deux apôtres.* VI. *Commentaire historique (Act. 18,23-28,31).* Études bibliques, n.s. 30. Paris: Gabalda, 1996.

Thomas, Christine. "At Home in the City of Artemis. Religion in Ephesos in the Literary Imagination of the Roman Period," in Helmut Koester, ed., *Ephesos. Metropolis of Asia. An Interdisciplinary Approach to its Archaeology, Religion, and Culture.* Harvard Theological Studies 41. Cambridge, MA: Harvard University Press, 2004, 81–117.

Tonneau, Raphael. "Éphèse au temps de saint Paul," *Revue Biblique* 38 (1929) 5–34, 321–63.

Tsetskhladze, Gocha. "Greeks beyond the Bosphorus," in Vassos Karageorghis, ed., *The Greeks beyond the Aegean.* New York: Onassis Foundation, 2003, 129–66.

White, Michael. "Urban Development and Social Change in Imperial Ephesos," in Helmut Koester, ed., *Ephesos. Metropolis of Asia. An Interdisciplinary Approach to its Archaeology, Religion, and Culture.* Harvard Theological Studies 41. Cambridge, MA: Harvard University Press, 2004, 27–80.

Winter, Erich. "Towards a Chronology of the Later Artemision at Ephesos," *American Journal of Archaeology* 84 (1980), 241.

Wiplinger, Gilbert, and Gudrun Wlach. *Ephesus: 100 Years of Austrian Research.* Vienna, Cologne, and Weimar: Böhlau, 1996.

Woodford, Susan. *The Parthenon*. Cambridge: Cambridge University Press, 1981.
Zabehlicky, Heinrich. "Preliminary Views of the Ephesian Harbour," in Helmut Koester, ed., *Ephesos. Metropolis of Asia. An Interdisciplinary Approach to its Archaeology, Religion, and Culture*. Harvard Theological Studies 41. Cambridge, MA: Harvard University Press, 2004, 201–16.

SUBJECT INDEX

CLASSICAL AUTHOR INDEX

NEW TESTAMENT INDEX